# Aho-Girl

\'ahô,gərl\ *Japanese, noun.*

A clueless girl.

## 5 | Hiroyuki

# CHARACTER PROFILES

## AHO-GIRL's Cast of Characters

Name **Akuru Akutsu (Akkun)**

Memo

Childhood friend of Yoshiko, who lives next door. Plays the aggravated straight man to Yoshiko's absurdity. Tries to cure Yoshiko of her stupidity, but despite all his effort, it's not going very well.

Name **Yoshiko Hanabatake**

Memo

An inexpressibly clueless high school girl. Favorite food: bananas. Has been friends with Akkun since they were kids and is in love with him. Lives entirely by impulse. Tends to enjoy life too much.

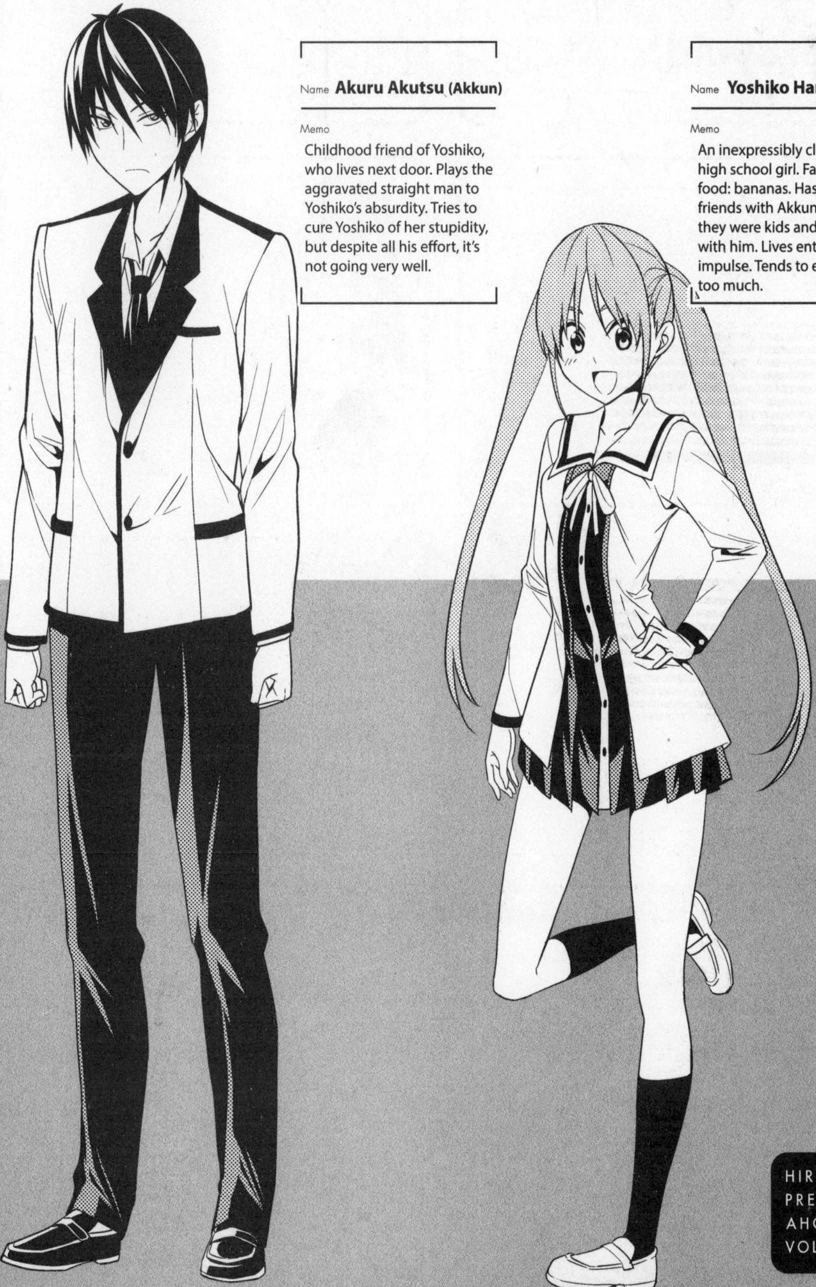

HIROYUKI PRESENTS AHO-GIRL VOLUME.5

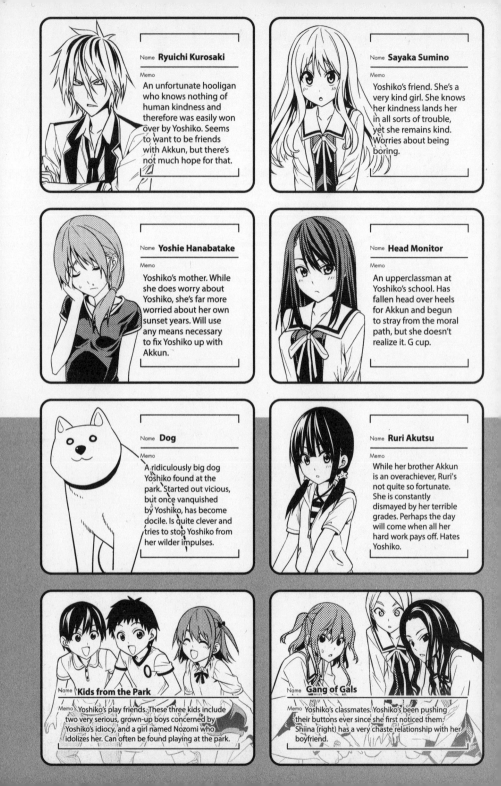

**Name** Ryuichi Kurosaki

**Memo**
An unfortunate hooligan who knows nothing of human kindness and therefore was easily won over by Yoshiko. Seems to want to be friends with Akkun, but there's not much hope for that.

**Name** Sayaka Sumino

**Memo**
Yoshiko's friend. She's a very kind girl. She knows her kindness lands her in all sorts of trouble, yet she remains kind. Worries about being boring.

**Name** Yoshie Hanabatake

**Memo**
Yoshiko's mother. While she does worry about Yoshiko, she's far more worried about her own sunset years. Will use any means necessary to fix Yoshiko up with Akkun.

**Name** Head Monitor

**Memo**
An upperclassman at Yoshiko's school. Has fallen head over heels for Akkun and begun to stray from the moral path, but she doesn't realize it. G cup.

**Name** Dog

**Memo**
A ridiculously big dog Yoshiko found at the park. Started out vicious, but once vanquished by Yoshiko, has become docile. Is quite clever and tries to stop Yoshiko from her wilder impulses.

**Name** Ruri Akutsu

**Memo**
While her brother Akkun is an overachiever, Ruri's not quite so fortunate. She is constantly dismayed by her terrible grades. Perhaps the day will come when all her hard work pays off. Hates Yoshiko.

**Name** Kids from the Park

**Memo** Yoshiko's play friends. These three kids include two very serious, grown-up boys concerned by Yoshiko's idiocy, and a girl named Nozomi who idolizes her. Can often be found playing at the park.

**Name** Gang of Gals

**Memo** Yoshiko's classmates. Yoshiko's been pushing their buttons ever since she first noticed them. Shiina (right) has a very chaste relationship with her boyfriend.

# AHO-GIRL CONTENTS



+ + = AHO-GIRL

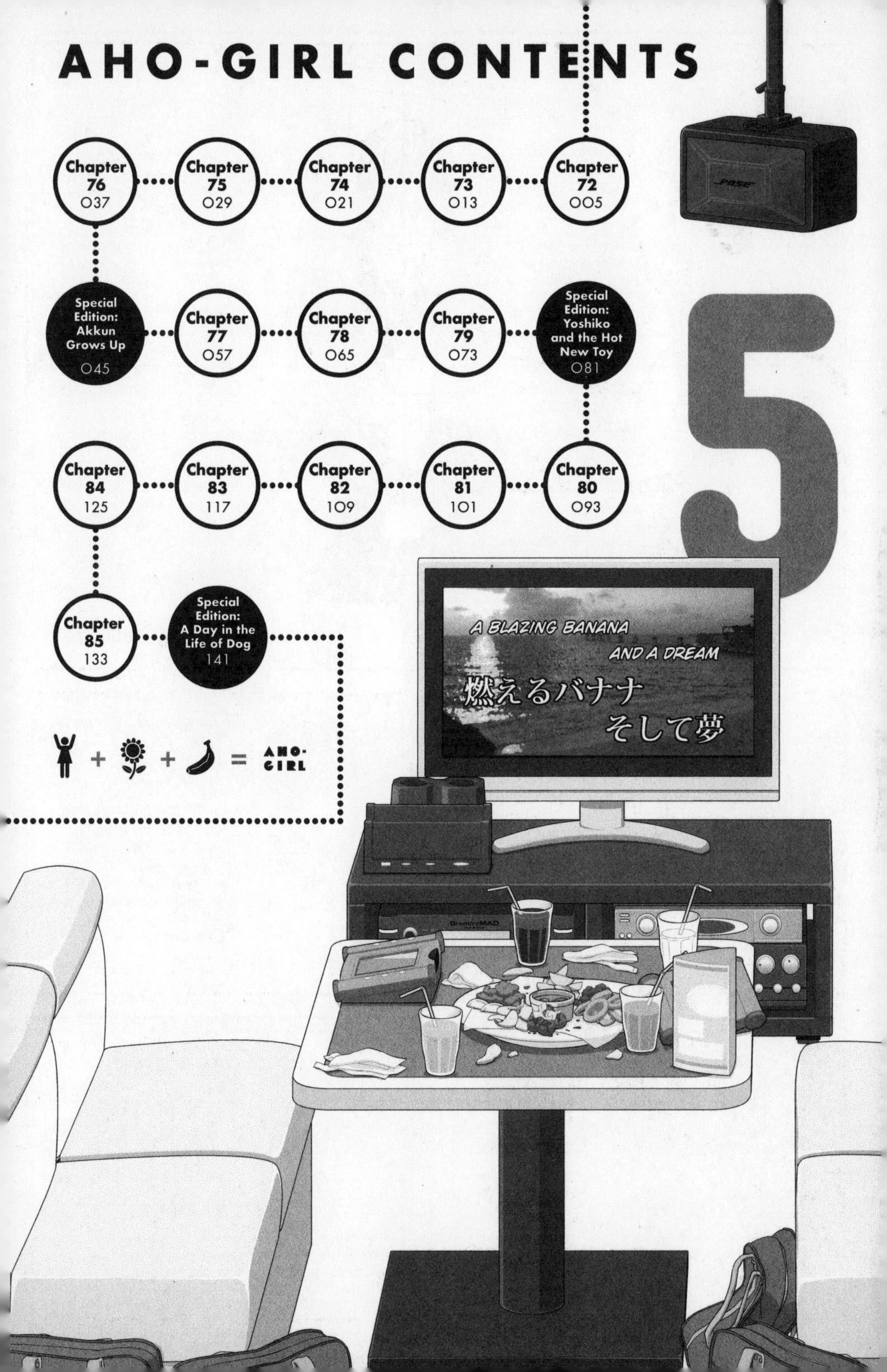

A BLAZING BANANA
AND A DREAM
燃えるバナナ
そして夢

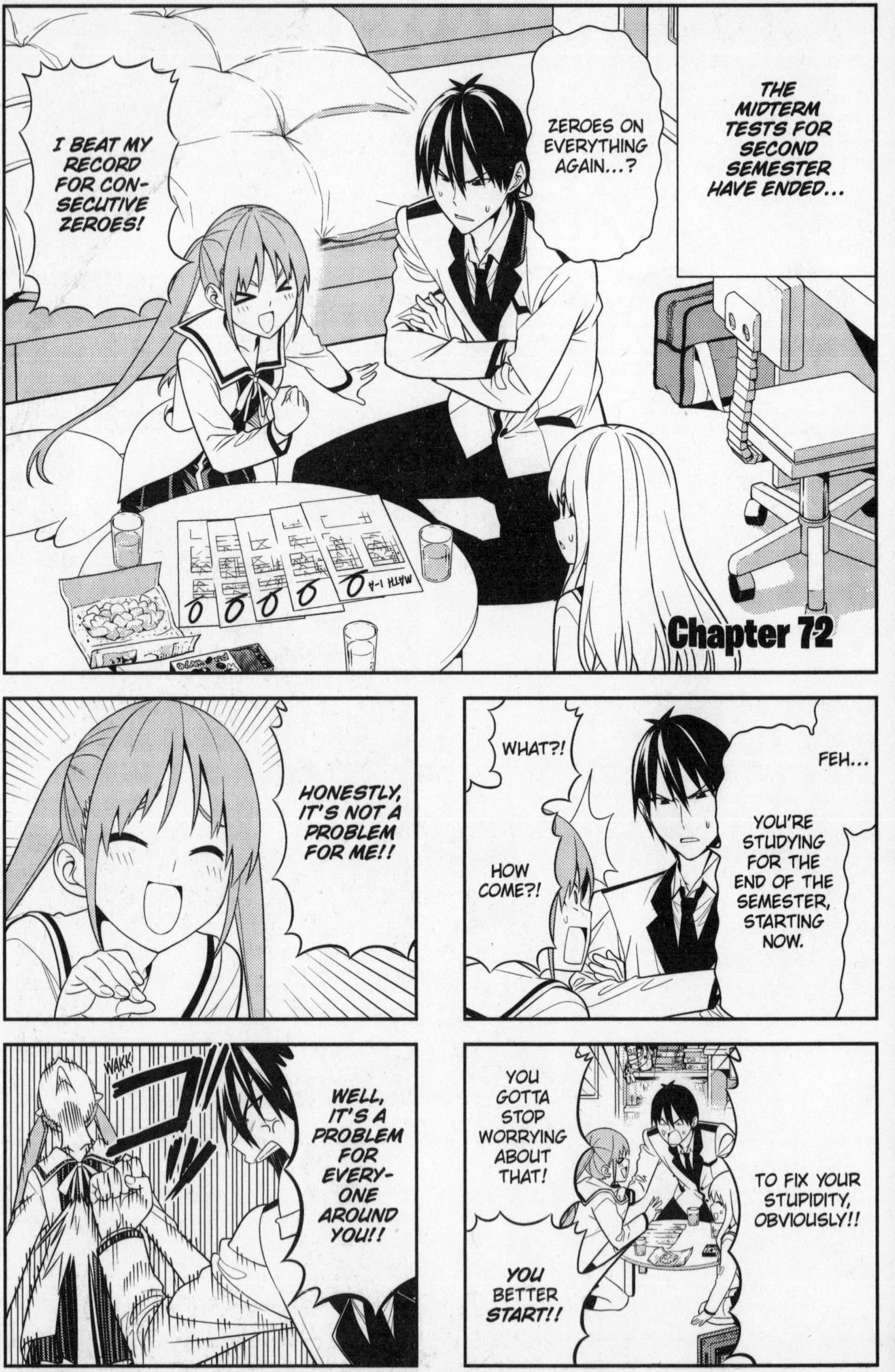
THE MIDTERM TESTS FOR SECOND SEMESTER HAVE ENDED...
ZEROES ON EVERYTHING AGAIN...?
I BEAT MY RECORD FOR CON-SECUTIVE ZEROES!
MATH I-A
Chapter 72
FEH...
YOU'RE STUDYING FOR THE END OF THE SEMESTER, STARTING NOW.
WHAT?!
HOW COME?!
HONESTLY, IT'S NOT A PROBLEM FOR ME!!
TO FIX YOUR STUPIDITY, OBVIOUSLY!!
YOU GOTTA STOP WORRYING ABOUT THAT!
YOU BETTER START!!
WELL, IT'S A PROBLEM FOR EVERY-ONE AROUND YOU!!
WAKK!

Once the Uniform's Off

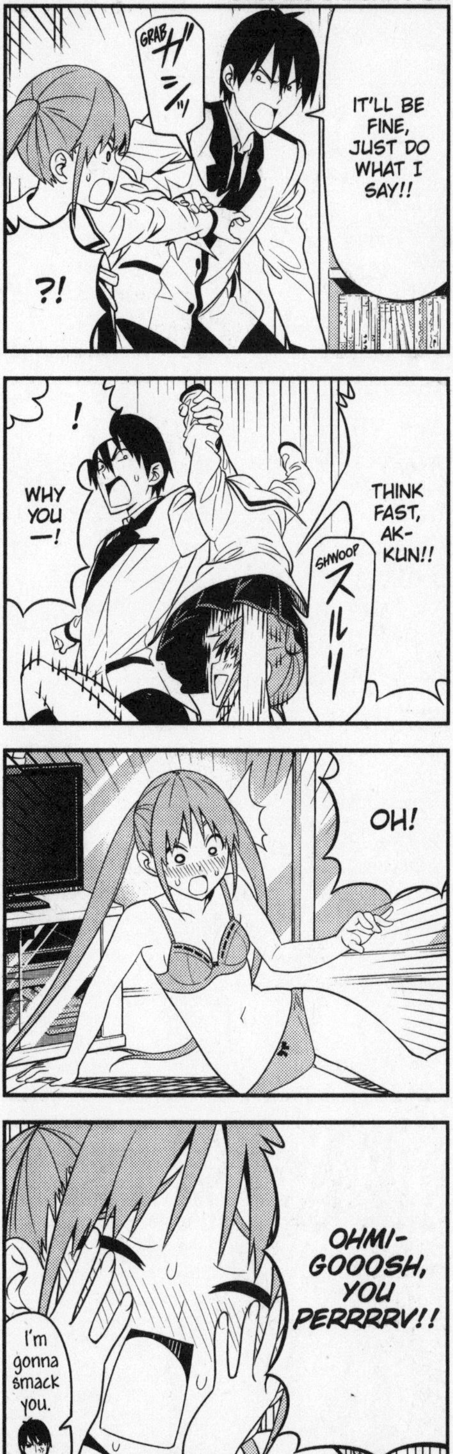
IT'LL BE FINE, JUST DO WHAT I SAY!!
GRAB
?!
THINK FAST, AK-KUN!!
SHWOOP
WHY YOU—!
!
OH!
OHMI-GOOOSH, YOU PERRRRV!!
I'm gonna smack you.

Now Let's Think About This

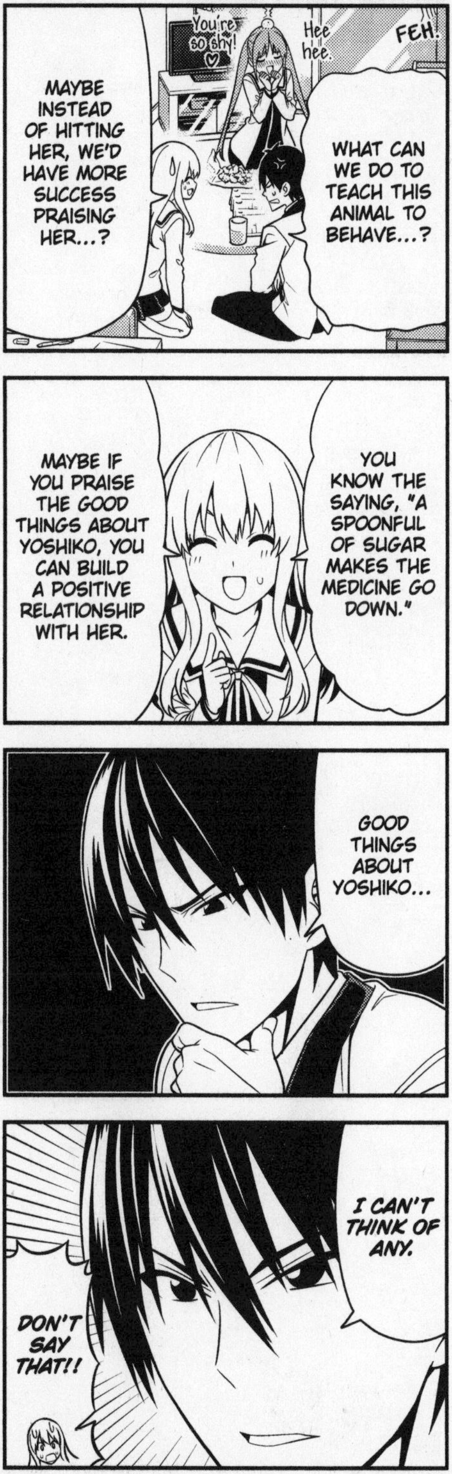
FEH.
WHAT CAN WE DO TO TEACH THIS ANIMAL TO BEHAVE...?
Hee hee.
You're so shy! ♥
MAYBE INSTEAD OF HITTING HER, WE'D HAVE MORE SUCCESS PRAISING HER...?
YOU KNOW THE SAYING, "A SPOONFUL OF SUGAR MAKES THE MEDICINE GO DOWN."
MAYBE IF YOU PRAISE THE GOOD THINGS ABOUT YOSHIKO, YOU CAN BUILD A POSITIVE RELATIONSHIP WITH HER.
GOOD THINGS ABOUT YOSHIKO...
I CAN'T THINK OF ANY.
DON'T SAY THAT!!

## You Can't Have It

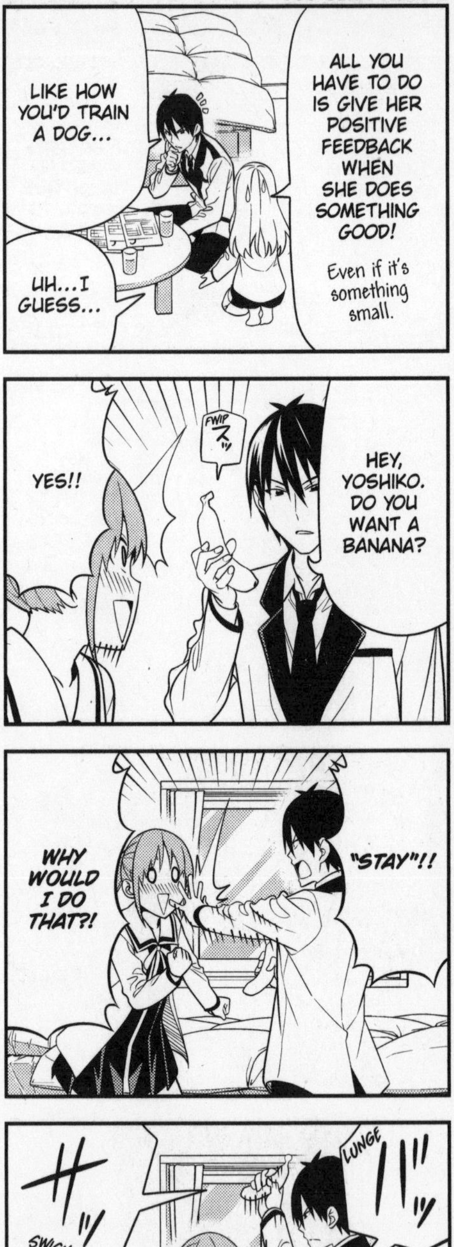
ALL YOU HAVE TO DO IS GIVE HER POSITIVE FEEDBACK WHEN SHE DOES SOMETHING GOOD!
Even if it's something small.
LIKE HOW YOU'D TRAIN A DOG...
UH...I GUESS...
HEY, YOSHIKO. DO YOU WANT A BANANA?
FWIP
YES!!
"STAY"!!
WHY WOULD I DO THAT?!
LUNGE
SWISH

## What Kind of Blood Runs in Your Veins?!

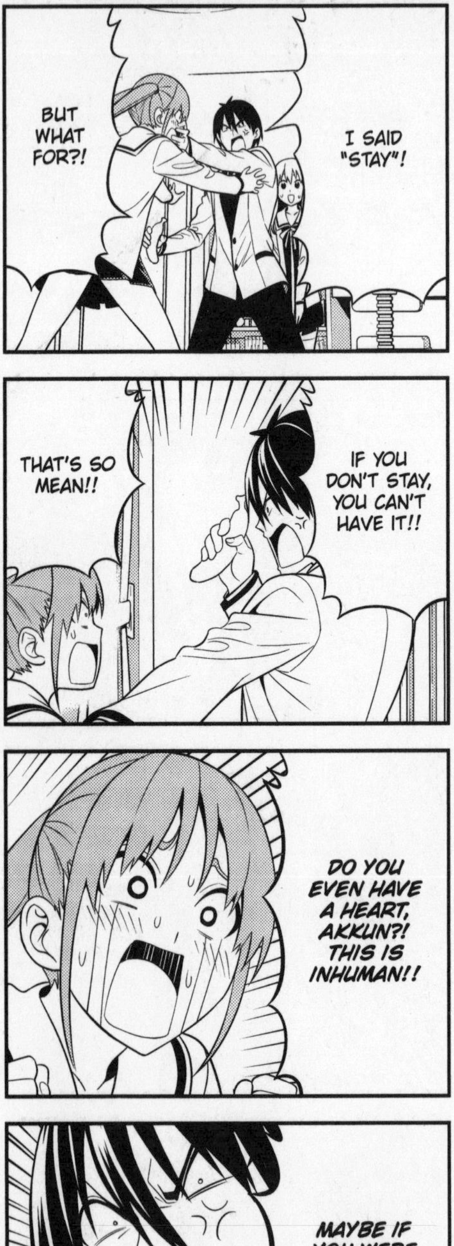
I SAID "STAY"!
BUT WHAT FOR?!
IF YOU DON'T STAY, YOU CAN'T HAVE IT!!
THAT'S SO MEAN!!
DO YOU EVEN HAVE A HEART, AKKUN?! THIS IS INHUMAN!!
MAYBE IF YOU WERE BETTER THAN A DOG AT ANYTHING!!

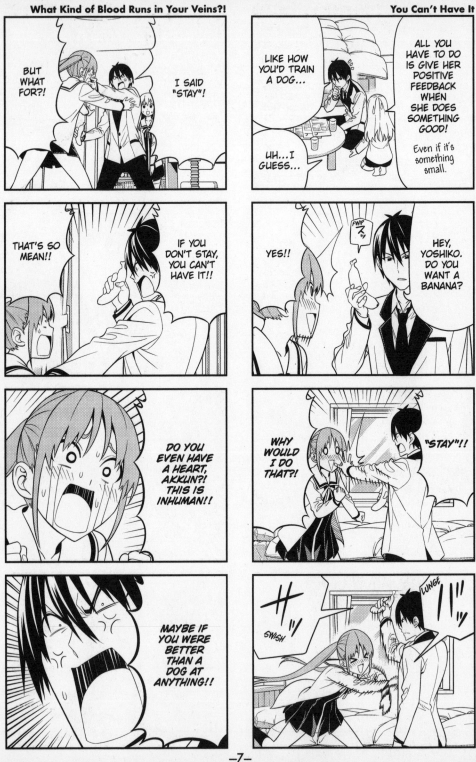

## Determination

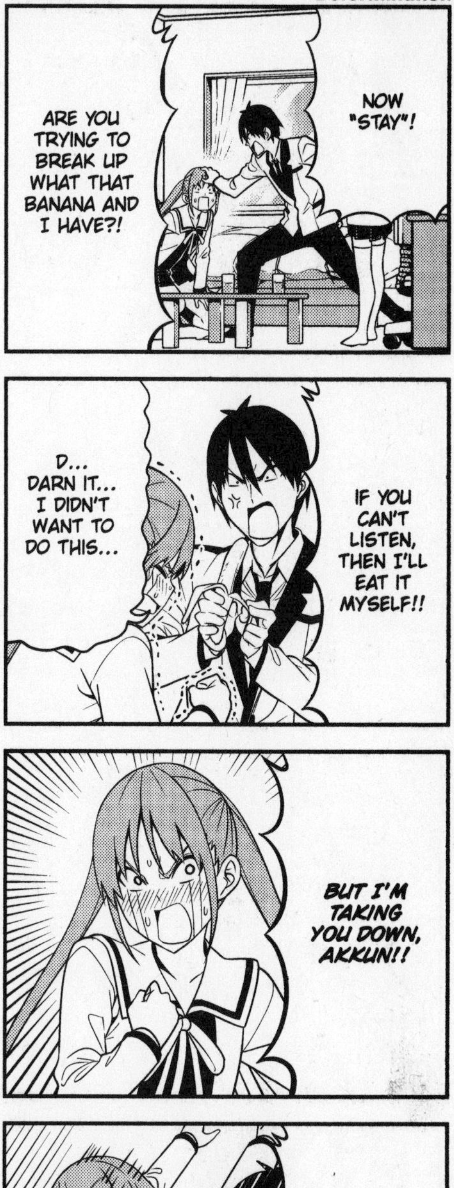
NOW "STAY"!
ARE YOU TRYING TO BREAK UP WHAT THAT BANANA AND I HAVE?!
IF YOU CAN'T LISTEN, THEN I'LL EAT IT MYSELF!!
D... DARN IT... I DIDN'T WANT TO DO THIS...
BUT I'M TAKING YOU DOWN, AKKUN!!
JUST "STAY"!!
AKKUN-SAN!
CHOK

## Yoshiko Makes a Break for It

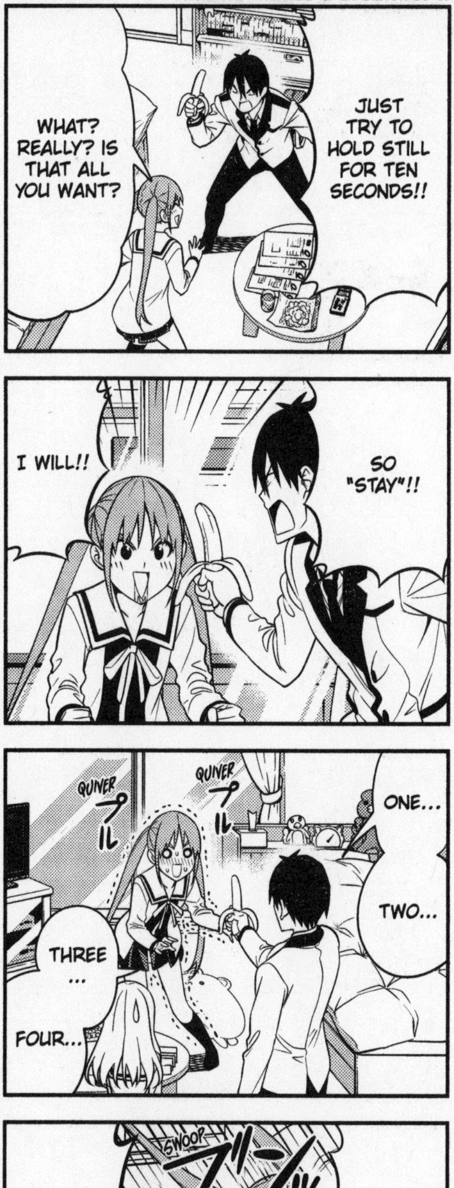
JUST TRY TO HOLD STILL FOR TEN SECONDS!!
WHAT? REALLY? IS THAT ALL YOU WANT?
SO "STAY"!!
I WILL!!
ONE...
QUIVER
QUIVER
TWO...
THREE ...
FOUR...
SWOOP
TEN!!
FIVE!!!
DUCK

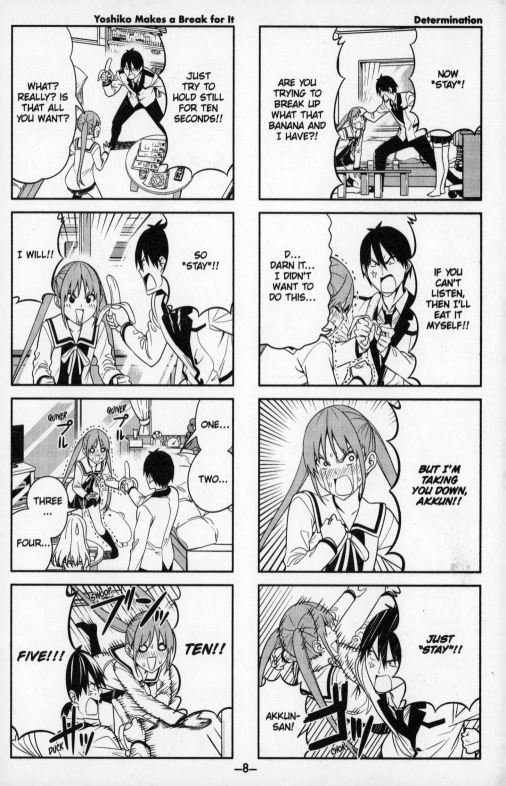

We're Powerless Before Time's March, But C'mon!

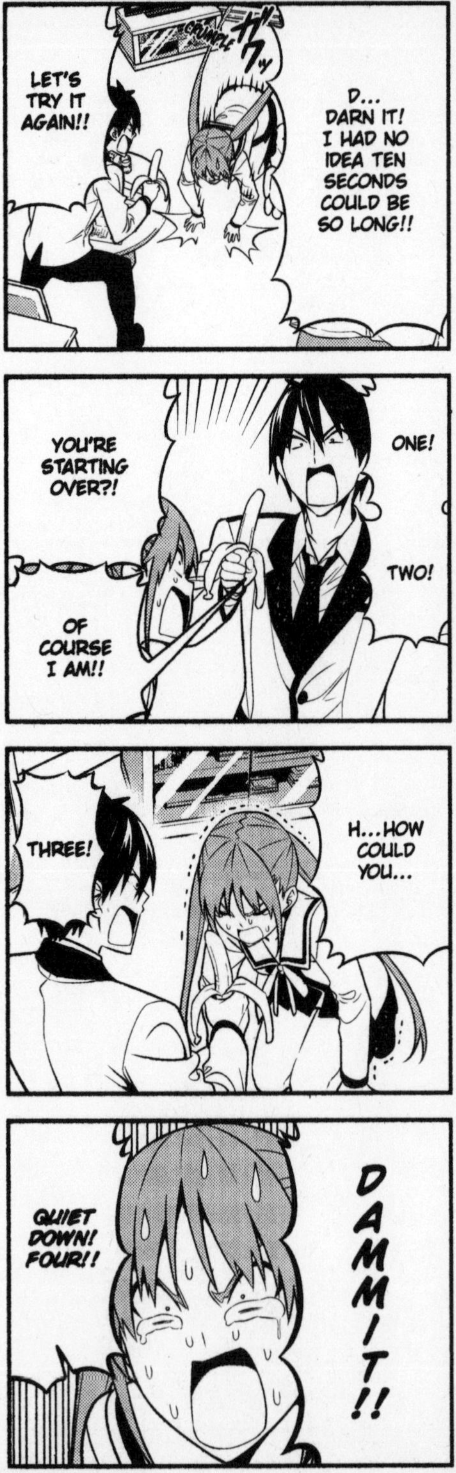
CRUMPLE
D... DARN IT! I HAD NO IDEA TEN SECONDS COULD BE SO LONG!!
LET'S TRY IT AGAIN!!
ONE!
YOU'RE STARTING OVER?!
TWO!
OF COURSE I AM!!
H...HOW COULD YOU...
THREE!
DAMMIT!!
QUIET DOWN! FOUR!!

Between Heaven and Hell

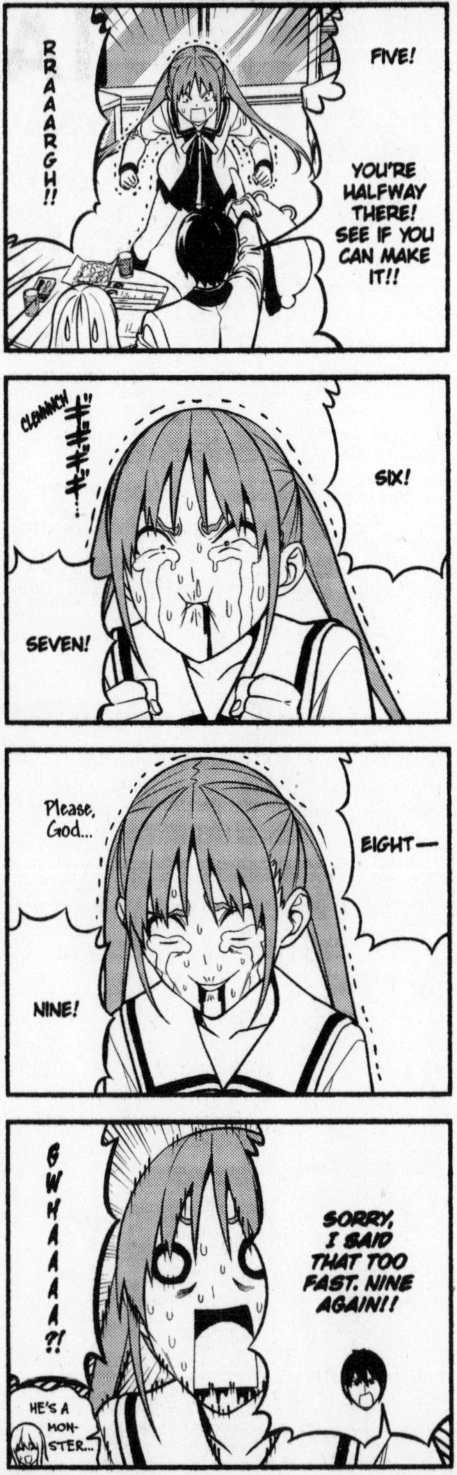
FIVE!
RRAAAARGH!!
YOU'RE HALFWAY THERE! SEE IF YOU CAN MAKE IT!!
SIX!
CLENNNCH
SEVEN!
EIGHT—
Please, God...
NINE!
SORRY, I SAID THAT TOO FAST. NINE AGAIN!!
GWHAAAAA?!
HE'S A MONSTER...

Not a Moment to Lose

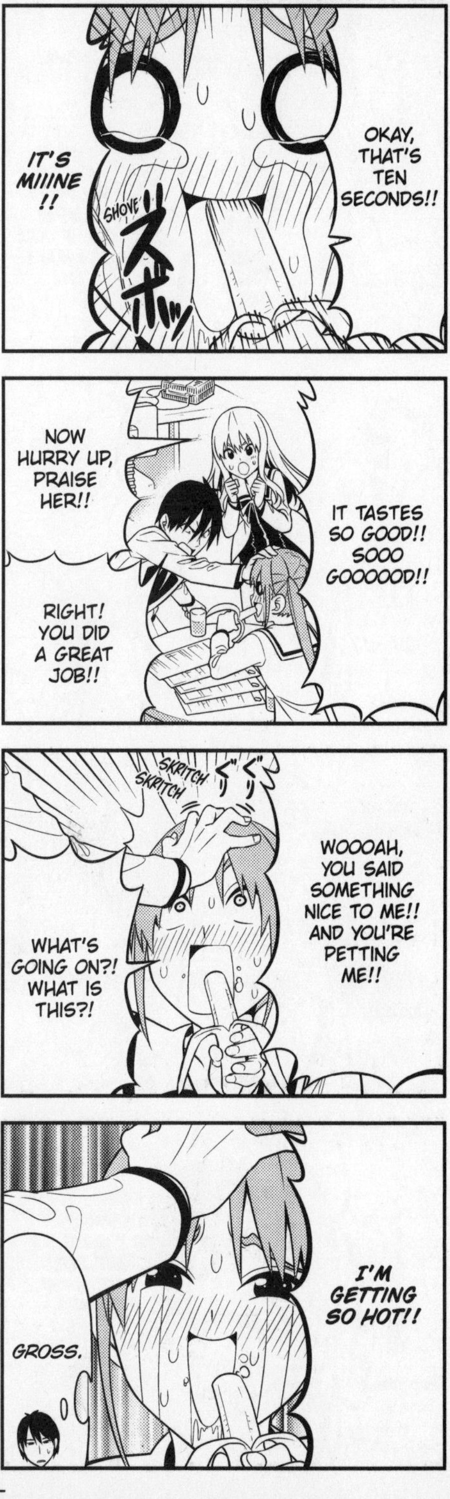
OKAY, THAT'S TEN SECONDS!!
SHOVE
IT'S MIIINE!!
IT TASTES SO GOOD!! SOOO GOOOOOD!!
NOW HURRY UP, PRAISE HER!!
RIGHT! YOU DID A GREAT JOB!!
SKRITCH SKRITCH
WOOOAH, YOU SAID SOMETHING NICE TO ME!! AND YOU'RE PETTING ME!!
WHAT'S GOING ON?! WHAT IS THIS?!
I'M GETTING SO HOT!!
GROSS.

Immediately

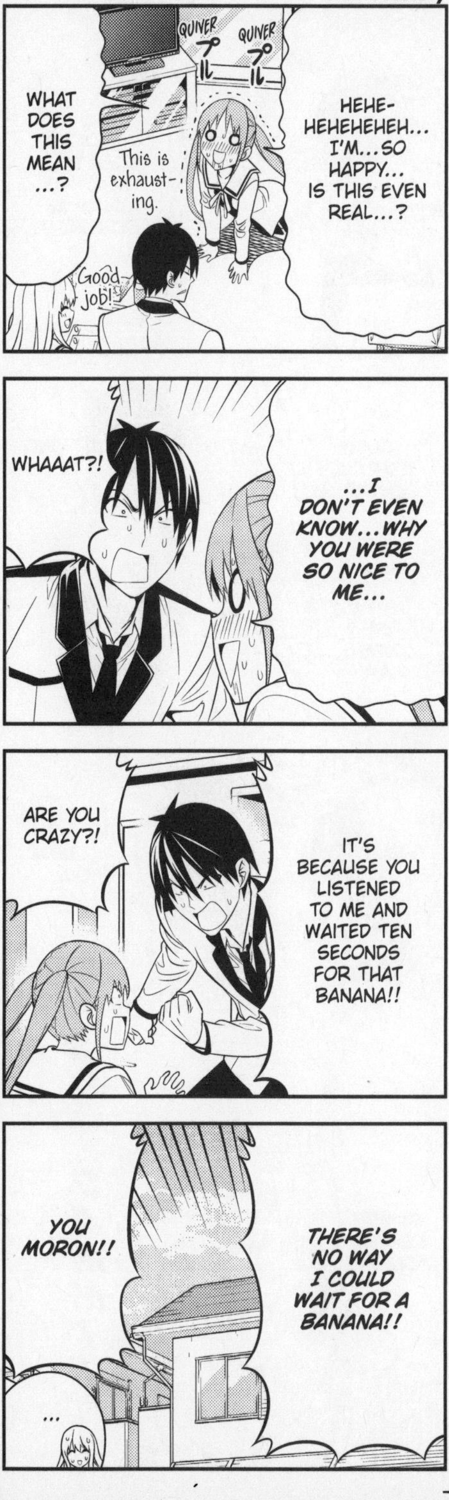
HEHE-HEHEHEHEH... I'M...SO HAPPY... IS THIS EVEN REAL...?
QUIVER
QUIVER
This is exhausting.
WHAT DOES THIS MEAN...?
Good job!
...I DON'T EVEN KNOW...WHY YOU WERE SO NICE TO ME...
WHAAAT?!
IT'S BECAUSE YOU LISTENED TO ME AND WAITED TEN SECONDS FOR THAT BANANA!!
ARE YOU CRAZY?!
THERE'S NO WAY I COULD WAIT FOR A BANANA!!
YOU MORON!!
...

**C'mon**

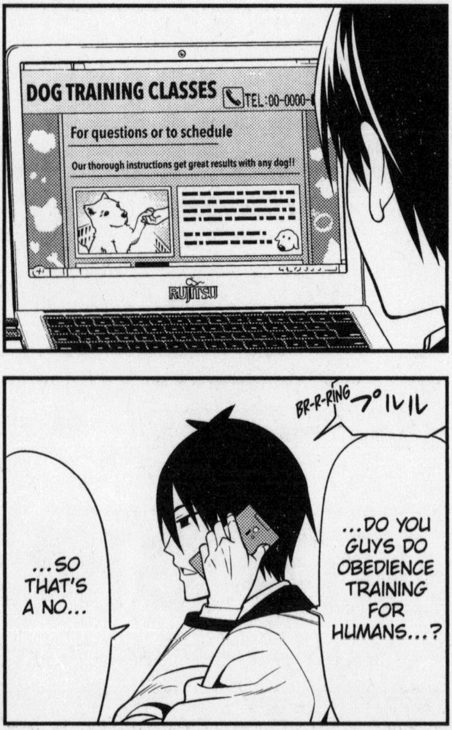
DOG TRAINING CLASSES
TEL:00-0000-
For questions or to schedule
Our thorough instructions get great results with any dog!!
BR-R-RING プルル
...DO YOU GUYS DO OBEDIENCE TRAINING FOR HUMANS...?
...SO THAT'S A NO...

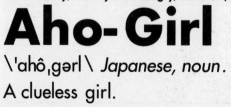
(Packed with nuts, sure to satisfy; when you're hungry, reach for)

# Aho-Girl

\\'ahô₁gərl\\ *Japanese, noun.*
A clueless girl.

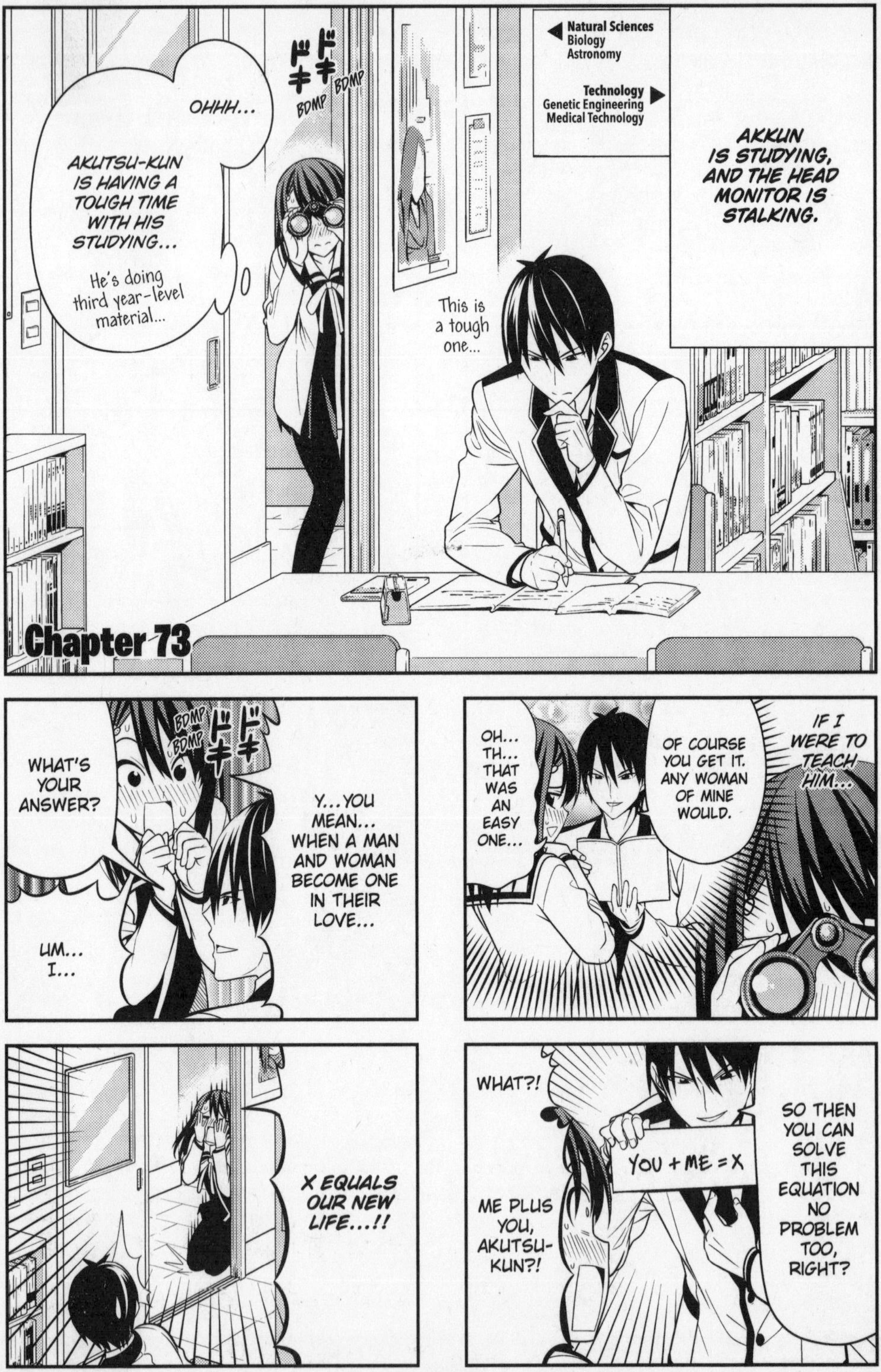

AKKUN IS STUDYING, AND THE HEAD MONITOR IS STALKING.
Natural Sciences
Biology
Astronomy
Technology
Genetic Engineering
Medical Technology
This is a tough one...
ドキドキ
BDMP BDMP
OHHH...
AKUTSU-KUN IS HAVING A TOUGH TIME WITH HIS STUDYING...
He's doing third year-level material...
Chapter 73
IF I WERE TO TEACH HIM...
OF COURSE YOU GET IT. ANY WOMAN OF MINE WOULD.
OH... TH... THAT WAS AN EASY ONE...
Y...YOU MEAN... WHEN A MAN AND WOMAN BECOME ONE IN THEIR LOVE...
ドキドキ
BDMP BDMP
WHAT'S YOUR ANSWER?
UM... I...
SO THEN YOU CAN SOLVE THIS EQUATION NO PROBLEM TOO, RIGHT?
YOU + ME = X
WHAT?!
ME PLUS YOU, AKUTSU-KUN?!
X EQUALS OUR NEW LIFE...!!

Oh—Really?!

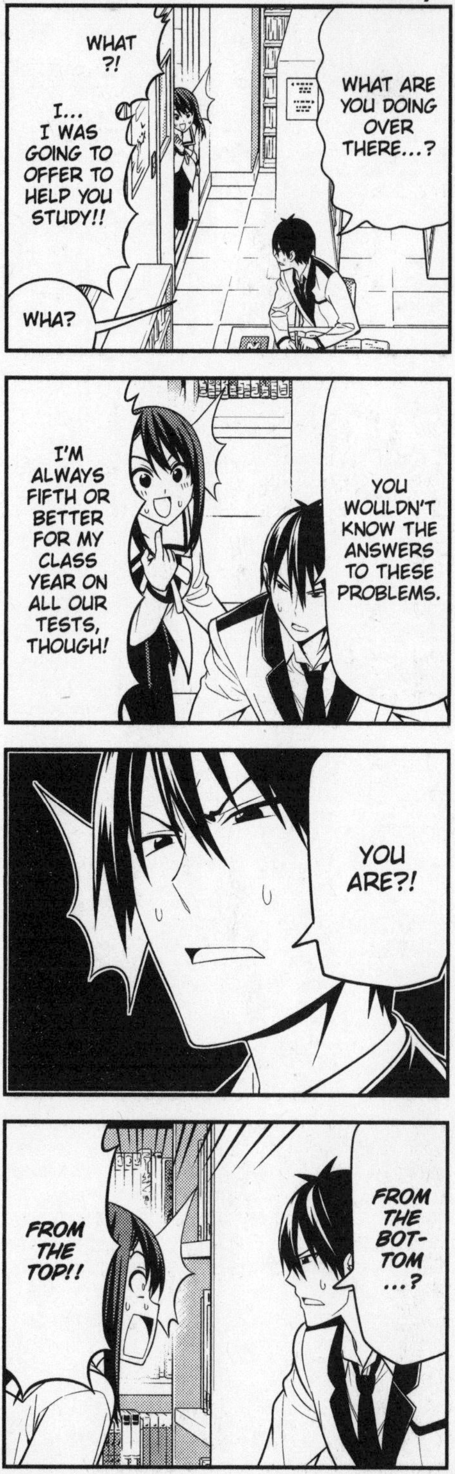
WHAT ARE YOU DOING OVER THERE...?
WHAT ?!
I... I WAS GOING TO OFFER TO HELP YOU STUDY!!
WHA?
YOU WOULDN'T KNOW THE ANSWERS TO THESE PROBLEMS.
I'M ALWAYS FIFTH OR BETTER FOR MY CLASS YEAR ON ALL OUR TESTS, THOUGH!
YOU ARE?!
FROM THE BOT-TOM ...?
FROM THE TOP!!

Proof of Her Intelligence

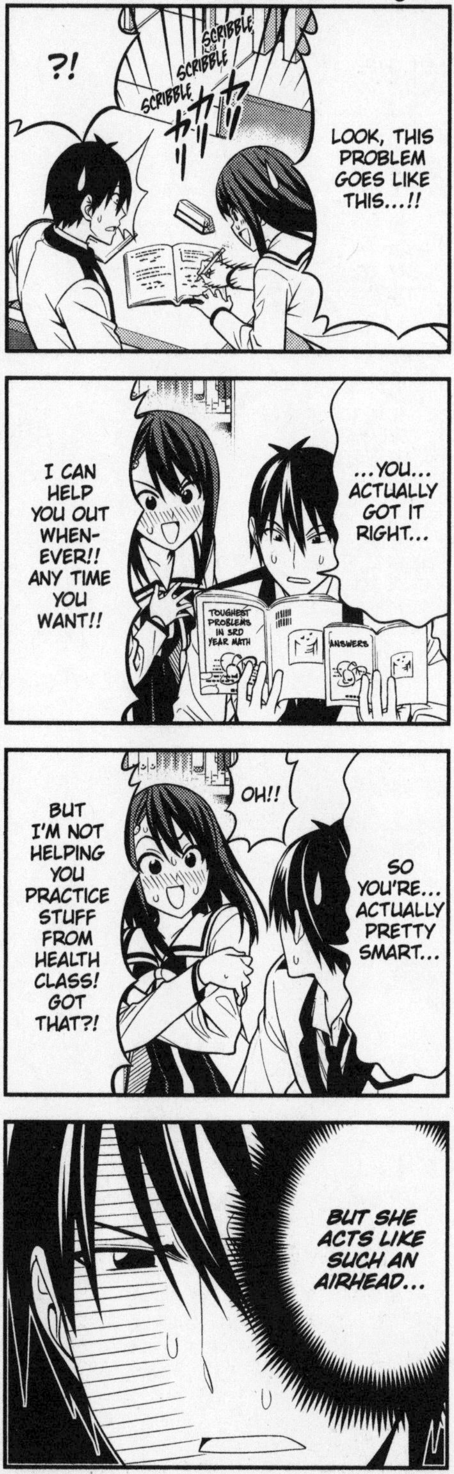
LOOK, THIS PROBLEM GOES LIKE THIS...!!
SCRIBBLE
SCRIBBLE
SCRIBBLE
?!
...YOU... ACTUALLY GOT IT RIGHT...
I CAN HELP YOU OUT WHEN-EVER!! ANY TIME YOU WANT!!
TOUGHEST PROBLEMS IN 3RD YEAR MATH
ANSWERS
SO YOU'RE... ACTUALLY PRETTY SMART...
OH!!
BUT I'M NOT HELPING YOU PRACTICE STUFF FROM HEALTH CLASS! GOT THAT?!
BUT SHE ACTS LIKE SUCH AN AIRHEAD...

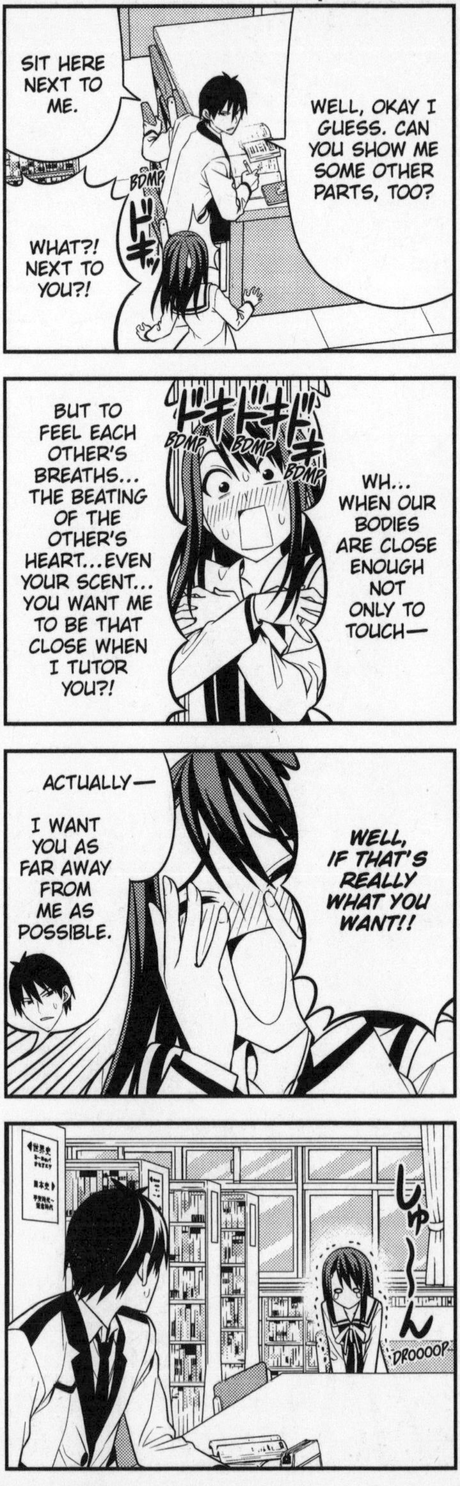
WELL, OKAY I GUESS. CAN YOU SHOW ME SOME OTHER PARTS, TOO?
SIT HERE NEXT TO ME.
ドキッ BDMP
WHAT?! NEXT TO YOU?!
WH... WHEN OUR BODIES ARE CLOSE ENOUGH NOT ONLY TO TOUCH—
ドキドキドキ BDMP BDMP BDMP
BUT TO FEEL EACH OTHER'S BREATHS... THE BEATING OF THE OTHER'S HEART...EVEN YOUR SCENT... YOU WANT ME TO BE THAT CLOSE WHEN I TUTOR YOU?!
WELL, IF THAT'S REALLY WHAT YOU WANT!!
ACTUALLY—
I WANT YOU AS FAR AWAY FROM ME AS POSSIBLE.
しゅ〜ん DROOOOP



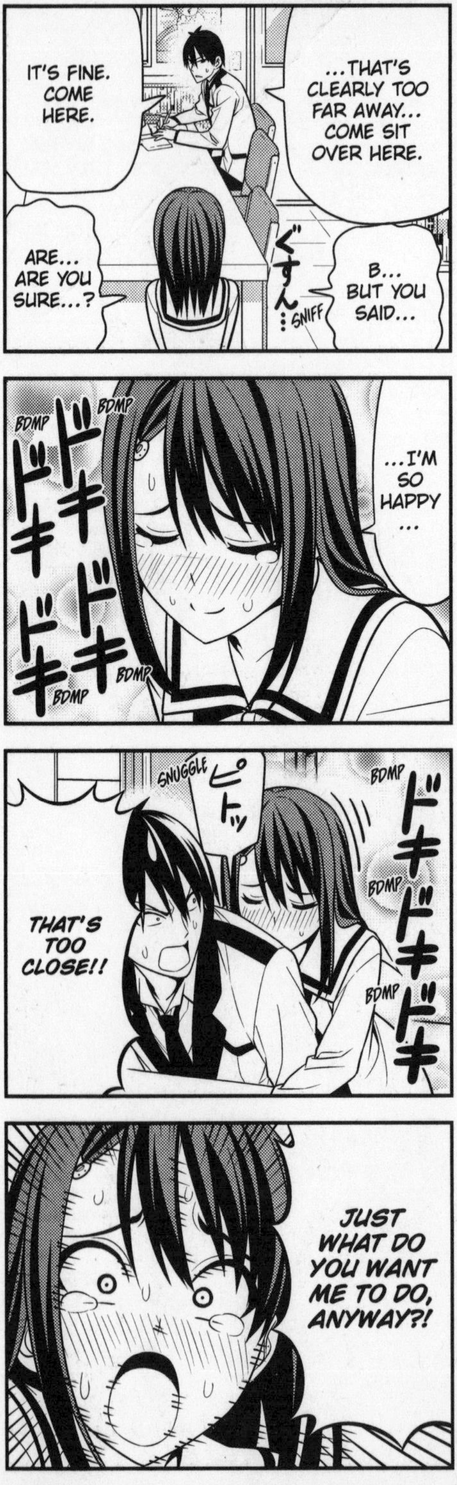
...THAT'S CLEARLY TOO FAR AWAY... COME SIT OVER HERE.
B... BUT YOU SAID...
ぐすん… SNIFF
IT'S FINE. COME HERE.
ARE... ARE YOU SURE...?
...I'M SO HAPPY...
ドキドキ BDMP BDMP
ドキドキ BDMP BDMP
THAT'S TOO CLOSE!!
ピトッ SNUGGLE
ドキドキドキ BDMP BDMP BDMP
JUST WHAT DO YOU WANT ME TO DO, ANYWAY?!

Turning Cold

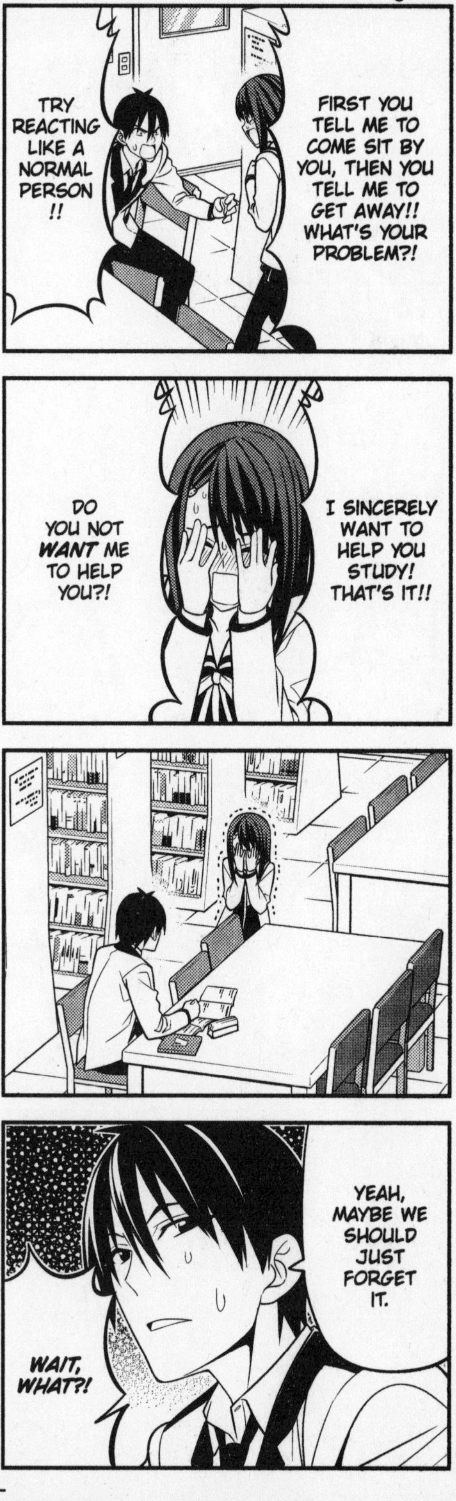
FIRST YOU TELL ME TO COME SIT BY YOU, THEN YOU TELL ME TO GET AWAY!! WHAT'S YOUR PROBLEM?!
TRY REACTING LIKE A NORMAL PERSON!!
I SINCERELY WANT TO HELP YOU STUDY! THAT'S IT!!
DO YOU NOT *WANT* ME TO HELP YOU?!
YEAH, MAYBE WE SHOULD JUST FORGET IT.
*WAIT, WHAT?!*

Compromise

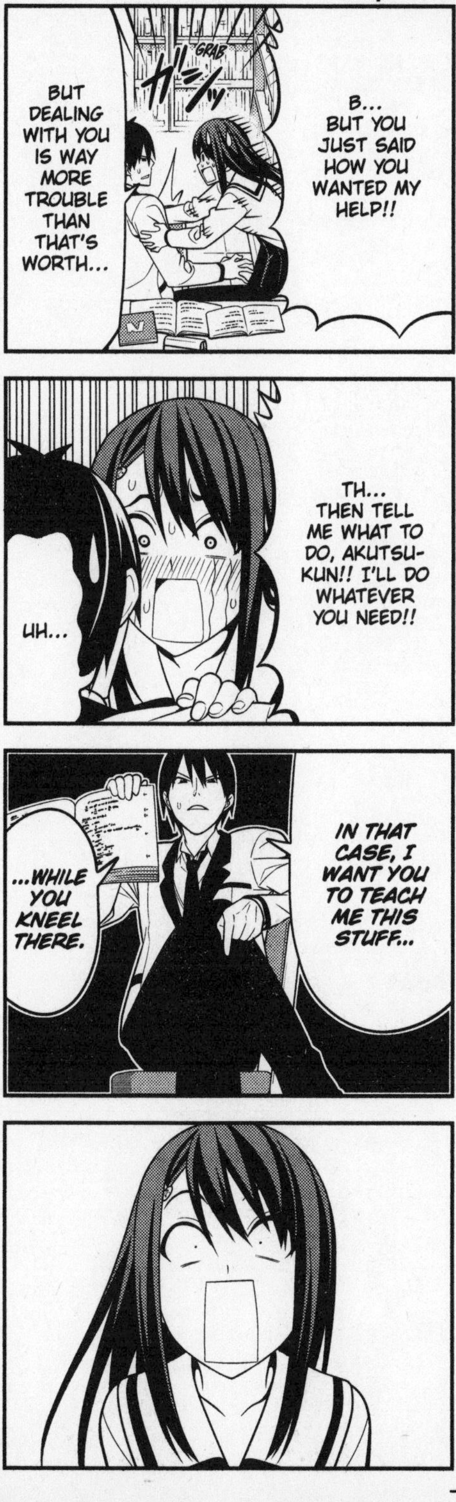
GRAB
B... BUT YOU JUST SAID HOW YOU WANTED MY HELP!!
BUT DEALING WITH YOU IS WAY MORE TROUBLE THAN THAT'S WORTH...
TH... THEN TELL ME WHAT TO DO, AKUTSU-KUN!! I'LL DO WHATEVER YOU NEED!!
UH...
*IN THAT CASE, I WANT YOU TO TEACH ME THIS STUFF...*
*...WHILE YOU KNEEL THERE.*

Smart Girls Lie

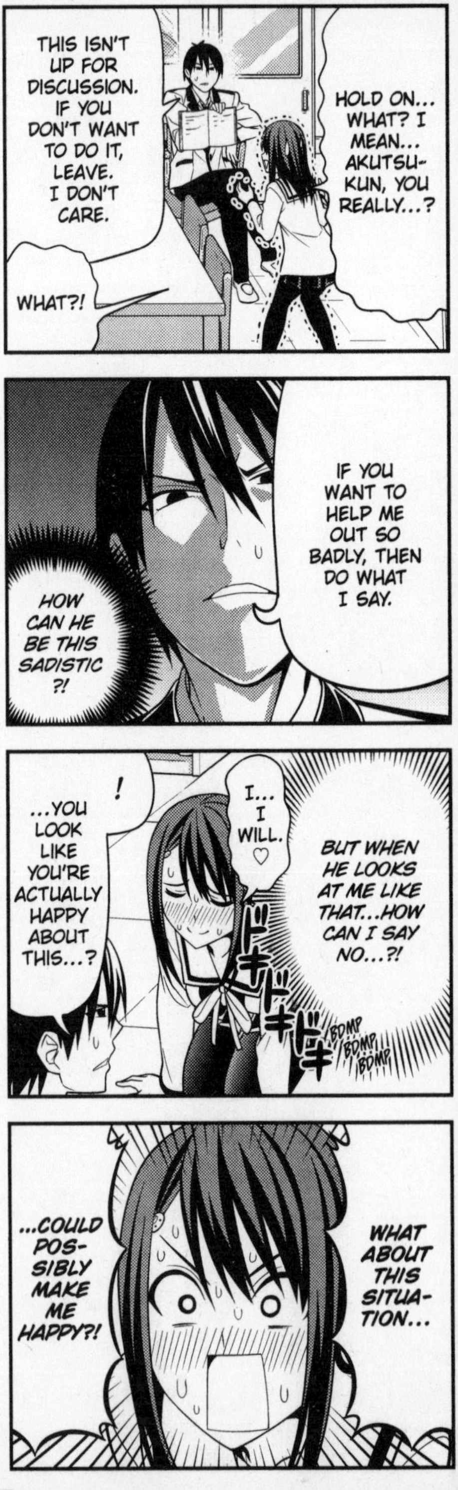
HOLD ON... WHAT? I MEAN... AKUTSU-KUN, YOU REALLY...?
THIS ISN'T UP FOR DISCUSSION. IF YOU DON'T WANT TO DO IT, LEAVE. I DON'T CARE.
WHAT?!
IF YOU WANT TO HELP ME OUT SO BADLY, THEN DO WHAT I SAY.
HOW CAN HE BE THIS SADISTIC ?!
I... I WILL. ♡
BUT WHEN HE LOOKS AT ME LIKE THAT...HOW CAN I SAY NO...?!
!
...YOU LOOK LIKE YOU'RE ACTUALLY HAPPY ABOUT THIS...?
ドキドキドキ
BDMP BDMP BDMP
WHAT ABOUT THIS SITUA-TION...
...COULD POS-SIBLY MAKE ME HAPPY?!

From the Bottom of My Heart

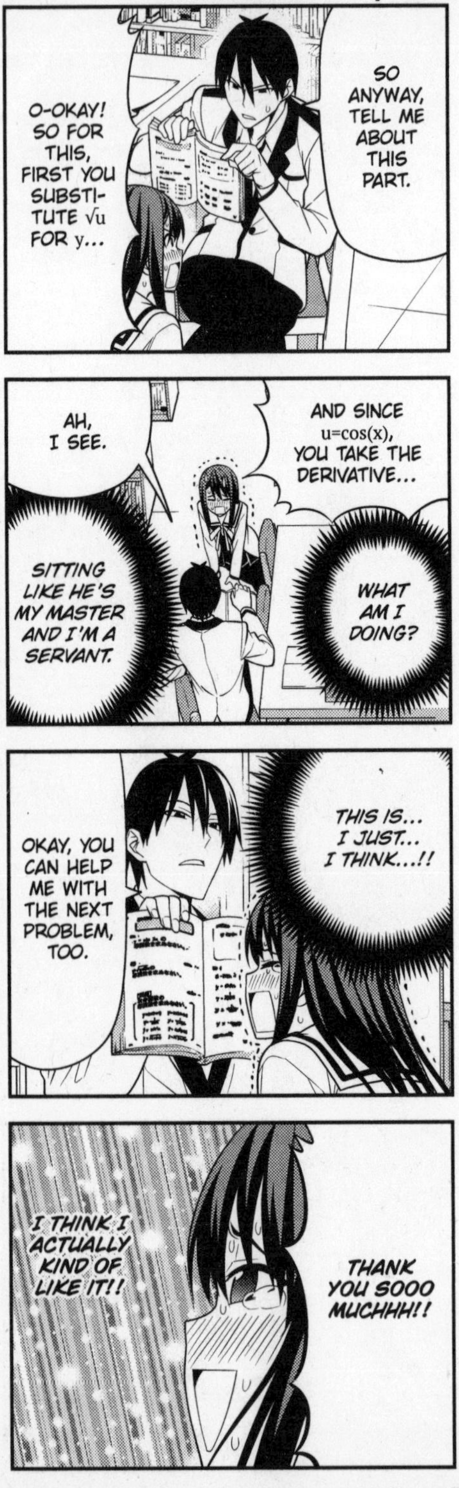
SO ANYWAY, TELL ME ABOUT THIS PART.
O-OKAY! SO FOR THIS, FIRST YOU SUBSTI-TUTE √u FOR y...
AND SINCE u=cos(x), YOU TAKE THE DERIVATIVE...
AH, I SEE.
WHAT AM I DOING?
SITTING LIKE HE'S MY MASTER AND I'M A SERVANT.
THIS IS... I JUST... I THINK...!!
OKAY, YOU CAN HELP ME WITH THE NEXT PROBLEM, TOO.
THANK YOU SOOO MUCHHH!!
I THINK I ACTUALLY KIND OF LIKE IT!!

More Than Happy

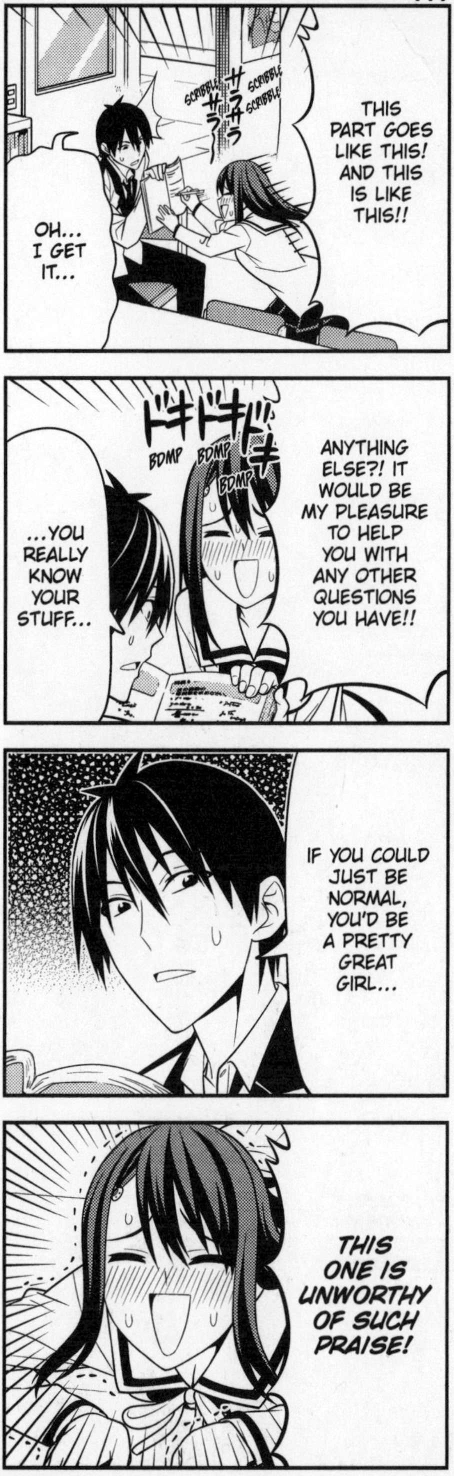
THIS PART GOES LIKE THIS! AND THIS IS LIKE THIS!!
SCRIBBLE SCRIBBLE SCRIBBLE
OH... I GET IT...
ANYTHING ELSE?! IT WOULD BE MY PLEASURE TO HELP YOU WITH ANY OTHER QUESTIONS YOU HAVE!!
BDMP BDMP BDMP
...YOU REALLY KNOW YOUR STUFF...
IF YOU COULD JUST BE NORMAL, YOU'D BE A PRETTY GREAT GIRL...
THIS ONE IS UNWORTHY OF SUCH PRAISE!

You Have My Pity, Head Monitor

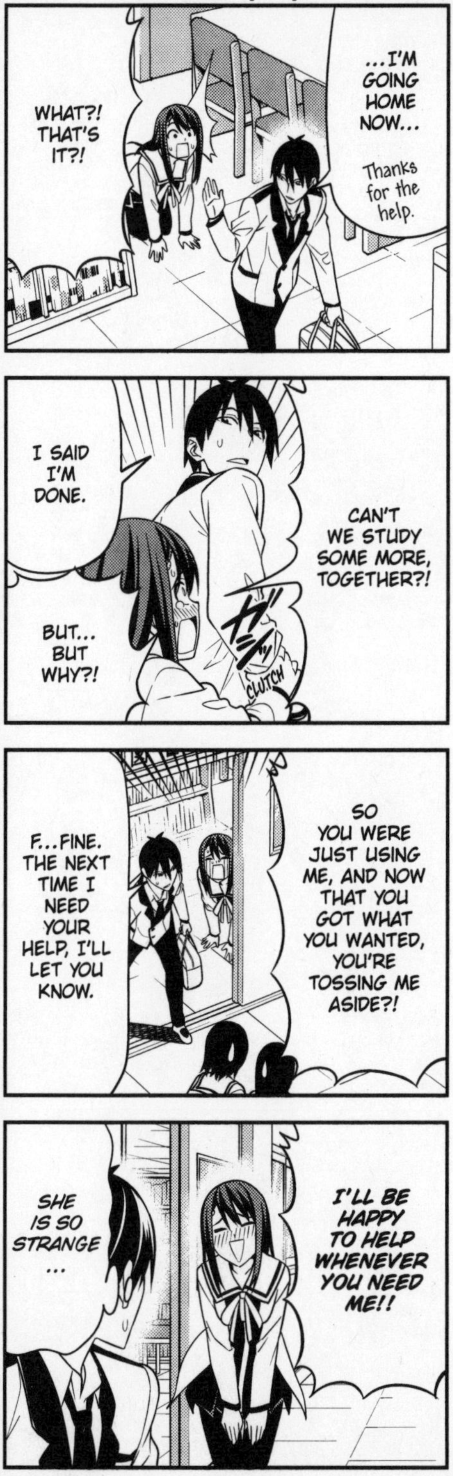
...I'M GOING HOME NOW... Thanks for the help.
WHAT?! THAT'S IT?!
CAN'T WE STUDY SOME MORE, TOGETHER?!
I SAID I'M DONE.
BUT... BUT WHY?!
CLUTCH
SO YOU WERE JUST USING ME, AND NOW THAT YOU GOT WHAT YOU WANTED, YOU'RE TOSSING ME ASIDE?!
F...FINE. THE NEXT TIME I NEED YOUR HELP, I'LL LET YOU KNOW.
I'LL BE HAPPY TO HELP WHENEVER YOU NEED ME!!
SHE IS SO STRANGE ...

The Gulf Continues to Widen

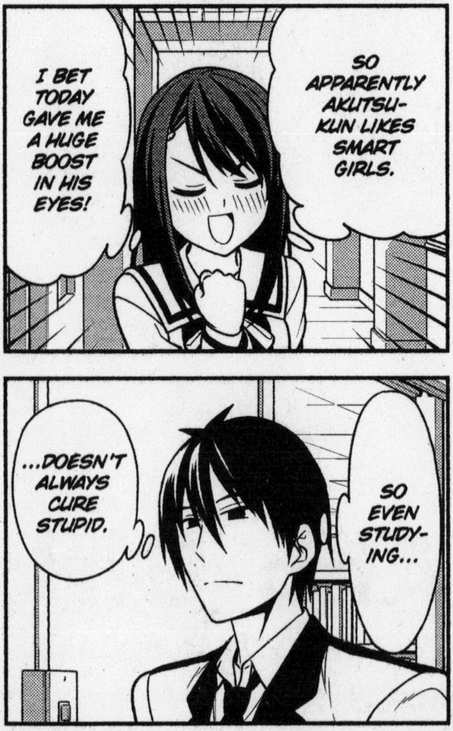
SO APPARENTLY AKUTSU-KUN LIKES SMART GIRLS.
I BET TODAY GAVE ME A HUGE BOOST IN HIS EYES!
SO EVEN STUDY-ING...
...DOESN'T ALWAYS CURE STUPID.

(Sine, cosine, and)

# Aho-Girl

\ˈahôˌgərl\ *Japanese, noun.*
A clueless girl.

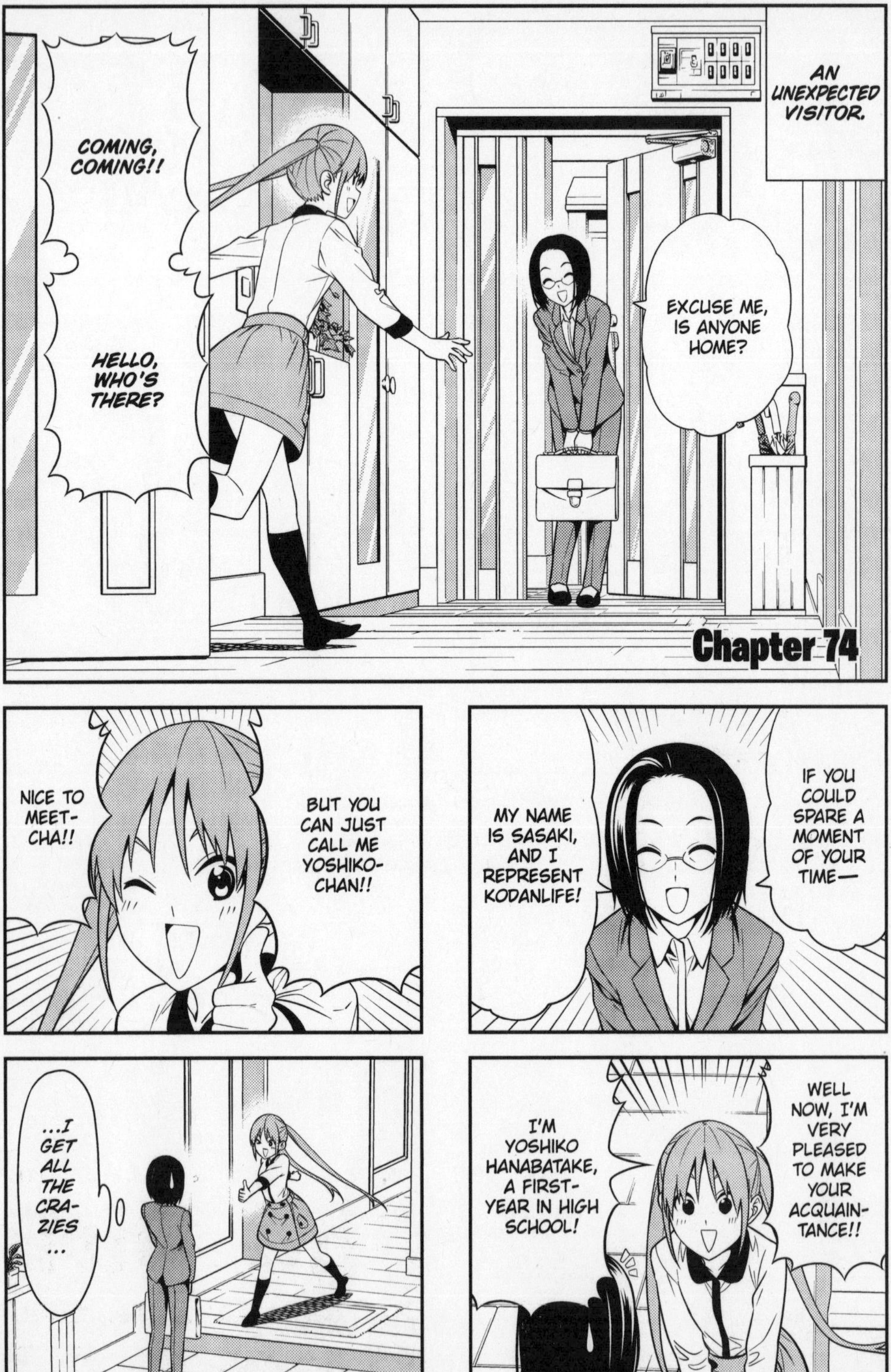
AN UNEXPECTED VISITOR.
EXCUSE ME, IS ANYONE HOME?
COMING, COMING!!
HELLO, WHO'S THERE?
Chapter 74
MY NAME IS SASAKI, AND I REPRESENT KODANLIFE!
IF YOU COULD SPARE A MOMENT OF YOUR TIME—
I'M YOSHIKO HANABATAKE, A FIRST-YEAR IN HIGH SCHOOL!
WELL NOW, I'M VERY PLEASED TO MAKE YOUR ACQUAINTANCE!!
NICE TO MEET-CHA!!
BUT YOU CAN JUST CALL ME YOSHIKO-CHAN!!
...I GET ALL THE CRAZIES...

Her Mom Can Leave Her Home Alone!

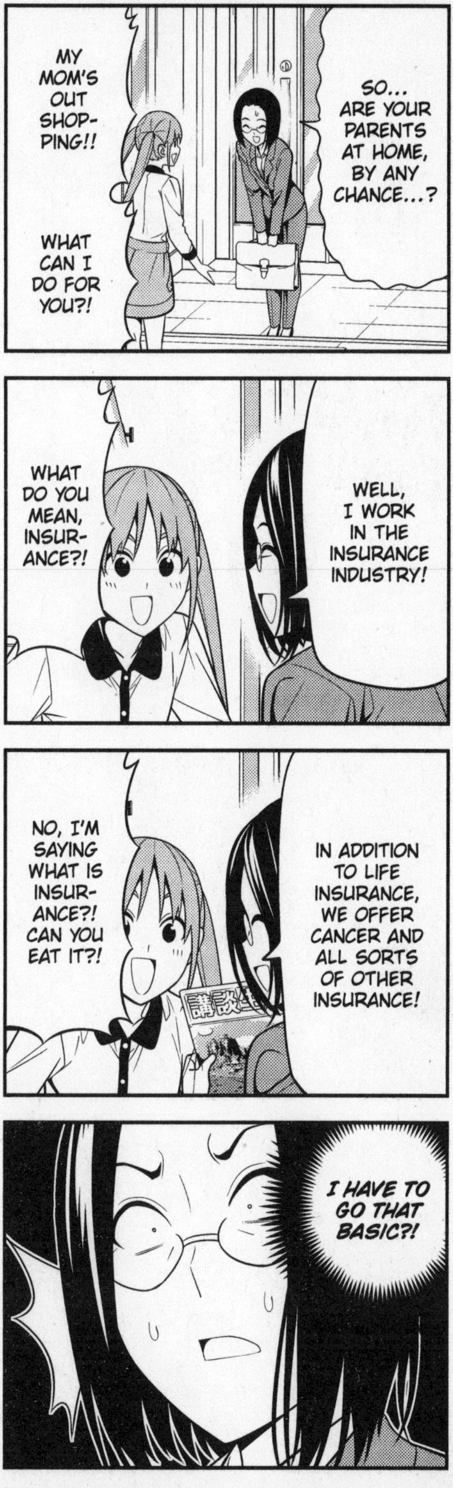
SO... ARE YOUR PARENTS AT HOME, BY ANY CHANCE...?
MY MOM'S OUT SHOP-PING!!
WHAT CAN I DO FOR YOU?!
WELL, I WORK IN THE INSURANCE INDUSTRY!
WHAT DO YOU MEAN, INSUR-ANCE?!
IN ADDITION TO LIFE INSURANCE, WE OFFER CANCER AND ALL SORTS OF OTHER INSURANCE!
NO, I'M SAYING WHAT IS INSUR-ANCE?! CAN YOU EAT IT?!
I HAVE TO GO THAT BASIC?!

Sink Your Claws In

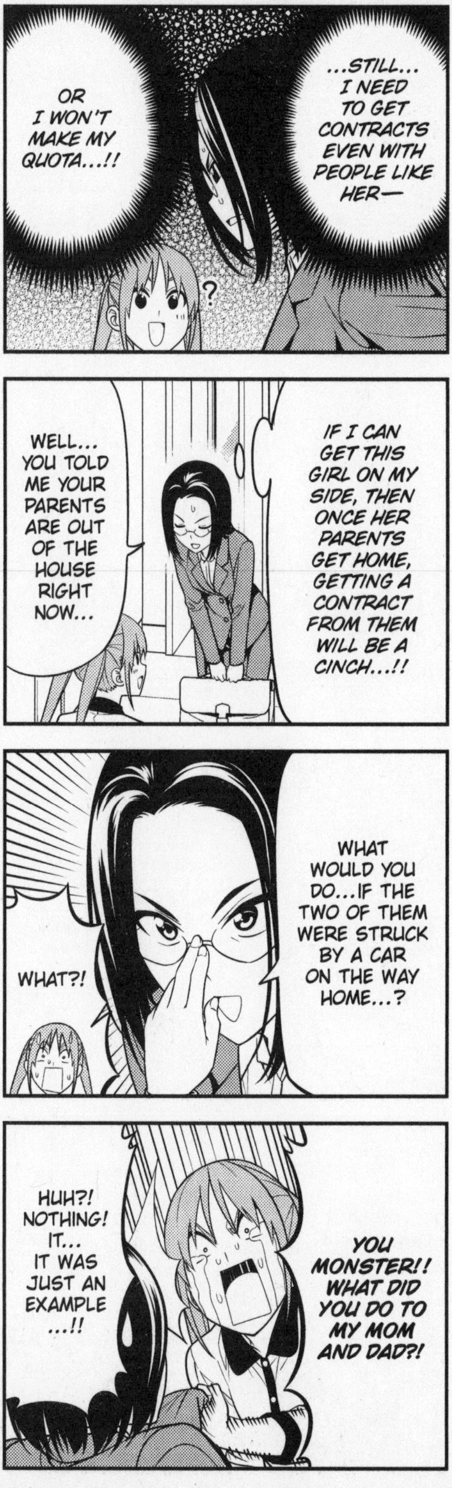
...STILL... I NEED TO GET CONTRACTS EVEN WITH PEOPLE LIKE HER—
OR I WON'T MAKE MY QUOTA...!!
?
IF I CAN GET THIS GIRL ON MY SIDE, THEN ONCE HER PARENTS GET HOME, GETTING A CONTRACT FROM THEM WILL BE A CINCH...!!
WELL... YOU TOLD ME YOUR PARENTS ARE OUT OF THE HOUSE RIGHT NOW...
WHAT WOULD YOU DO...IF THE TWO OF THEM WERE STRUCK BY A CAR ON THE WAY HOME...?
WHAT?!
YOU MONSTER!! WHAT DID YOU DO TO MY MOM AND DAD?!
HUH?! NOTHING! IT... IT WAS JUST AN EXAMPLE ...!!

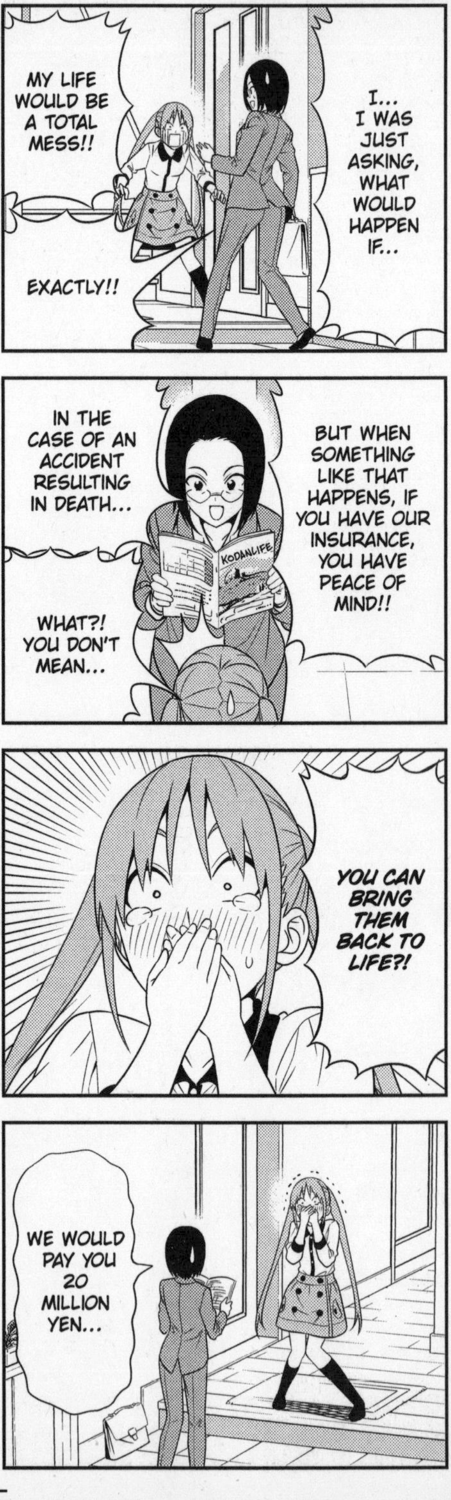
I... I WAS JUST ASKING, WHAT WOULD HAPPEN IF...
MY LIFE WOULD BE A TOTAL MESS!!
EXACTLY!!
BUT WHEN SOMETHING LIKE THAT HAPPENS, IF YOU HAVE OUR INSURANCE, YOU HAVE PEACE OF MIND!!
KODANLIFE
IN THE CASE OF AN ACCIDENT RESULTING IN DEATH...
WHAT?! YOU DON'T MEAN...
YOU CAN BRING THEM BACK TO LIFE?!
WE WOULD PAY YOU 20 MILLION YEN...



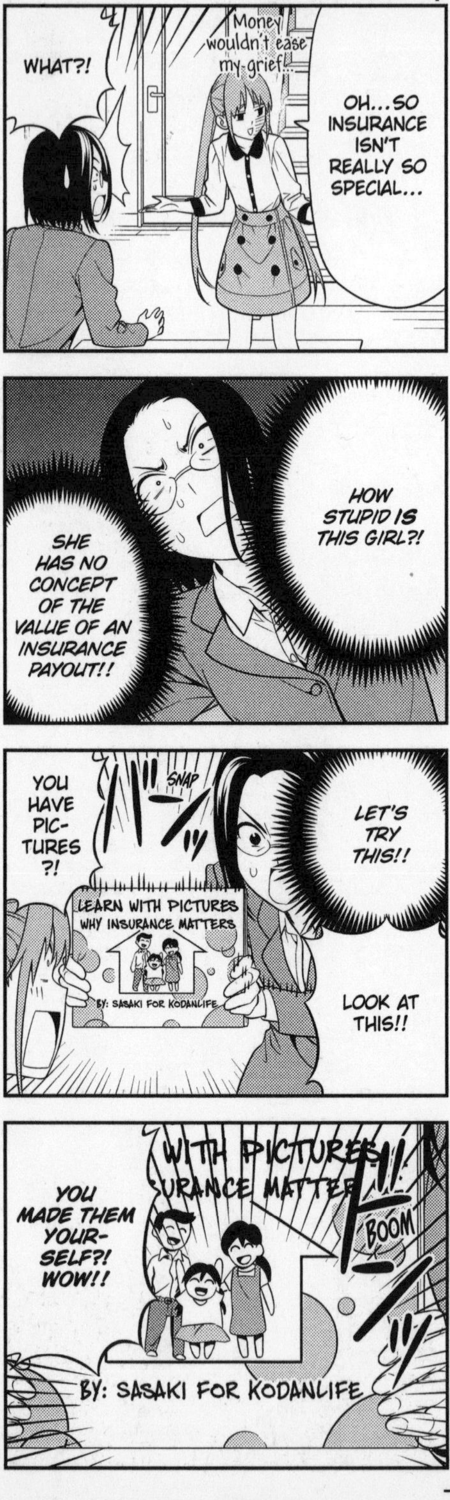
OH...SO INSURANCE ISN'T REALLY SO SPECIAL...
Money wouldn't ease my grief...
WHAT?!
HOW STUPID IS THIS GIRL?!
SHE HAS NO CONCEPT OF THE VALUE OF AN INSURANCE PAYOUT!!
LET'S TRY THIS!!
SNAP
YOU HAVE PIC-TURES?!
LEARN WITH PICTURES WHY INSURANCE MATTERS
BY: SASAKI FOR KODANLIFE
LOOK AT THIS!!
WITH PICTURES
BOOM
YOU MADE THEM YOUR-SELF?! WOW!!
BY: SASAKI FOR KODANLIFE

Things Take a Gruesome Turn

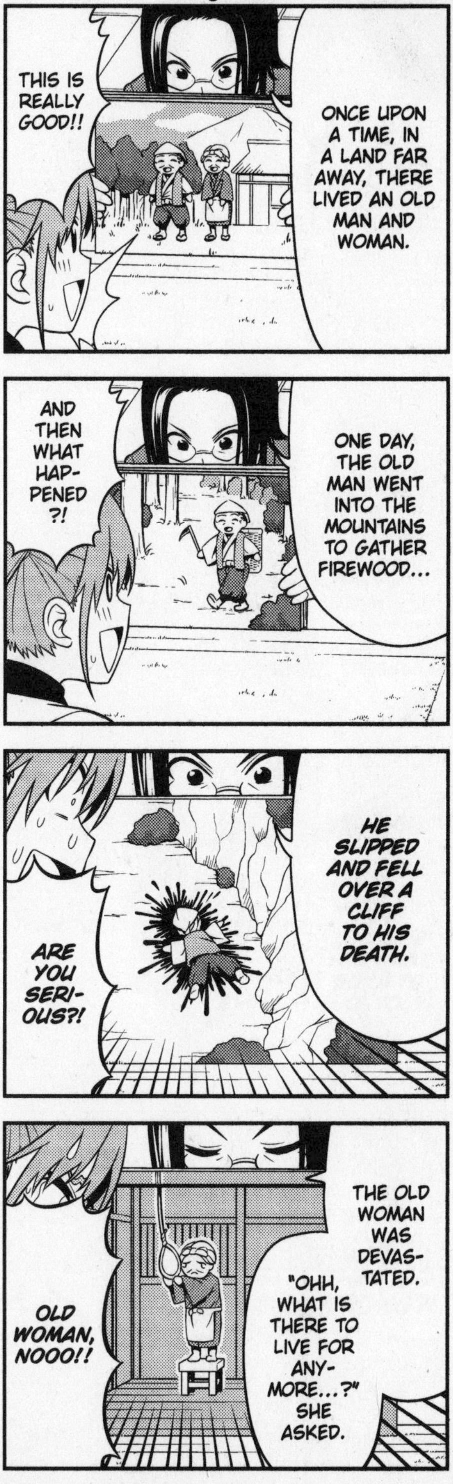
ONCE UPON A TIME, IN A LAND FAR AWAY, THERE LIVED AN OLD MAN AND WOMAN.
THIS IS REALLY GOOD!!
ONE DAY, THE OLD MAN WENT INTO THE MOUNTAINS TO GATHER FIREWOOD...
AND THEN WHAT HAPPENED?!
HE SLIPPED AND FELL OVER A CLIFF TO HIS DEATH.
ARE YOU SERIOUS?!
THE OLD WOMAN WAS DEVASTATED.
"OHH, WHAT IS THERE TO LIVE FOR ANYMORE...?" SHE ASKED.
OLD WOMAN, NOOO!!

An Emotional Ending

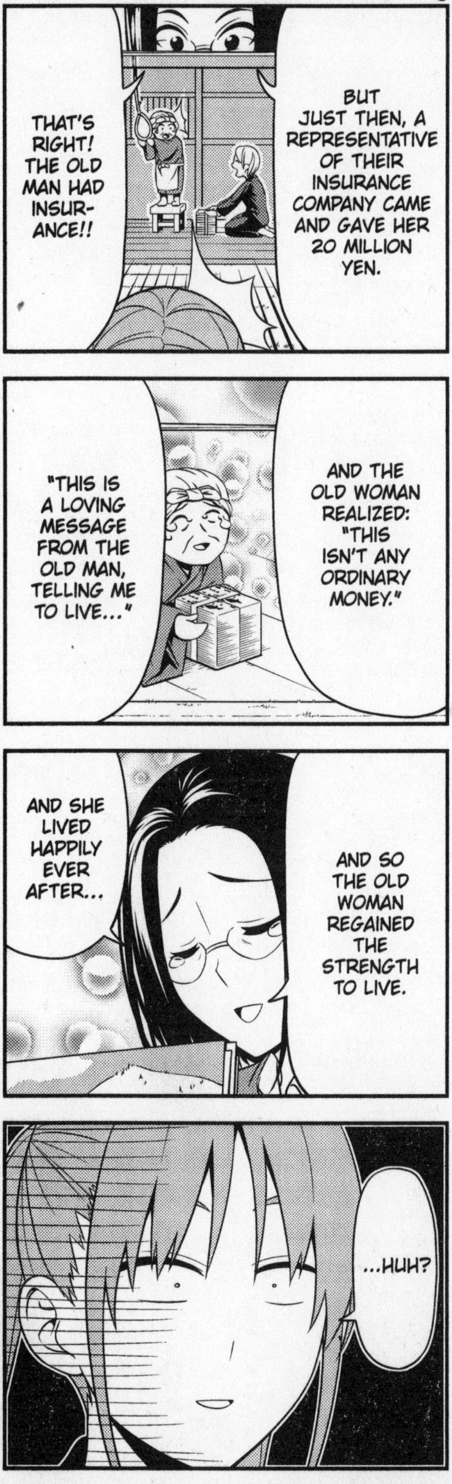
BUT JUST THEN, A REPRESENTATIVE OF THEIR INSURANCE COMPANY CAME AND GAVE HER 20 MILLION YEN.
THAT'S RIGHT! THE OLD MAN HAD INSURANCE!!
AND THE OLD WOMAN REALIZED: "THIS ISN'T ANY ORDINARY MONEY."
"THIS IS A LOVING MESSAGE FROM THE OLD MAN, TELLING ME TO LIVE..."
AND SO THE OLD WOMAN REGAINED THE STRENGTH TO LIVE.
AND SHE LIVED HAPPILY EVER AFTER...
...HUH?

**I Have Something to Say**

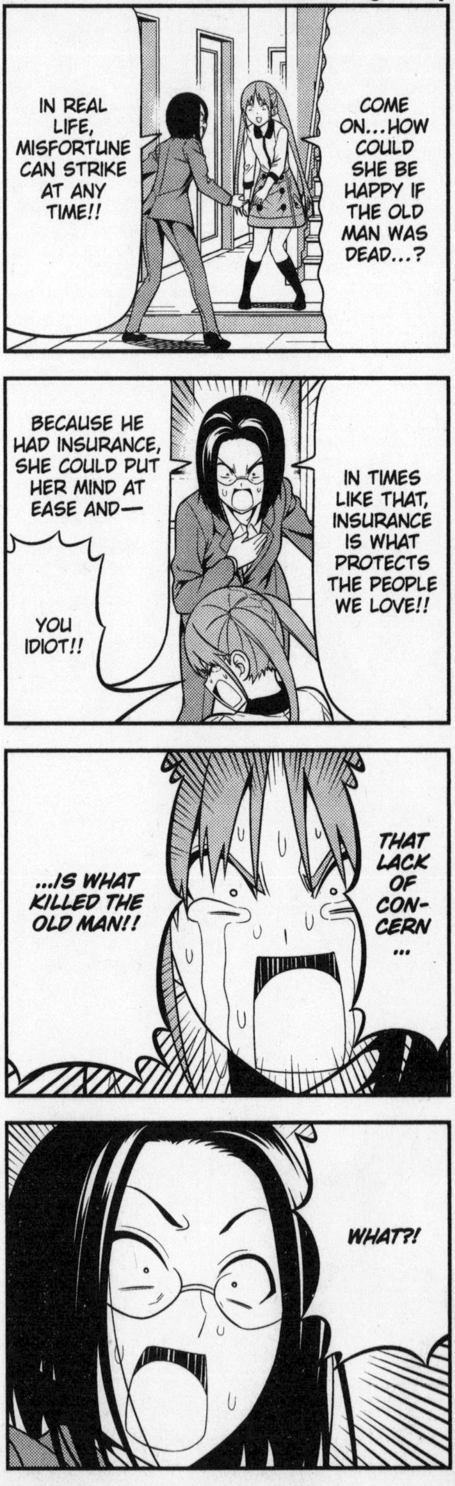
COME ON...HOW COULD SHE BE HAPPY IF THE OLD MAN WAS DEAD...?
IN REAL LIFE, MISFORTUNE CAN STRIKE AT ANY TIME!!
IN TIMES LIKE THAT, INSURANCE IS WHAT PROTECTS THE PEOPLE WE LOVE!!
BECAUSE HE HAD INSURANCE, SHE COULD PUT HER MIND AT EASE AND—
YOU IDIOT!!
THAT LACK OF CON-CERN...
...IS WHAT KILLED THE OLD MAN!!
WHAT?!

**The Heart of the Problem**

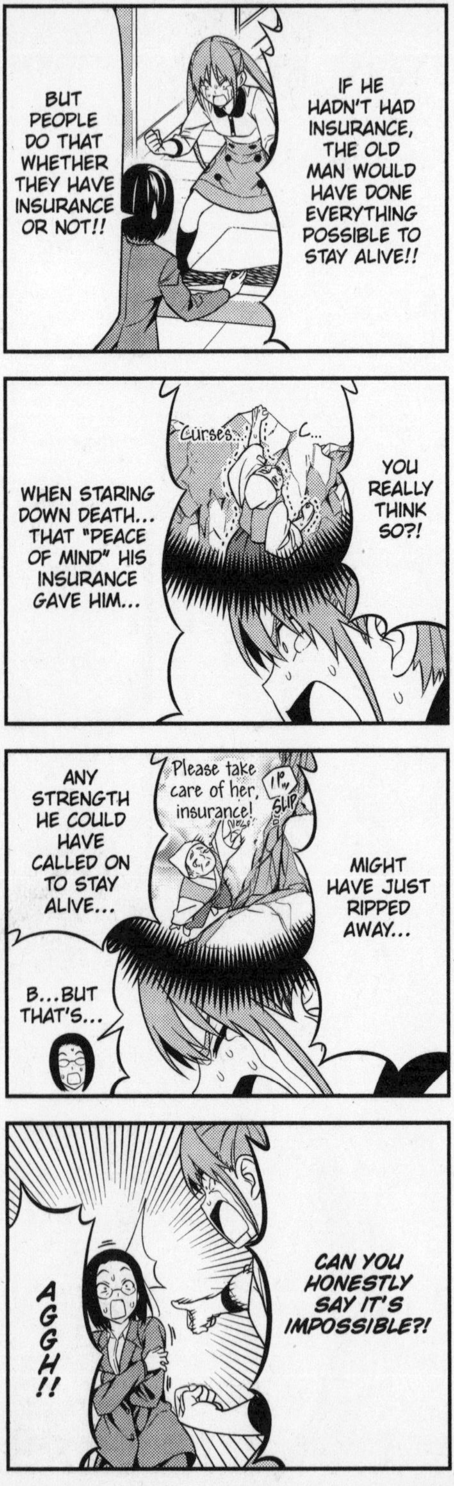
IF HE HADN'T HAD INSURANCE, THE OLD MAN WOULD HAVE DONE EVERYTHING POSSIBLE TO STAY ALIVE!!
BUT PEOPLE DO THAT WHETHER THEY HAVE INSURANCE OR NOT!!
YOU REALLY THINK SO?!
Curses...
C...
WHEN STARING DOWN DEATH... THAT "PEACE OF MIND" HIS INSURANCE GAVE HIM...
MIGHT HAVE JUST RIPPED AWAY...
SLIP
Please take care of her, insurance!
ANY STRENGTH HE COULD HAVE CALLED ON TO STAY ALIVE...
B...BUT THAT'S...
CAN YOU HONESTLY SAY IT'S IMPOSSIBLE?!
AGGH!!

## A Revolution in Insurance

## If It Were Real, I'd Buy It

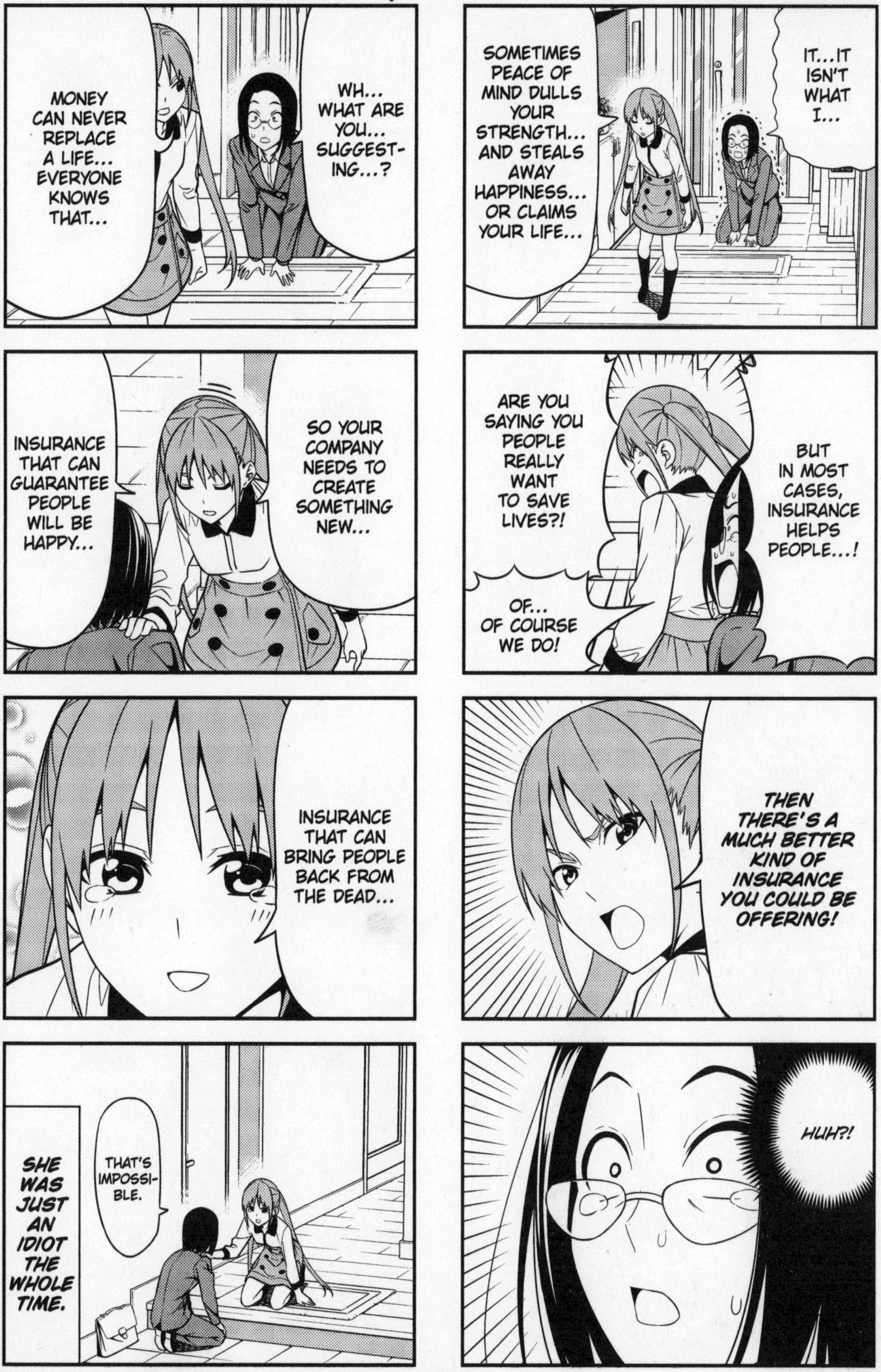
IT...IT ISN'T WHAT I...
SOMETIMES PEACE OF MIND DULLS YOUR STRENGTH... AND STEALS AWAY HAPPINESS... OR CLAIMS YOUR LIFE...
BUT IN MOST CASES, INSURANCE HELPS PEOPLE...!
ARE YOU SAYING YOU PEOPLE REALLY WANT TO SAVE LIVES?!
OF... OF COURSE WE DO!
THEN THERE'S A MUCH BETTER KIND OF INSURANCE YOU COULD BE OFFERING!
HUH?!
WH... WHAT ARE YOU... SUGGEST-ING...?
MONEY CAN NEVER REPLACE A LIFE... EVERYONE KNOWS THAT...
SO YOUR COMPANY NEEDS TO CREATE SOMETHING NEW...
INSURANCE THAT CAN GUARANTEE PEOPLE WILL BE HAPPY...
INSURANCE THAT CAN BRING PEOPLE BACK FROM THE DEAD...
THAT'S IMPOSSI-BLE.
SHE WAS JUST AN IDIOT THE WHOLE TIME.

**Say it as Many Times as it Takes**

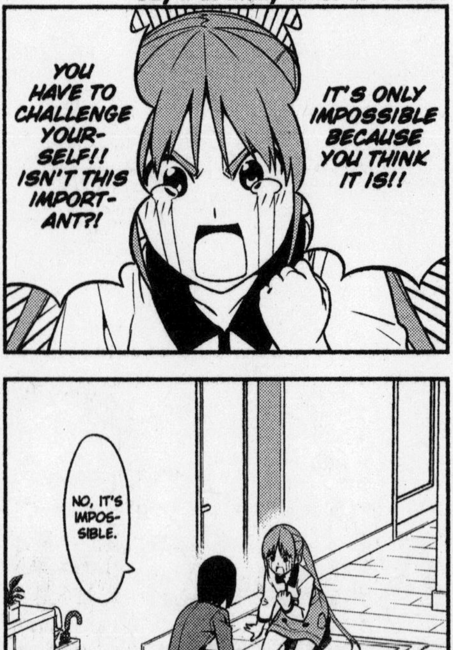
IT'S ONLY IMPOSSIBLE BECAUSE YOU THINK IT IS!!
YOU HAVE TO CHALLENGE YOUR-SELF!! ISN'T THIS IMPORT-ANT?!
NO, IT'S IMPOS-SIBLE.

(It's incredibly important. They took care of my hospital stay, and)

# Aho-Girl

\ˈahôˌgərl \ *Japanese, noun.*

A clueless girl.

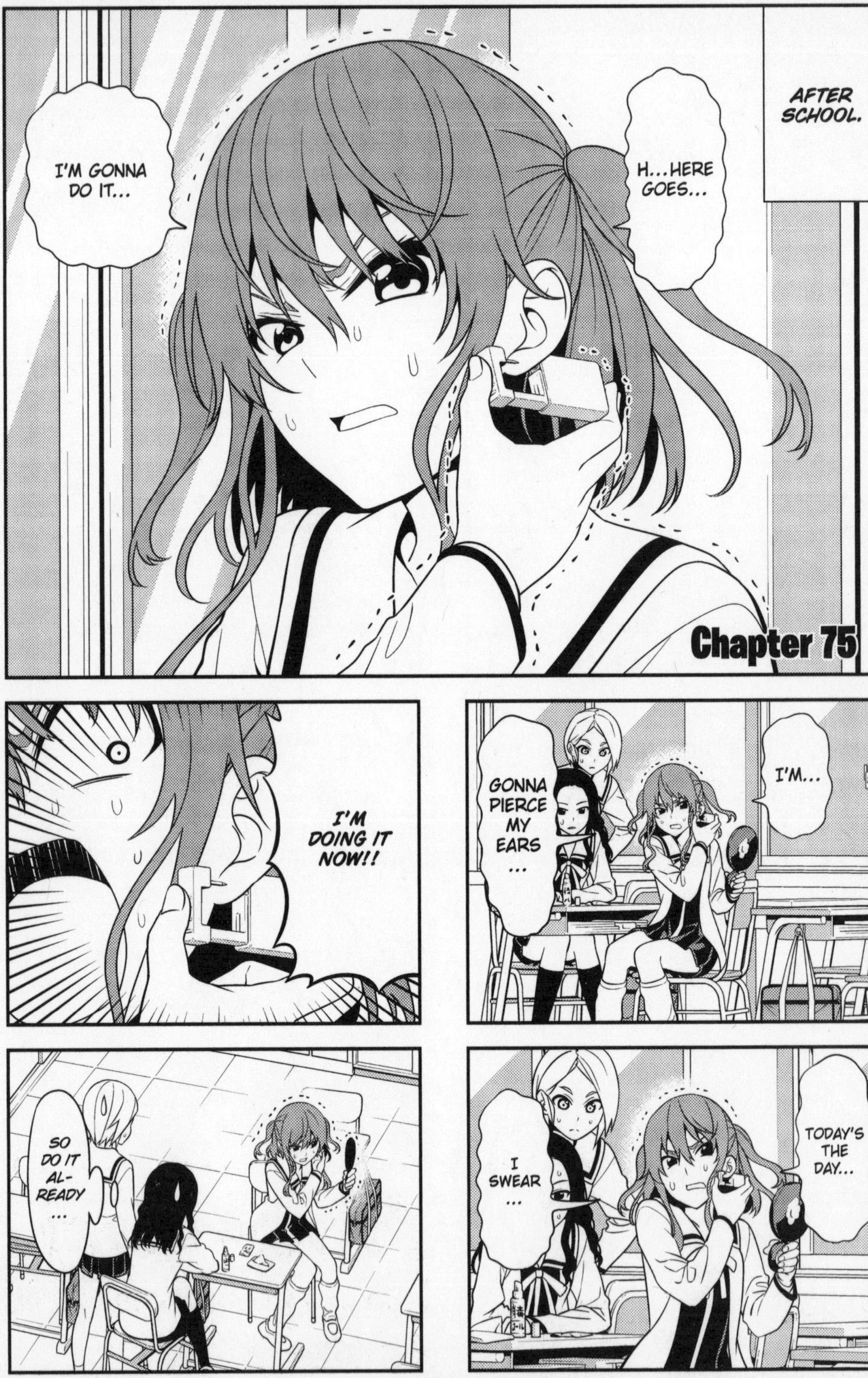
AFTER SCHOOL.
H...HERE GOES...
I'M GONNA DO IT...
Chapter 75
I'M...
GONNA PIERCE MY EARS ...
I'M DOING IT NOW!!
TODAY'S THE DAY...
I SWEAR ...
SO DO IT AL-READY ...

The Road to Hell Is Paved with Good Intentions

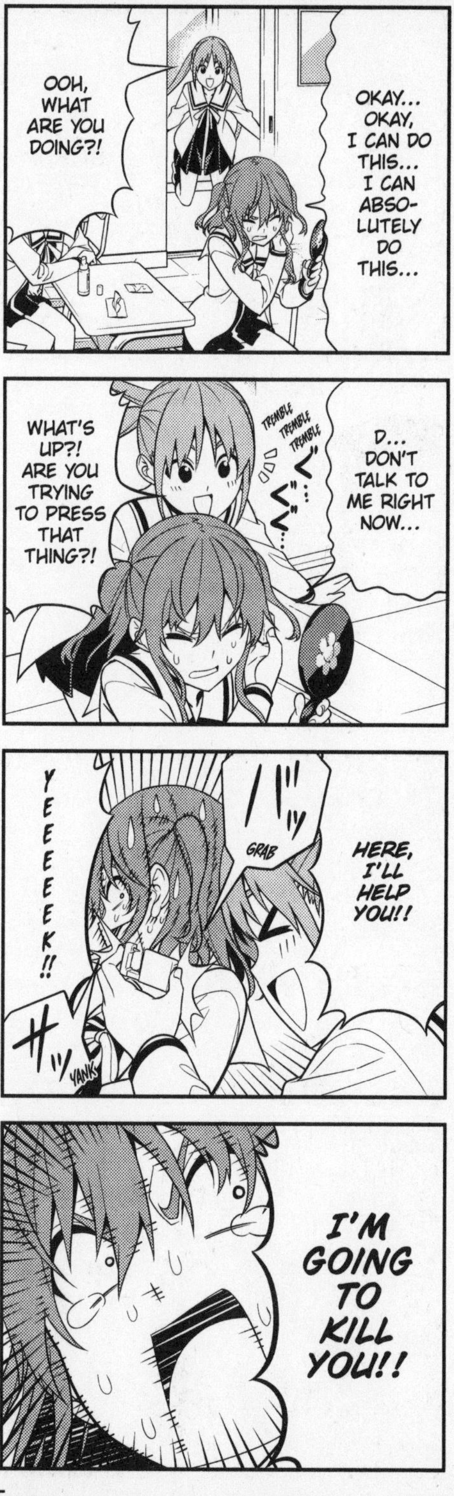
OKAY... OKAY, I CAN DO THIS... I CAN ABSOLUTELY DO THIS...
OOH, WHAT ARE YOU DOING?!
D... DON'T TALK TO ME RIGHT NOW...
TREMBLE TREMBLE TREMBLE
WHAT'S UP?! ARE YOU TRYING TO PRESS THAT THING?!
HERE, I'LL HELP YOU!!
GRAB
YEEEEEEK!!
YANK
I'M GOING TO KILL YOU!!

Not a Great Explanation

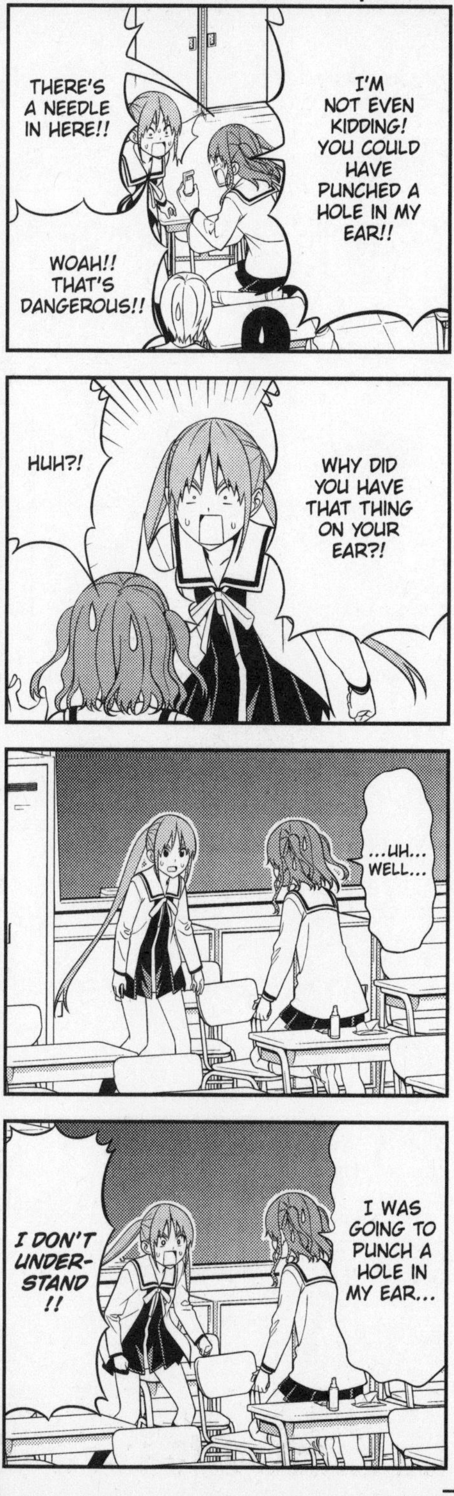
I'M NOT EVEN KIDDING! YOU COULD HAVE PUNCHED A HOLE IN MY EAR!!
THERE'S A NEEDLE IN HERE!!
WOAH!! THAT'S DANGEROUS!!
WHY DID YOU HAVE THAT THING ON YOUR EAR?!
HUH?!
...UH... WELL...
I WAS GOING TO PUNCH A HOLE IN MY EAR...
I DON'T UNDERSTAND!!

## You're Headed for a Bad End

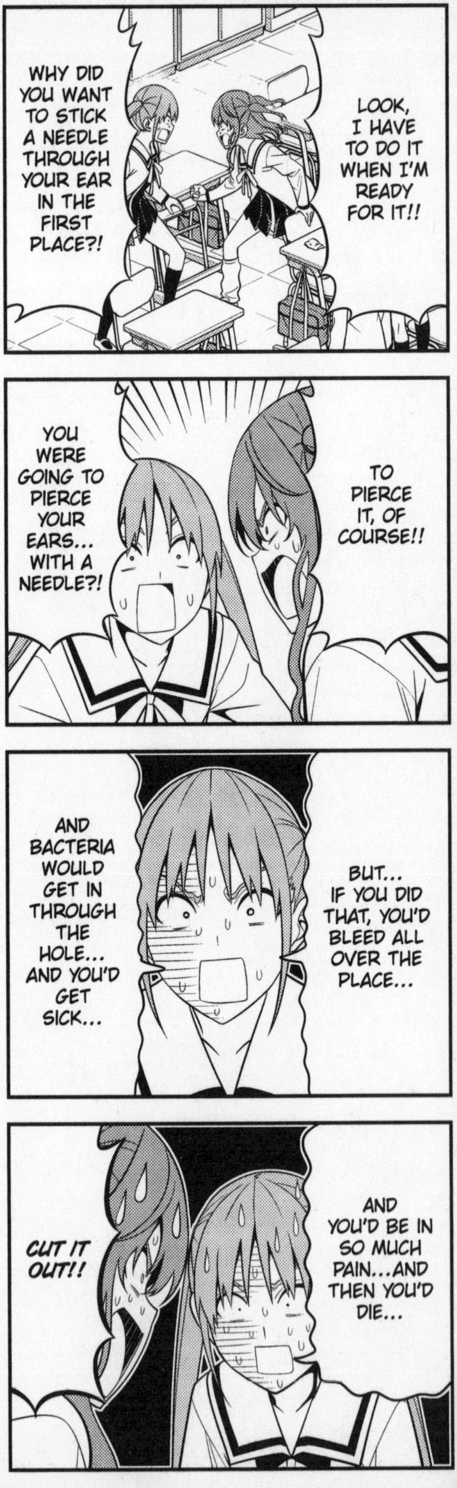
LOOK, I HAVE TO DO IT WHEN I'M READY FOR IT!!
WHY DID YOU WANT TO STICK A NEEDLE THROUGH YOUR EAR IN THE FIRST PLACE?!
TO PIERCE IT, OF COURSE!!
YOU WERE GOING TO PIERCE YOUR EARS... WITH A NEEDLE?!
BUT... IF YOU DID THAT, YOU'D BLEED ALL OVER THE PLACE...
AND BACTERIA WOULD GET IN THROUGH THE HOLE... AND YOU'D GET SICK...
AND YOU'D BE IN SO MUCH PAIN...AND THEN YOU'D DIE...
CUT IT OUT!!

## Yes

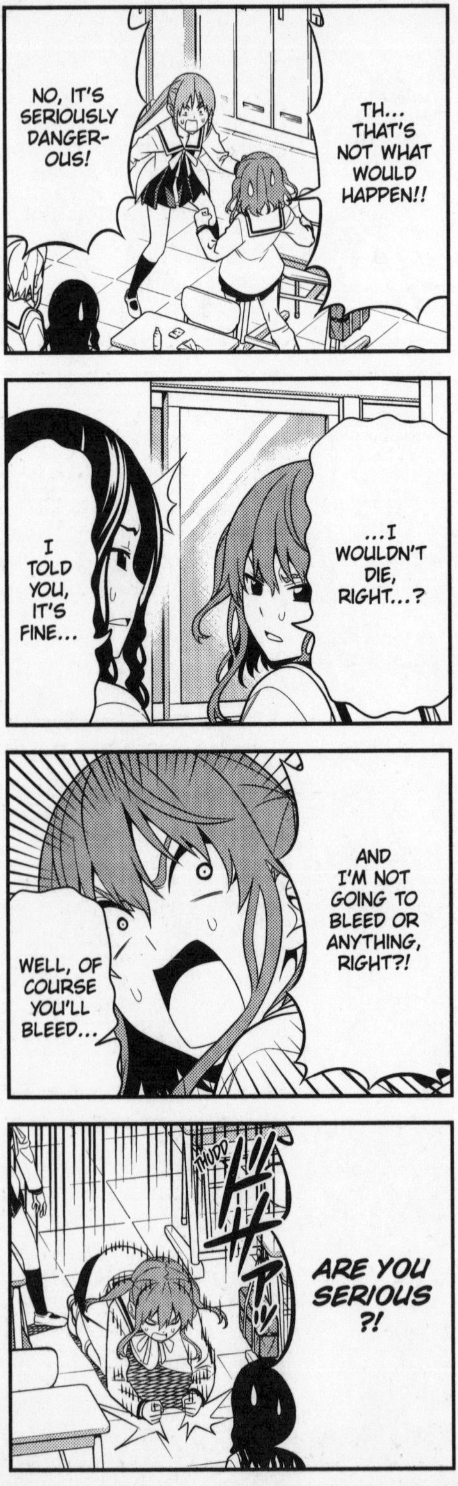
TH... THAT'S NOT WHAT WOULD HAPPEN!!
NO, IT'S SERIOUSLY DANGER-OUS!
...I WOULDN'T DIE, RIGHT...?
I TOLD YOU, IT'S FINE...
AND I'M NOT GOING TO BLEED OR ANYTHING, RIGHT?!
WELL, OF COURSE YOU'LL BLEED...
THUDD
ARE YOU SERIOUS?!

No, It's Not Wrong

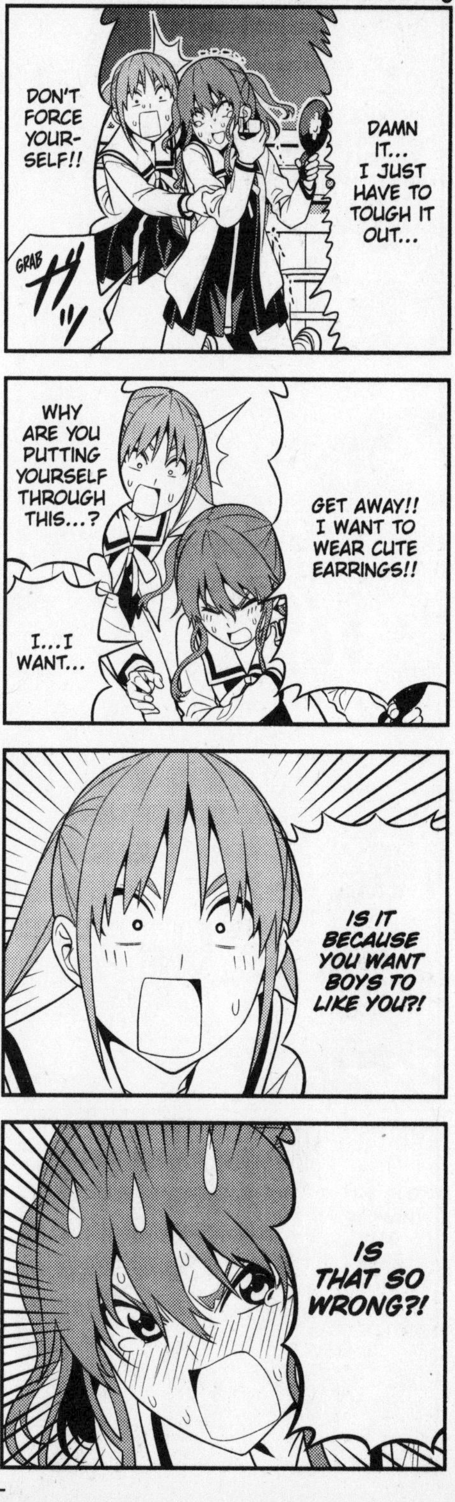
DAMN IT... I JUST HAVE TO TOUGH IT OUT...
DON'T FORCE YOURSELF!!
GRAB
WHY ARE YOU PUTTING YOURSELF THROUGH THIS...?
GET AWAY!! I WANT TO WEAR CUTE EARRINGS!!
I...I WANT...
IS IT BECAUSE YOU WANT BOYS TO LIKE YOU?!
IS THAT SO WRONG?!

I'm Not Sure Those Things Are Related

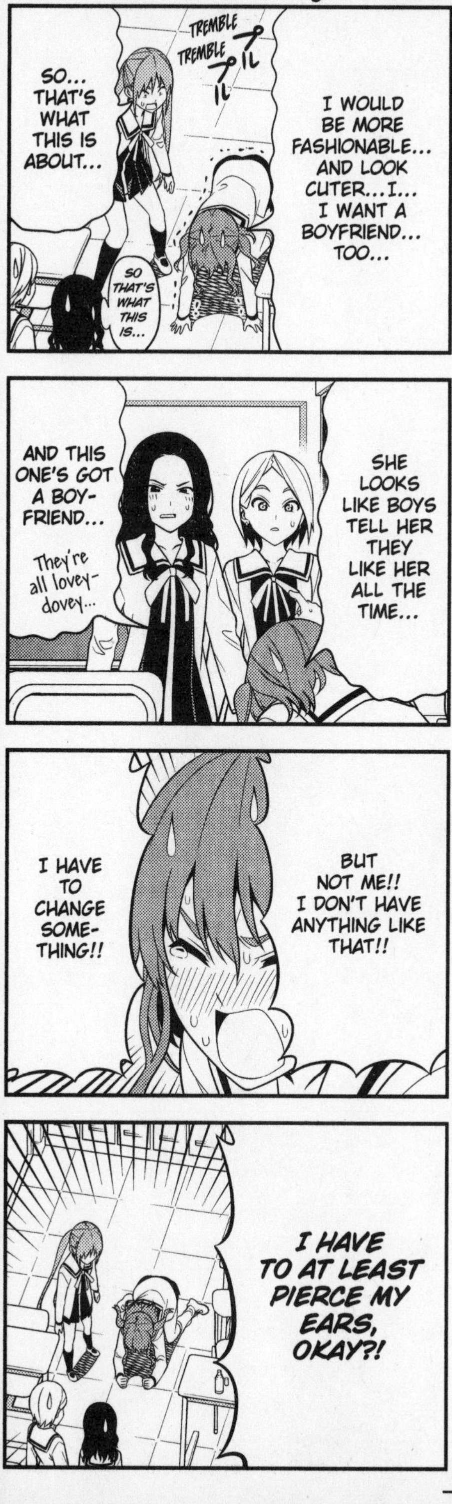
I WOULD BE MORE FASHIONABLE... AND LOOK CUTER... I... I WANT A BOYFRIEND... TOO...
TREMBLE
TREMBLE
SO... THAT'S WHAT THIS IS ABOUT...
SO THAT'S WHAT THIS IS...
SHE LOOKS LIKE BOYS TELL HER THEY LIKE HER ALL THE TIME...
AND THIS ONE'S GOT A BOYFRIEND...
They're all lovey-dovey...
BUT NOT ME!! I DON'T HAVE ANYTHING LIKE THAT!!
I HAVE TO CHANGE SOMETHING!!
I HAVE TO AT LEAST PIERCE MY EARS, OKAY?!

A Gentle Hand

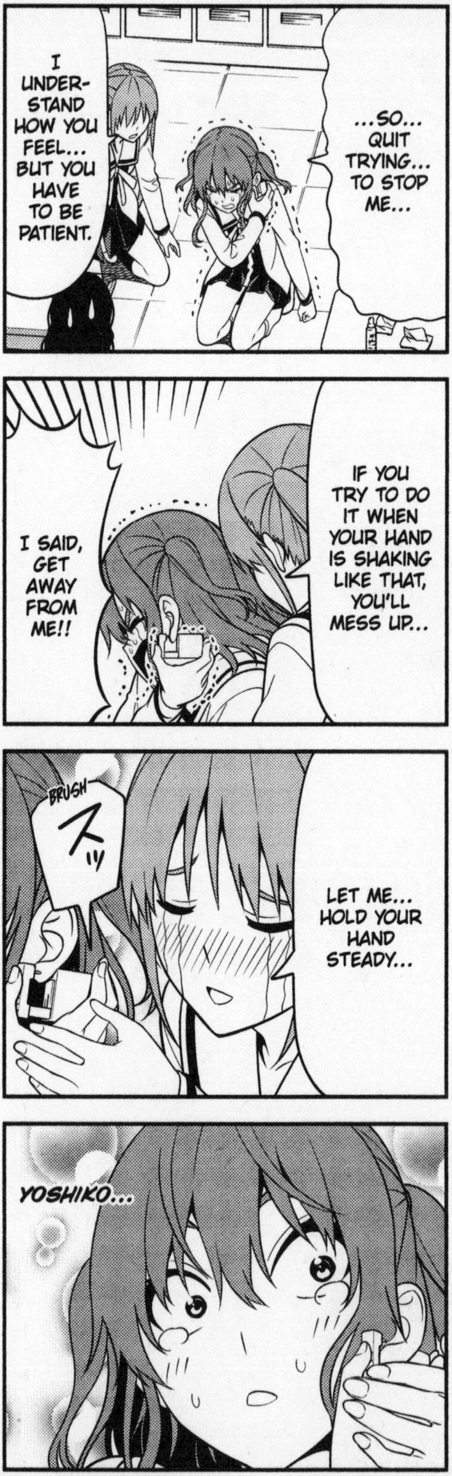
...SO... QUIT TRYING... TO STOP ME...
I UNDERSTAND HOW YOU FEEL... BUT YOU HAVE TO BE PATIENT.
IF YOU TRY TO DO IT WHEN YOUR HAND IS SHAKING LIKE THAT, YOU'LL MESS UP...
I SAID, GET AWAY FROM ME!!
LET ME... HOLD YOUR HAND STEADY...
BRUSH
YOSHIKO...

Let's Do This!

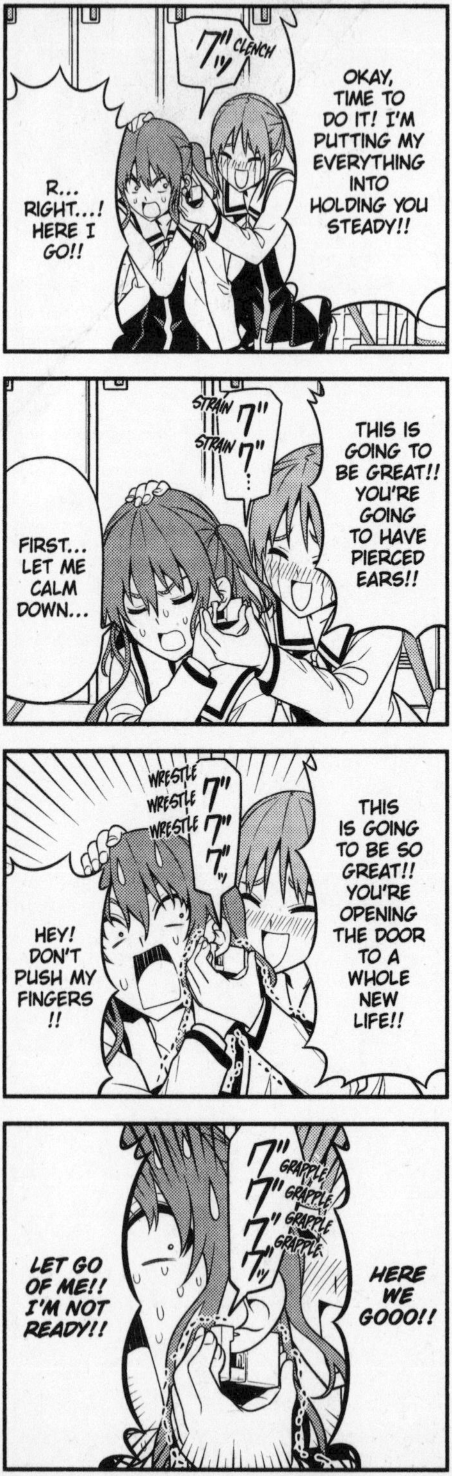
CLENCH
OKAY, TIME TO DO IT! I'M PUTTING MY EVERYTHING INTO HOLDING YOU STEADY!!
R... RIGHT...! HERE I GO!!
STRAIN
STRAIN
THIS IS GOING TO BE GREAT!! YOU'RE GOING TO HAVE PIERCED EARS!!
FIRST... LET ME CALM DOWN...
WRESTLE
WRESTLE
WRESTLE
THIS IS GOING TO BE SO GREAT!! YOU'RE OPENING THE DOOR TO A WHOLE NEW LIFE!!
HEY! DON'T PUSH MY FINGERS!!
GRAPPLE
GRAPPLE
GRAPPLE
GRAPPLE
HERE WE GOOO!!
LET GO OF ME!! I'M NOT READY!!

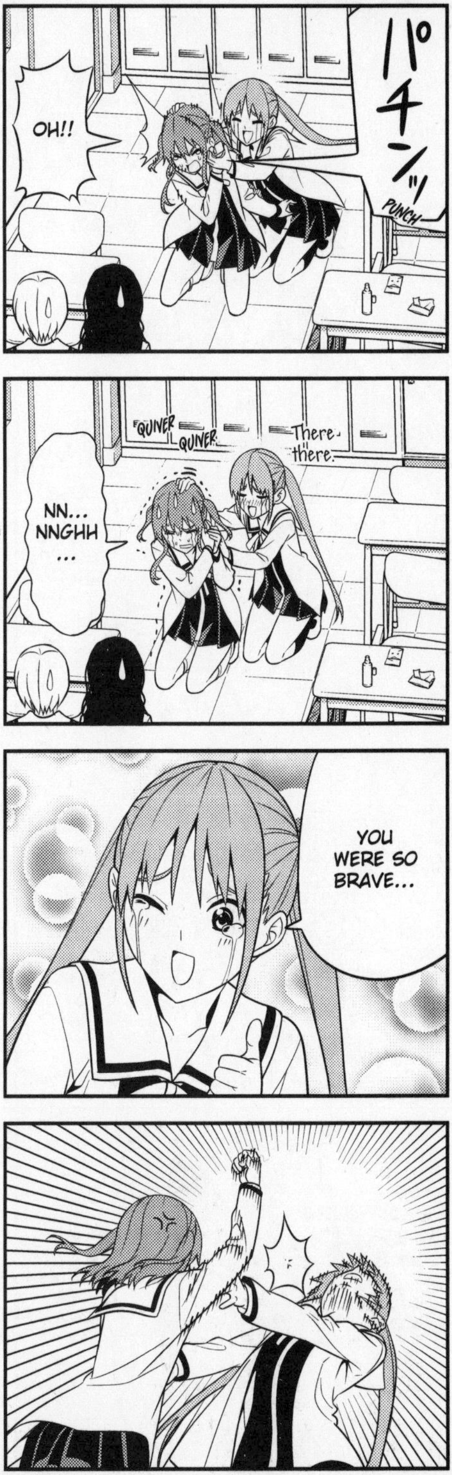
パチンッ
PUNCH
OH!!
There there.
QUIVER QUIVER
NN... NNGHH ...
YOU WERE SO BRAVE...



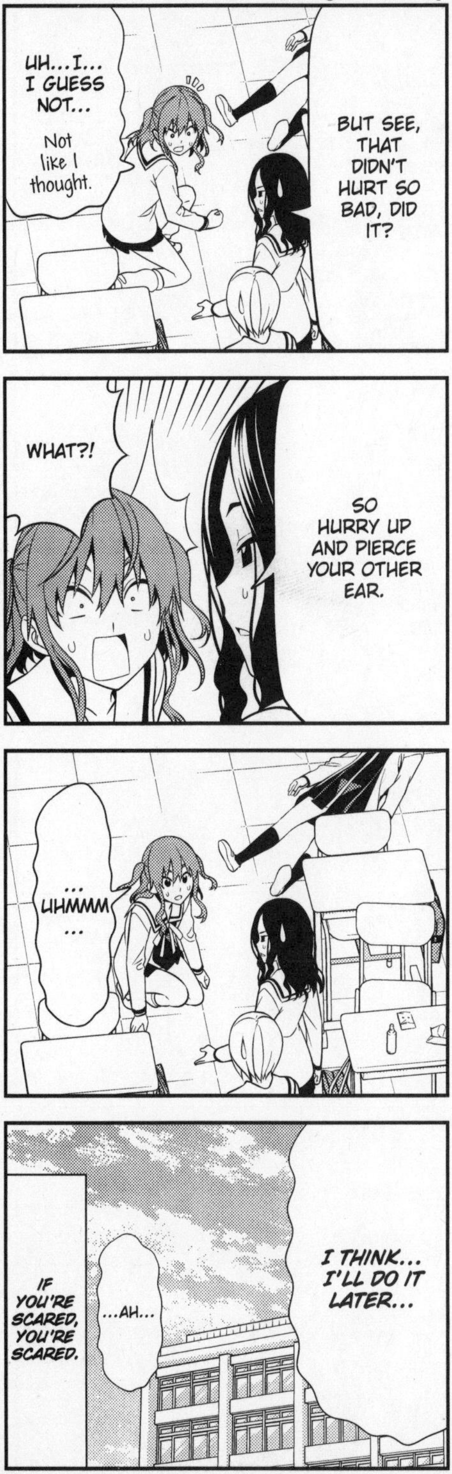
BUT SEE, THAT DIDN'T HURT SO BAD, DID IT?
UH...I... I GUESS NOT...
Not like I thought.
SO HURRY UP AND PIERCE YOUR OTHER EAR.
WHAT?!
... UHMMM ...
I THINK... I'LL DO IT LATER...
...AH...
IF YOU'RE SCARED, YOU'RE SCARED.

**Who Knew?**

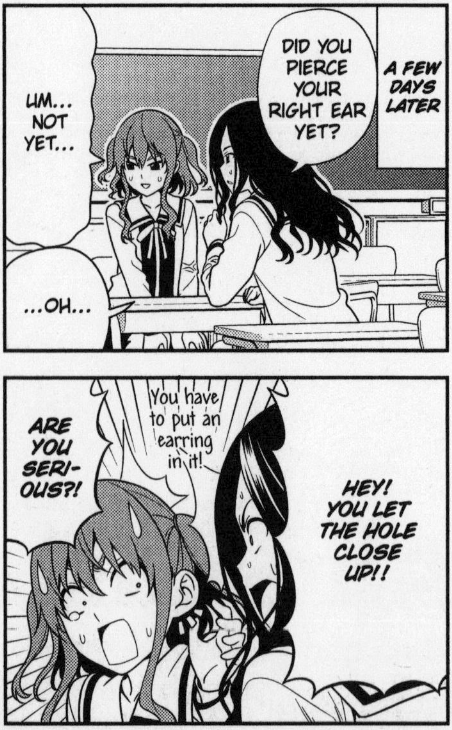
A FEW DAYS LATER
DID YOU PIERCE YOUR RIGHT EAR YET?
UM... NOT YET...
...OH...
HEY! YOU LET THE HOLE CLOSE UP!!
You have to put an earring in it!
ARE YOU SERI-OUS?!

**(In the trendy, popular "gal" mold)**

# Aho-Girl

\ˈahôˌɡərl \ *Japanese, noun.*
A clueless girl.

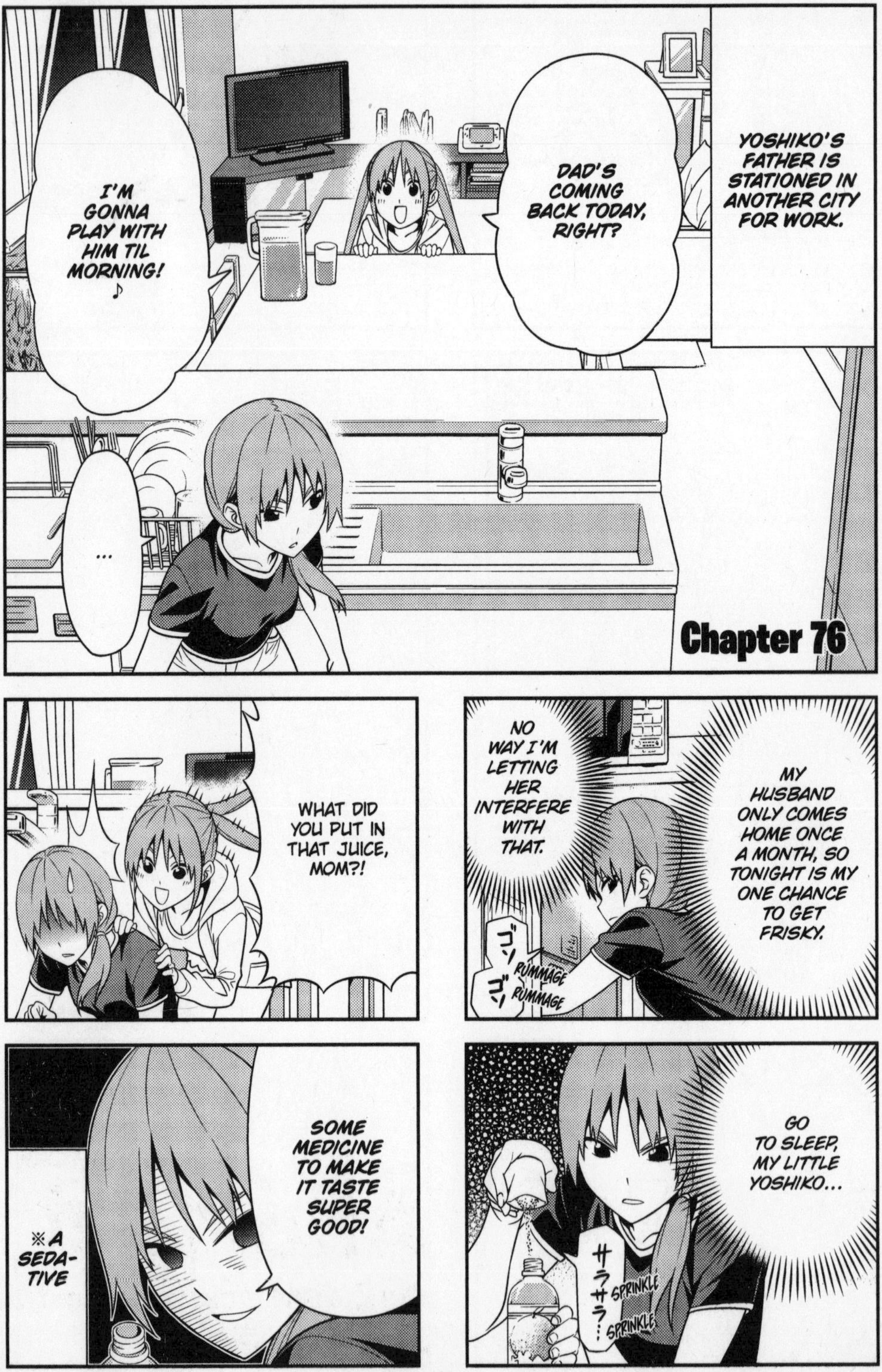
YOSHIKO'S FATHER IS STATIONED IN ANOTHER CITY FOR WORK.
DAD'S COMING BACK TODAY, RIGHT?
I'M GONNA PLAY WITH HIM TIL MORNING! ♪
...
Chapter 76
MY HUSBAND ONLY COMES HOME ONCE A MONTH, SO TONIGHT IS MY ONE CHANCE TO GET FRISKY.
NO WAY I'M LETTING HER INTERFERE WITH THAT.
ゴソ RUMMAGE
ゴソ RUMMAGE
WHAT DID YOU PUT IN THAT JUICE, MOM?!
GO TO SLEEP, MY LITTLE YOSHIKO...
サラサラ… SPRINKLE SPRINKLE
SOME MEDICINE TO MAKE IT TASTE SUPER GOOD!
※A SEDA-TIVE

Her Preferred Method

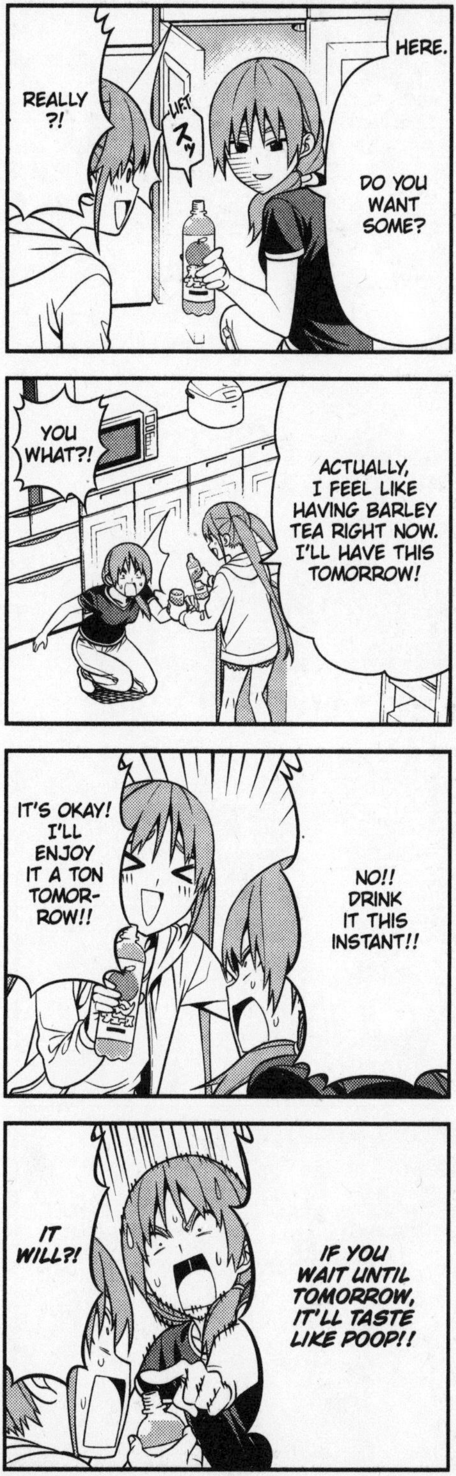
HERE.
DO YOU WANT SOME?
LIFT スッ
REALLY?!
ACTUALLY, I FEEL LIKE HAVING BARLEY TEA RIGHT NOW. I'LL HAVE THIS TOMORROW!
YOU WHAT?!
NO!! DRINK IT THIS INSTANT!!
IT'S OKAY! I'LL ENJOY IT A TON TOMORROW!!
IF YOU WAIT UNTIL TOMORROW, IT'LL TASTE LIKE POOP!!
IT WILL?!

Unstoppable Curiosity

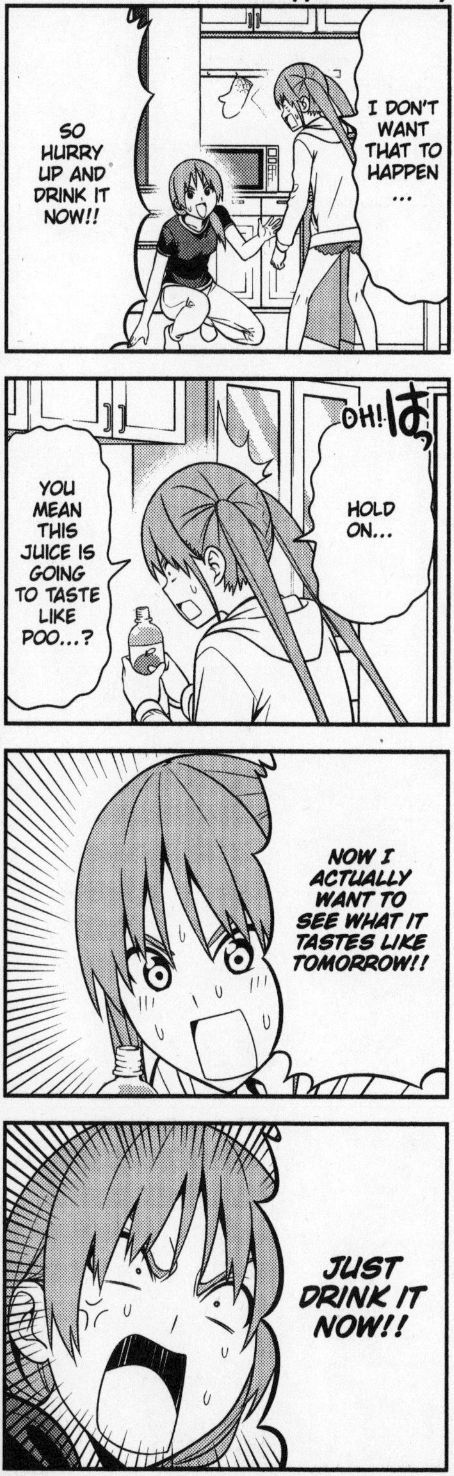
I DON'T WANT THAT TO HAPPEN ...
SO HURRY UP AND DRINK IT NOW!!
OH! は
HOLD ON...
YOU MEAN THIS JUICE IS GOING TO TASTE LIKE POO...?
NOW I ACTUALLY WANT TO SEE WHAT IT TASTES LIKE TOMORROW!!
JUST DRINK IT NOW!!

The Father Appears

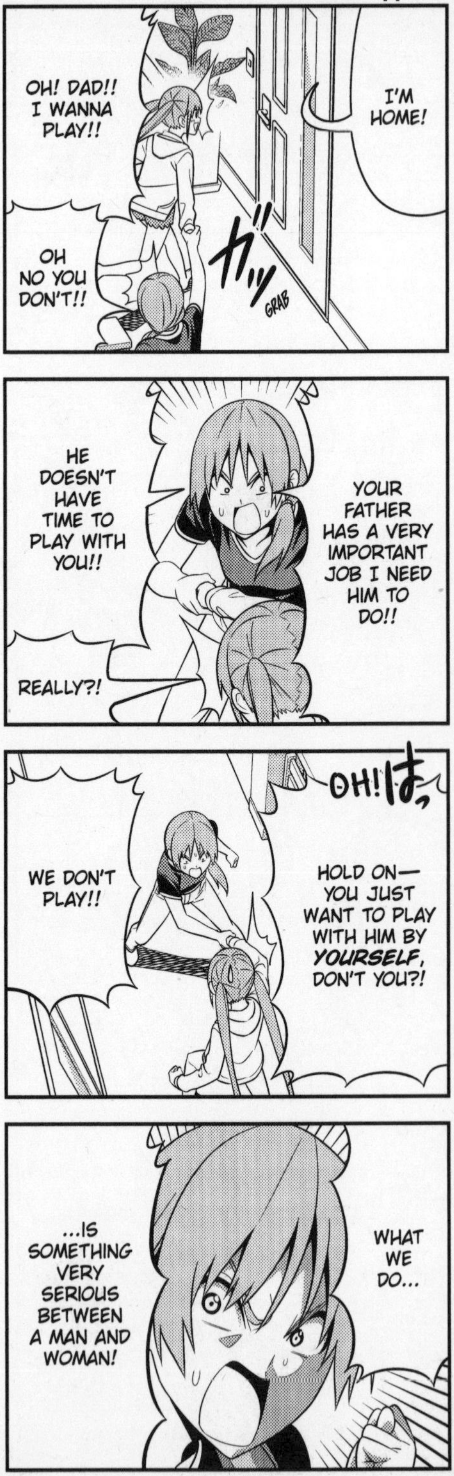
I'M HOME!
OH! DAD!! I WANNA PLAY!!
OH NO YOU DON'T!!
ガッ
GRAB
YOUR FATHER HAS A VERY IMPORTANT JOB I NEED HIM TO DO!!
HE DOESN'T HAVE TIME TO PLAY WITH YOU!!
REALLY?!
OH! はっ
HOLD ON— YOU JUST WANT TO PLAY WITH HIM BY **YOURSELF**, DON'T YOU?!
WE DON'T PLAY!!
WHAT WE DO...
...IS SOMETHING VERY SERIOUS BETWEEN A MAN AND WOMAN!

Outmatched in Ultimate Battle

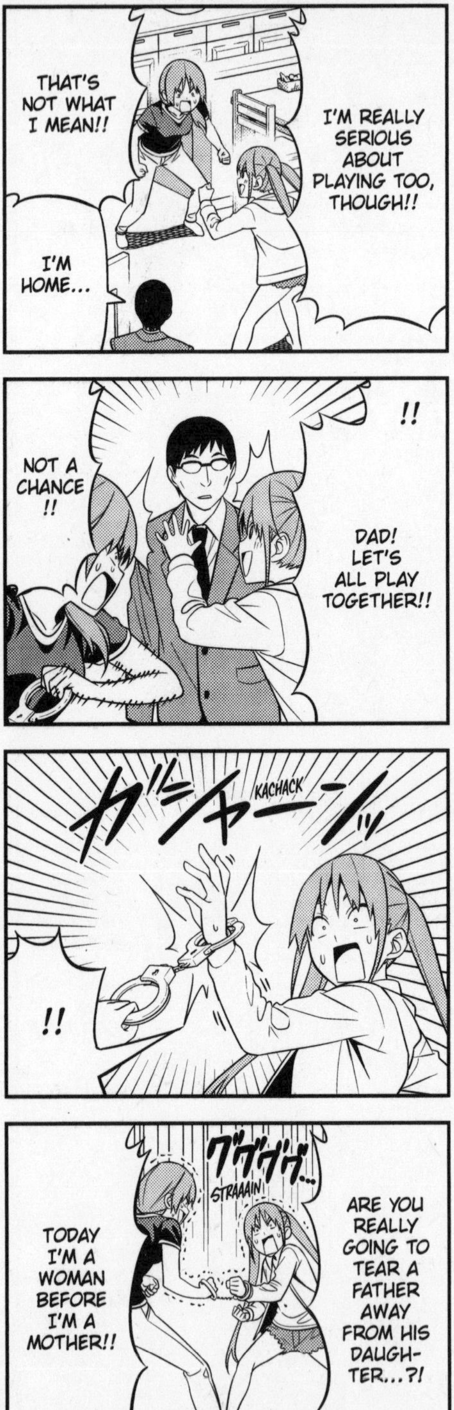
I'M REALLY SERIOUS ABOUT PLAYING TOO, THOUGH!!
THAT'S NOT WHAT I MEAN!!
I'M HOME...
!!
DAD! LET'S ALL PLAY TOGETHER!!
NOT A CHANCE!!
ガシャーンッ
KACHACK
!!
ググググ...
STRAAAIN
ARE YOU REALLY GOING TO TEAR A FATHER AWAY FROM HIS DAUGHTER...?!
TODAY I'M A WOMAN BEFORE I'M A MOTHER!!

## From This Day Forward

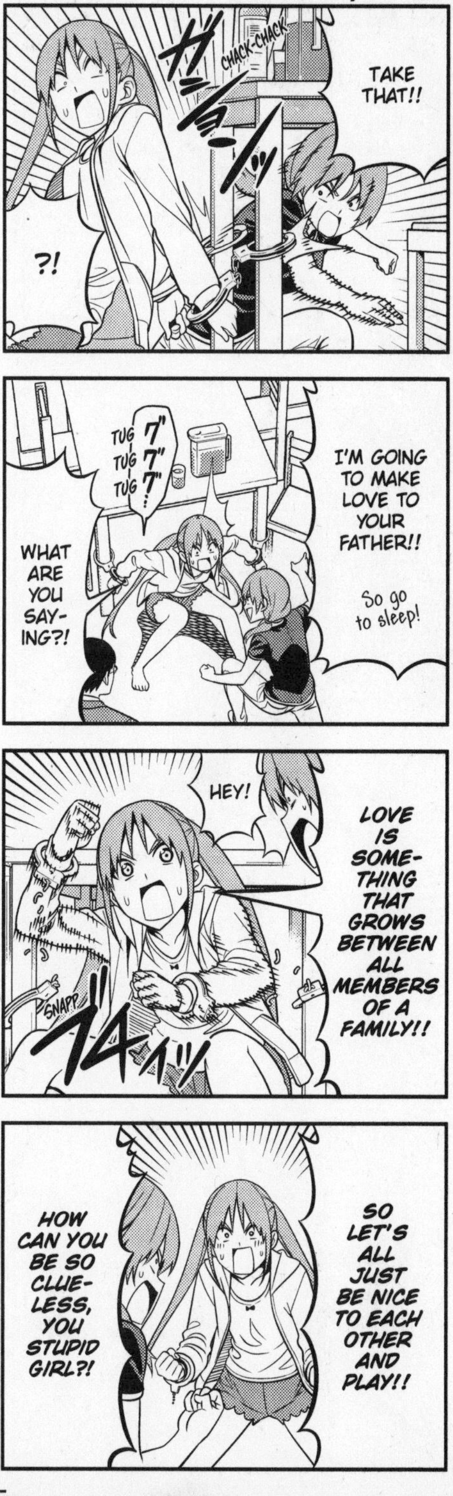
CHACK-CHACK
TAKE THAT!!
?!
I'M GOING TO MAKE LOVE TO YOUR FATHER!!
So go to sleep!
TUG TUG TUG
WHAT ARE YOU SAYING?!
LOVE IS SOMETHING THAT GROWS BETWEEN ALL MEMBERS OF A FAMILY!!
HEY!
SNAPP
SO LET'S ALL JUST BE NICE TO EACH OTHER AND PLAY!!
HOW CAN YOU BE SO CLUELESS, YOU STUPID GIRL?!

## Watch Carefully—What Do Your Senses Tell You?

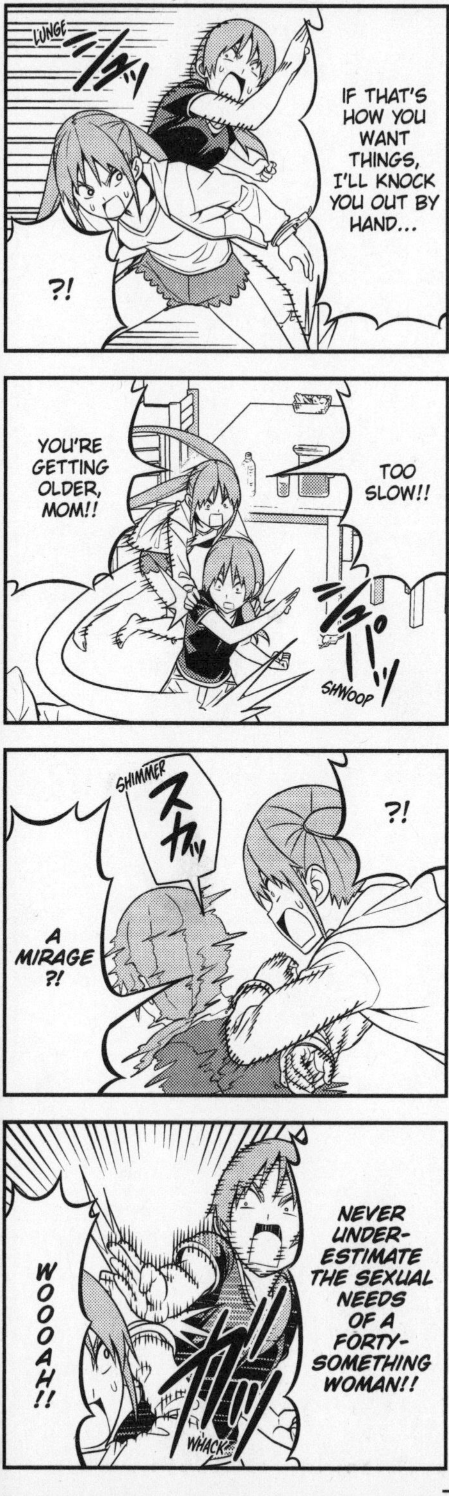
IF THAT'S HOW YOU WANT THINGS, I'LL KNOCK YOU OUT BY HAND...
LUNGE
?!
TOO SLOW!!
YOU'RE GETTING OLDER, MOM!!
SHWOOP
?!
SHIMMER
A MIRAGE?!
NEVER UNDERESTIMATE THE SEXUAL NEEDS OF A FORTY-SOMETHING WOMAN!!
WOOOOAH!!
WHACK

Cast Off

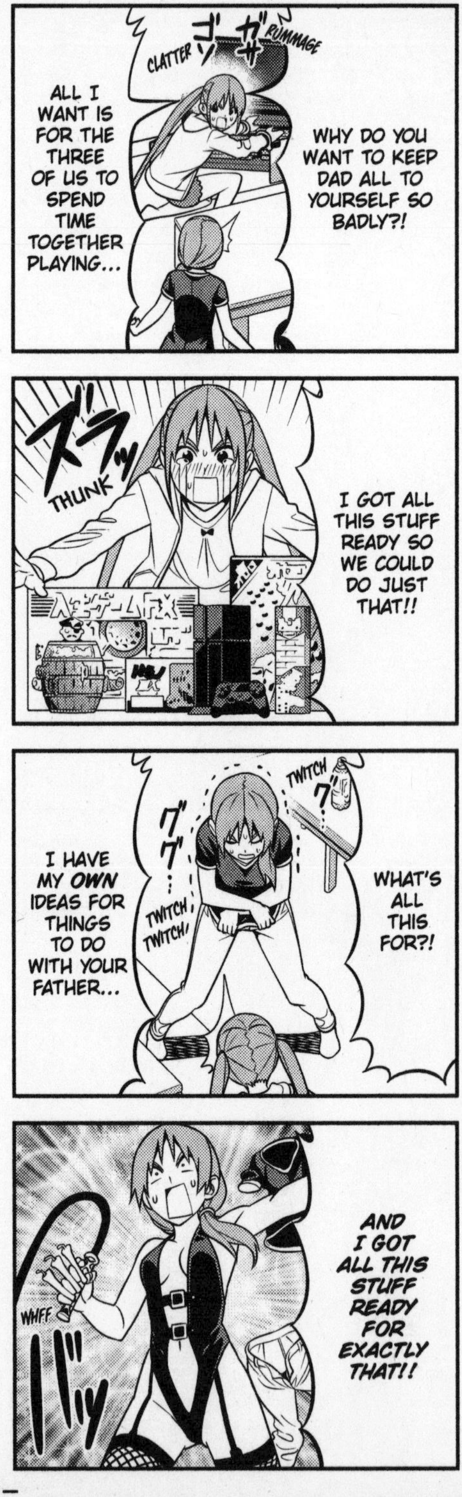
CLATTER
RUMMAGE
WHY DO YOU WANT TO KEEP DAD ALL TO YOURSELF SO BADLY?!
ALL I WANT IS FOR THE THREE OF US TO SPEND TIME TOGETHER PLAYING...
THUNK
I GOT ALL THIS STUFF READY SO WE COULD DO JUST THAT!!
WHAT'S ALL THIS FOR?!
TWITCH
TWITCH TWITCH
I HAVE MY OWN IDEAS FOR THINGS TO DO WITH YOUR FATHER...
AND I GOT ALL THIS STUFF READY FOR EXACTLY THAT!!
WHFF

A Growing Gulf

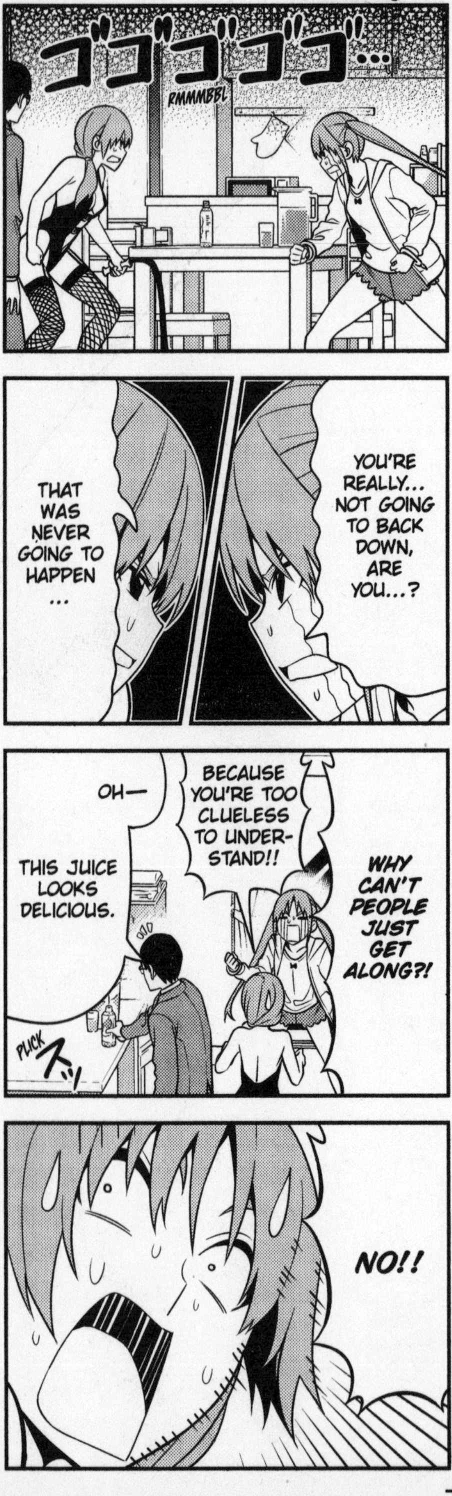
RMMMBBL
YOU'RE REALLY... NOT GOING TO BACK DOWN, ARE YOU...?
THAT WAS NEVER GOING TO HAPPEN...
WHY CAN'T PEOPLE JUST GET ALONG?!
BECAUSE YOU'RE TOO CLUELESS TO UNDER-STAND!!
OH— THIS JUICE LOOKS DELICIOUS.
PLICK
NO!!

## A Growing Miscalculation

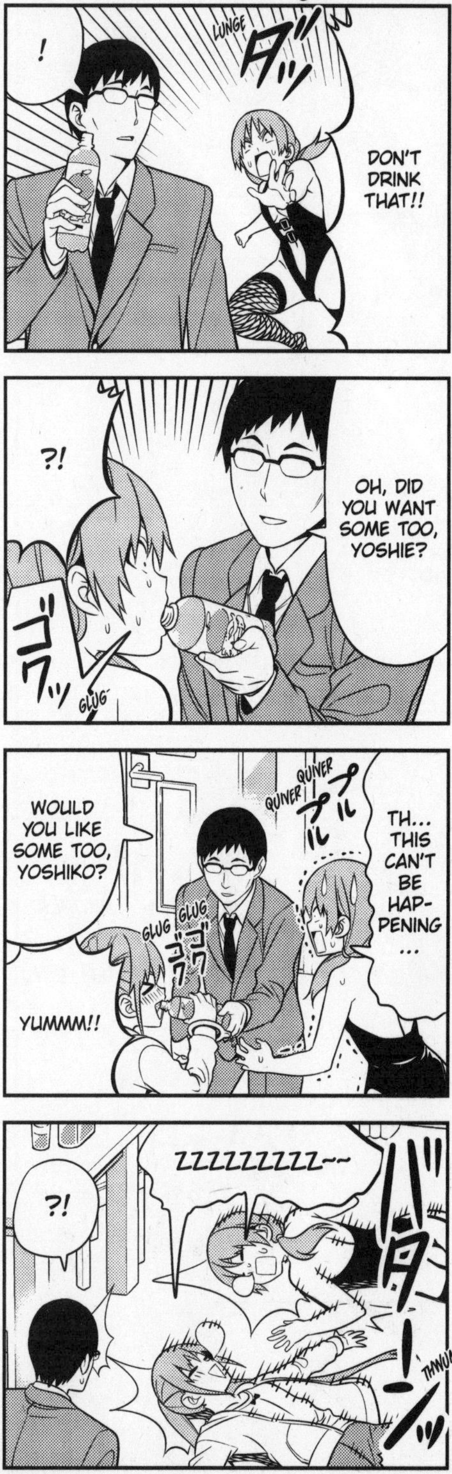
ダッ
LUNGE
DON'T DRINK THAT!!
!
OH, DID YOU WANT SOME TOO, YOSHIE?
?!
ゴクッ
GLUG
プルプル
QUIVER QUIVER
TH... THIS CAN'T BE HAP-PENING...
WOULD YOU LIKE SOME TOO, YOSHIKO?
ゴクゴク
GLUG GLUG
YUMMM!!
バタ!ッ
THWUMP
ZZZZZZZZZ~~
?!

## Dad's Opinion

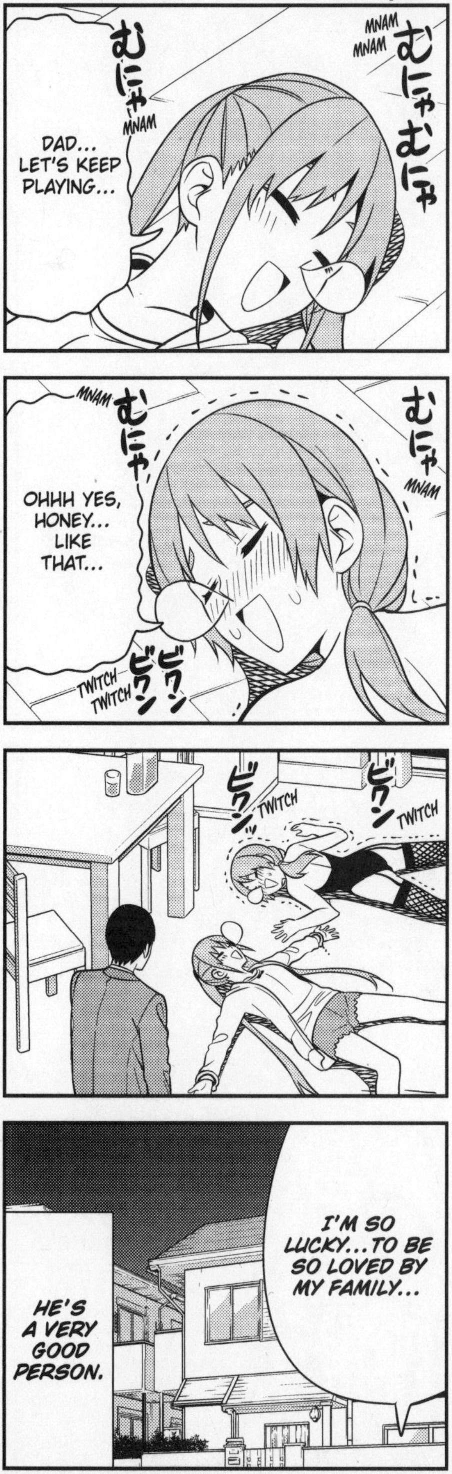
むにゃむにゃ
MNAM MNAM
むにゃ
MNAM
DAD... LET'S KEEP PLAYING...
むにゃ
MNAM
むにゃ
MNAM
OHHH YES, HONEY... LIKE THAT...
ビクンビクン
TWITCH TWITCH
ビクン
TWITCH
ビクンッ
TWITCH
I'M SO LUCKY...TO BE SO LOVED BY MY FAMILY...
HE'S A VERY GOOD PERSON.

A Reasonable Question

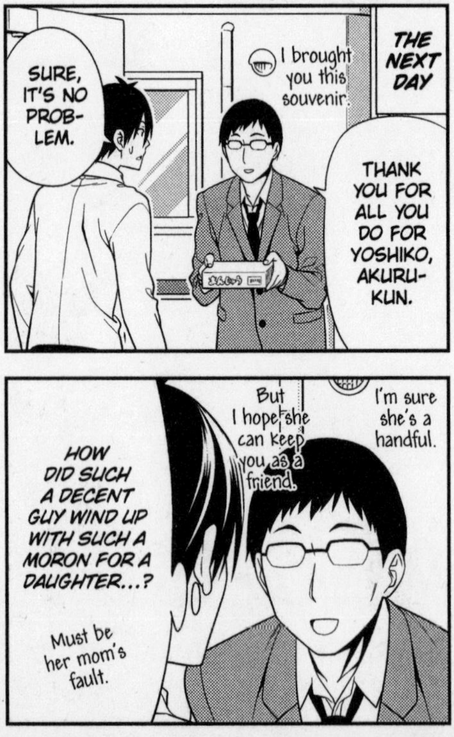
THE NEXT DAY
THANK YOU FOR ALL YOU DO FOR YOSHIKO, AKURU-KUN.
I brought you this souvenir.
SURE, IT'S NO PROB-LEM.
I'm sure she's a handful.
But I hope she can keep you as a friend.
HOW DID SUCH A DECENT GUY WIND UP WITH SUCH A MORON FOR A DAUGHTER...?
Must be her mom's fault.

# Aho-Girl

\ˈahôˌgərl\ *Japanese, noun.*
A clueless girl.

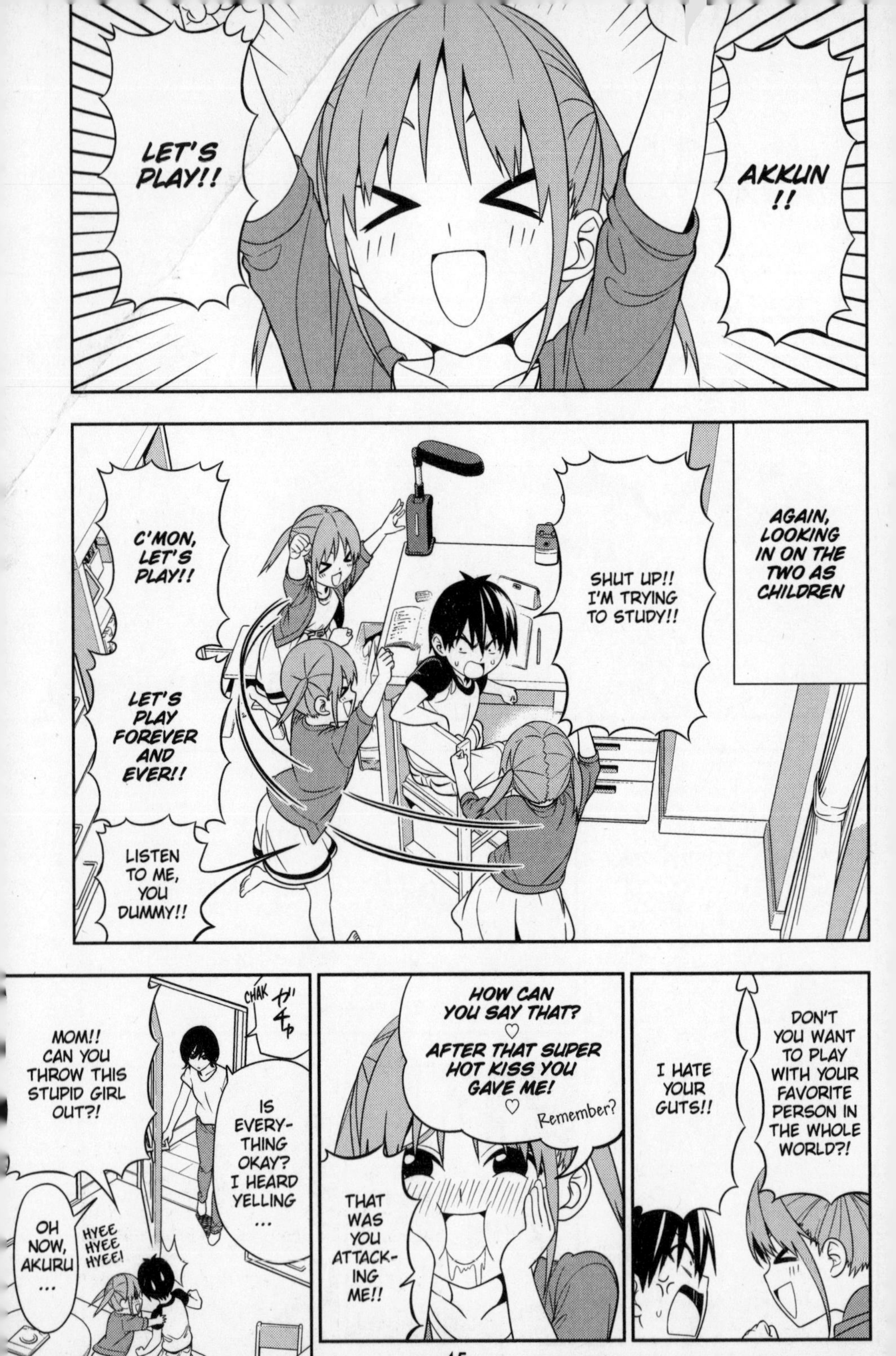
AKKUN !!
LET'S PLAY!!
AGAIN, LOOKING IN ON THE TWO AS CHILDREN
SHUT UP!! I'M TRYING TO STUDY!!
C'MON, LET'S PLAY!!
LET'S PLAY FOREVER AND EVER!!
LISTEN TO ME, YOU DUMMY!!
DON'T YOU WANT TO PLAY WITH YOUR FAVORITE PERSON IN THE WHOLE WORLD?!
I HATE YOUR GUTS!!
HOW CAN YOU SAY THAT? ♡ AFTER THAT SUPER HOT KISS YOU GAVE ME! ♡
Remember?
THAT WAS YOU ATTACKING ME!!
CHAK
IS EVERYTHING OKAY? I HEARD YELLING ...
MOM!! CAN YOU THROW THIS STUPID GIRL OUT?!
HYEE HYEE HYEE!
OH NOW, AKURU ...

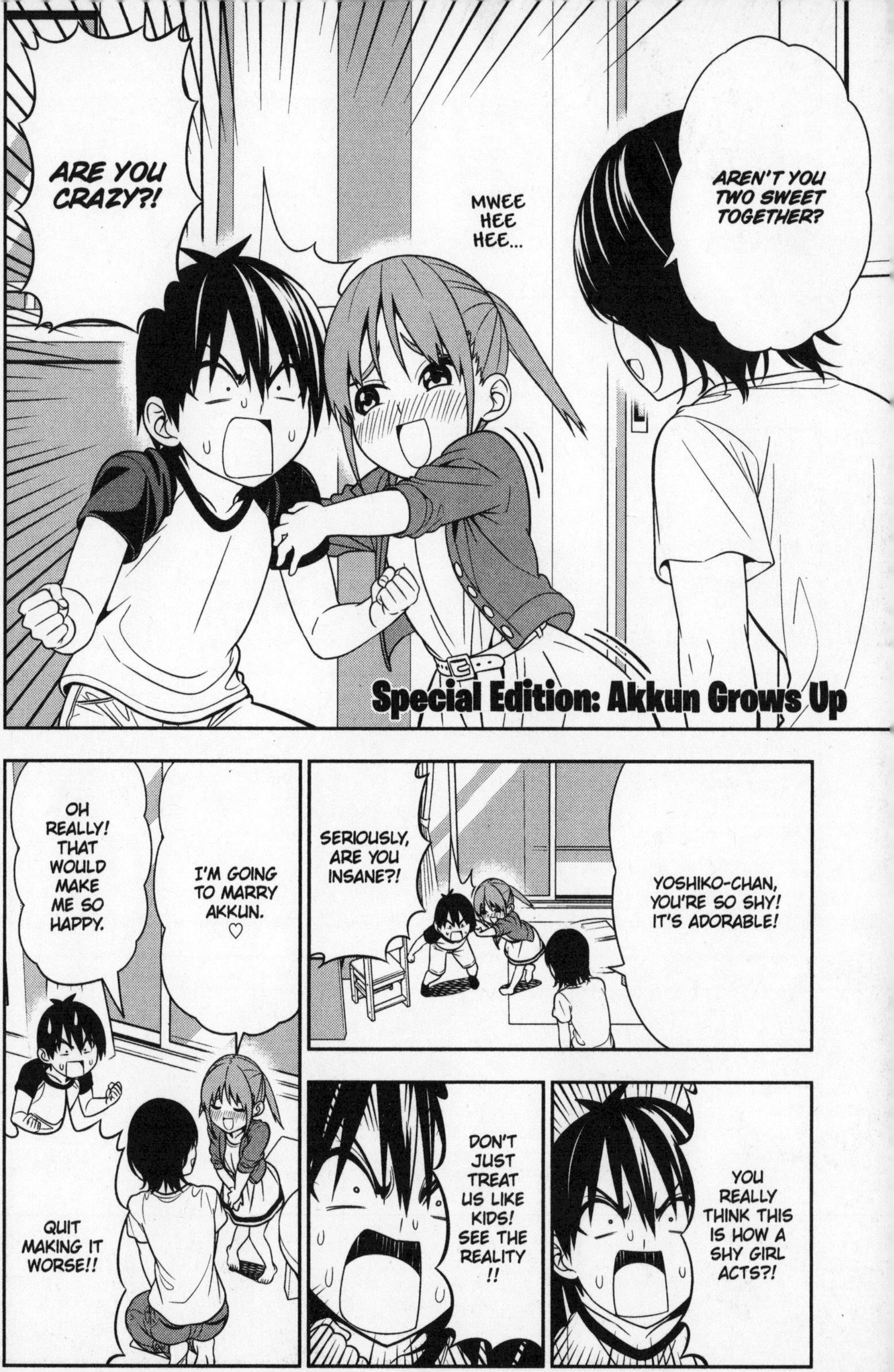
AREN'T YOU TWO SWEET TOGETHER?
MWEE HEE HEE...
ARE YOU CRAZY?!
Special Edition: Akkun Grows Up
YOSHIKO-CHAN, YOU'RE SO SHY! IT'S ADORABLE!
SERIOUSLY, ARE YOU INSANE?!
YOU REALLY THINK THIS IS HOW A SHY GIRL ACTS?!
DON'T JUST TREAT US LIKE KIDS! SEE THE REALITY !!
I'M GOING TO MARRY AKKUN. ♡
OH REALLY! THAT WOULD MAKE ME SO HAPPY.
QUIT MAKING IT WORSE!!

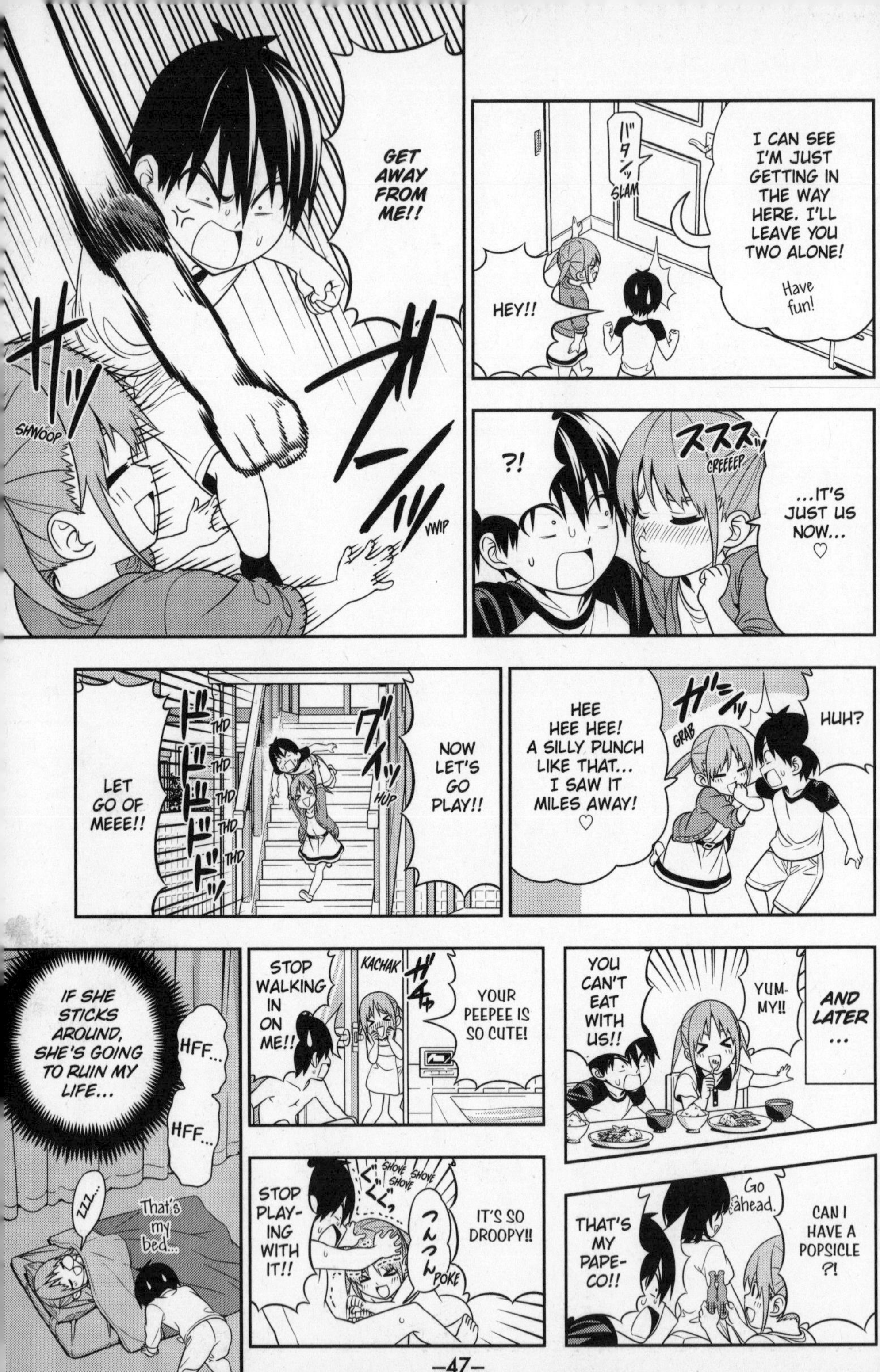
I CAN SEE I'M JUST GETTING IN THE WAY HERE. I'LL LEAVE YOU TWO ALONE!
Have fun!
バタンッ
SLAM
HEY!!
...IT'S JUST US NOW... ♡
ススス
CREEEEP
?!
GET AWAY FROM ME!!
VWIP
サッ
SHWOOP
HUH?
ガシィッ
GRAB
HEE HEE HEE! A SILLY PUNCH LIKE THAT... I SAW IT MILES AWAY! ♡
NOW LET'S GO PLAY!!
グイッ
HUP
THD THD THD THD THD
LET GO OF MEEE!!
AND LATER...
YUM-MY!!
YOU CAN'T EAT WITH US!!
YOUR PEEPEE IS SO CUTE!
KACHAK
STOP WALKING IN ON ME!!
CAN I HAVE A POPSICLE?!
Go ahead.
THAT'S MY PAPE-CO!!
IT'S SO DROOPY!!
つんつん
POKE
SHOVE SHOVE SHOVE
STOP PLAY-ING WITH IT!!
IF SHE STICKS AROUND, SHE'S GOING TO RUIN MY LIFE...
HFF...
HFF...
That's my bed...
ZZZ...

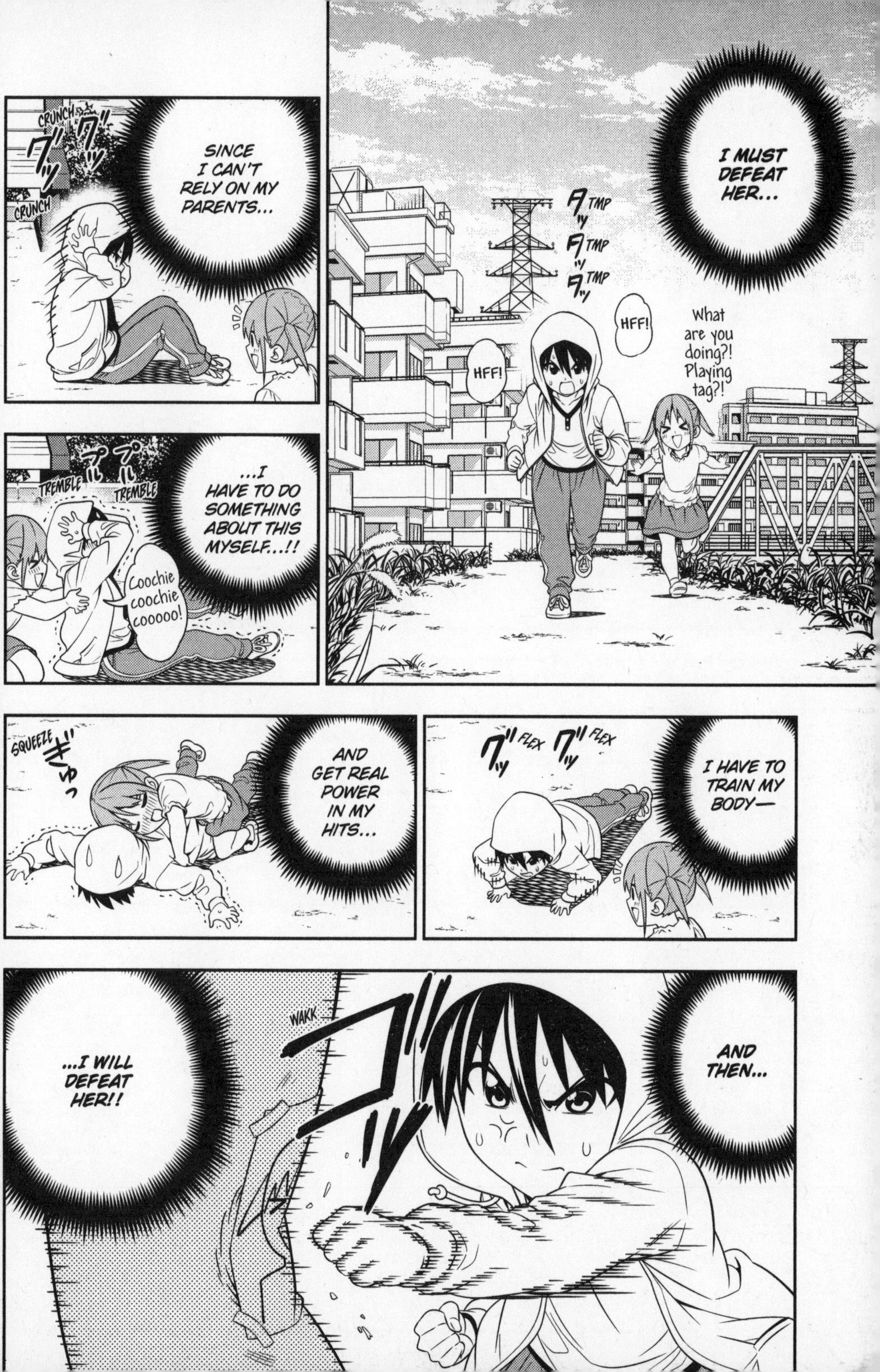
I MUST DEFEAT HER...
TMP
TMP
TMP
HFF!
HFF!
What are you doing?! Playing tag?!
CRUNCH
CRUNCH
SINCE I CAN'T RELY ON MY PARENTS...
TREMBLE
TREMBLE
...I HAVE TO DO SOMETHING ABOUT THIS MYSELF...!!
Coochie coochie cooooo!
FLEX
FLEX
I HAVE TO TRAIN MY BODY—
SQUEEZE
AND GET REAL POWER IN MY HITS...
AND THEN...
WAKK
...I WILL DEFEAT HER!!

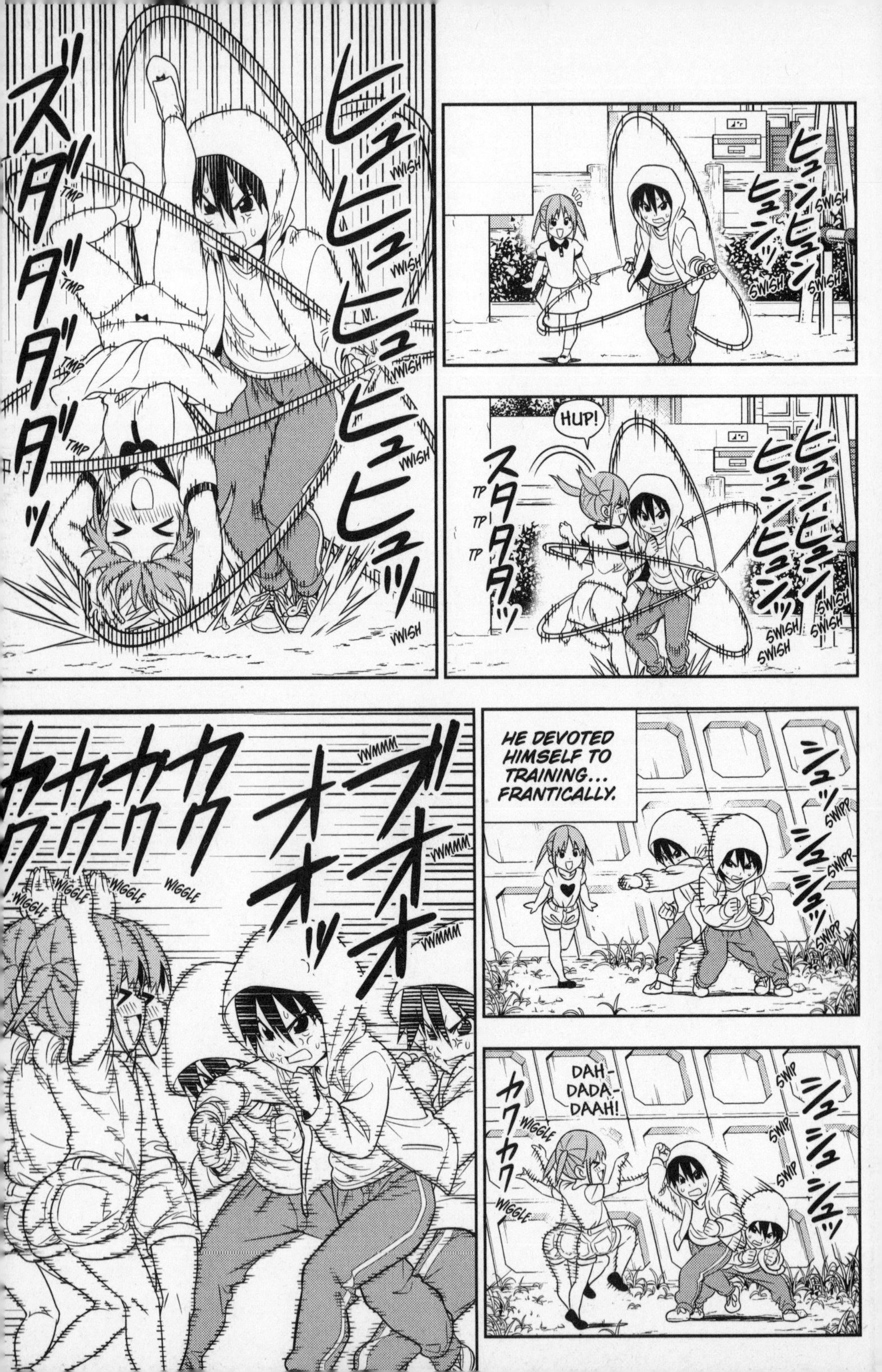
ヒュンヒュンヒュンッ
SWISH
SWISH
SWISH
HUP!
ヒュンヒュンヒュンッ
SWISH
SWISH
SWISH
SWISH
スタタタッ
TP
TP
TP
ヒュヒュヒュヒュヒュッ
VWISH
VWISH
VWISH
VWISH
VWISH
ズダダダダッ
TMP
TMP
TMP
TMP
HE DEVOTED HIMSELF TO TRAINING... FRANTICALLY.
シュッシュシュッ
SWIPP
SWIPP
SWIPP
DAH-DADA-DAAH!
シュシュシュッ
SWIP
SWIP
SWIP
カクカク
WIGGLE
WIGGLE
ブオオオッ
VWMMM
VWMMM
VWMMM
カクカクカクカク
WIGGLE
WIGGLE
WIGGLE
WIGGLE

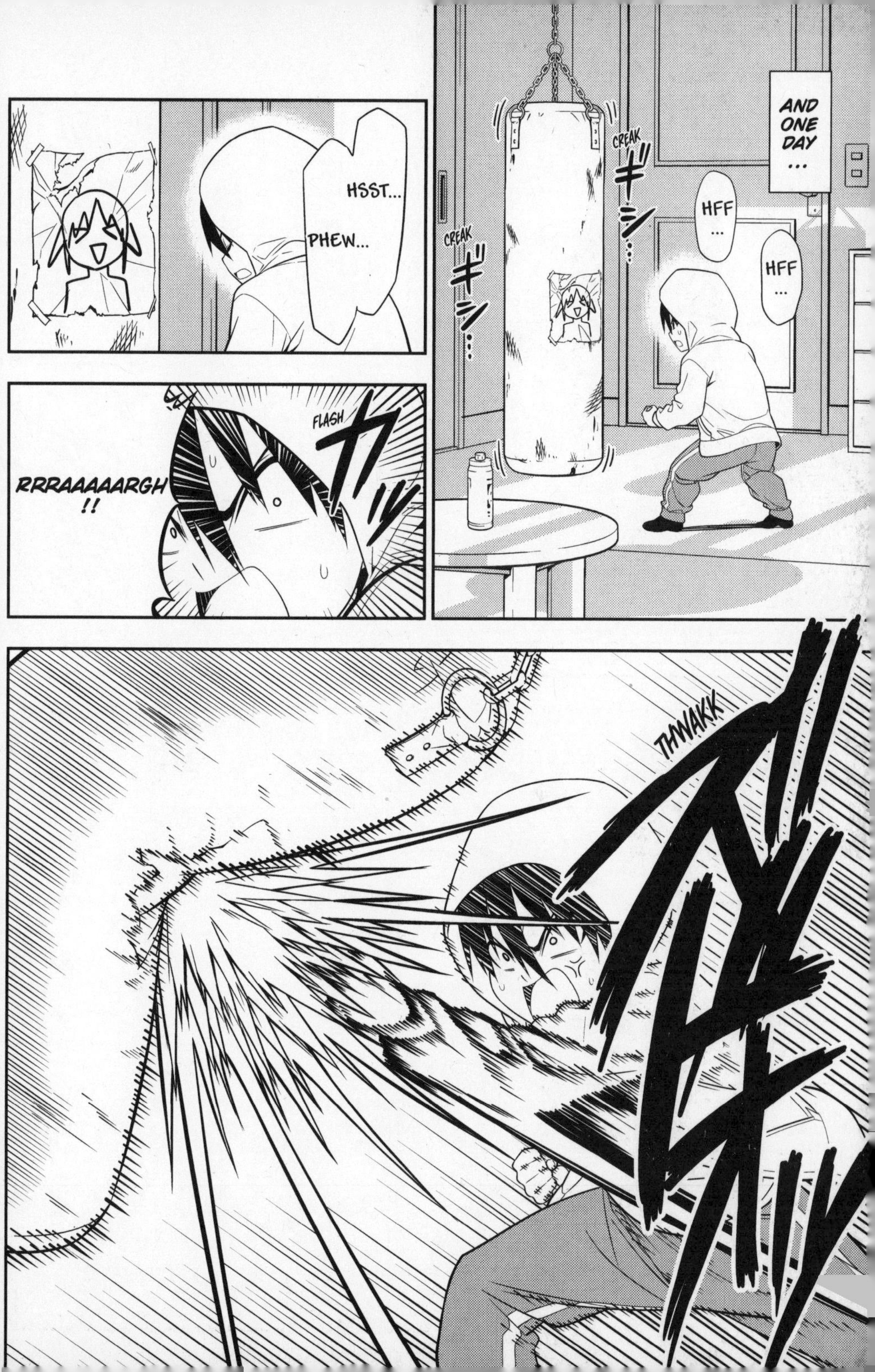
AND ONE DAY ...
HFF ...
HFF ...
CREAK
CREAK
HSST...
PHEW...
FLASH
RRRAAAAARGH !!
THWAKK

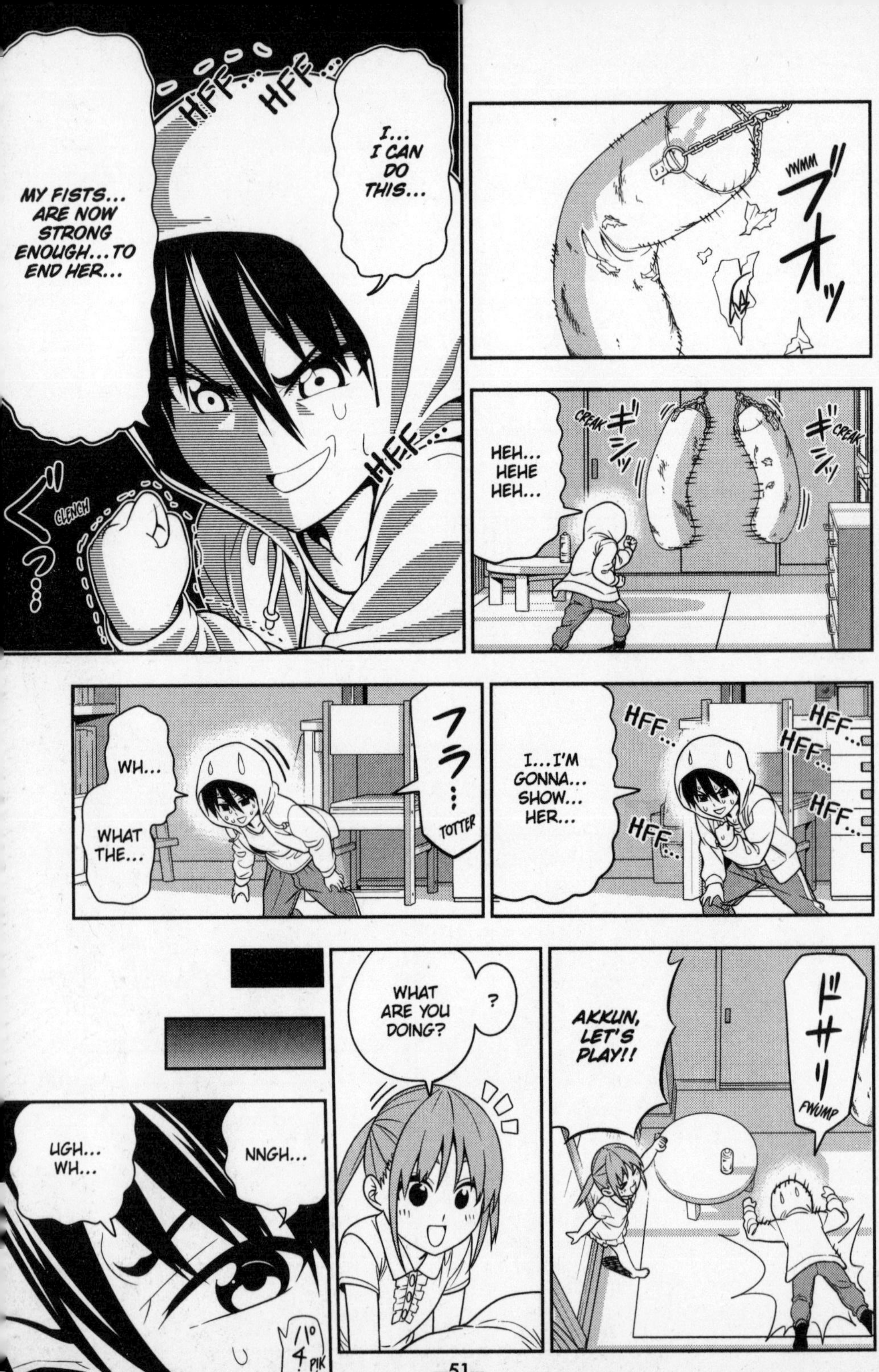
VMM
ブオッ
CREAK
ギシッ
HEH... HEHE HEH...
ギシッ
CREAK
HFF... HFF...
I... I CAN DO THIS...
MY FISTS... ARE NOW STRONG ENOUGH...TO END HER...
HFF...
ぐっ...
CLENCH
HFF...
I...I'M GONNA... SHOW... HER...
HFF...
HFF...
HFF...
HFF...
フラ...
TOTTER
WH...
WHAT THE...
AKKUN, LET'S PLAY!!
ドサリ
FWUMP
WHAT ARE YOU DOING?
?
NNGH...
UGH... WH...
パチ...
PIK

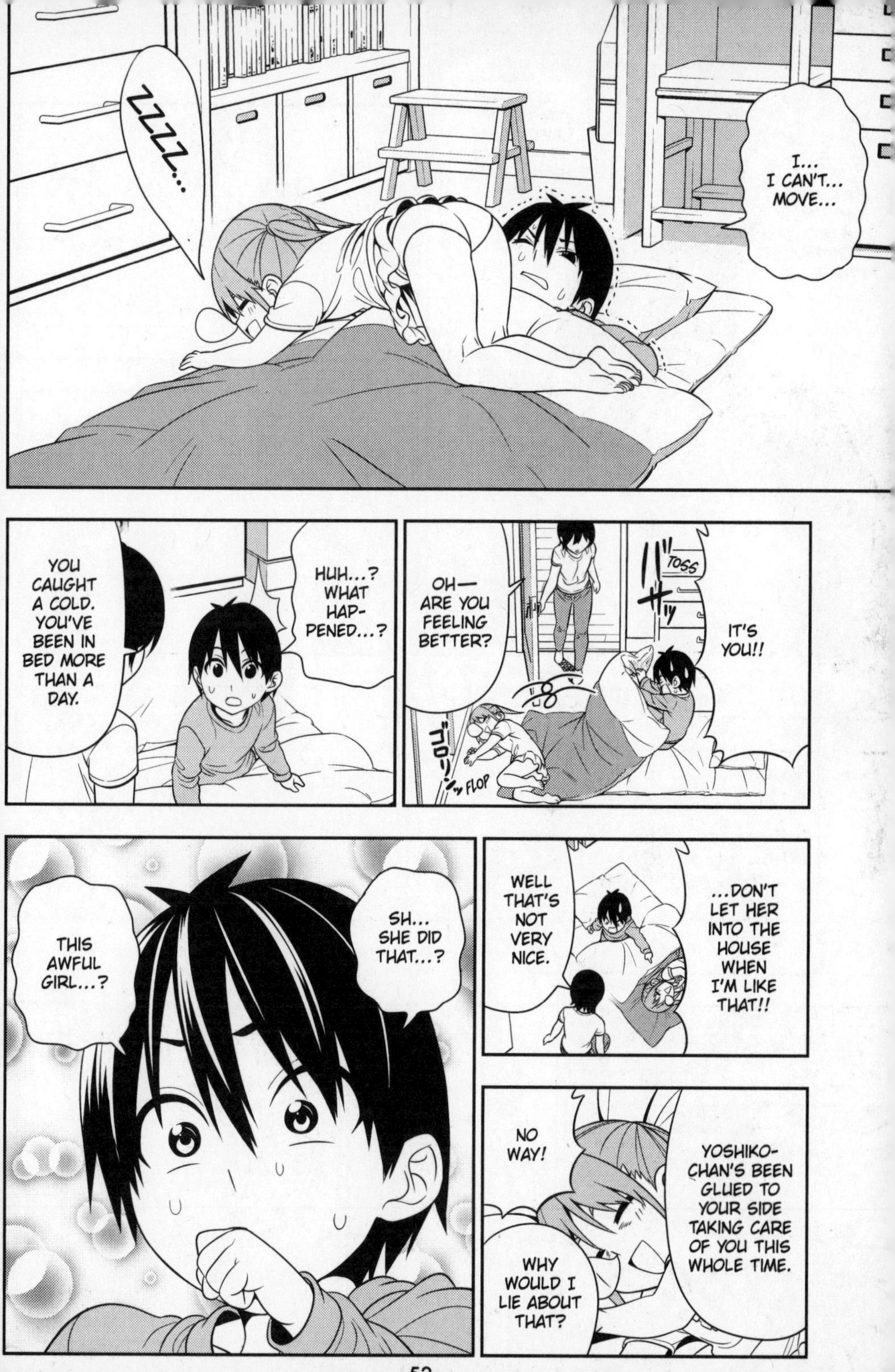
I... I CAN'T... MOVE...
ZZZZ...
TOSS
IT'S YOU!!
OH— ARE YOU FEELING BETTER?
FLOP
HUH...? WHAT HAP-PENED...?
YOU CAUGHT A COLD. YOU'VE BEEN IN BED MORE THAN A DAY.
...DON'T LET HER INTO THE HOUSE WHEN I'M LIKE THAT!!
WELL THAT'S NOT VERY NICE.
YOSHIKO-CHAN'S BEEN GLUED TO YOUR SIDE TAKING CARE OF YOU THIS WHOLE TIME.
NO WAY!
WHY WOULD I LIE ABOUT THAT?
SH... SHE DID THAT...?
THIS AWFUL GIRL...?

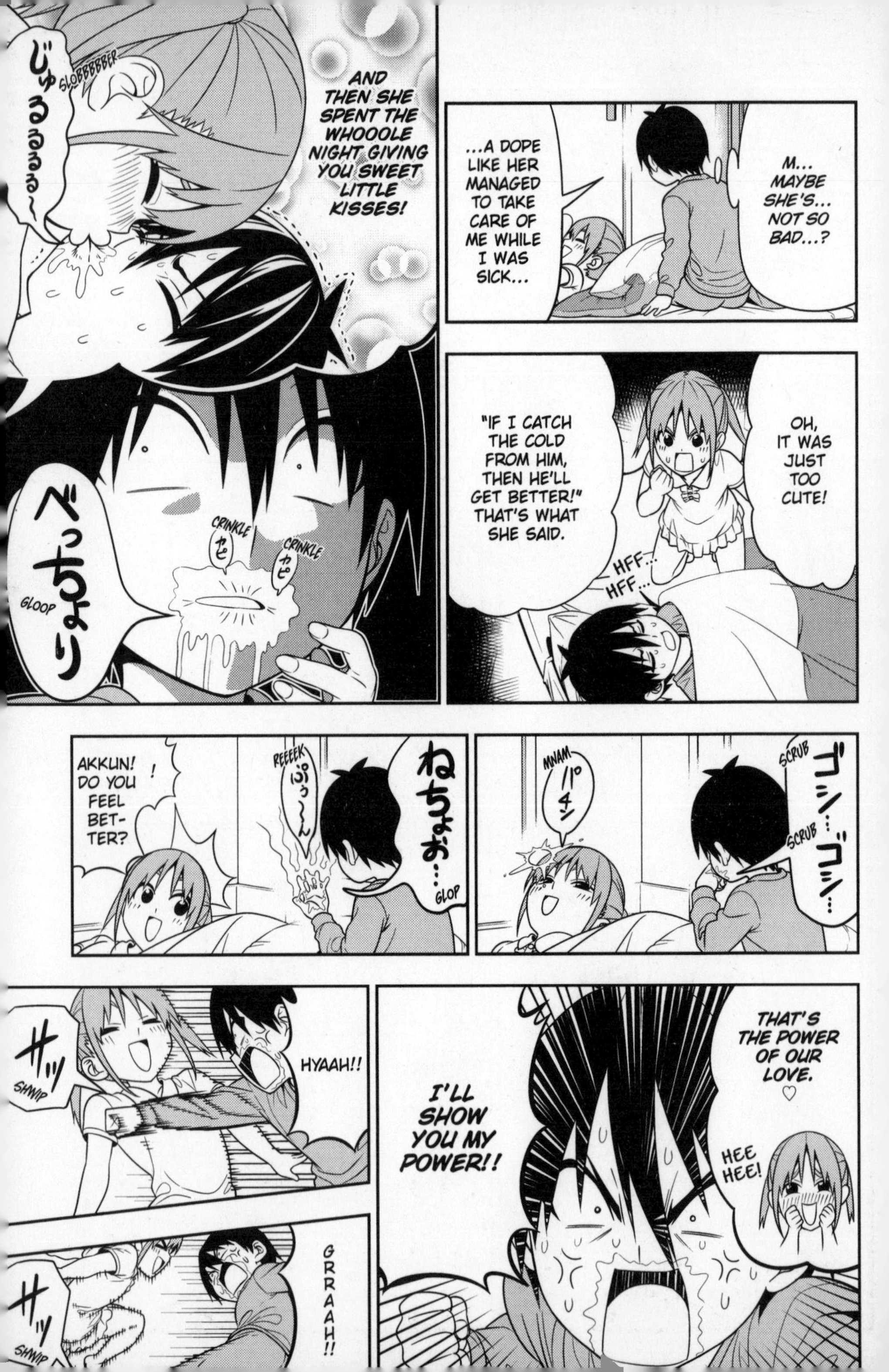
M... MAYBE SHE'S... NOT SO BAD...?
...A DOPE LIKE HER MANAGED TO TAKE CARE OF ME WHILE I WAS SICK...
OH, IT WAS JUST TOO CUTE!
"IF I CATCH THE COLD FROM HIM, THEN HE'LL GET BETTER!" THAT'S WHAT SHE SAID.
HFF... HFF...
AND THEN SHE SPENT THE WHOOOLE NIGHT GIVING YOU SWEET LITTLE KISSES!
じゅるるるる~
SLOBBBBBER
カピ
CRINKLE
カピ
CRINKLE
べっちょり
GLOOP
ゴシ...ゴシ...
SCRUB
SCRUB
パチン
MNAM
ねちょぉ...
GLOP
ぷぅ~ん
REEEEK
AKKUN! DO YOU FEEL BET-TER?
!
THAT'S THE POWER OF OUR LOVE. ♡
HEE HEE!
I'LL SHOW YOU MY POWER!!
HYAAH!!
サッ
SHWIP
GRRAAH!!
サッ
SHWIP

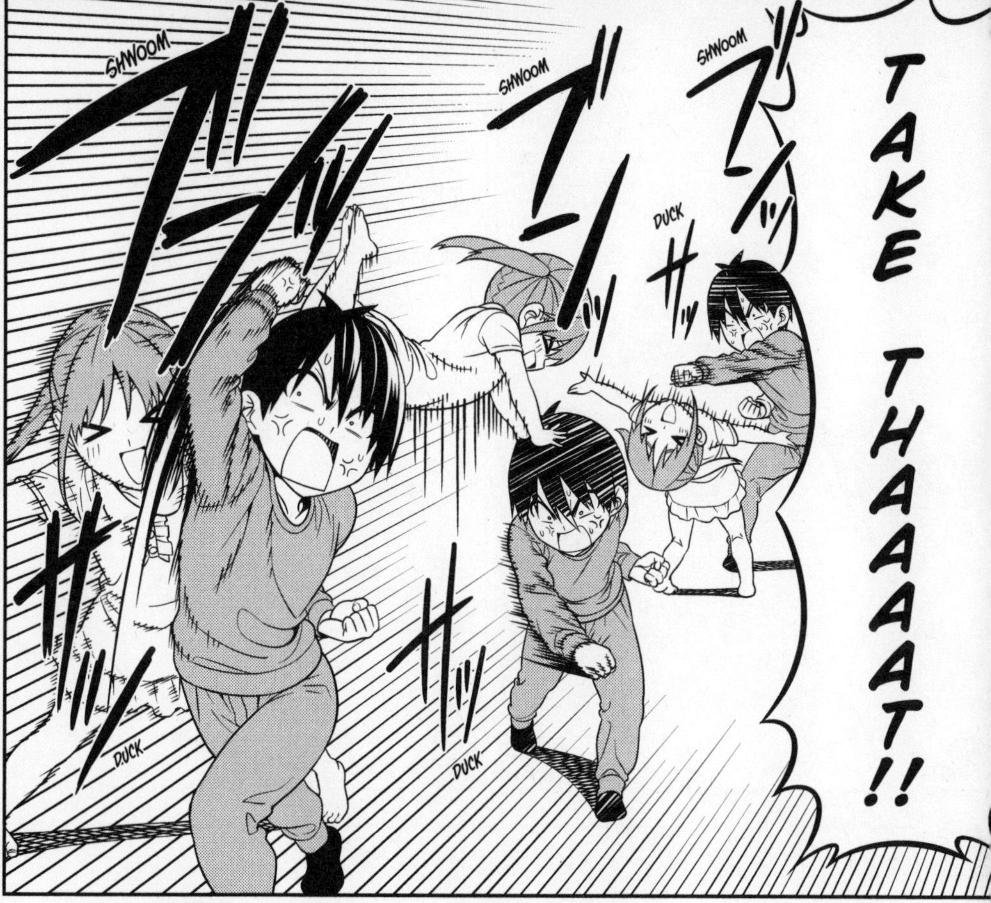
TAKE THAAAAAT!!
SHWOOM
SHWOOM
DUCK
SHWOOM
DUCK
DUCK

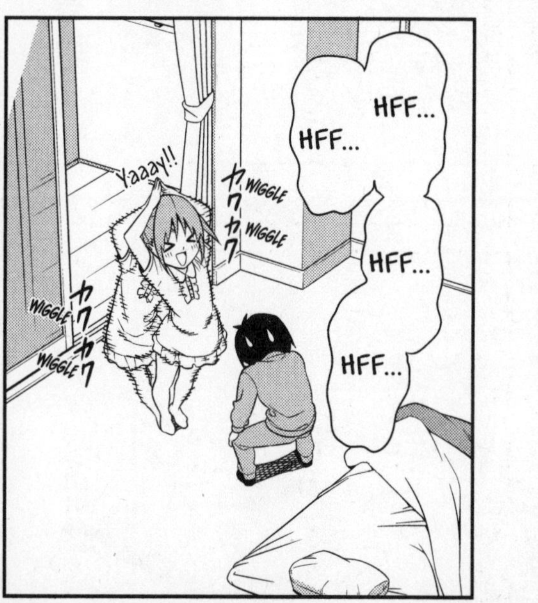
HFF...
HFF...
HFF...
HFF...
WIGGLE
WIGGLE
Yaaay!!
WIGGLE
WIGGLE

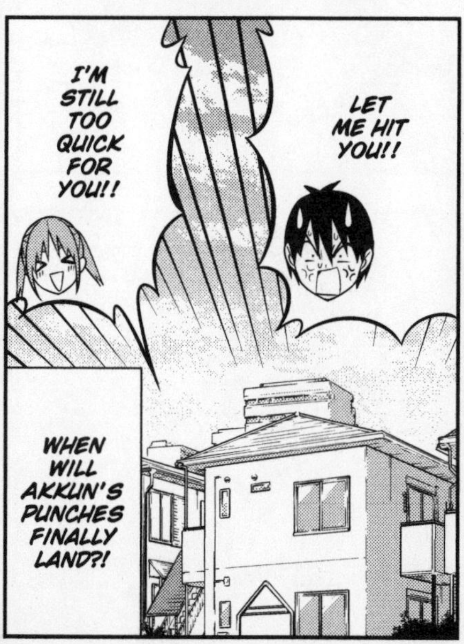
LET ME HIT YOU!!
I'M STILL TOO QUICK FOR YOU!!
WHEN WILL AKKUN'S PUNCHES FINALLY LAND?!

## He's Only Five

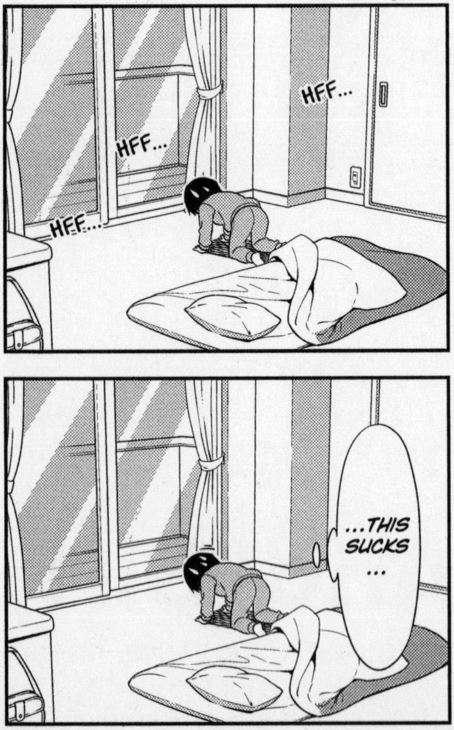
HFF...
HFF...
HFF...
...THIS SUCKS ...

(Kids Return)

# Aho-Girl

\\'ahô͵gərl\\ *Japanese, noun.*
A clueless girl.

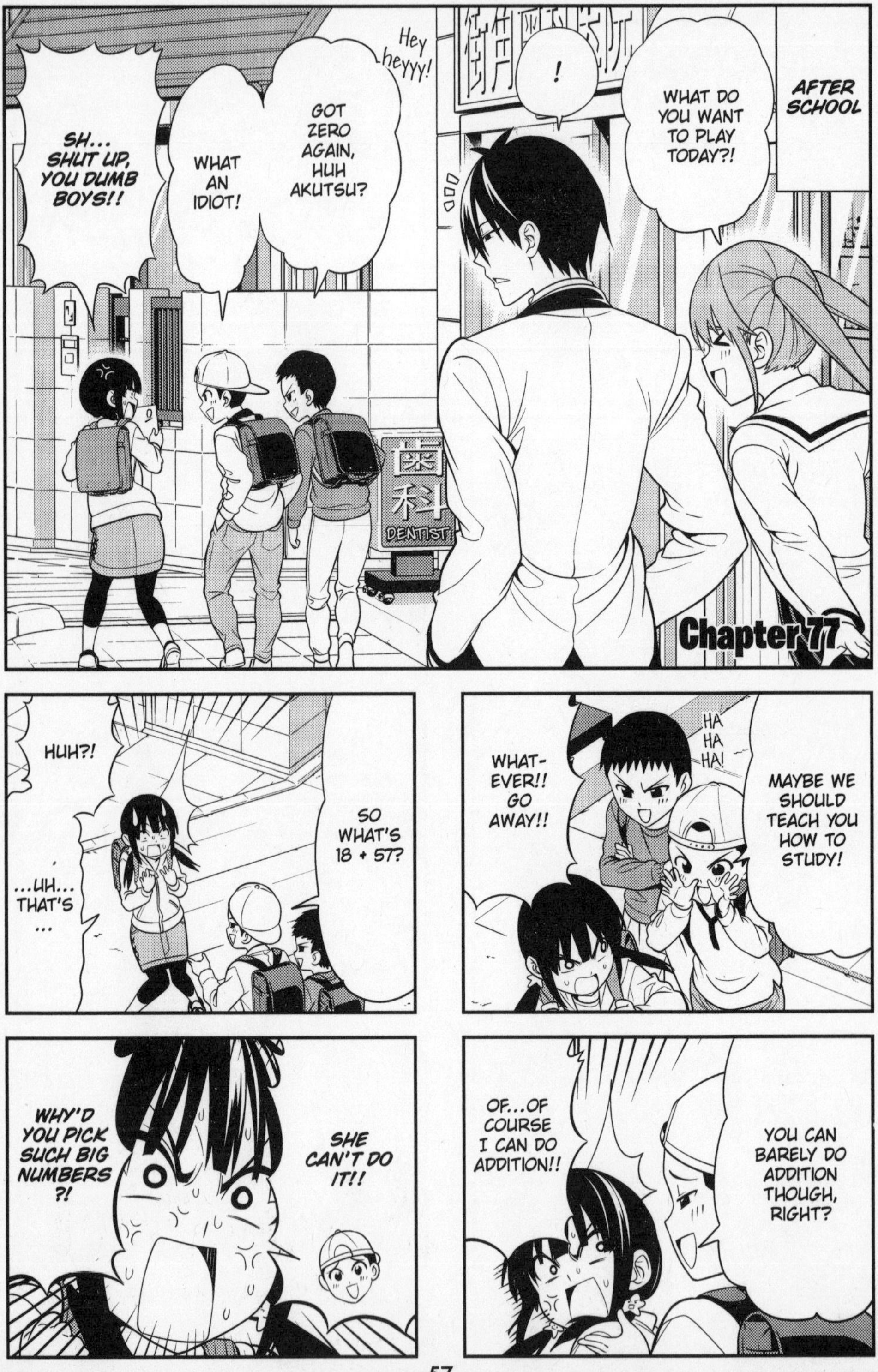
AFTER SCHOOL
WHAT DO YOU WANT TO PLAY TODAY?!
!
Hey heyyy!
GOT ZERO AGAIN, HUH AKUTSU?
WHAT AN IDIOT!
SH... SHUT UP, YOU DUMB BOYS!!
DENTIST
Chapter 77
MAYBE WE SHOULD TEACH YOU HOW TO STUDY!
HA HA HA!
WHAT-EVER!! GO AWAY!!
SO WHAT'S 18 + 57?
HUH?!
...UH... THAT'S ...
YOU CAN BARELY DO ADDITION THOUGH, RIGHT?
OF...OF COURSE I CAN DO ADDITION!!
SHE CAN'T DO IT!!
WHY'D YOU PICK SUCH BIG NUMBERS ?!

## This Is My Weak Arm

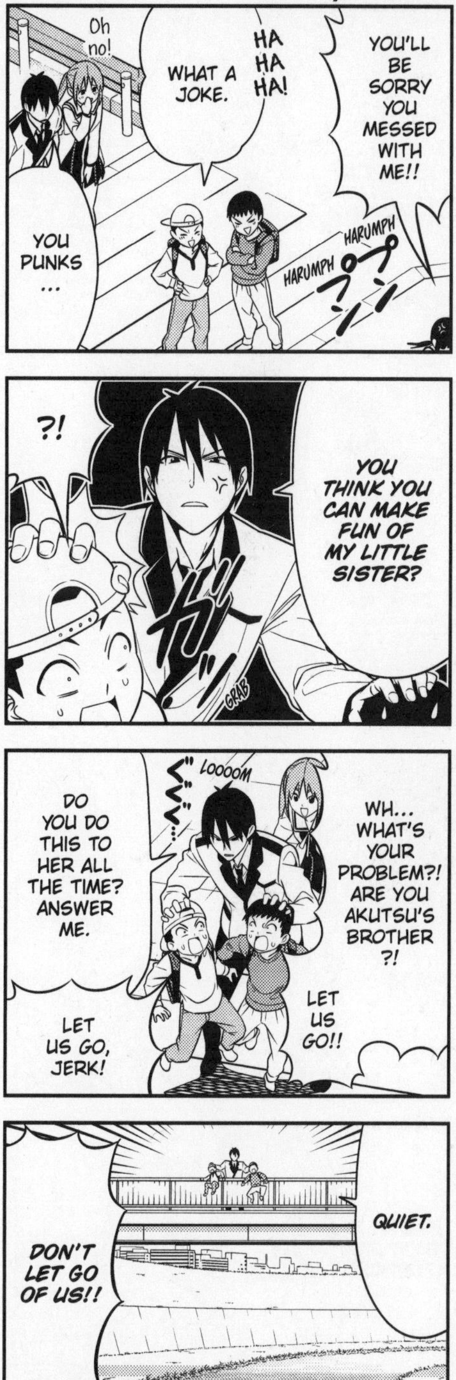
YOU'LL BE SORRY YOU MESSED WITH ME!!
HA HA HA!
WHAT A JOKE.
Oh no!
HARUMPH
HARUMPH
YOU PUNKS ...
YOU THINK YOU CAN MAKE FUN OF MY LITTLE SISTER?
?!
GRAB
WH... WHAT'S YOUR PROBLEM?! ARE YOU AKUTSU'S BROTHER?!
LOOOOM
DO YOU DO THIS TO HER ALL THE TIME? ANSWER ME.
LET US GO!!
LET US GO, JERK!
QUIET.
DON'T LET GO OF US!!

## That Was Fast

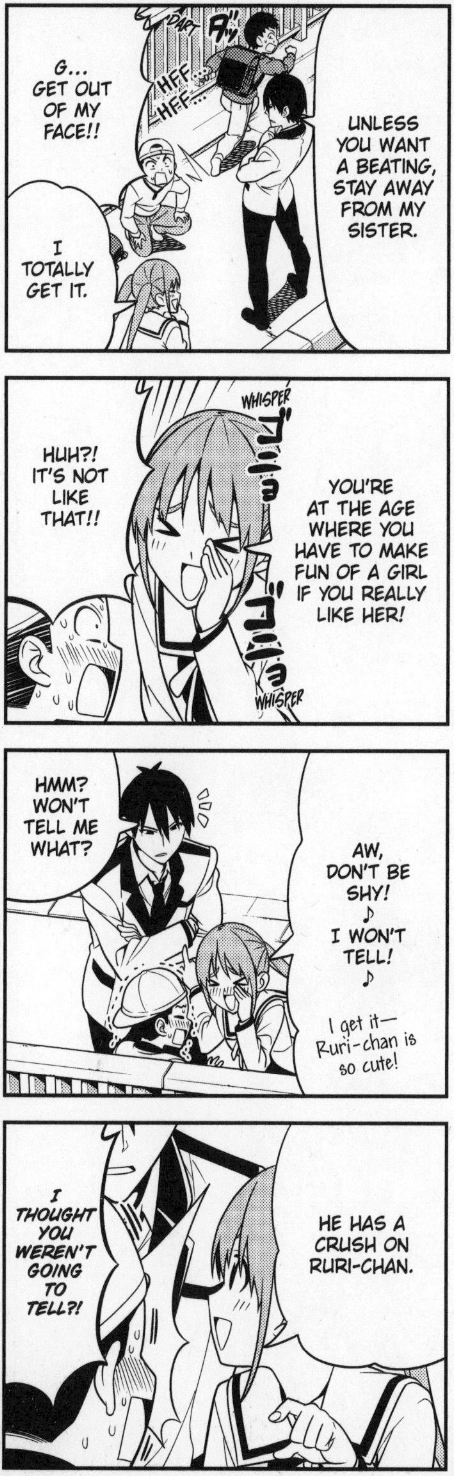
UNLESS YOU WANT A BEATING, STAY AWAY FROM MY SISTER.
DART
HFF... HFF...
G... GET OUT OF MY FACE!!
I TOTALLY GET IT.
YOU'RE AT THE AGE WHERE YOU HAVE TO MAKE FUN OF A GIRL IF YOU REALLY LIKE HER!
WHISPER
WHISPER
HUH?! IT'S NOT LIKE THAT!!
AW, DON'T BE SHY! ♪ I WON'T TELL! ♪
I get it— Ruri-chan is so cute!
HMM? WON'T TELL ME WHAT?
HE HAS A CRUSH ON RURI-CHAN.
I THOUGHT YOU WEREN'T GOING TO TELL?!

## A Terrifying Guardian

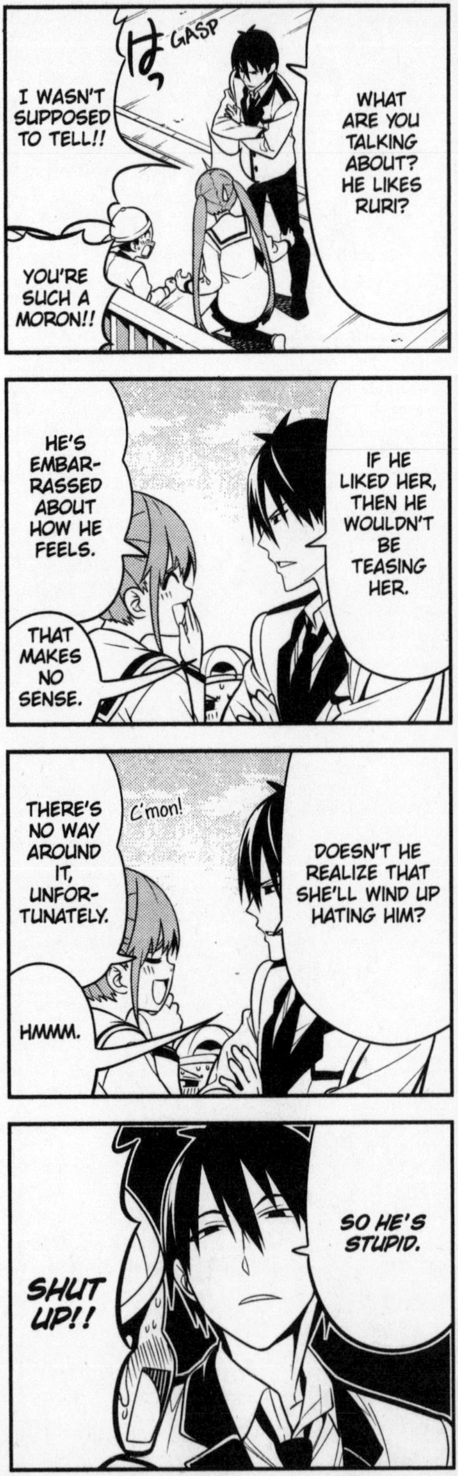

WHAT ARE YOU TALKING ABOUT? HE LIKES RURI?
はっ GASP
I WASN'T SUPPOSED TO TELL!!
YOU'RE SUCH A MORON!!
IF HE LIKED HER, THEN HE WOULDN'T BE TEASING HER.
HE'S EMBARRASSED ABOUT HOW HE FEELS.
THAT MAKES NO SENSE.
DOESN'T HE REALIZE THAT SHE'LL WIND UP HATING HIM?
C'mon!
THERE'S NO WAY AROUND IT, UNFORTUNATELY.
HMMM.
SO HE'S STUPID.
SHUT UP!!


## Way, Way Too Terrifying a Guardian

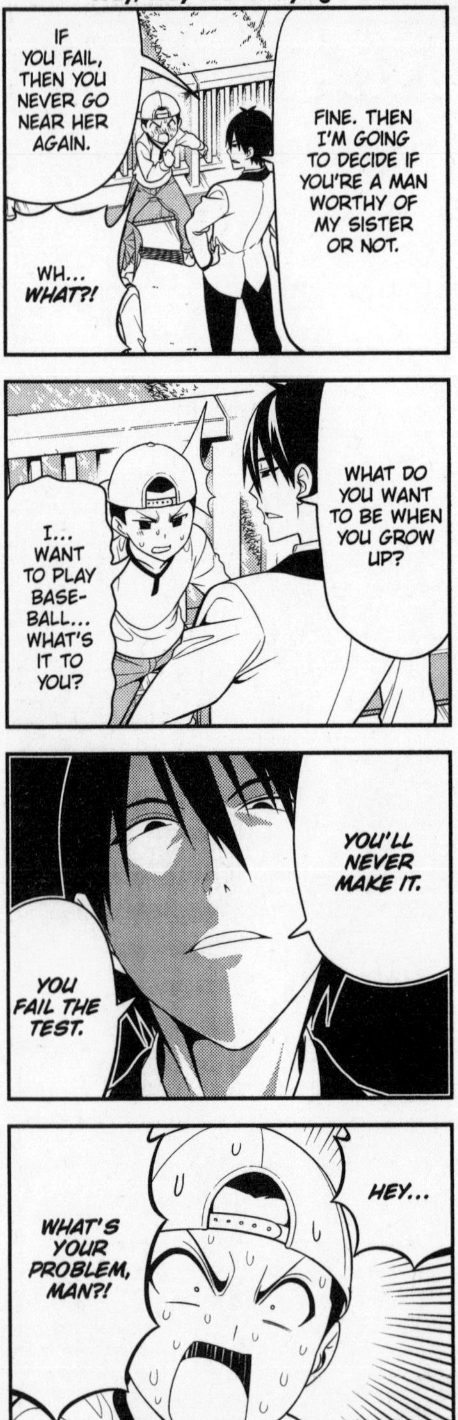

FINE. THEN I'M GOING TO DECIDE IF YOU'RE A MAN WORTHY OF MY SISTER OR NOT.
IF YOU FAIL, THEN YOU NEVER GO NEAR HER AGAIN.
WH... WHAT?!
WHAT DO YOU WANT TO BE WHEN YOU GROW UP?
I... WANT TO PLAY BASE-BALL... WHAT'S IT TO YOU?
YOU'LL NEVER MAKE IT.
YOU FAIL THE TEST.
HEY...
WHAT'S YOUR PROBLEM, MAN?!

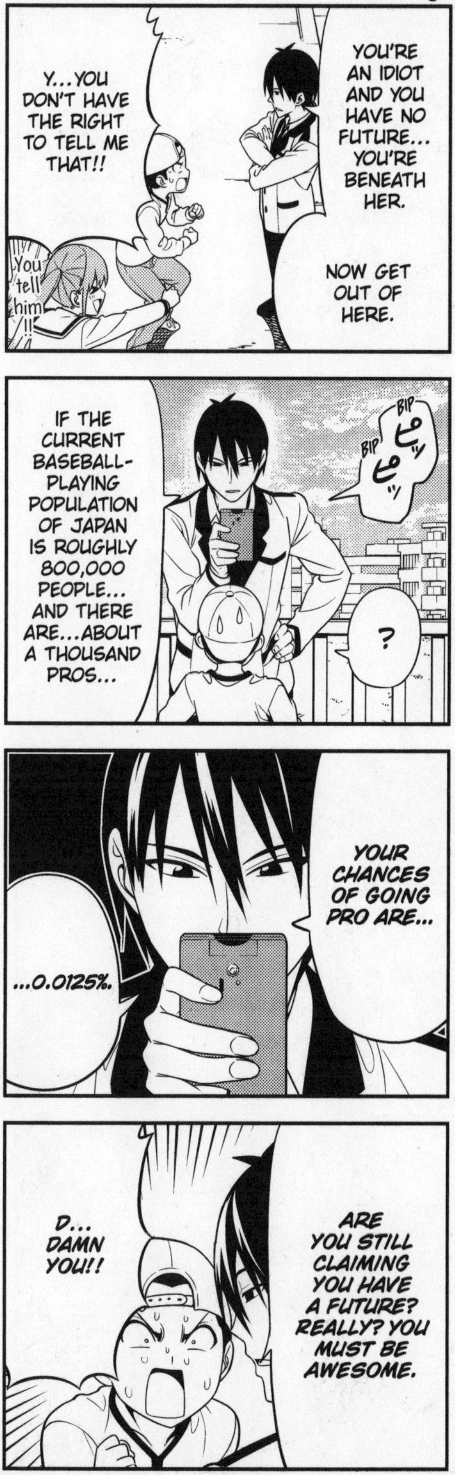
YOU'RE AN IDIOT AND YOU HAVE NO FUTURE... YOU'RE BENEATH HER.
NOW GET OUT OF HERE.
Y...YOU DON'T HAVE THE RIGHT TO TELL ME THAT!!
You tell him!!
BIP ピッ
BIP ピッ
IF THE CURRENT BASEBALL-PLAYING POPULATION OF JAPAN IS ROUGHLY 800,000 PEOPLE... AND THERE ARE...ABOUT A THOUSAND PROS...
?
YOUR CHANCES OF GOING PRO ARE...
...0.0125%.
ARE YOU STILL CLAIMING YOU HAVE A FUTURE? REALLY? YOU MUST BE AWESOME.
D... DAMN YOU!!



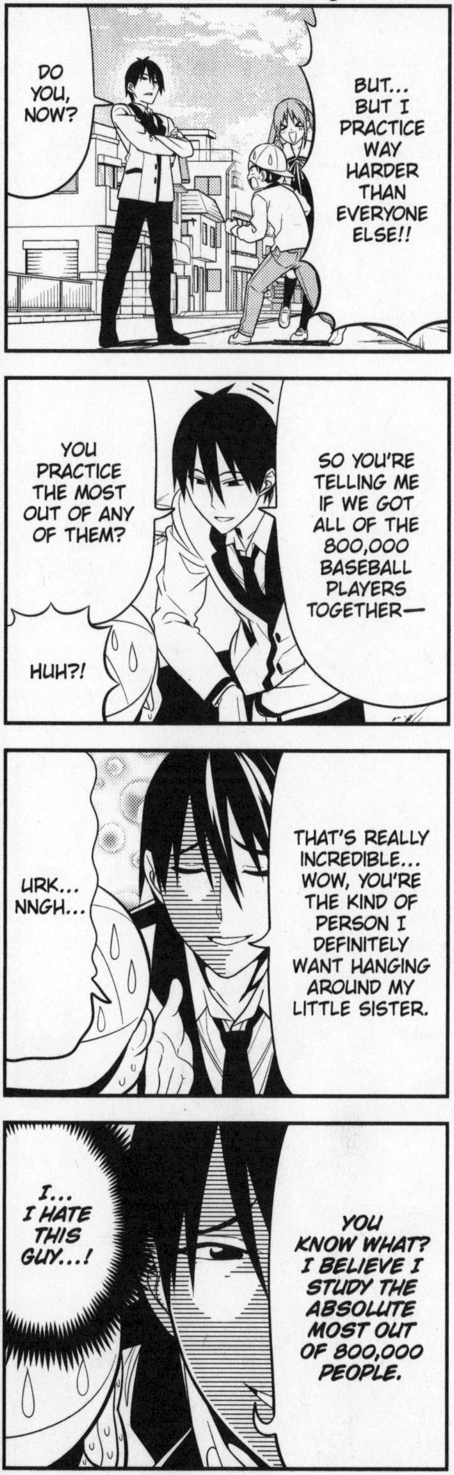
BUT... BUT I PRACTICE WAY HARDER THAN EVERYONE ELSE!!
DO YOU, NOW?
SO YOU'RE TELLING ME IF WE GOT ALL OF THE 800,000 BASEBALL PLAYERS TOGETHER—
YOU PRACTICE THE MOST OUT OF ANY OF THEM?
HUH?!
THAT'S REALLY INCREDIBLE... WOW, YOU'RE THE KIND OF PERSON I DEFINITELY WANT HANGING AROUND MY LITTLE SISTER.
URK... NNGH...
YOU KNOW WHAT? I BELIEVE I STUDY THE ABSOLUTE MOST OUT OF 800,000 PEOPLE.
I... I HATE THIS GUY...!

Total Break with Logic

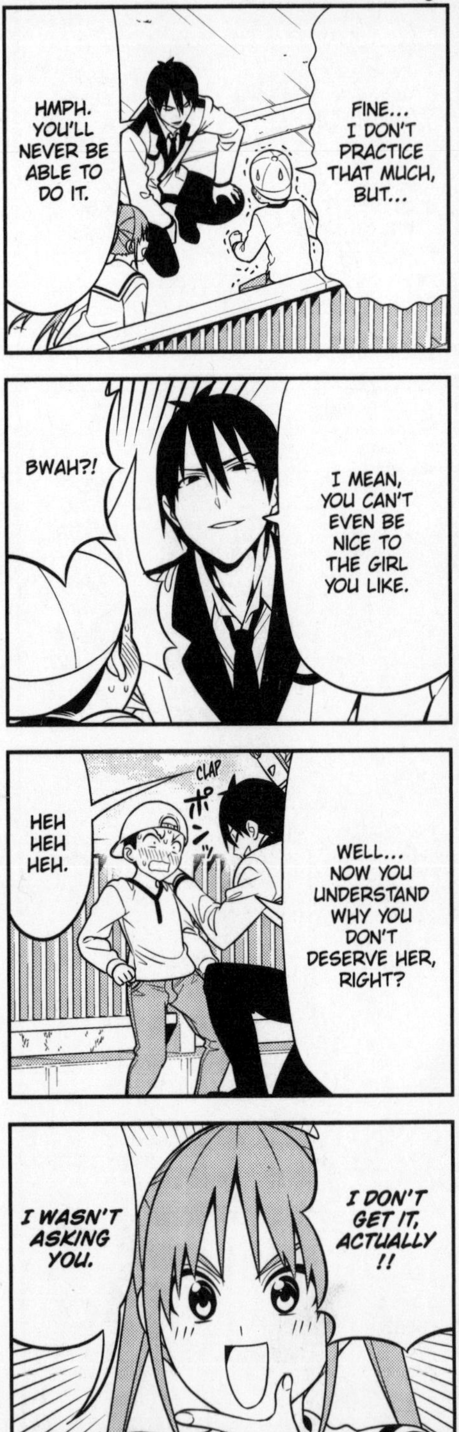
FINE... I DON'T PRACTICE THAT MUCH, BUT...
HMPH. YOU'LL NEVER BE ABLE TO DO IT.
I MEAN, YOU CAN'T EVEN BE NICE TO THE GIRL YOU LIKE.
BWAH?!
ポンッ
CLAP
WELL... NOW YOU UNDERSTAND WHY YOU DON'T DESERVE HER, RIGHT?
HEH HEH HEH.
I DON'T GET IT, ACTUALLY!!
I WASN'T ASKING YOU.

He Fights Back!

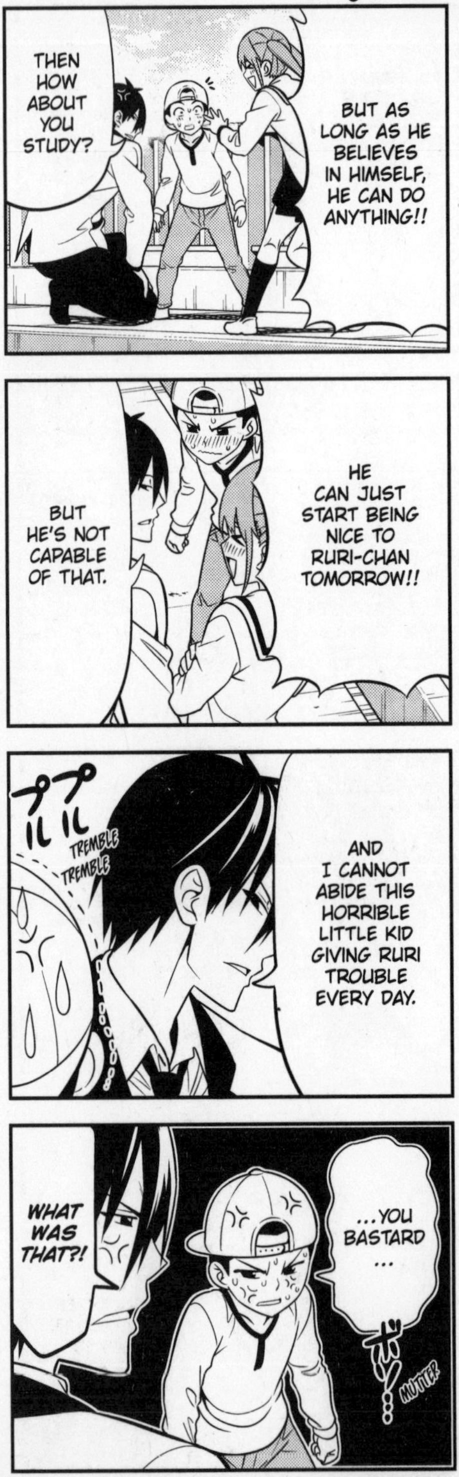
BUT AS LONG AS HE BELIEVES IN HIMSELF, HE CAN DO ANYTHING!!
THEN HOW ABOUT YOU STUDY?
HE CAN JUST START BEING NICE TO RURI-CHAN TOMORROW!!
BUT HE'S NOT CAPABLE OF THAT.
AND I CANNOT ABIDE THIS HORRIBLE LITTLE KID GIVING RURI TROUBLE EVERY DAY.
プルプル
TREMBLE TREMBLE
...YOU BASTARD ...
ボソ...
MUTTER
WHAT WAS THAT?!

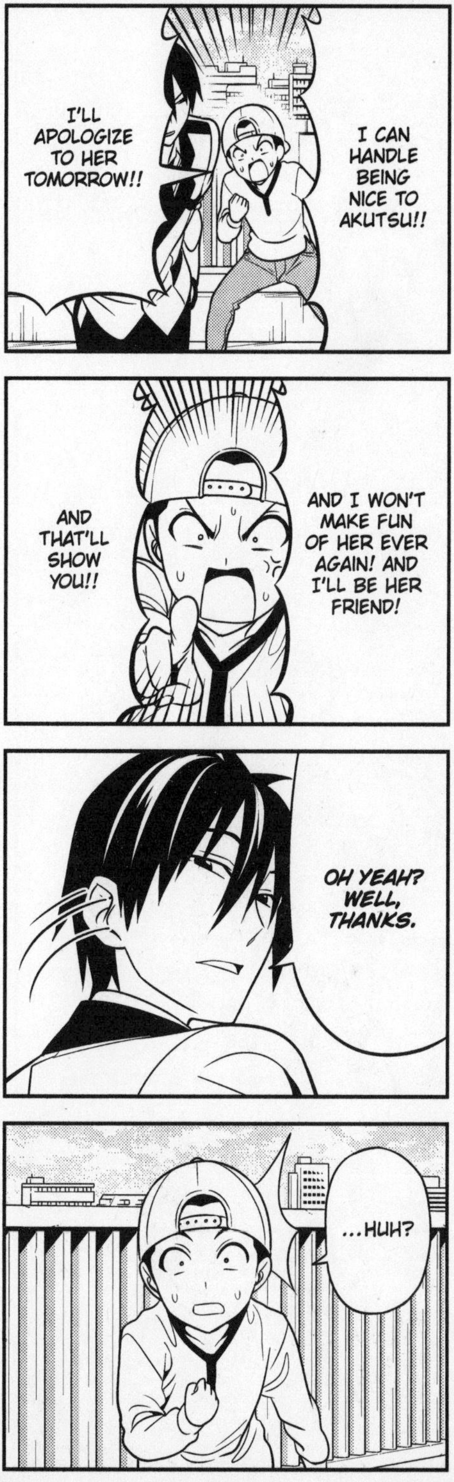
I CAN HANDLE BEING NICE TO AKUTSU!!
I'LL APOLOGIZE TO HER TOMORROW!!
AND I WON'T MAKE FUN OF HER EVER AGAIN! AND I'LL BE HER FRIEND!
AND THAT'LL SHOW YOU!!
OH YEAH? WELL, THANKS.
...HUH?



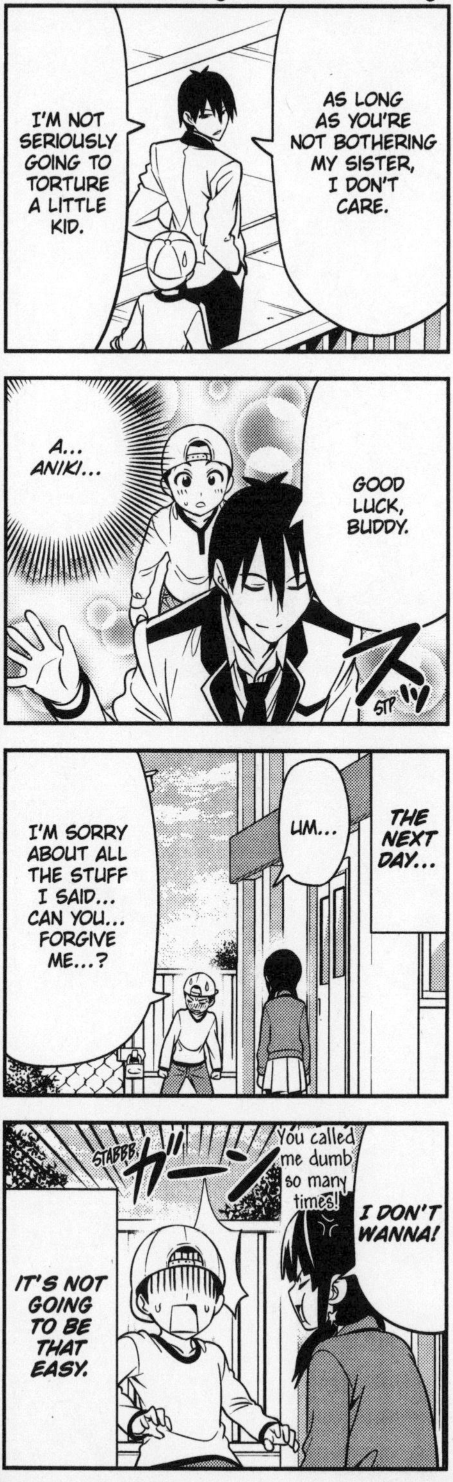
AS LONG AS YOU'RE NOT BOTHERING MY SISTER, I DON'T CARE.
I'M NOT SERIOUSLY GOING TO TORTURE A LITTLE KID.
GOOD LUCK, BUDDY.
スッ
STP
A... ANIKI...
THE NEXT DAY...
UM...
I'M SORRY ABOUT ALL THE STUFF I SAID... CAN YOU... FORGIVE ME...?
I DON'T WANNA!
You called me dumb so many times!
ガーン
STABBB
IT'S NOT GOING TO BE THAT EASY.

**No Way!**

UM... ANIKI... HOW CAN I GET AKUTSU TO LIKE ME...?
HOW SHOULD I KNOW?
I NEED HELP WITH THAT MYSELF.
SHE HATES YOU, TOO?!

(No way I can go see my clients like this, man. That'd be)

# Aho-Girl

\ˈahô͵gərl\ *Japanese, noun.*
A clueless girl.

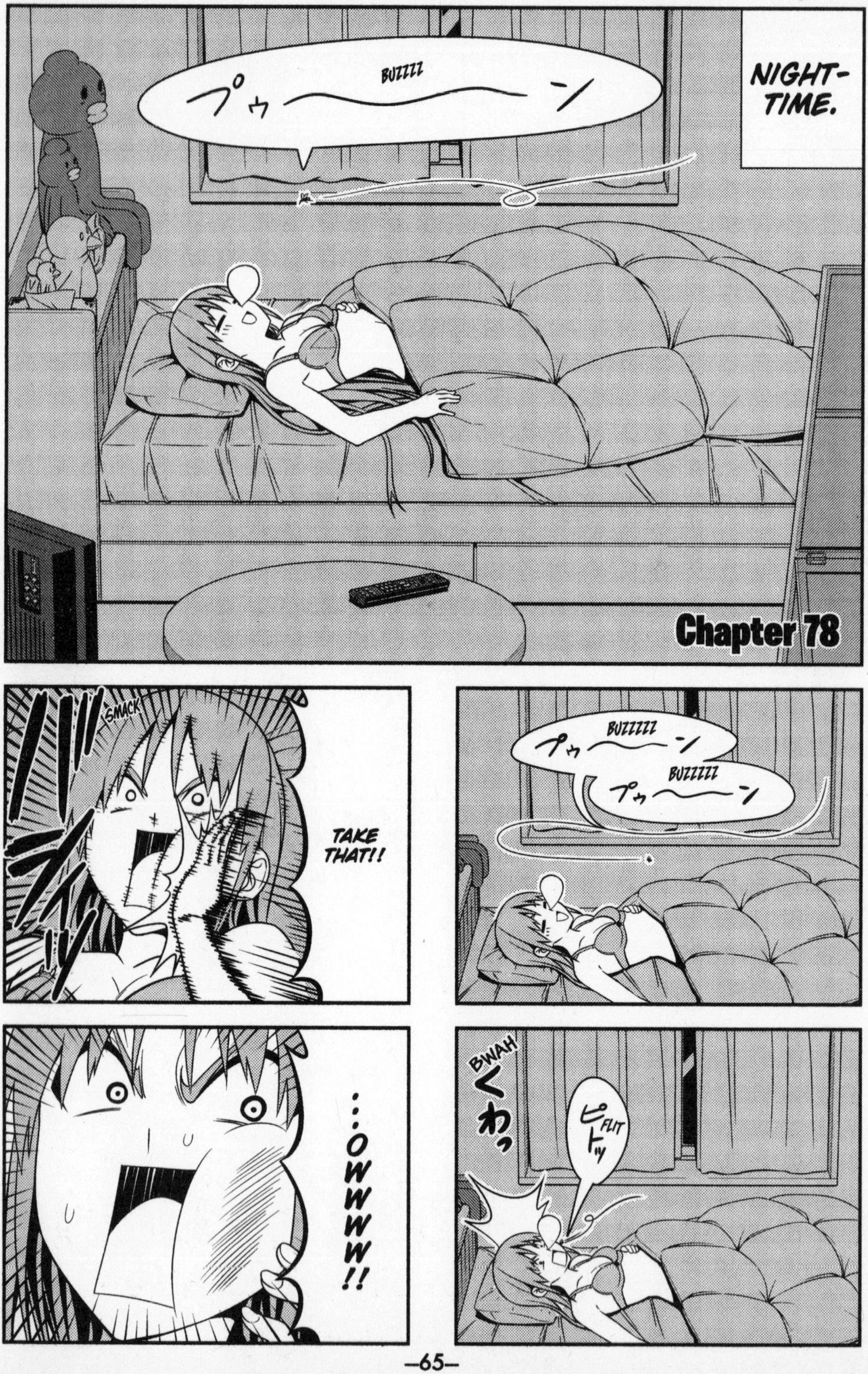
NIGHT-TIME.
プゥ〜〜〜〜ン
BUZZZZ
Chapter 78
プゥ〜〜ン
BUZZZZZ
プゥ〜〜ン
BUZZZZZ
SMACK
TAKE THAT!!
くわっ
BWAH
ピトッ
FLIT
...OWWWWW!!

It's Not Getting Better!

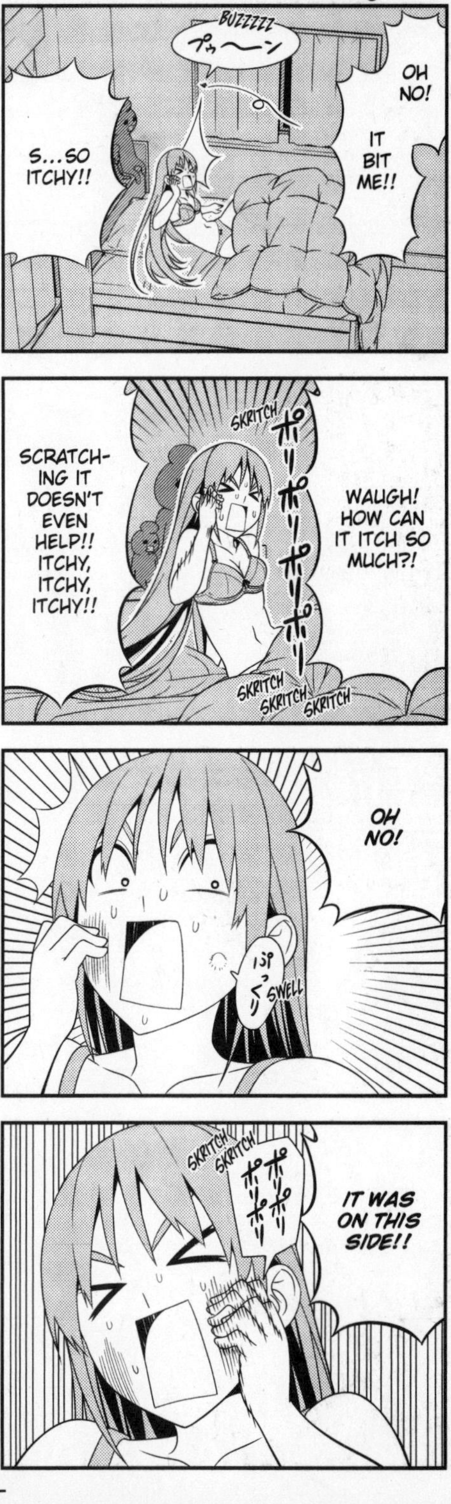
BUZZZZZ
プゥ〜ン
OH NO!
IT BIT ME!!
S...SO ITCHY!!
SKRITCH
WAUGH! HOW CAN IT ITCH SO MUCH?!
SCRATCHING IT DOESN'T EVEN HELP!! ITCHY, ITCHY, ITCHY!!
SKRITCH SKRITCH SKRITCH
OH NO!
SWELL
IT WAS ON THIS SIDE!!
SKRITCH SKRITCH

Showdown

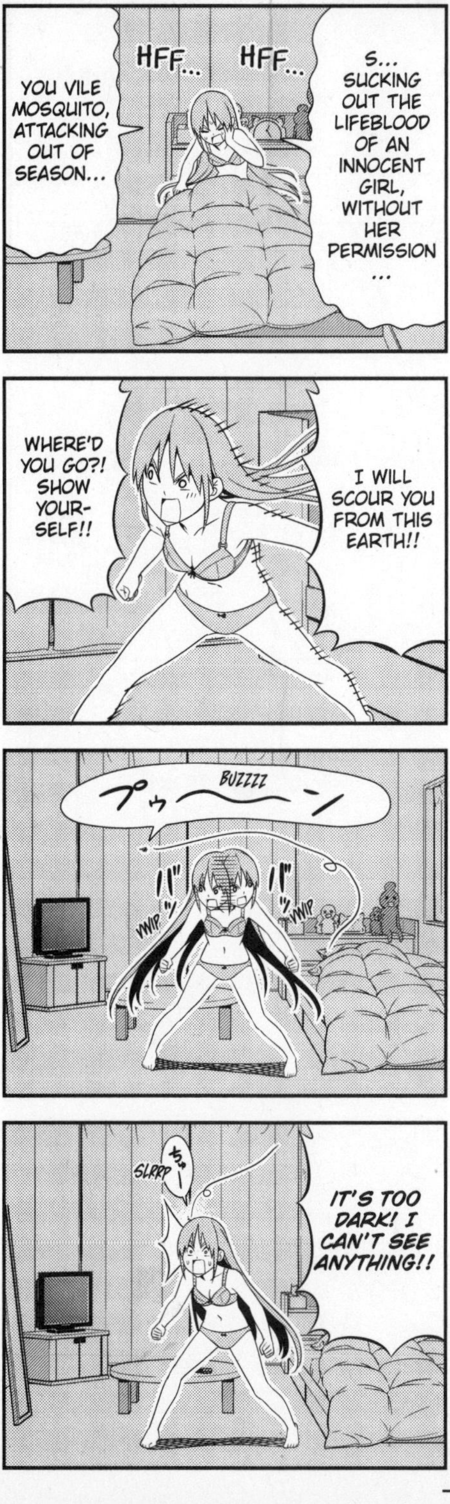
S... SUCKING OUT THE LIFEBLOOD OF AN INNOCENT GIRL, WITHOUT HER PERMISSION...
HFF... HFF...
YOU VILE MOSQUITO, ATTACKING OUT OF SEASON...
I WILL SCOUR YOU FROM THIS EARTH!!
WHERE'D YOU GO?! SHOW YOURSELF!!
BUZZZZ
プゥ〜〜ン
VWIP
VWIP
IT'S TOO DARK! I CAN'T SEE ANYTHING!!
SLRRP

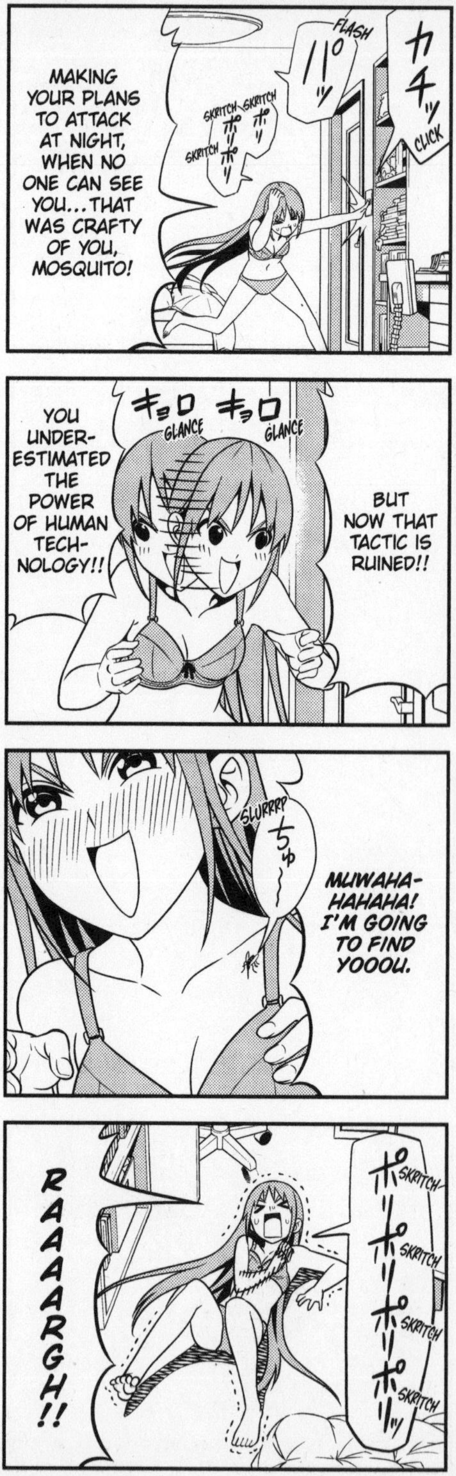
カチッ
CLICK
パッ
FLASH
ポリ ポリ ポリ
SKRITCH SKRITCH SKRITCH
MAKING YOUR PLANS TO ATTACK AT NIGHT, WHEN NO ONE CAN SEE YOU...THAT WAS CRAFTY OF YOU, MOSQUITO!
BUT NOW THAT TACTIC IS RUINED!!
キョロ キョロ
GLANCE GLANCE
YOU UNDER-ESTIMATED THE POWER OF HUMAN TECH-NOLOGY!!
MUWAHA-HAHAHA! I'M GOING TO FIND YOOOU.
ちゅ~
SLURRRP
ポリポリポリポリッ
SKRITCH SKRITCH SKRITCH SKRITCH
RAAAAARGH!!



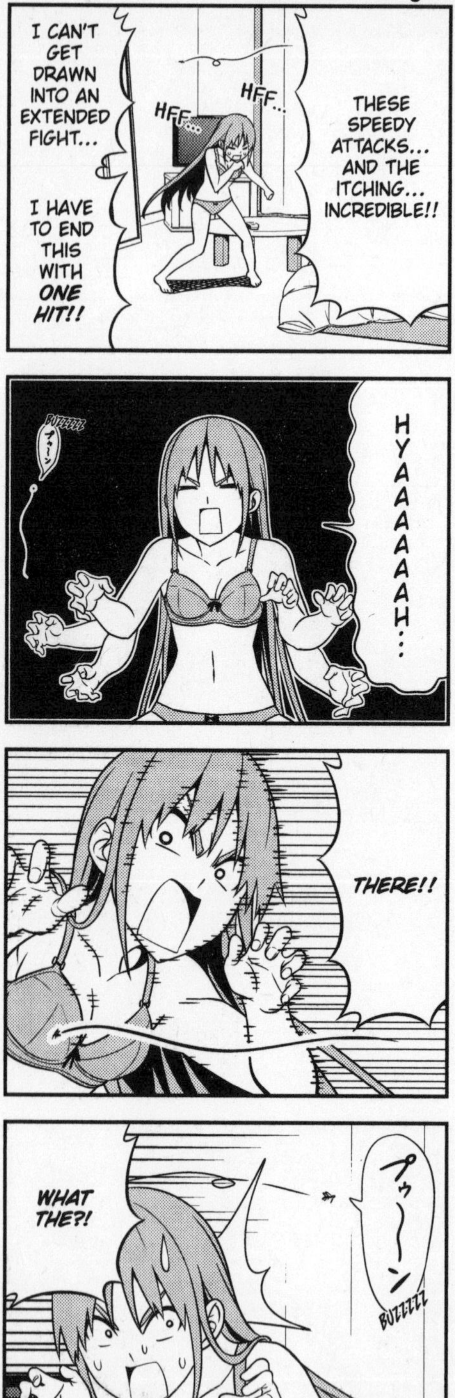
THESE SPEEDY ATTACKS... AND THE ITCHING... INCREDIBLE!!
HFF...
HFF...
I CAN'T GET DRAWN INTO AN EXTENDED FIGHT...
I HAVE TO END THIS WITH ONE HIT!!
HYAAAAAAAH...
プ~ン
BUZZZZZ
THERE!!
プゥ~~ン
BUZZZZZ
WHAT THE?!

The Truth Is Wilder Than Anything You Could Imagine

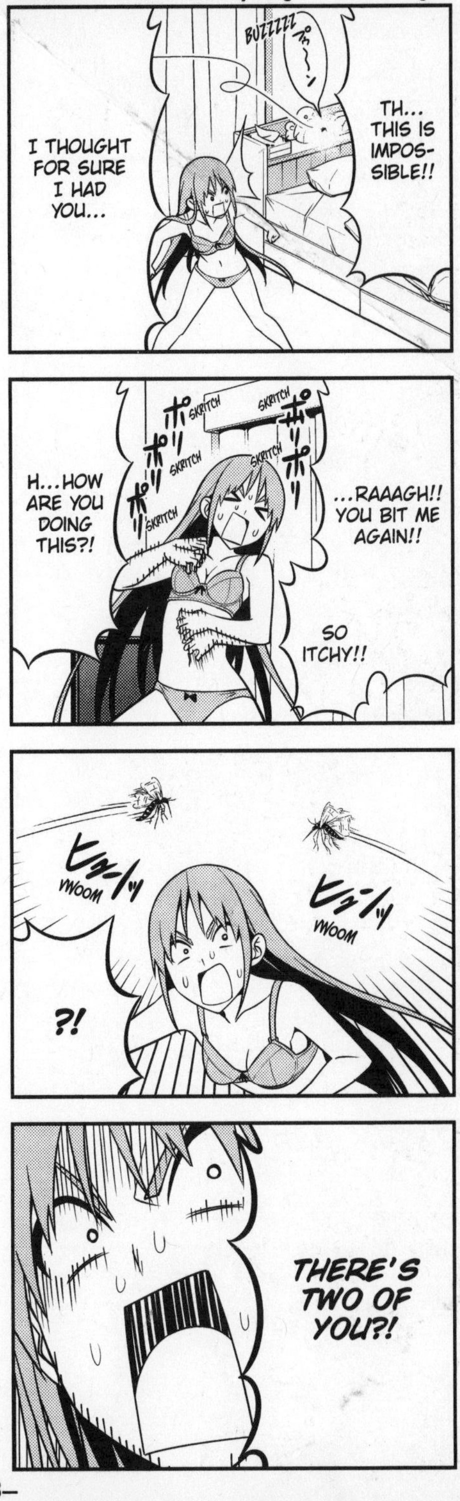
BUZZZZZ
プゥ〜ン
TH... THIS IS IMPOSSIBLE!!
I THOUGHT FOR SURE I HAD YOU...
ポリ
SKRITCH
ポリ
SKRITCH
...RAAAGH!! YOU BIT ME AGAIN!!
SO ITCHY!!
ポリ
SKRITCH
ポリ
SKRITCH
H...HOW ARE YOU DOING THIS?!
ヒューンッ
VWOOM
ヒューンッ
VWOOM
?!
THERE'S TWO OF YOU?!

It's Two on One

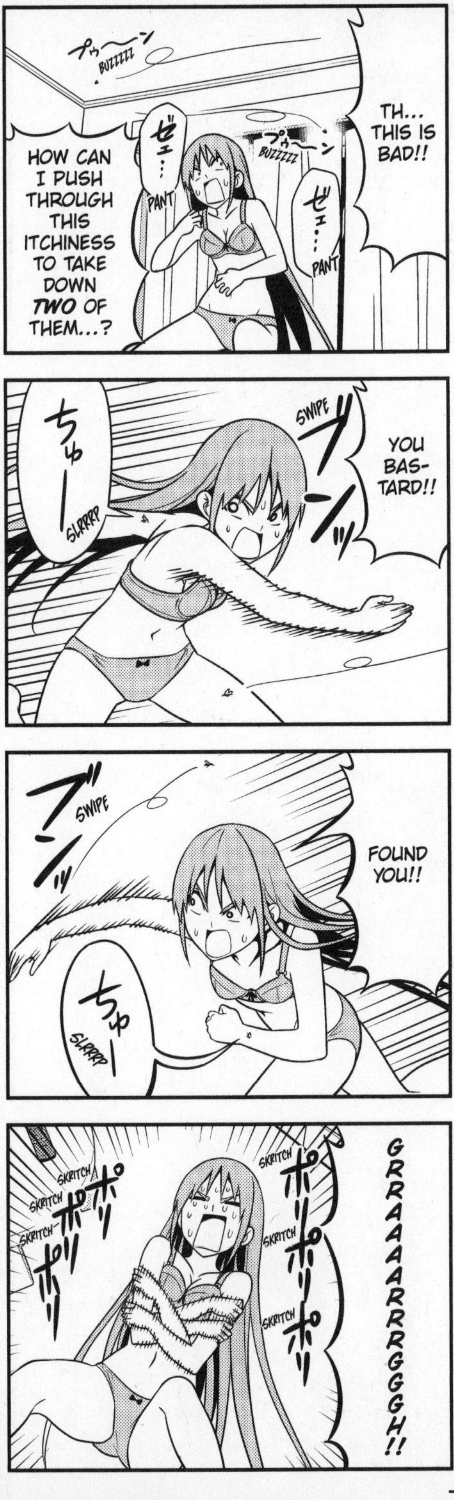
プゥ〜ン
BUZZZZZ
TH... THIS IS BAD!!
ゼェ…
PANT
プゥ〜ン
BUZZZZZ
ゼェ…
PANT
HOW CAN I PUSH THROUGH THIS ITCHINESS TO TAKE DOWN TWO OF THEM...?
SWIPE
ブンッ
YOU BASTARD!!
ちゅー
SLRRRP
FOUND YOU!!
ブンッ
SWIPE
ちゅー
SLRRRP
GRRAAAARRRGGGH!!
ポリポリ
SKRITCH
ポリポリ
SKRITCH
ポリ
SKRITCH
ポリ
SKRITCH

Secret Technique for the Upset

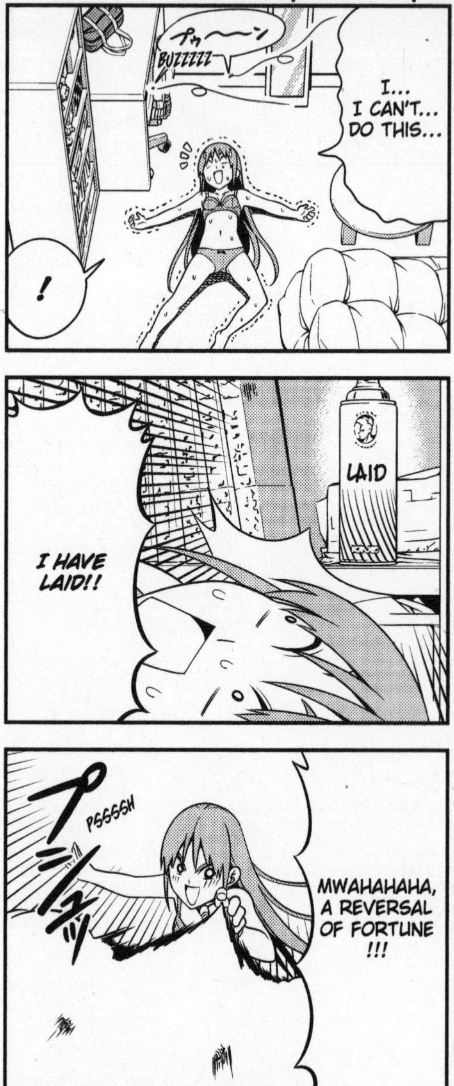
I... I CAN'T... DO THIS...
プゥ〜〜ン
BUZZZZZ
!
LAID
I HAVE LAID!!
MWAHAHAHA, A REVERSAL OF FORTUNE !!!
PSSSSH
プシュッ
VICTORY IS MINE!!

Yoshiko Regrets Her Actions

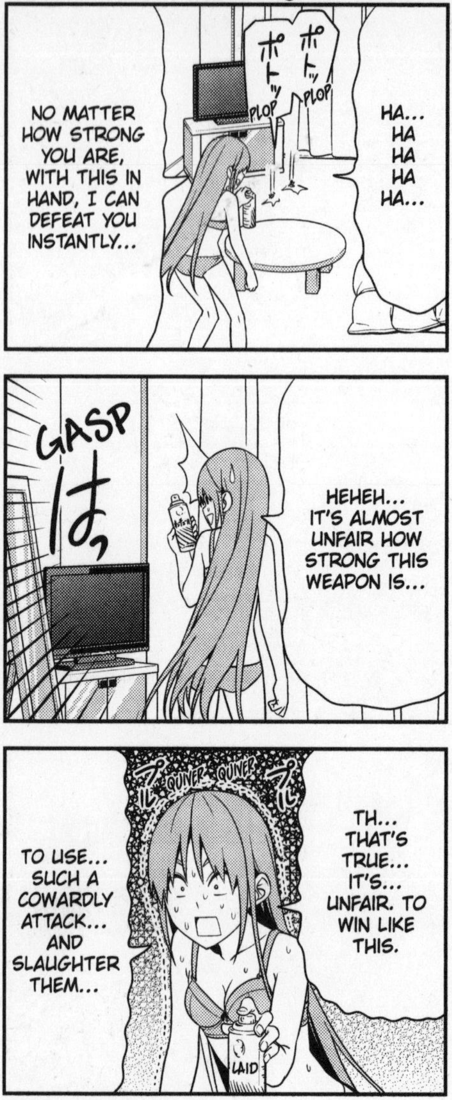
HA... HA HA HA HA...
ポトッ
PLOP
ポトッ
PLOP
NO MATTER HOW STRONG YOU ARE, WITH THIS IN HAND, I CAN DEFEAT YOU INSTANTLY...
HEHEH... IT'S ALMOST UNFAIR HOW STRONG THIS WEAPON IS...
GASP
はっ
ブル
QUIVER
QUIVER
ブル
TH... THAT'S TRUE... IT'S... UNFAIR. TO WIN LIKE THIS.
TO USE... SUCH A COWARDLY ATTACK... AND SLAUGHTER THEM...
LAID
THIS IS NO VICTORY!!
ダーン
SLAM

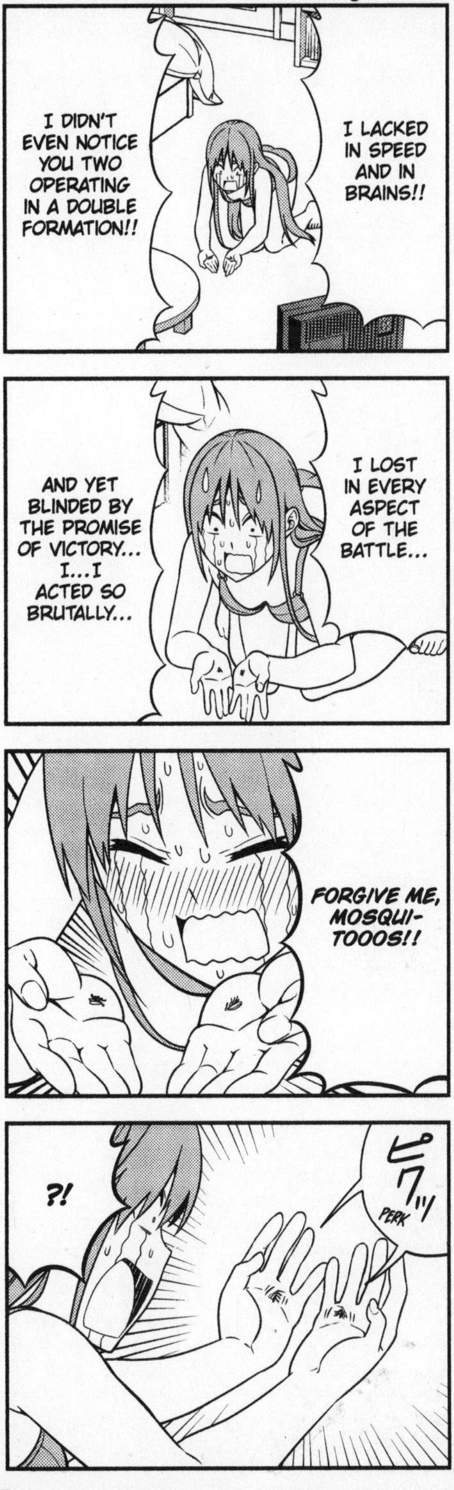
I LACKED IN SPEED AND IN BRAINS!!
I DIDN'T EVEN NOTICE YOU TWO OPERATING IN A DOUBLE FORMATION!!
I LOST IN EVERY ASPECT OF THE BATTLE...
AND YET BLINDED BY THE PROMISE OF VICTORY... I...I ACTED SO BRUTALLY...
FORGIVE ME, MOSQUI-TOOOS!!
ピクッ
PERK
?!



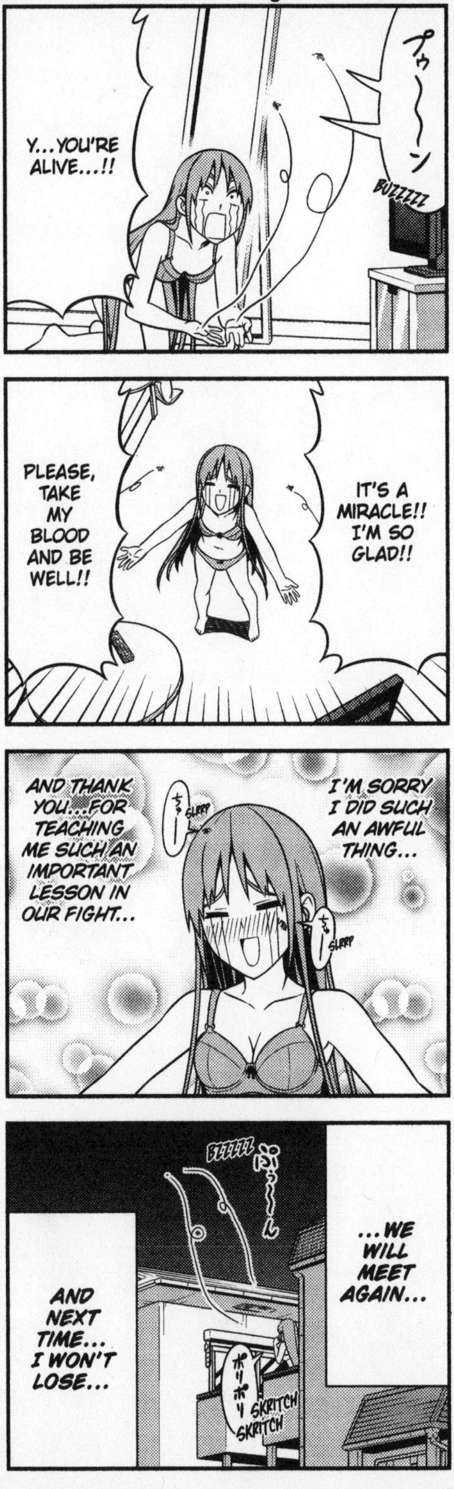
プゥ～～ン
BUZZZZZ
Y...YOU'RE ALIVE...!!
IT'S A MIRACLE!! I'M SO GLAD!!
PLEASE, TAKE MY BLOOD AND BE WELL!!
I'M SORRY I DID SUCH AN AWFUL THING...
ちゅー
SLRRP
ちゅー
SLRRP
AND THANK YOU...FOR TEACHING ME SUCH AN IMPORTANT LESSON IN OUR FIGHT...
...WE WILL MEET AGAIN...
ぷ～～ん
BZZZZZ
ポリポリ
SKRITCH SKRITCH
AND NEXT TIME... I WON'T LOSE...

The Kindness of Sayaka-chan

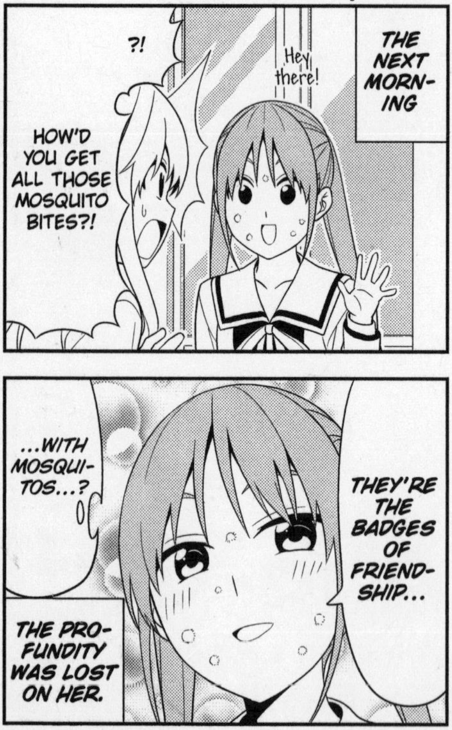
THE NEXT MORNING
Hey there!
?!
HOW'D YOU GET ALL THOSE MOSQUITO BITES?!
THEY'RE THE BADGES OF FRIENDSHIP...
...WITH MOSQUITOS...?
THE PROFUNDITY WAS LOST ON HER.

(You brought it)

# Aho-Girl

\\'ahô͵gərl\\ *Japanese, noun.*
A clueless girl.

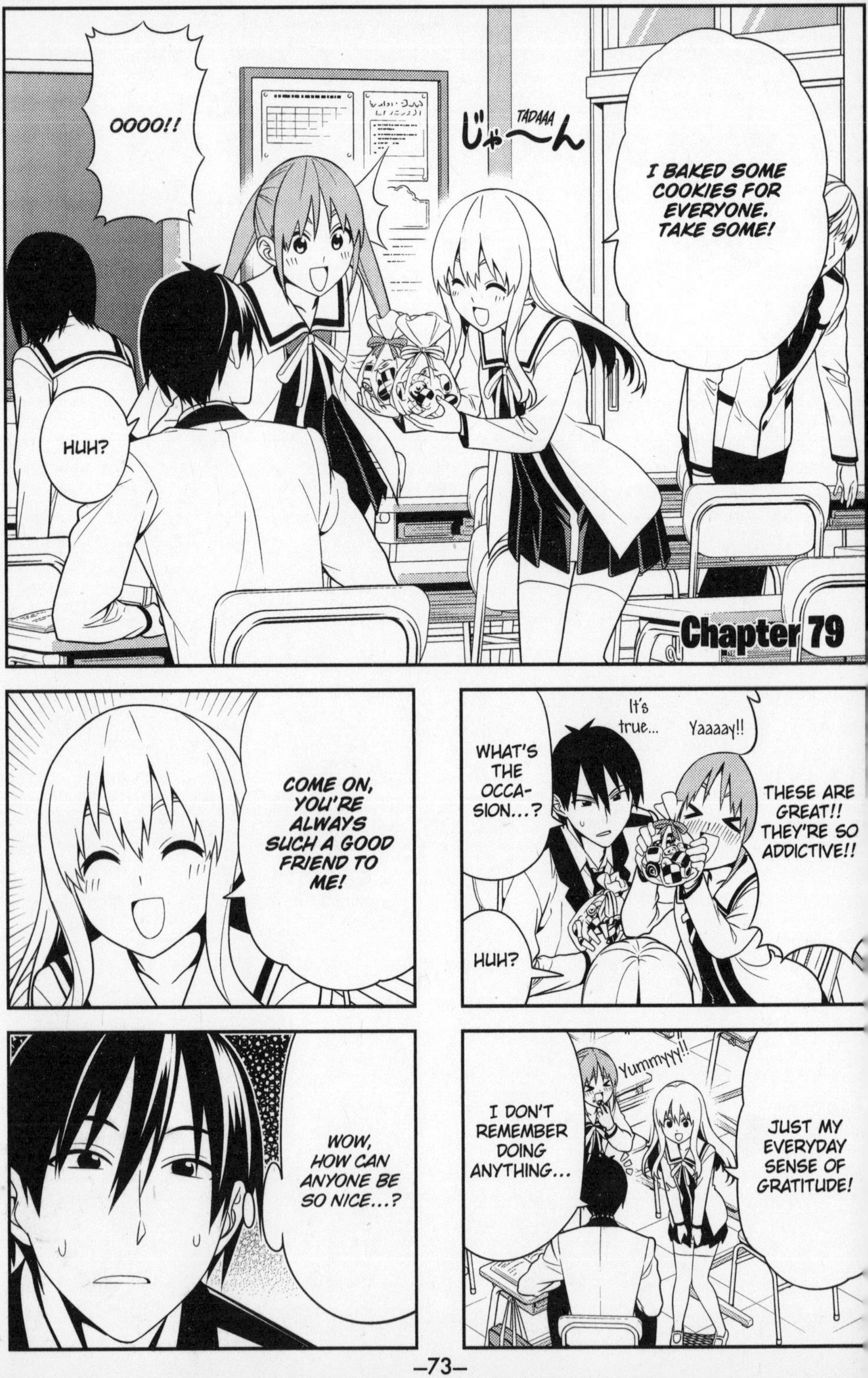
I BAKED SOME COOKIES FOR EVERYONE. TAKE SOME!
じゃ〜ん TADAAA
OOOO!!
HUH?
Chapter 79
THESE ARE GREAT!! THEY'RE SO ADDICTIVE!!
Yaaaay!!
It's true...
WHAT'S THE OCCASION...?
HUH?
COME ON, YOU'RE ALWAYS SUCH A GOOD FRIEND TO ME!
JUST MY EVERYDAY SENSE OF GRATITUDE!
Yummyyy!!
I DON'T REMEMBER DOING ANYTHING...
WOW, HOW CAN ANYONE BE SO NICE...?

## That's Not It

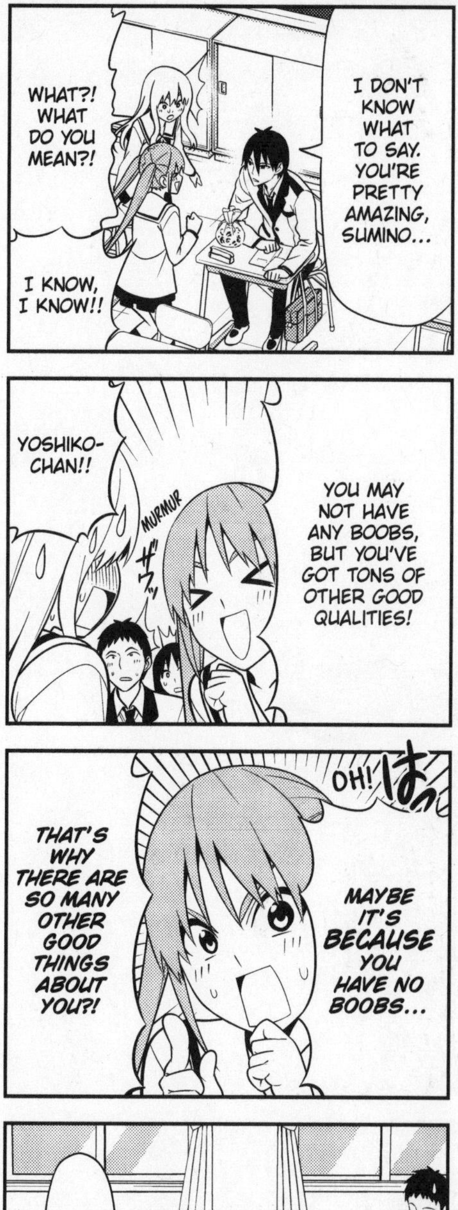
I DON'T KNOW WHAT TO SAY. YOU'RE PRETTY AMAZING, SUMINO...
WHAT?! WHAT DO YOU MEAN?!
I KNOW, I KNOW!!
YOU MAY NOT HAVE ANY BOOBS, BUT YOU'VE GOT TONS OF OTHER GOOD QUALITIES!
MURMUR
ザワッ
YOSHIKO-CHAN!!
OH! はっ
MAYBE IT'S BECAUSE YOU HAVE NO BOOBS...
THAT'S WHY THERE ARE SO MANY OTHER GOOD THINGS ABOUT YOU?!
NOPE.

## Think Reeeally Hard

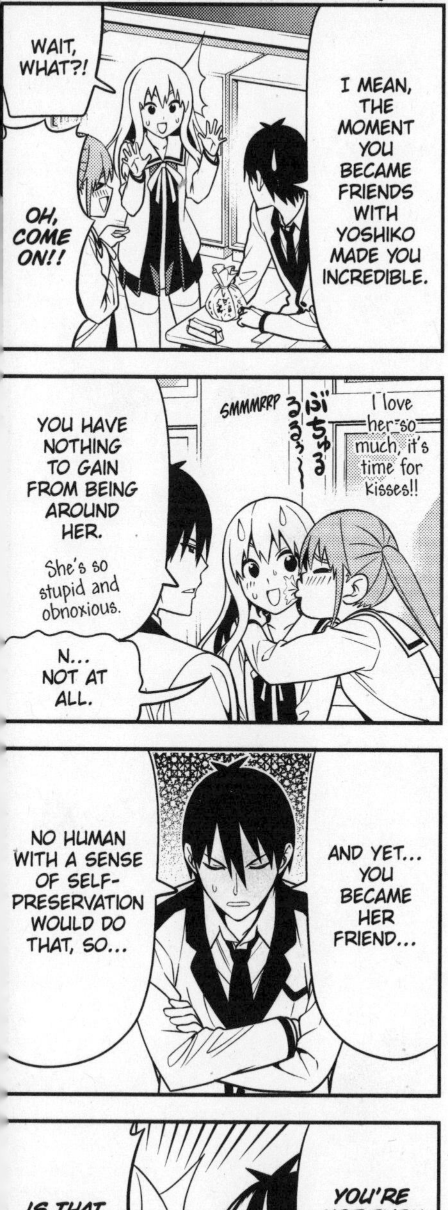
I MEAN, THE MOMENT YOU BECAME FRIENDS WITH YOSHIKO MADE YOU INCREDIBLE.
WAIT, WHAT?!
OH, COME ON!!
I love her so much, it's time for kisses!!
ぶちゅるるるぅ~
SMMMRRP
YOU HAVE NOTHING TO GAIN FROM BEING AROUND HER.
She's so stupid and obnoxious.
N... NOT AT ALL.
AND YET... YOU BECAME HER FRIEND...
NO HUMAN WITH A SENSE OF SELF-PRESERVATION WOULD DO THAT, SO...
YOU'RE NOT EVEN HUMAN TO ME.
IS THAT SUPPOSED TO BE A COMPLIMENT?!

Compliments, Compliments, Compliments

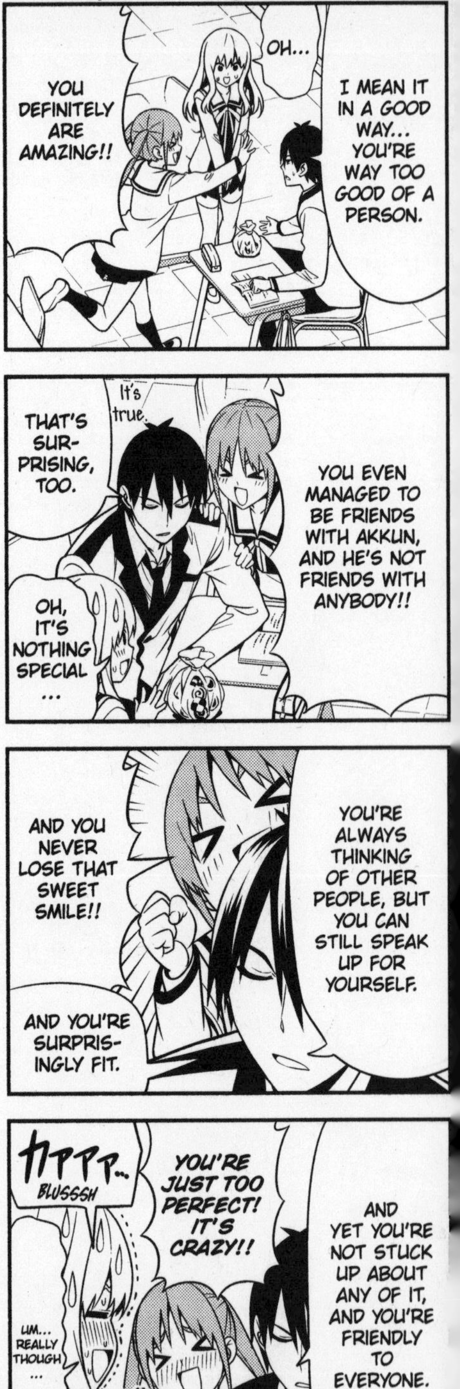
I MEAN IT IN A GOOD WAY... YOU'RE WAY TOO GOOD OF A PERSON.
OH...
YOU DEFINITELY ARE AMAZING!!
YOU EVEN MANAGED TO BE FRIENDS WITH AKKUN, AND HE'S NOT FRIENDS WITH ANYBODY!!
It's true.
THAT'S SUR-PRISING, TOO.
OH, IT'S NOTHING SPECIAL ...
YOU'RE ALWAYS THINKING OF OTHER PEOPLE, BUT YOU CAN STILL SPEAK UP FOR YOURSELF.
AND YOU NEVER LOSE THAT SWEET SMILE!!
AND YOU'RE SURPRIS-INGLY FIT.
AND YET YOU'RE NOT STUCK UP ABOUT ANY OF IT, AND YOU'RE FRIENDLY TO EVERYONE.
YOU'RE JUST TOO PERFECT! IT'S CRAZY!!
BLUSSSH
UM... REALLY THOUGH ...

Less Than Goddess, But More Than Human

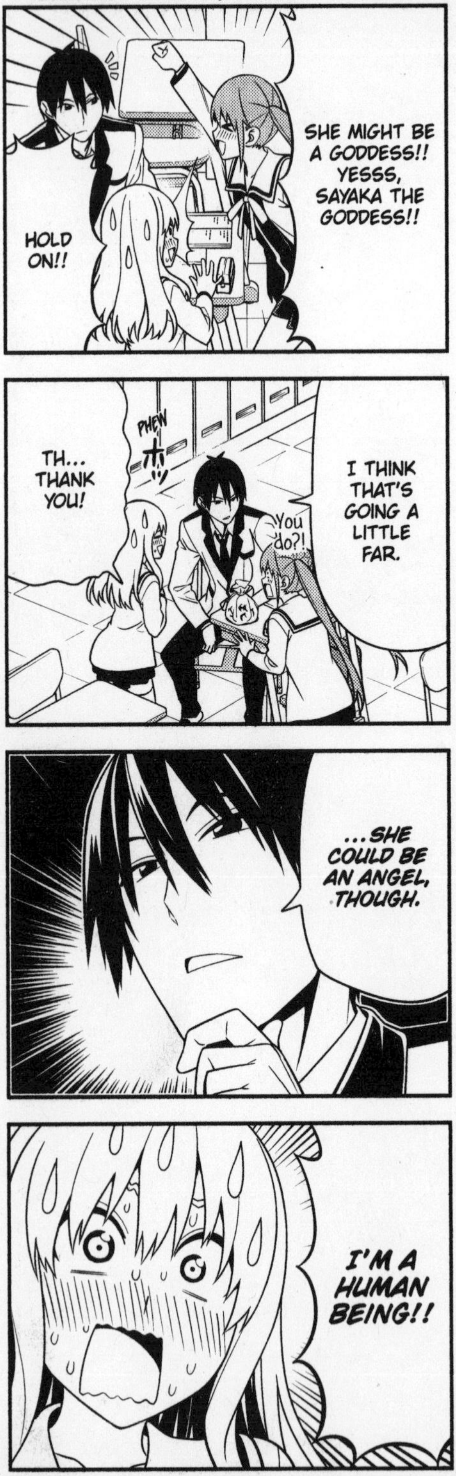
SHE MIGHT BE A GODDESS!! YESSS, SAYAKA THE GODDESS!!
HOLD ON!!
I THINK THAT'S GOING A LITTLE FAR.
You do?!
PHEW
TH... THANK YOU!
...SHE COULD BE AN ANGEL, THOUGH.
I'M A HUMAN BEING!!

## Everyday Gratitude

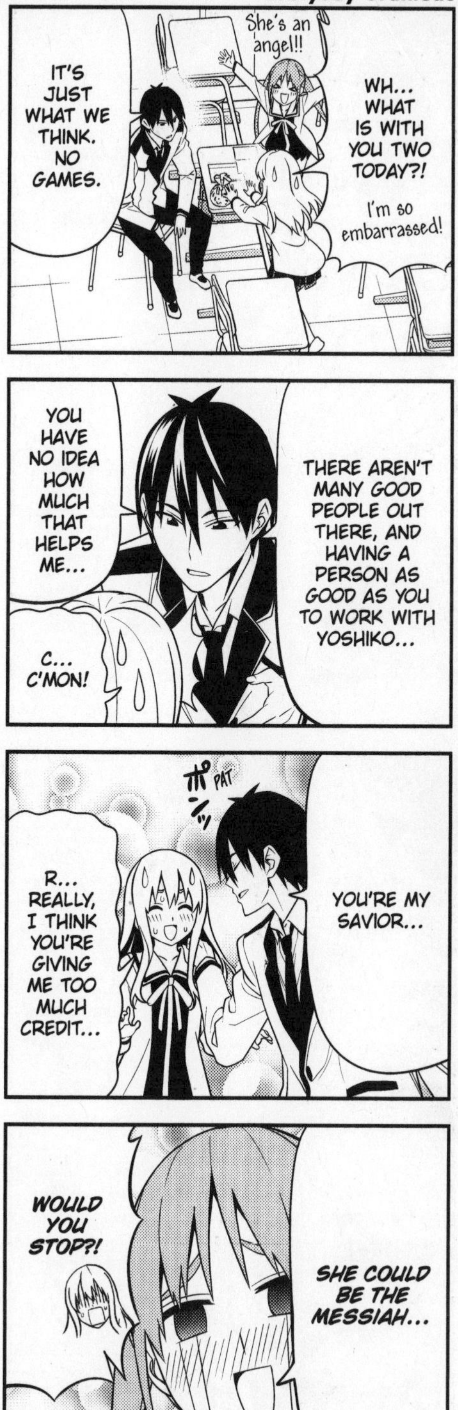

She's an angel!!
WH... WHAT IS WITH YOU TWO TODAY?!
I'm so embarrassed!
IT'S JUST WHAT WE THINK. NO GAMES.
THERE AREN'T MANY GOOD PEOPLE OUT THERE, AND HAVING A PERSON AS GOOD AS YOU TO WORK WITH YOSHIKO...
YOU HAVE NO IDEA HOW MUCH THAT HELPS ME...
C... C'MON!
YOU'RE MY SAVIOR...
ポンッ PAT
R... REALLY, I THINK YOU'RE GIVING ME TOO MUCH CREDIT...
SHE COULD BE THE MESSIAH...
WOULD YOU STOP?!


## Gratitude That Sends Sparks Flying

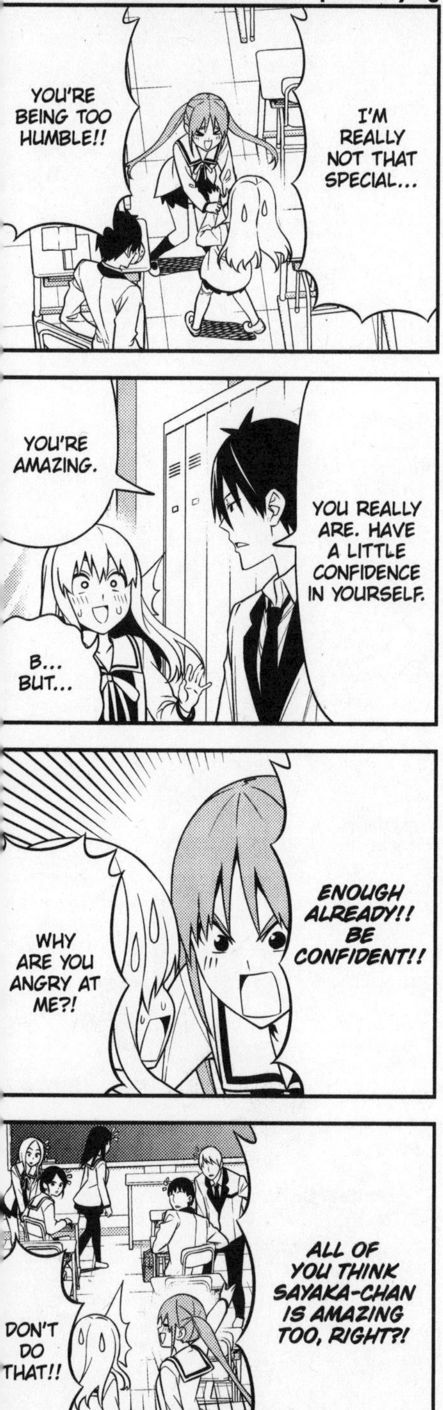

I'M REALLY NOT THAT SPECIAL...
YOU'RE BEING TOO HUMBLE!!
YOU'RE AMAZING.
YOU REALLY ARE. HAVE A LITTLE CONFIDENCE IN YOURSELF.
B... BUT...
ENOUGH ALREADY!! BE CONFIDENT!!
WHY ARE YOU ANGRY AT ME?!
ALL OF YOU THINK SAYAKA-CHAN IS AMAZING TOO, RIGHT?!
DON'T DO THAT!!

They All Do

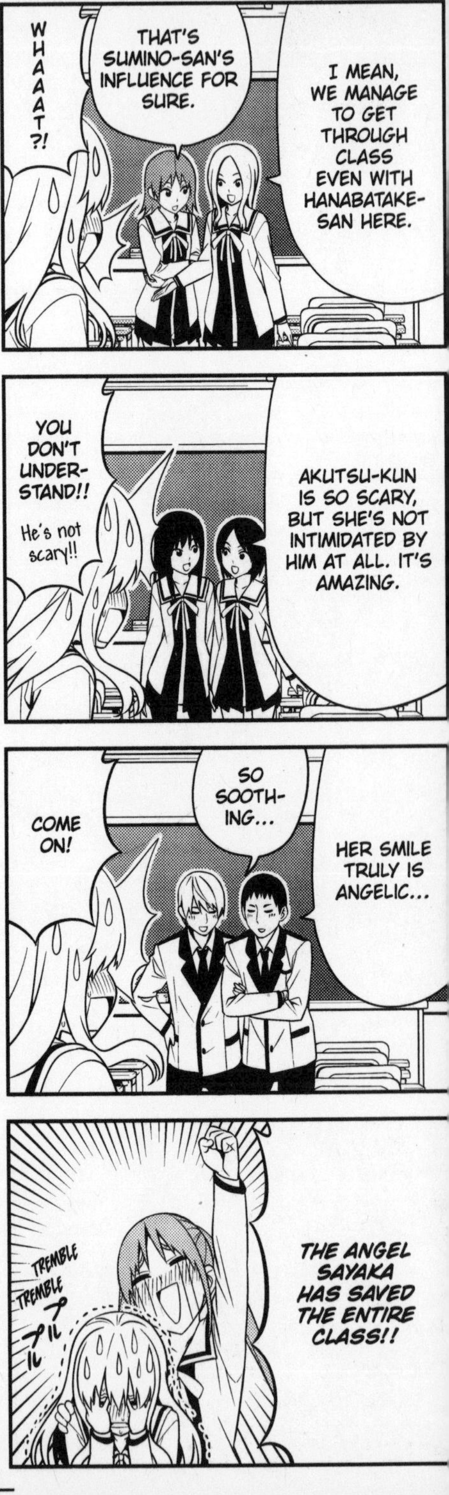
I MEAN, WE MANAGE TO GET THROUGH CLASS EVEN WITH HANABATAKE-SAN HERE.
THAT'S SUMINO-SAN'S INFLUENCE FOR SURE.
WHAAAAT?!
AKUTSU-KUN IS SO SCARY, BUT SHE'S NOT INTIMIDATED BY HIM AT ALL. IT'S AMAZING.
YOU DON'T UNDER-STAND!!
He's not scary!!
HER SMILE TRULY IS ANGELIC...
SO SOOTH-ING...
COME ON!
THE ANGEL SAYAKA HAS SAVED THE ENTIRE CLASS!!
TREMBLE
TREMBLE
プル
プル

Go On, Say It

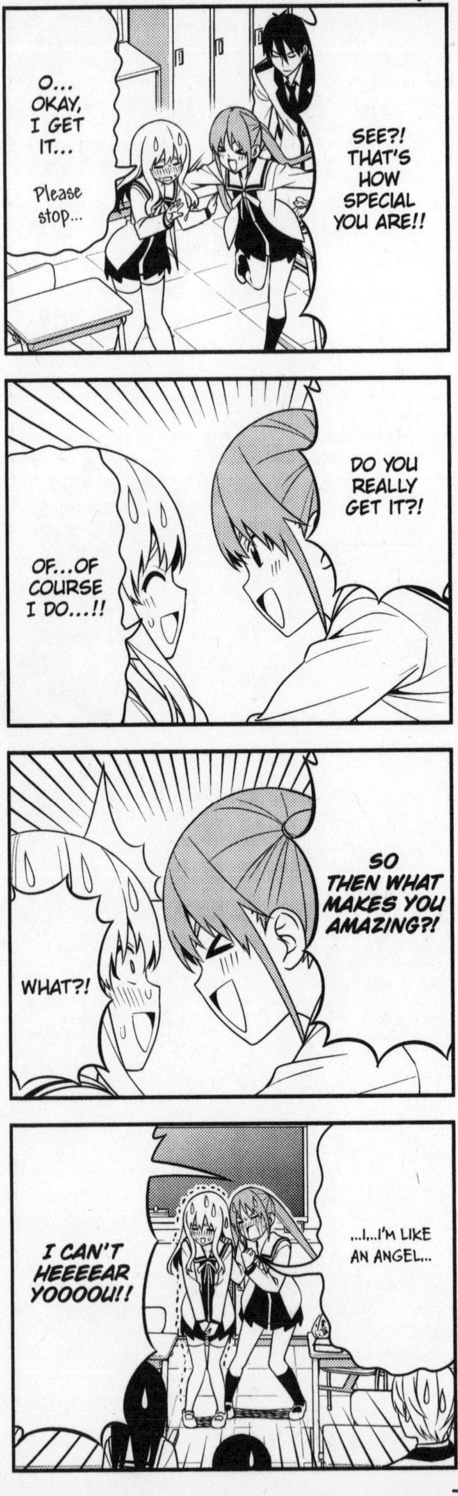
SEE?! THAT'S HOW SPECIAL YOU ARE!!
O... OKAY, I GET IT...
Please stop...
DO YOU REALLY GET IT?!
OF...OF COURSE I DO...!!
SO THEN WHAT MAKES YOU AMAZING?!
WHAT?!
...I...I'M LIKE AN ANGEL...
I CAN'T HEEEEAR YOOOOU!!

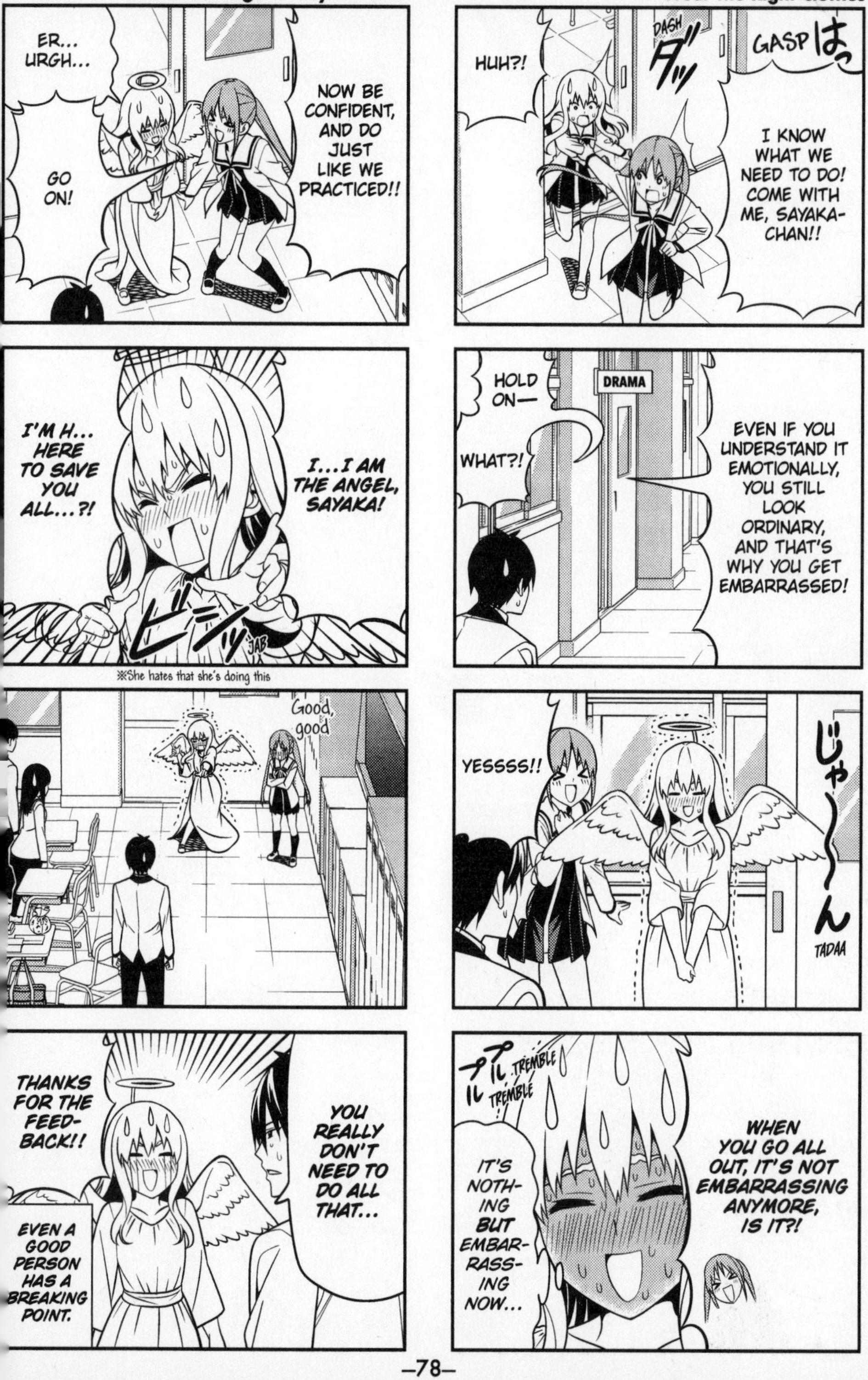
GASP はっ
DASH ダッ
I KNOW WHAT WE NEED TO DO! COME WITH ME, SAYAKA-CHAN!!
HUH?!
EVEN IF YOU UNDERSTAND IT EMOTIONALLY, YOU STILL LOOK ORDINARY, AND THAT'S WHY YOU GET EMBARRASSED!
DRAMA
HOLD ON—
WHAT?!
じゃ～～ん
TADAA
YESSSS!!
プル TREMBLE
プル TREMBLE
WHEN YOU GO ALL OUT, IT'S NOT EMBARRASSING ANYMORE, IS IT?!
IT'S NOTHING BUT EMBARRASSING NOW...
NOW BE CONFIDENT, AND DO JUST LIKE WE PRACTICED!!
ER... URGH...
GO ON!
I...I AM THE ANGEL, SAYAKA!
I'M H... HERE TO SAVE YOU ALL...?!
ビシッ
JAB
※She hates that she's doing this
Good, good
YOU REALLY DON'T NEED TO DO ALL THAT...
THANKS FOR THE FEEDBACK!!
EVEN A GOOD PERSON HAS A BREAKING POINT.

**The Blush Never Fades from Sayaka-chan**

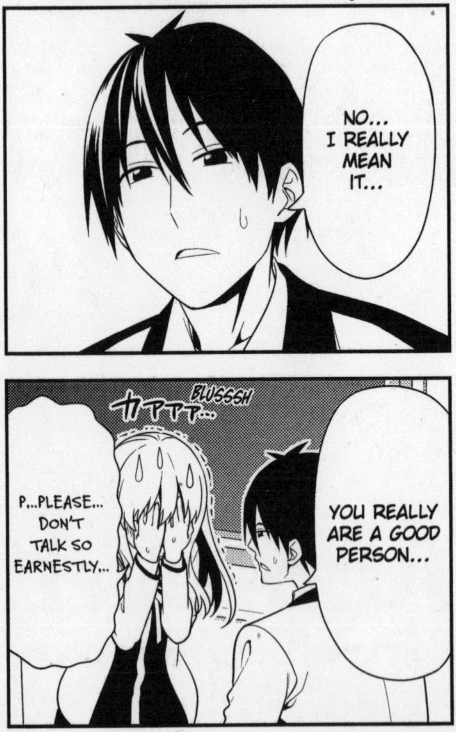
NO... I REALLY MEAN IT...
YOU REALLY ARE A GOOD PERSON...
BLUSSSH
カァァァ...
P...PLEASE... DON'T TALK SO EARNESTLY...

(To live in eternal suffering until the anointed one's return)

# Aho-Girl

\\ˈahô͵gərl \\ *Japanese, noun.*
A clueless girl.

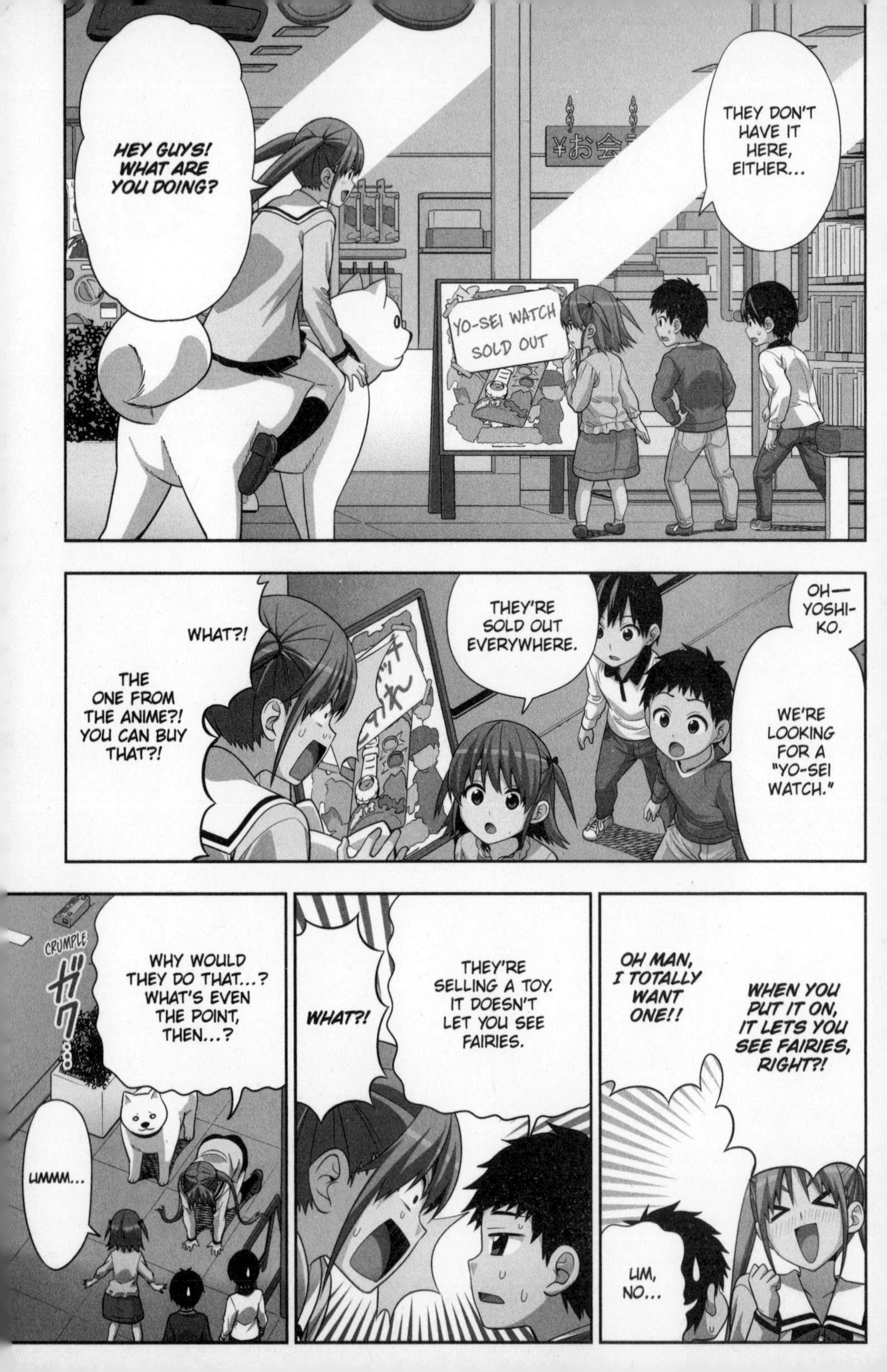
THEY DON'T HAVE IT HERE, EITHER...
HEY GUYS! WHAT ARE YOU DOING?
YO-SEI WATCH SOLD OUT
OH— YOSHIKO.
WE'RE LOOKING FOR A "YO-SEI WATCH."
THEY'RE SOLD OUT EVERYWHERE.
WHAT?!
THE ONE FROM THE ANIME?! YOU CAN BUY THAT?!
WHEN YOU PUT IT ON, IT LETS YOU SEE FAIRIES, RIGHT?!
OH MAN, I TOTALLY WANT ONE!!
UM, NO...
THEY'RE SELLING A TOY. IT DOESN'T LET YOU SEE FAIRIES.
WHAT?!
WHY WOULD THEY DO THAT...? WHAT'S EVEN THE POINT, THEN...?
CRUMPLE
ガク…
UMMM...

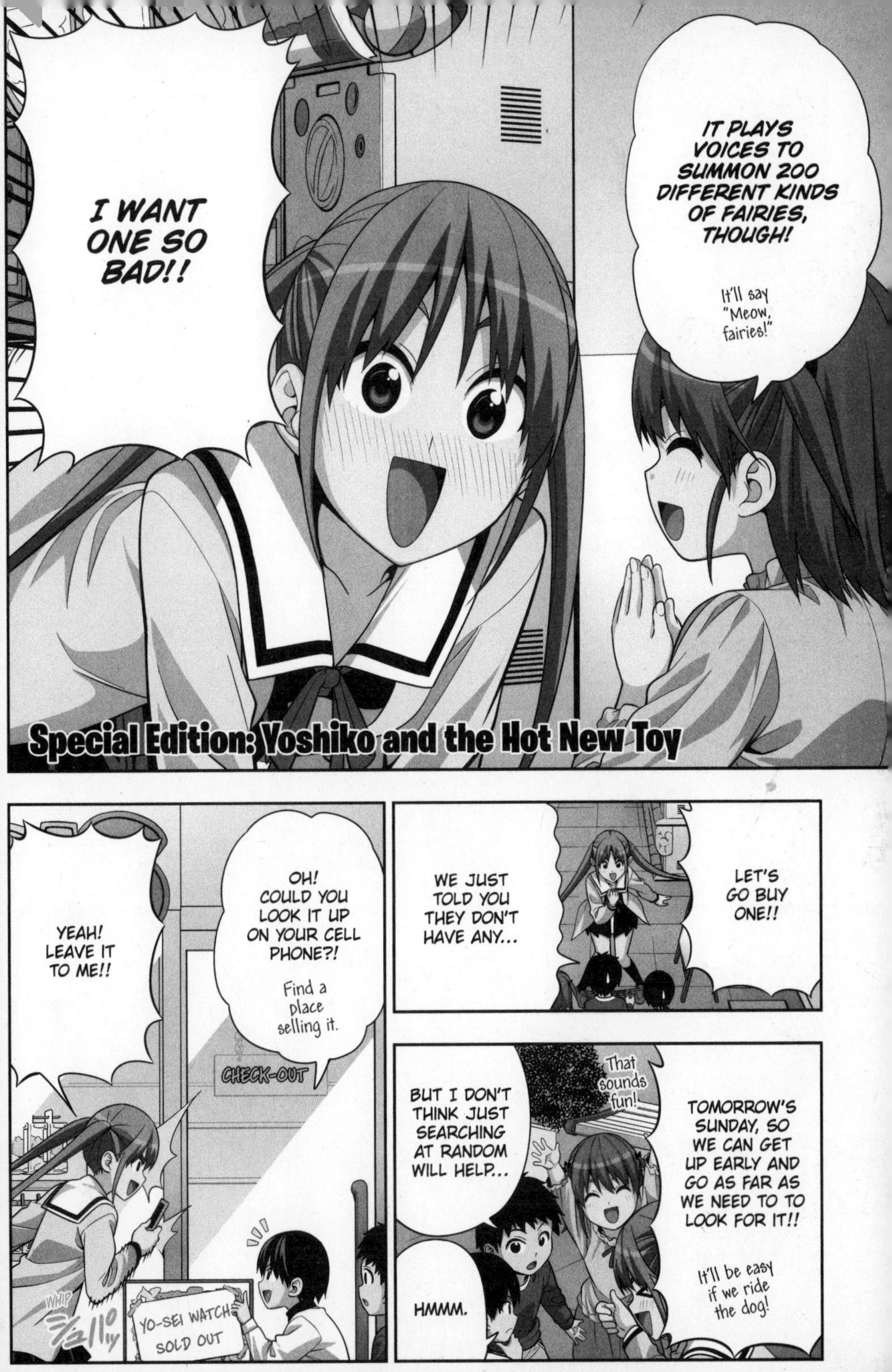
IT PLAYS VOICES TO SUMMON 200 DIFFERENT KINDS OF FAIRIES, THOUGH!
It'll say "Meow, fairies!"
I WANT ONE SO BAD!!
Special Edition: Yoshiko and the Hot New Toy
LET'S GO BUY ONE!!
WE JUST TOLD YOU THEY DON'T HAVE ANY...
TOMORROW'S SUNDAY, SO WE CAN GET UP EARLY AND GO AS FAR AS WE NEED TO TO LOOK FOR IT!!
It'll be easy if we ride the dog!
That sounds fun!
BUT I DON'T THINK JUST SEARCHING AT RANDOM WILL HELP...
HMMM.
OH! COULD YOU LOOK IT UP ON YOUR CELL PHONE?!
Find a place selling it.
YEAH! LEAVE IT TO ME!!
CHECK-OUT
WHIP
YO-SEI WATCH
SOLD OUT

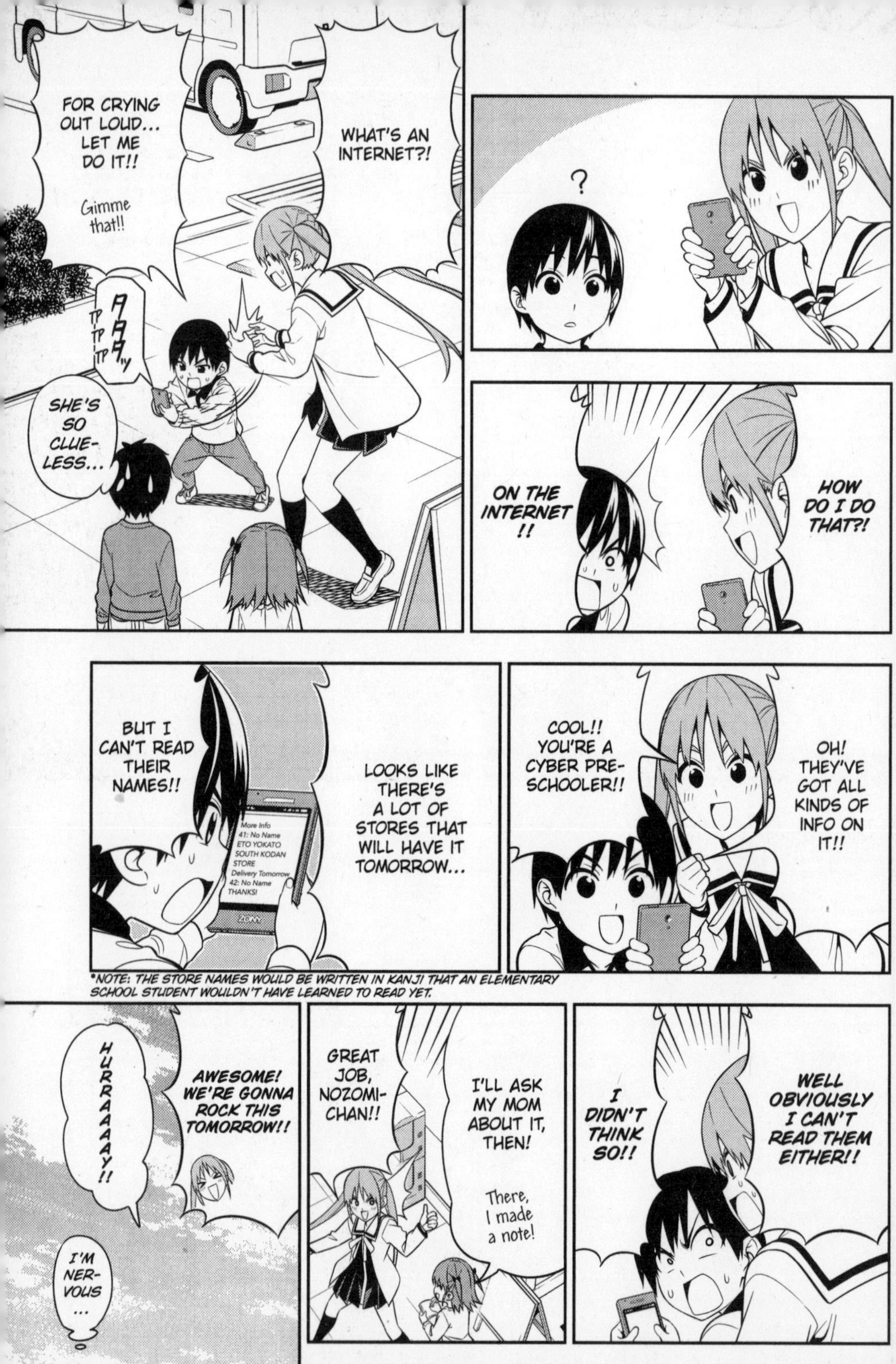
?
HOW DO I DO THAT?!
ON THE INTERNET!!
WHAT'S AN INTERNET?!
FOR CRYING OUT LOUD... LET ME DO IT!!
Gimme that!!
TP TP TP
タタタッ
SHE'S SO CLUELESS...
OH! THEY'VE GOT ALL KINDS OF INFO ON IT!!
COOL!! YOU'RE A CYBER PRE-SCHOOLER!!
LOOKS LIKE THERE'S A LOT OF STORES THAT WILL HAVE IT TOMORROW...
BUT I CAN'T READ THEIR NAMES!!
More Info
41: No Name
ETO YOKATO
SOUTH KODAN
STORE
Delivery Tomorrow
42: No Name
THANKS!
ZONY
*NOTE: THE STORE NAMES WOULD BE WRITTEN IN KANJI THAT AN ELEMENTARY SCHOOL STUDENT WOULDN'T HAVE LEARNED TO READ YET.
WELL OBVIOUSLY I CAN'T READ THEM EITHER!!
I DIDN'T THINK SO!!
I'LL ASK MY MOM ABOUT IT, THEN!
GREAT JOB, NOZOMI-CHAN!!
There, I made a note!
AWESOME! WE'RE GONNA ROCK THIS TOMORROW!!
HURRAAAAY!!
I'M NERVOUS...

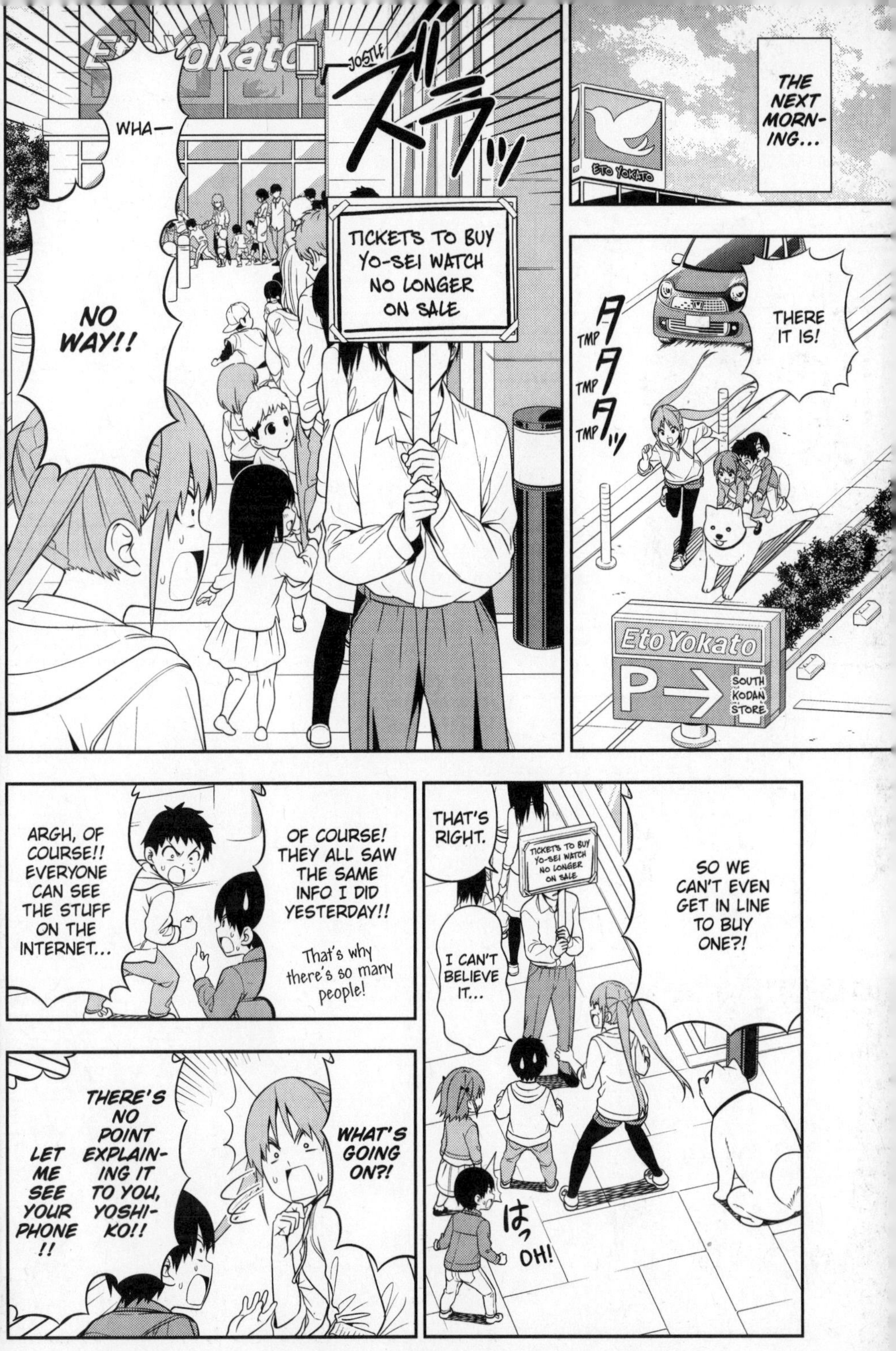
THE NEXT MORNING...
ETO YOKATO
THERE IT IS!
タタタッ
TMP TMP TMP
Eto Yokato
P
SOUTH KODAN STORE
Eto Yokato
ズラッ
JOSTLE
WHA—
TICKETS TO BUY YO-SEI WATCH NO LONGER ON SALE
NO WAY!!
SO WE CAN'T EVEN GET IN LINE TO BUY ONE?!
THAT'S RIGHT.
TICKETS TO BUY YO-SEI WATCH NO LONGER ON SALE
I CAN'T BELIEVE IT...
はっ
OH!
OF COURSE! THEY ALL SAW THE SAME INFO I DID YESTERDAY!!
That's why there's so many people!
ARGH, OF COURSE!! EVERYONE CAN SEE THE STUFF ON THE INTERNET...
WHAT'S GOING ON?!
THERE'S NO POINT EXPLAINING IT TO YOU, YOSHIKO!!
LET ME SEE YOUR PHONE!!

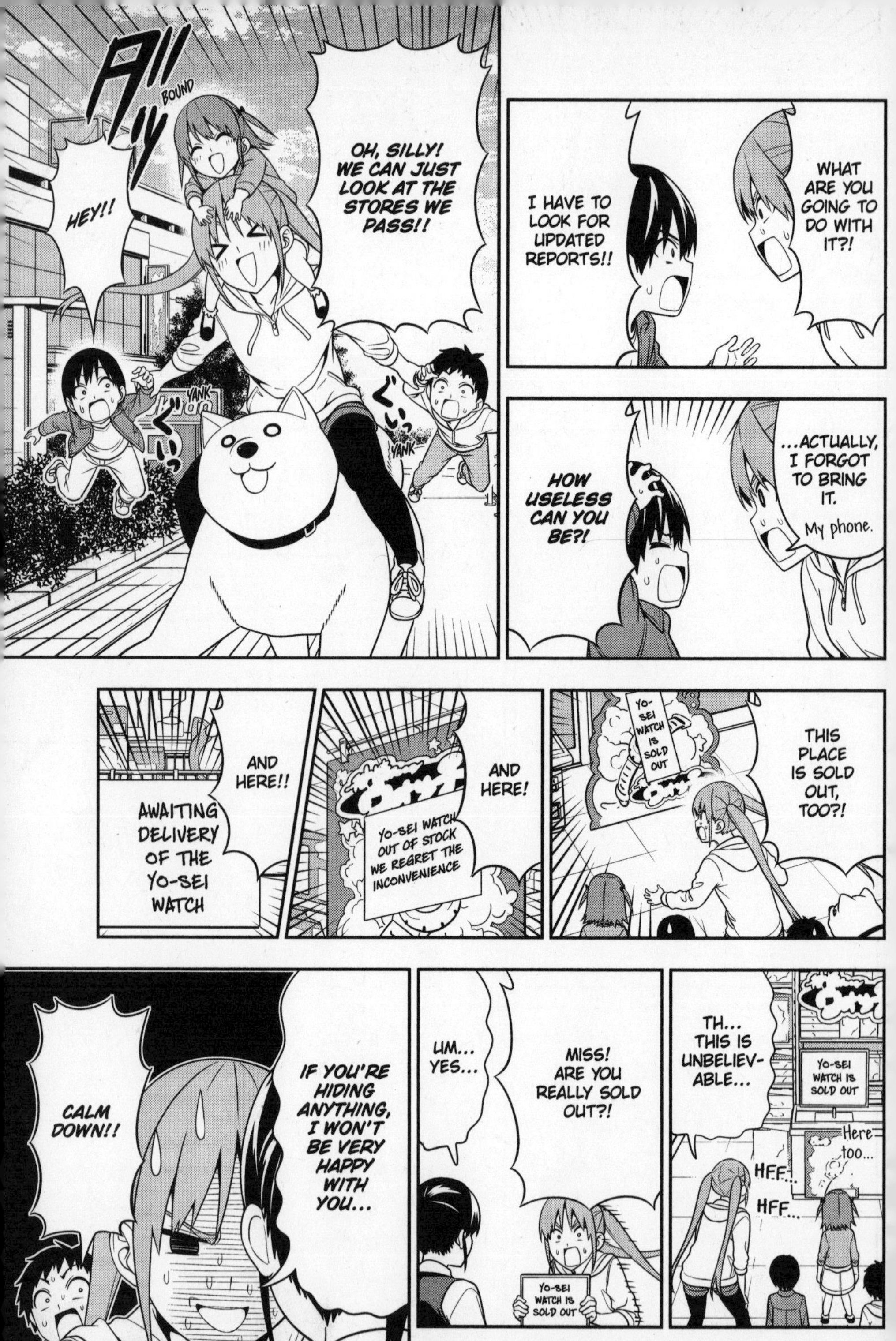
WHAT ARE YOU GOING TO DO WITH IT?!
I HAVE TO LOOK FOR UPDATED REPORTS!!
...ACTUALLY, I FORGOT TO BRING IT.
My phone.
HOW USELESS CAN YOU BE?!
OH, SILLY! WE CAN JUST LOOK AT THE STORES WE PASS!!
BOUND
YANK
YANK
HEY!!
THIS PLACE IS SOLD OUT, TOO?!
YO-SEI WATCH IS SOLD OUT
AND HERE!
YO-SEI WATCH OUT OF STOCK WE REGRET THE INCONVENIENCE
AND HERE!!
AWAITING DELIVERY OF THE YO-SEI WATCH
TH... THIS IS UNBELIEV-ABLE...
YO-SEI WATCH IS SOLD OUT
Here too...
HFF...
HFF...
MISS! ARE YOU REALLY SOLD OUT?!
UM... YES...
YO-SEI WATCH IS SOLD OUT
IF YOU'RE HIDING ANYTHING, I WON'T BE VERY HAPPY WITH YOU...
CALM DOWN!!

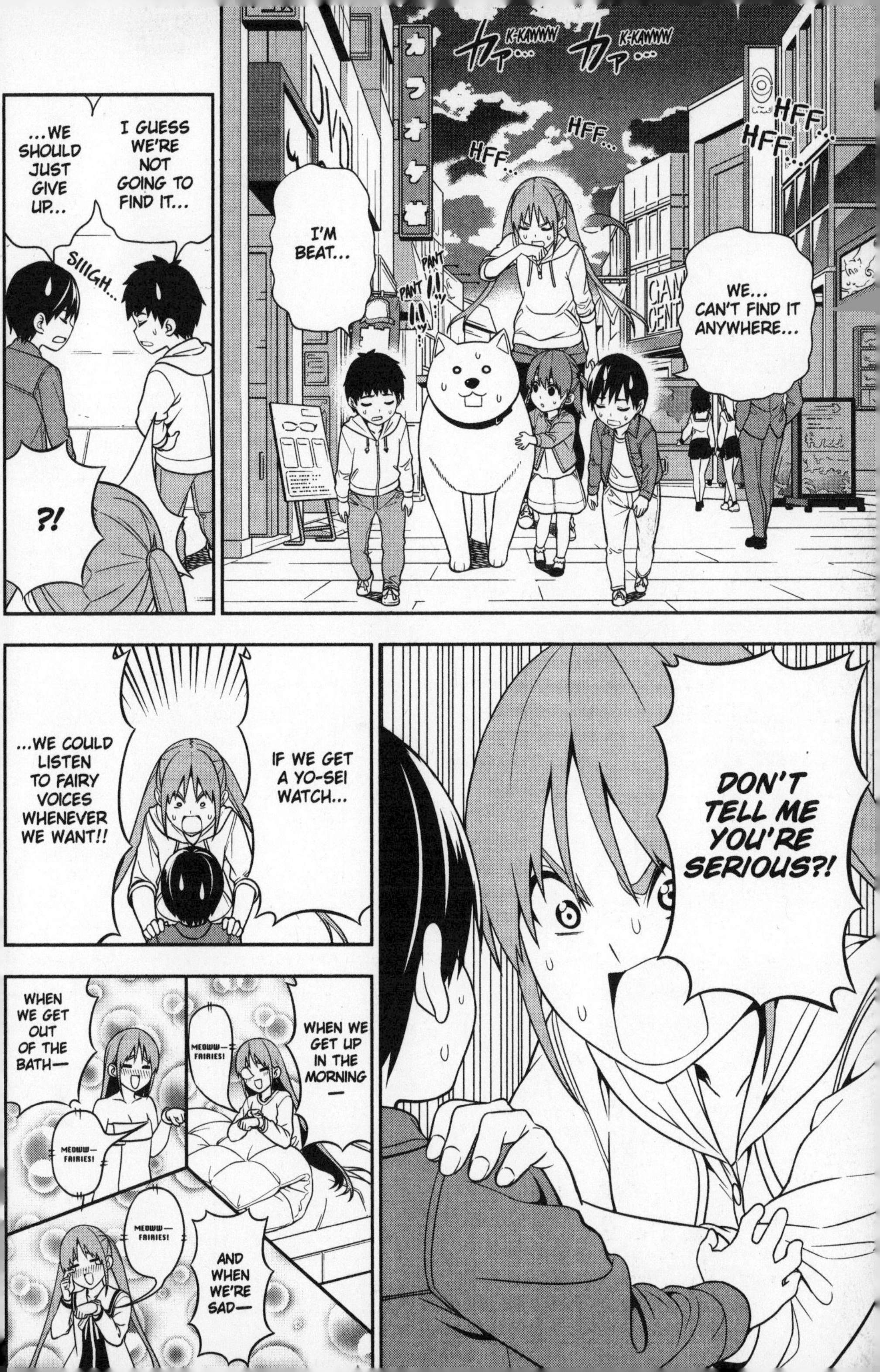
カァ… K-KAWWW
カァ… K-KAWWW
HFF...
HFF...
HFF...
HFF...
WE... CAN'T FIND IT ANYWHERE...
I'M BEAT...
PANT PANT
I GUESS WE'RE NOT GOING TO FIND IT...
...WE SHOULD JUST GIVE UP...
SIIIGH...
?!
DON'T TELL ME YOU'RE SERIOUS?!
IF WE GET A YO-SEI WATCH...
...WE COULD LISTEN TO FAIRY VOICES WHENEVER WE WANT!!
WHEN WE GET UP IN THE MORNING—
MEOWW— FAIRIES!
WHEN WE GET OUT OF THE BATH—
MEOWW— FAIRIES!
AND WHEN WE'RE SAD—
MEOWW— FAIRIES!

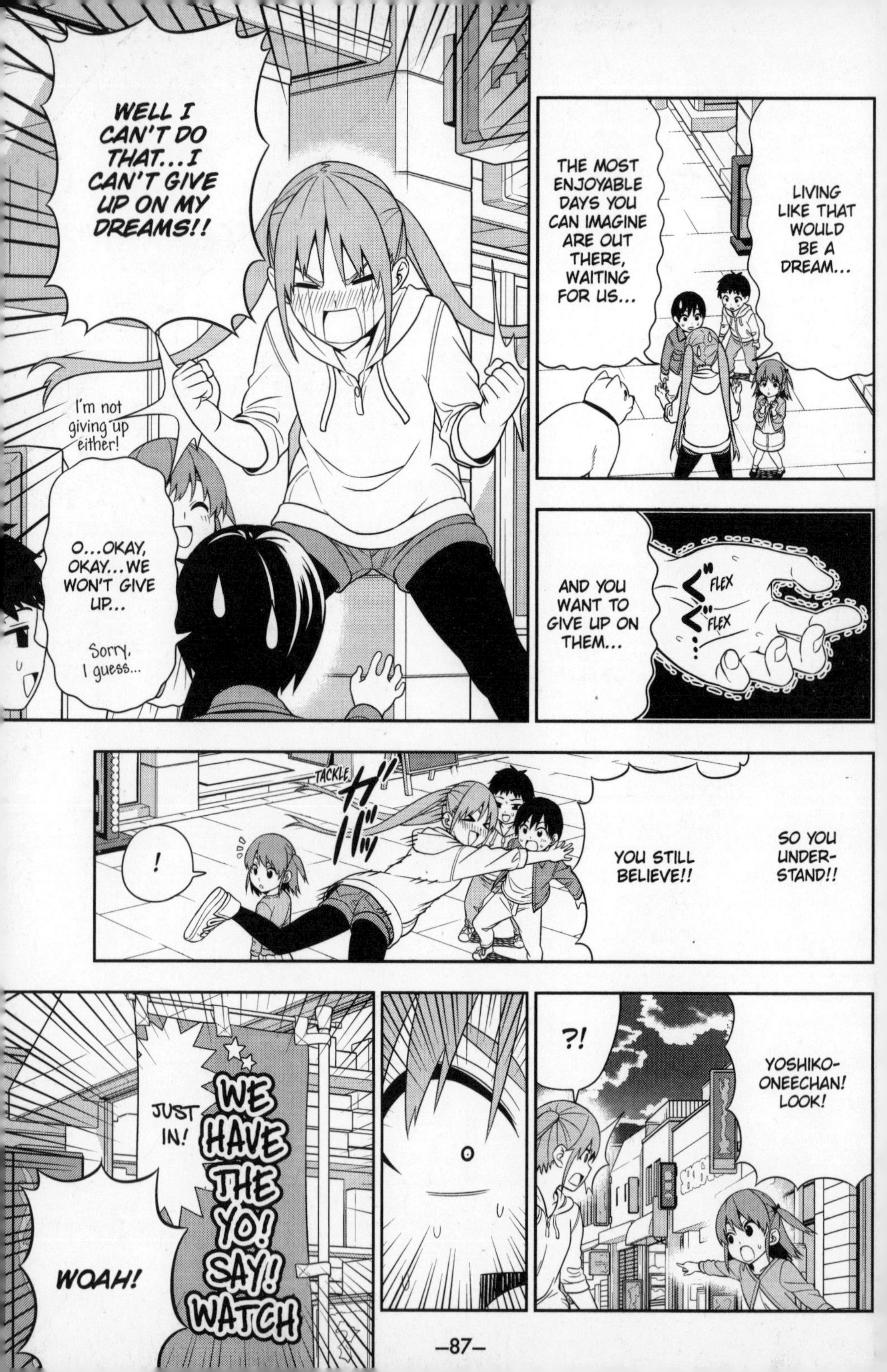
LIVING LIKE THAT WOULD BE A DREAM...
THE MOST ENJOYABLE DAYS YOU CAN IMAGINE ARE OUT THERE, WAITING FOR US...
FLEX
FLEX
AND YOU WANT TO GIVE UP ON THEM...
WELL I CAN'T DO THAT...I CAN'T GIVE UP ON MY DREAMS!!
O...OKAY, OKAY...WE WON'T GIVE UP...
Sorry, I guess...
I'm not giving up either!
SO YOU UNDER-STAND!!
YOU STILL BELIEVE!!
TACKLE
!
YOSHIKO-ONEECHAN! LOOK!
?!
WE HAVE THE YO! SAY! WATCH
JUST IN!
WOAH!

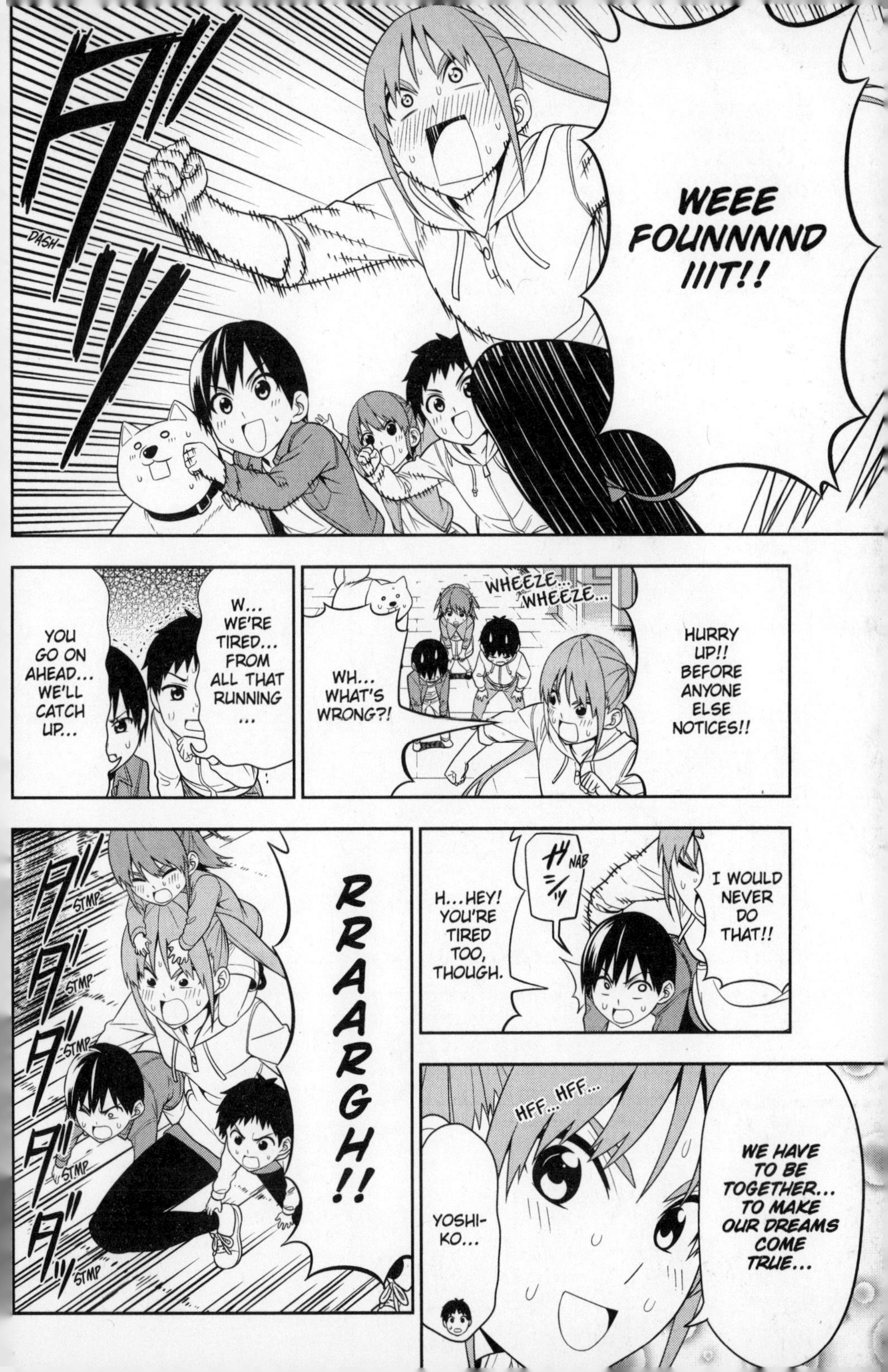
WEEE FOUNNNND IIIT!!
DASH
WHEEZE... WHEEZE...
HURRY UP!! BEFORE ANYONE ELSE NOTICES!!
WH... WHAT'S WRONG?!
W... WE'RE TIRED... FROM ALL THAT RUNNING ...
YOU GO ON AHEAD... WE'LL CATCH UP...
I WOULD NEVER DO THAT!!
NAB
H...HEY! YOU'RE TIRED TOO, THOUGH.
WE HAVE TO BE TOGETHER... TO MAKE OUR DREAMS COME TRUE...
HFF... HFF...
YOSHI-KO...
RRAARGH!!
STMP
STMP
STMP
STMP
STMP

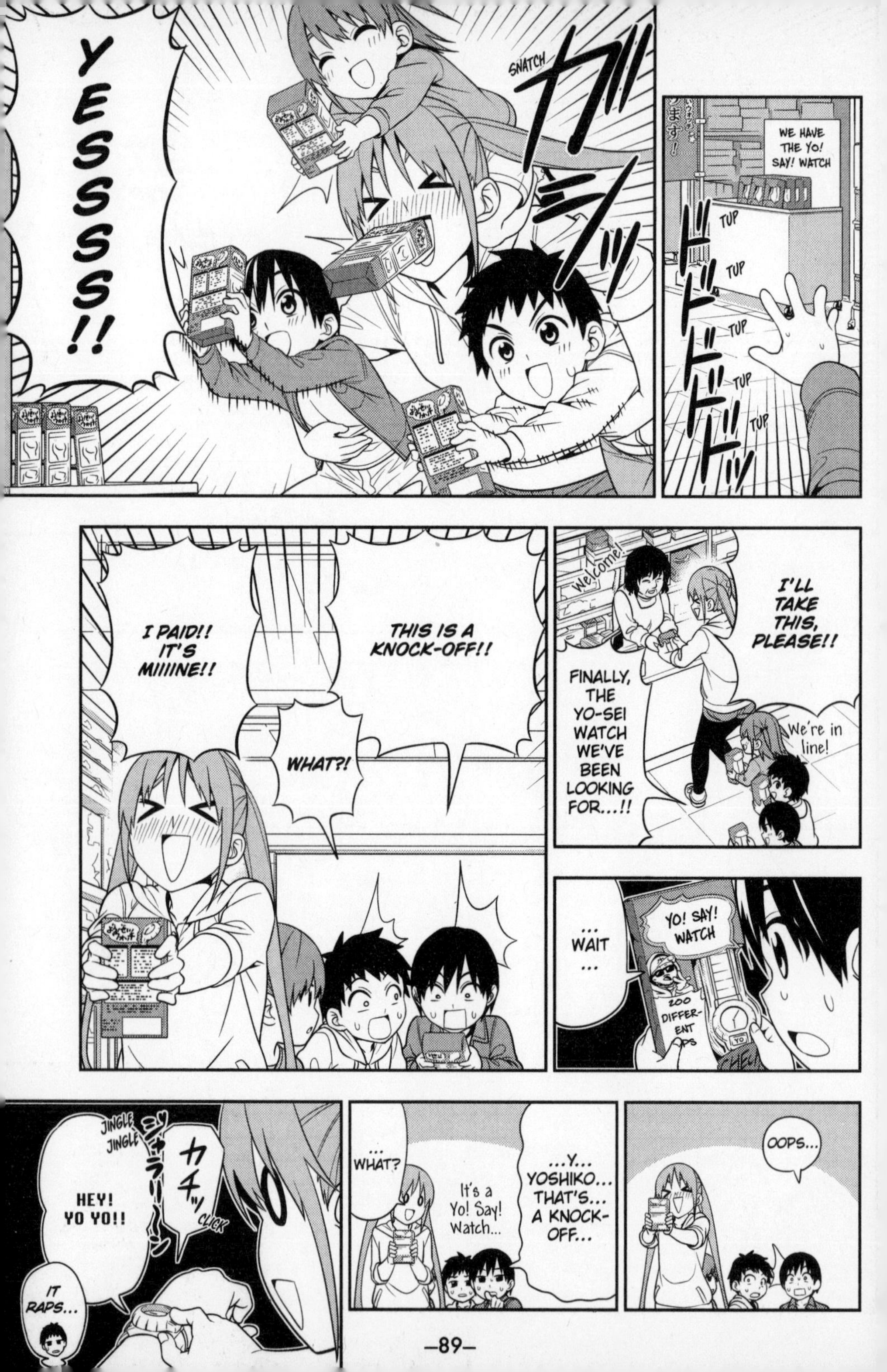
WE HAVE THE Yo! SAY! WATCH
TUP
TUP
TUP
TUP
TUP
SNATCH
YESSSSS!!
I'LL TAKE THIS, PLEASE!!
welcome!
FINALLY, THE YO-SEI WATCH WE'VE BEEN LOOKING FOR...!!
We're in line!
...WAIT...
YO! SAY! WATCH
THIS IS A KNOCK-OFF!!
I PAID!! IT'S MIIIINE!!
WHAT?!
OOPS...
...Y... YOSHIKO... THAT'S... A KNOCK-OFF...
It's a Yo! Say! Watch...
...WHAT?
JINGLE JINGLE
CLICK
HEY! YO YO!!
IT RAPS...

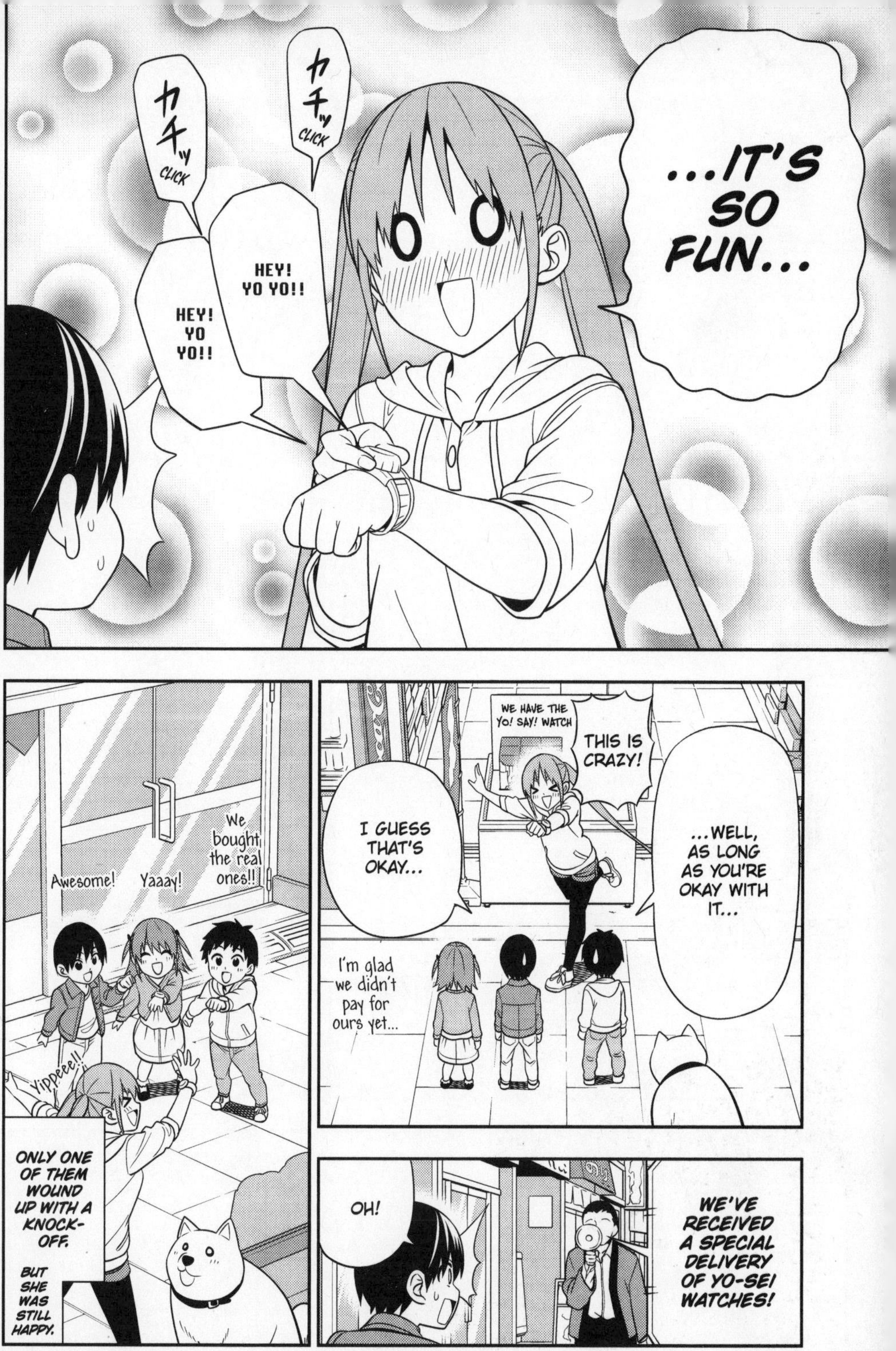
...IT'S SO FUN...
カチッ CLICK
HEY! YO YO!!
カチッ CLICK
HEY! YO YO!!
...WELL, AS LONG AS YOU'RE OKAY WITH IT...
WE HAVE THE YO! SAY! WATCH
THIS IS CRAZY!
I GUESS THAT'S OKAY...
I'm glad we didn't pay for ours yet...
WE'VE RECEIVED A SPECIAL DELIVERY OF YO-SEI WATCHES!
OH!
We bought the real ones!!
Yaaay!
Awesome!
Yippeee!!
ONLY ONE OF THEM WOUND UP WITH A KNOCK-OFF.
BUT SHE WAS STILL HAPPY.

## An Adult View

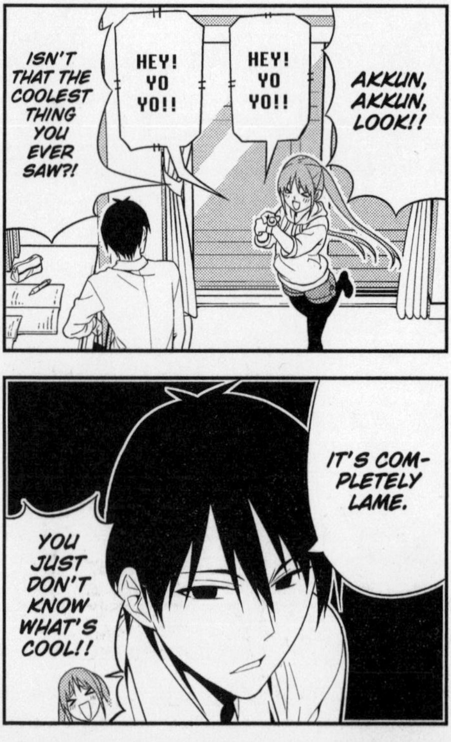
AKKUN, AKKUN, LOOK!!
HEY! YO YO!!
HEY! YO YO!!
ISN'T THAT THE COOLEST THING YOU EVER SAW?!
IT'S COM-PLETELY LAME.
YOU JUST DON'T KNOW WHAT'S COOL!!

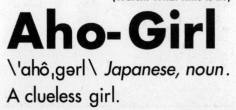

(Watch! What time is it?)

# Aho-Girl

\ˈahôˌɡərl\ *Japanese, noun*.
A clueless girl.

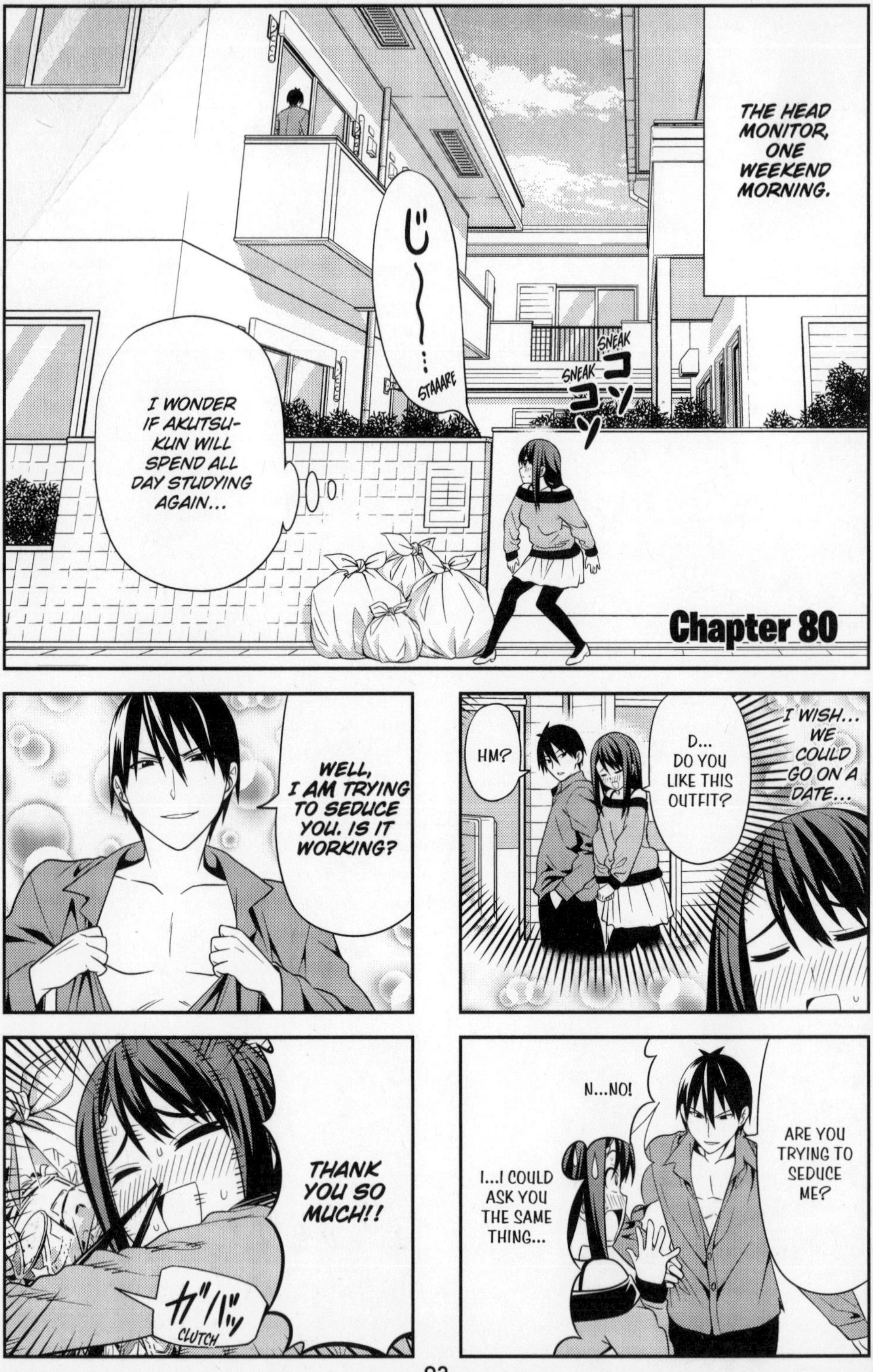
THE HEAD MONITOR, ONE WEEKEND MORNING.
SNEAK SNEAK
コソコソ
じ〜〜…
STAAARE
I WONDER IF AKUTSU-KUN WILL SPEND ALL DAY STUDYING AGAIN...
Chapter 80
I WISH... WE COULD GO ON A DATE...
D... DO YOU LIKE THIS OUTFIT?
HM?
WELL, I AM TRYING TO SEDUCE YOU. IS IT WORKING?
ARE YOU TRYING TO SEDUCE ME?
N...NO!
I...I COULD ASK YOU THE SAME THING...
THANK YOU SO MUCH!!
ガバッ
CLUTCH

I'll Do It for Him

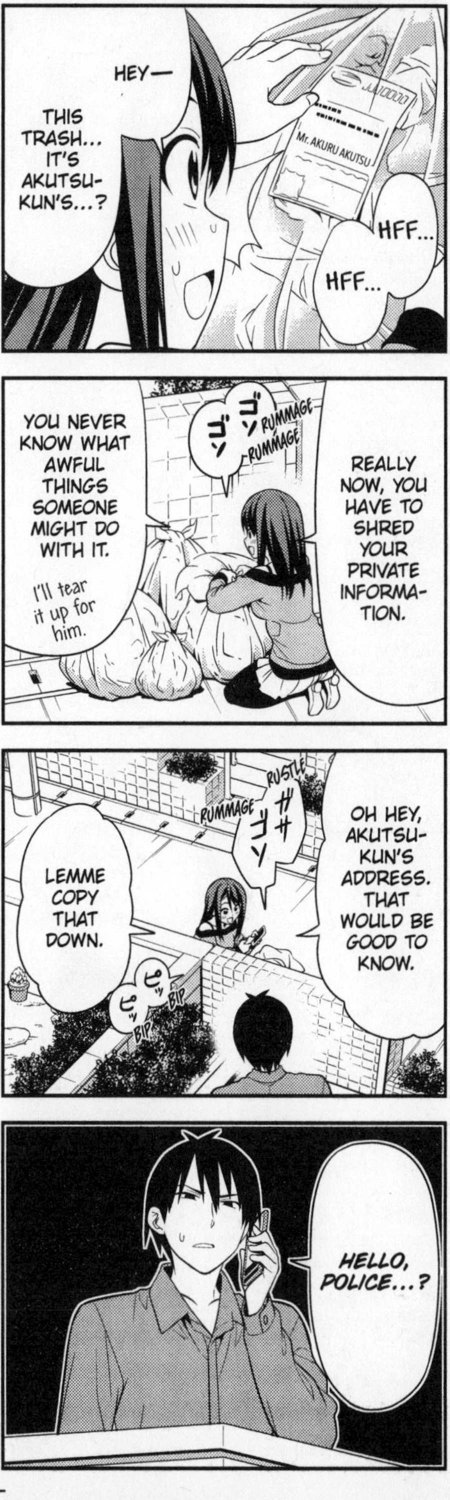
HEY—
THIS TRASH... IT'S AKUTSU-KUN'S...?
Mr. AKURU AKUTSU
HFF...
HFF...
REALLY NOW, YOU HAVE TO SHRED YOUR PRIVATE INFORMATION.
ゴソ ゴソ
RUMMAGE RUMMAGE
YOU NEVER KNOW WHAT AWFUL THINGS SOMEONE MIGHT DO WITH IT.
I'll tear it up for him.
OH HEY, AKUTSU-KUN'S ADDRESS. THAT WOULD BE GOOD TO KNOW.
RUSTLE ガサ
ゴソ RUMMAGE
LEMME COPY THAT DOWN.
ピッ ピッ
BIP BIP
HELLO, POLICE...?

Head Monitor, Behind You!! Behind You!!

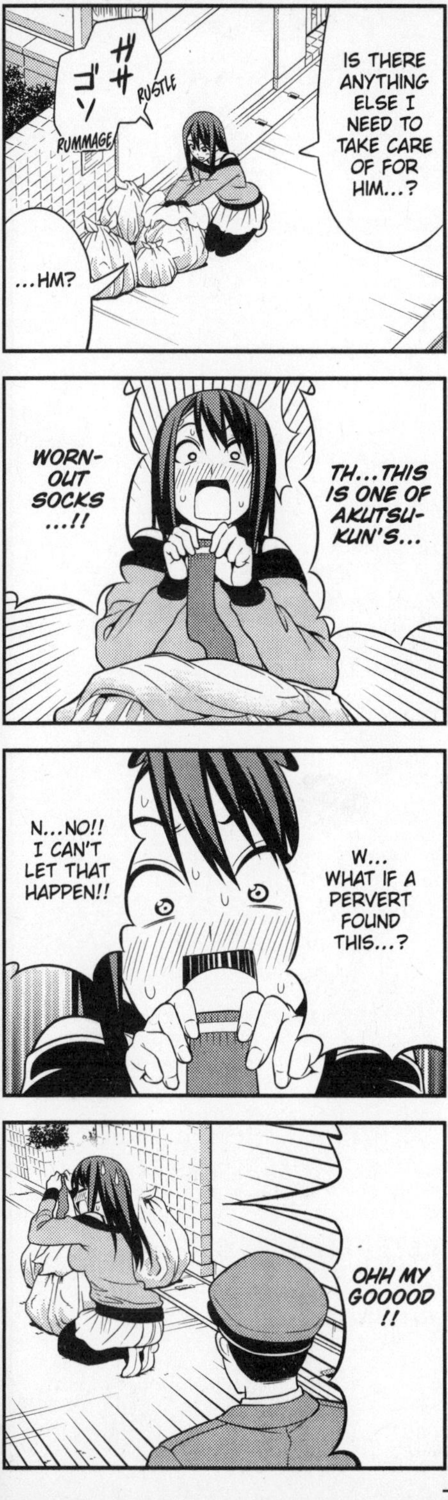
IS THERE ANYTHING ELSE I NEED TO TAKE CARE OF FOR HIM...?
ガサ ゴソ
RUSTLE
RUMMAGE
...HM?
TH...THIS IS ONE OF AKUTSU-KUN'S...
WORN-OUT SOCKS...!!
W... WHAT IF A PERVERT FOUND THIS...?
N...NO!! I CAN'T LET THAT HAPPEN!!
OHH MY GOOOOD!!

Justice vs. Morality

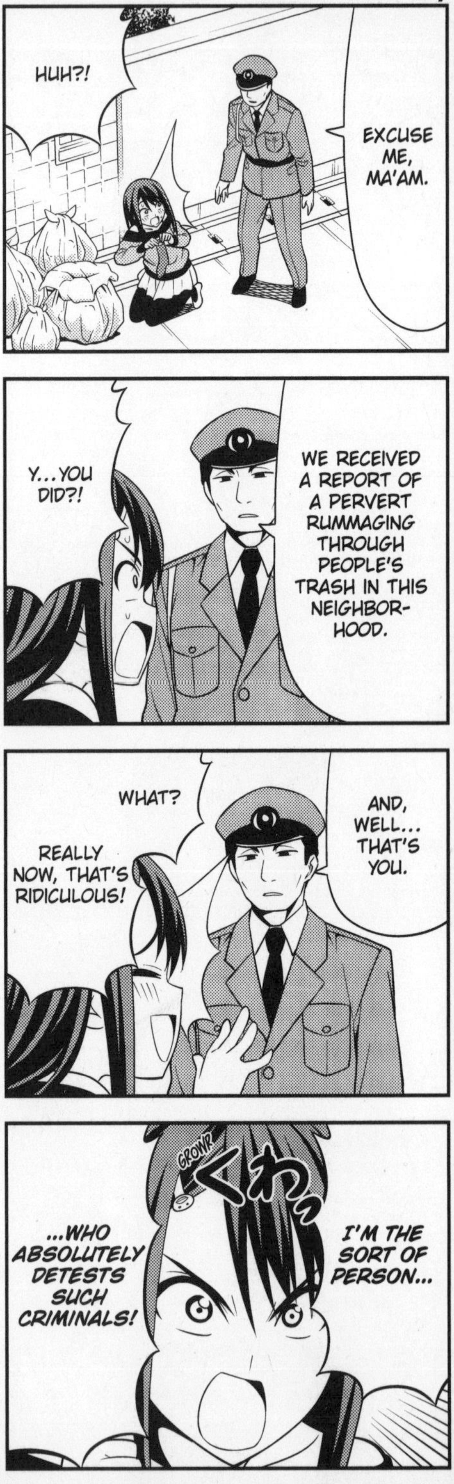
EXCUSE ME, MA'AM.
HUH?!
WE RECEIVED A REPORT OF A PERVERT RUMMAGING THROUGH PEOPLE'S TRASH IN THIS NEIGHBOR-HOOD.
Y...YOU DID?!
AND, WELL... THAT'S YOU.
WHAT?
REALLY NOW, THAT'S RIDICULOUS!
I'M THE SORT OF PERSON...
GROWR くわっ
...WHO ABSOLUTELY DETESTS SUCH CRIMINALS!

Reinforcements Have Arrived!

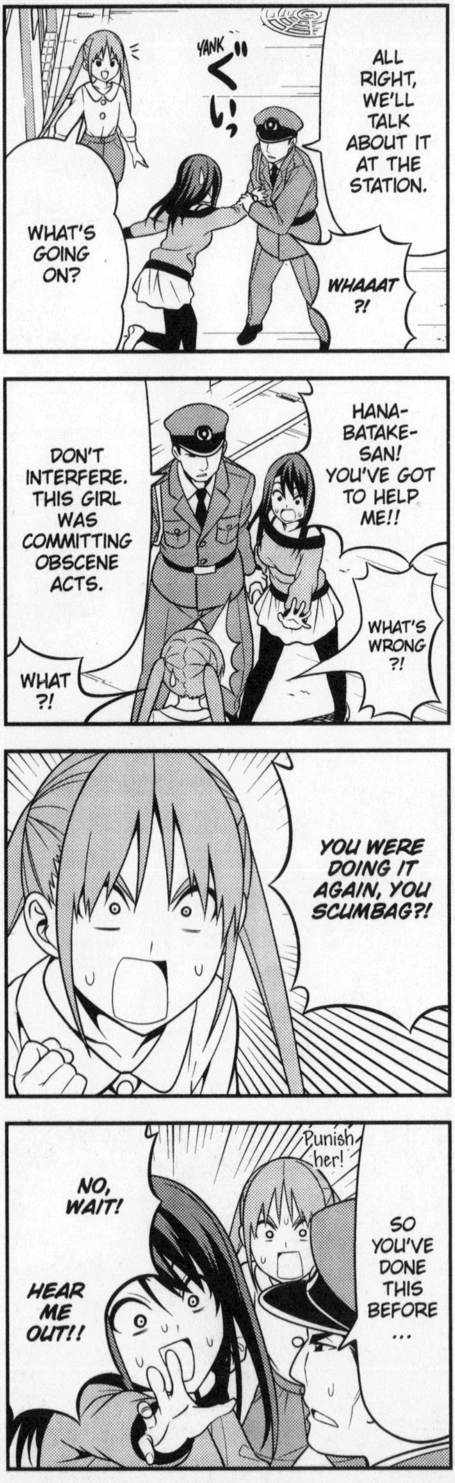
ALL RIGHT, WE'LL TALK ABOUT IT AT THE STATION.
YANK ぐいっ
WHAAAT?!
WHAT'S GOING ON?
HANA-BATAKE-SAN! YOU'VE GOT TO HELP ME!!
DON'T INTERFERE. THIS GIRL WAS COMMITTING OBSCENE ACTS.
WHAT'S WRONG?!
WHAT?!
YOU WERE DOING IT AGAIN, YOU SCUMBAG?!
SO YOU'VE DONE THIS BEFORE...
Punish her!
NO, WAIT!
HEAR ME OUT!!

So Cliché

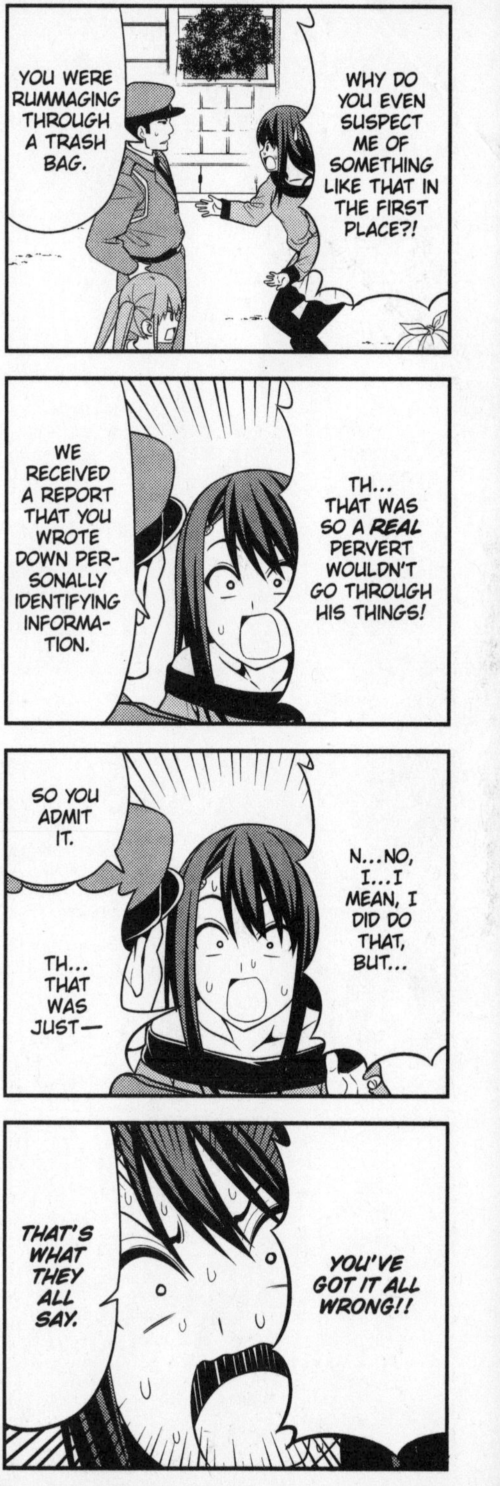
WHY DO YOU EVEN SUSPECT ME OF SOMETHING LIKE THAT IN THE FIRST PLACE?!
YOU WERE RUMMAGING THROUGH A TRASH BAG.
TH... THAT WAS SO A *REAL* PERVERT WOULDN'T GO THROUGH HIS THINGS!
WE RECEIVED A REPORT THAT YOU WROTE DOWN PERSONALLY IDENTIFYING INFORMATION.
N...NO, I...I MEAN, I DID DO THAT, BUT...
SO YOU ADMIT IT.
TH... THAT WAS JUST—
YOU'VE GOT IT ALL WRONG!!
THAT'S WHAT THEY ALL SAY.

He's the One Who Called

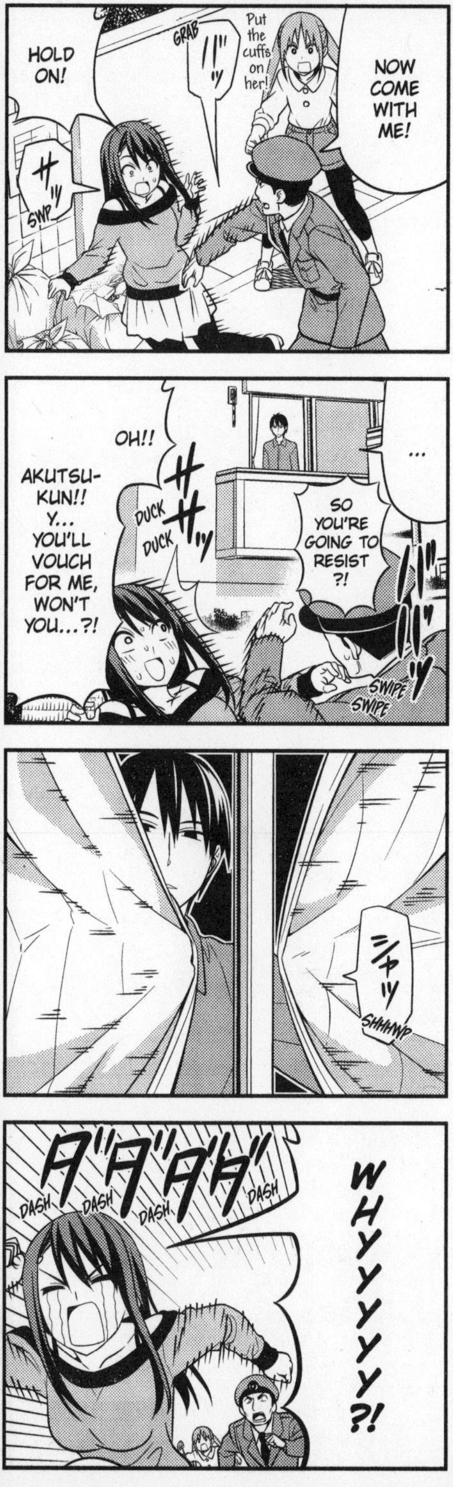
NOW COME WITH ME!
Put the cuffs on her!
GRAB
HOLD ON!
SWP
...
SO YOU'RE GOING TO RESIST?!
OH!!
AKUTSU-KUN!! Y... YOU'LL VOUCH FOR ME, WON'T YOU...?!
DUCK DUCK
SWIPE SWIPE
SHHHNP
WHYYYYYYY?!
DASH DASH DASH DASH

## Head Monitor: Action Star

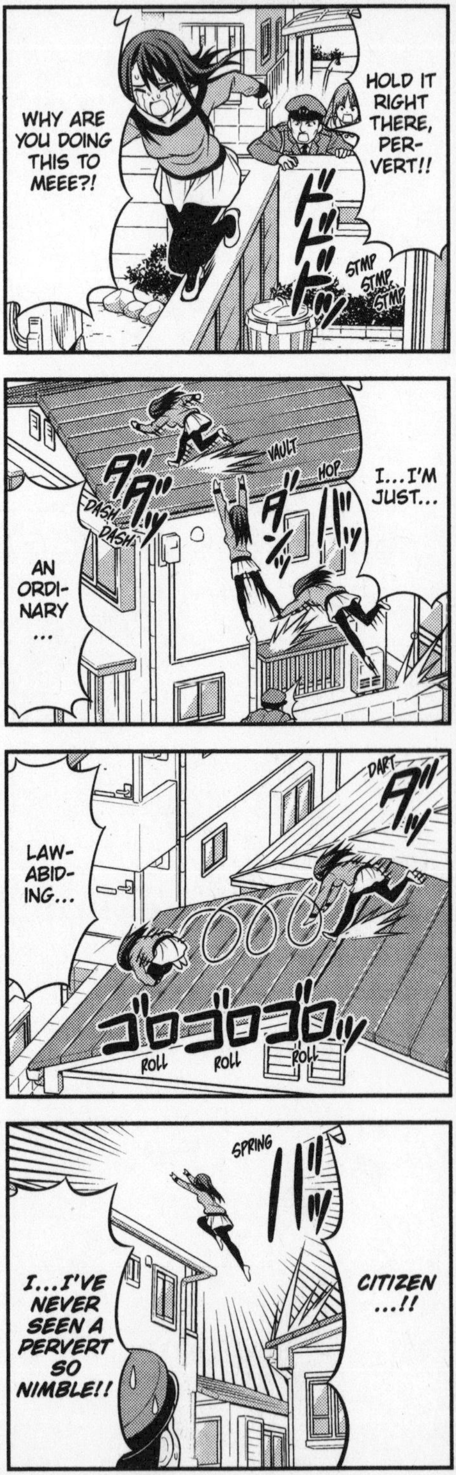

HOLD IT RIGHT THERE, PER-VERT!!
WHY ARE YOU DOING THIS TO MEEE?!
STMP STMP STMP
VAULT
HOP
I...I'M JUST...
DASH DASH
AN ORDI-NARY ...
DART
LAW-ABID-ING...
ROLL ROLL ROLL
SPRING
CITIZEN ...!!
I...I'VE NEVER SEEN A PERVERT SO NIMBLE!!


## But I Still Wasn't Doing Anything

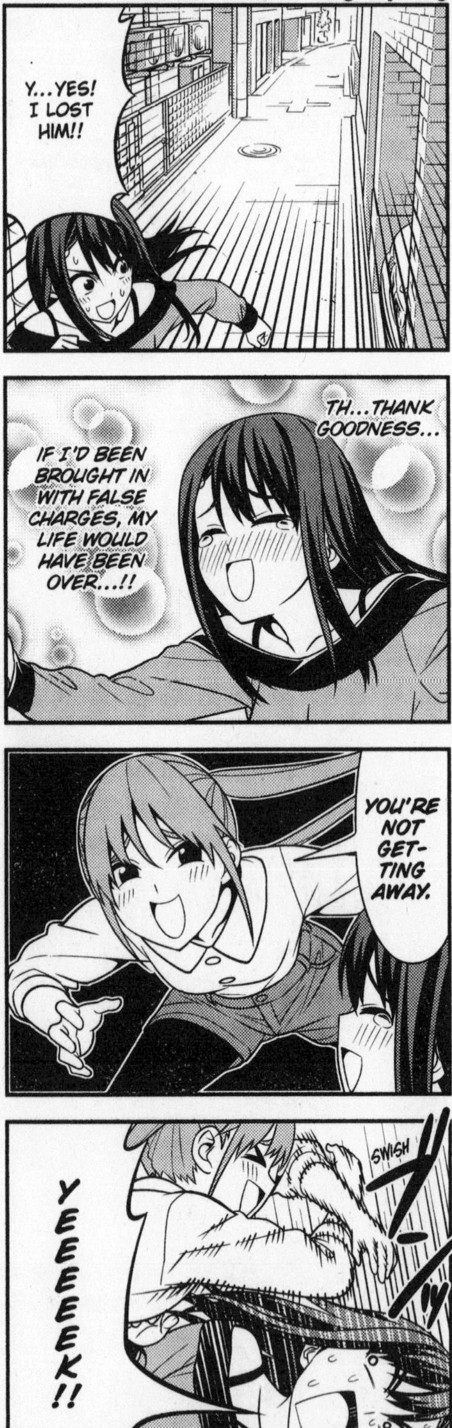

Y...YES! I LOST HIM!!
TH...THANK GOODNESS...
IF I'D BEEN BROUGHT IN WITH FALSE CHARGES, MY LIFE WOULD HAVE BEEN OVER...!!
YOU'RE NOT GET-TING AWAY.
SWISH
YEEEEEK!!

She Knows Not Fatigue

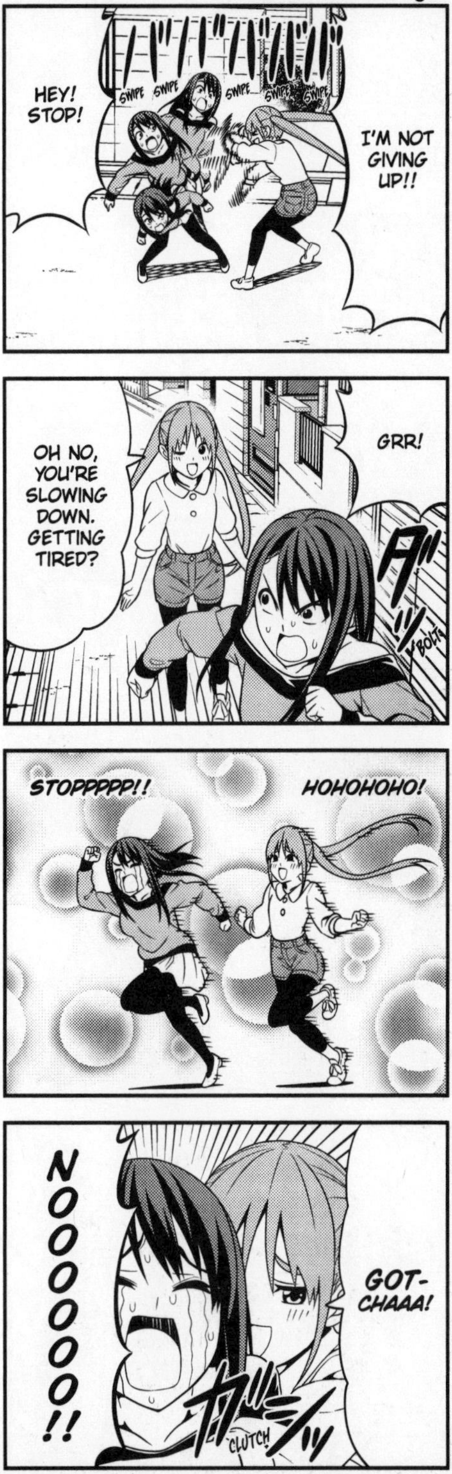
I'M NOT GIVING UP!!
SWIPE SWIPE SWIPE SWIPE SWIPE
HEY! STOP!
GRR!
BOLT
OH NO, YOU'RE SLOWING DOWN. GETTING TIRED?
HOHOHOHO!
STOPPPPP!!
GOT-CHAAA!
CLUTCH
NOOOOOOO!!

She Went Home, Obviously

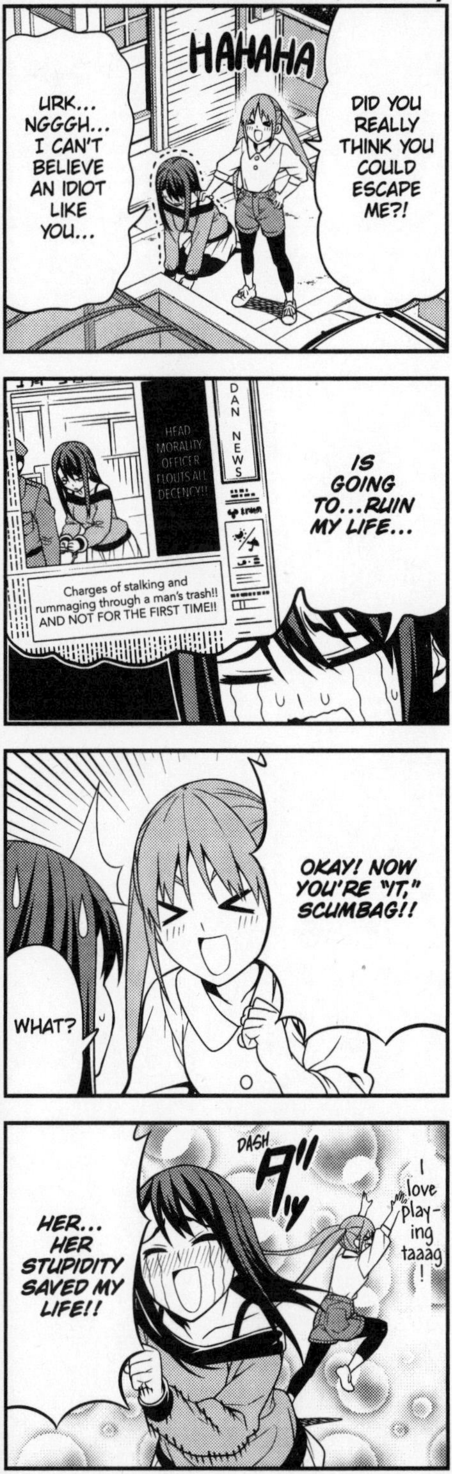
HAHAHA
DID YOU REALLY THINK YOU COULD ESCAPE ME?!
URK... NGGGH... I CAN'T BELIEVE AN IDIOT LIKE YOU...
IS GOING TO...RUIN MY LIFE...
DAN NEWS
HEAD MORALITY OFFICER FLOUTS ALL DECENCY!!
Charges of stalking and rummaging through a man's trash!! AND NOT FOR THE FIRST TIME!!
OKAY! NOW YOU'RE "IT," SCUMBAG!!
WHAT?
DASH
I love playing taaag!
HER... HER STUPIDITY SAVED MY LIFE!!

**Completely Unaware**

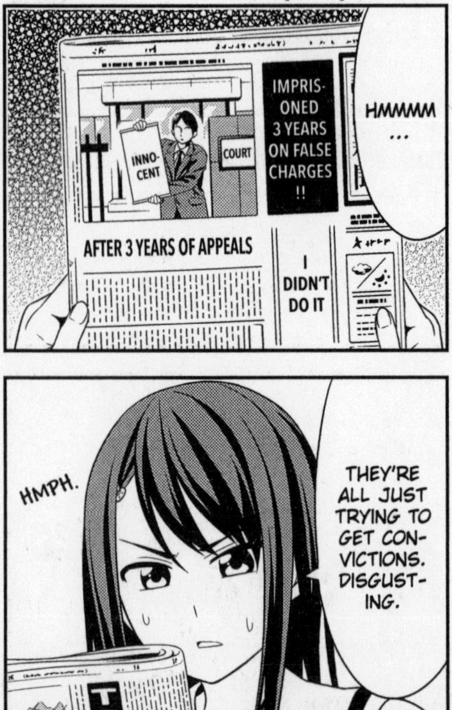
HMMMM ...
IMPRIS-ONED 3 YEARS ON FALSE CHARGES !!
COURT
INNO-CENT
AFTER 3 YEARS OF APPEALS
I DIDN'T DO IT
THEY'RE ALL JUST TRYING TO GET CON-VICTIONS. DISGUST-ING.
HMPH.

# Aho-Girl

\ˈahôˌgərl \ *Japanese, noun.*
A clueless girl.

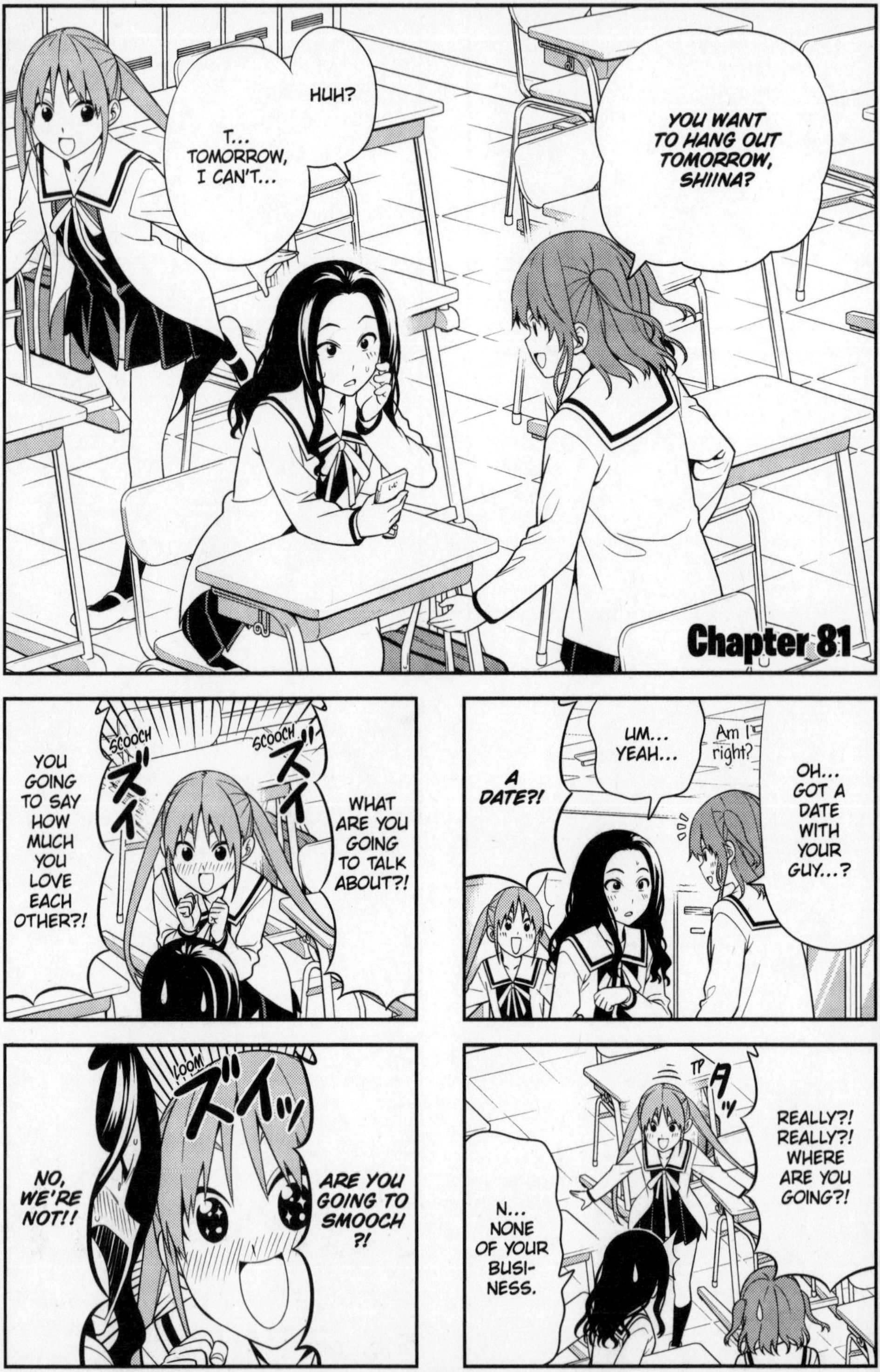
YOU WANT TO HANG OUT TOMORROW, SHIINA?
HUH?
T... TOMORROW, I CAN'T...
Chapter 81
OH... GOT A DATE WITH YOUR GUY...?
Am I right?
UM... YEAH...
A DATE?!
SCOOCH ズイ
WHAT ARE YOU GOING TO TALK ABOUT?!
SCOOCH ズイ
YOU GOING TO SAY HOW MUCH YOU LOVE EACH OTHER?!
TP タッ
REALLY?! REALLY?! WHERE ARE YOU GOING?!
N... NONE OF YOUR BUSI-NESS.
LOOM ズイッ
ARE YOU GOING TO SMOOCH?!
NO, WE'RE NOT!!

We Need an Explanation

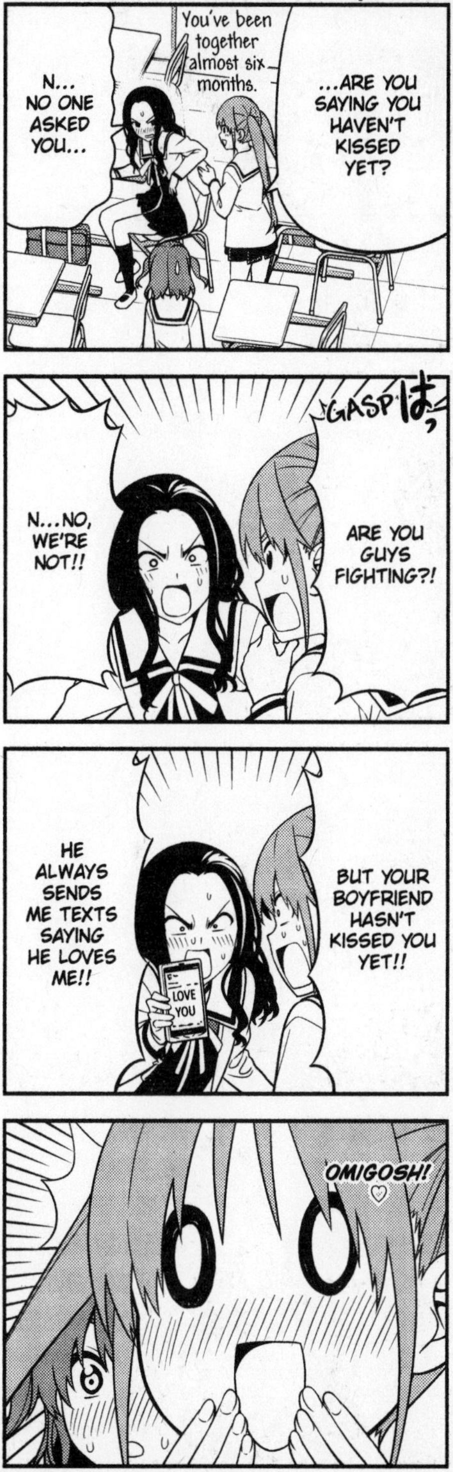
...ARE YOU SAYING YOU HAVEN'T KISSED YET?
You've been together almost six months.
N... NO ONE ASKED YOU...
GASP
は,
ARE YOU GUYS FIGHTING?!
N...NO, WE'RE NOT!!
BUT YOUR BOYFRIEND HASN'T KISSED YOU YET!!
HE ALWAYS SENDS ME TEXTS SAYING HE LOVES ME!!
LOVE YOU
OMIGOSH! ♡

Answer Honestly

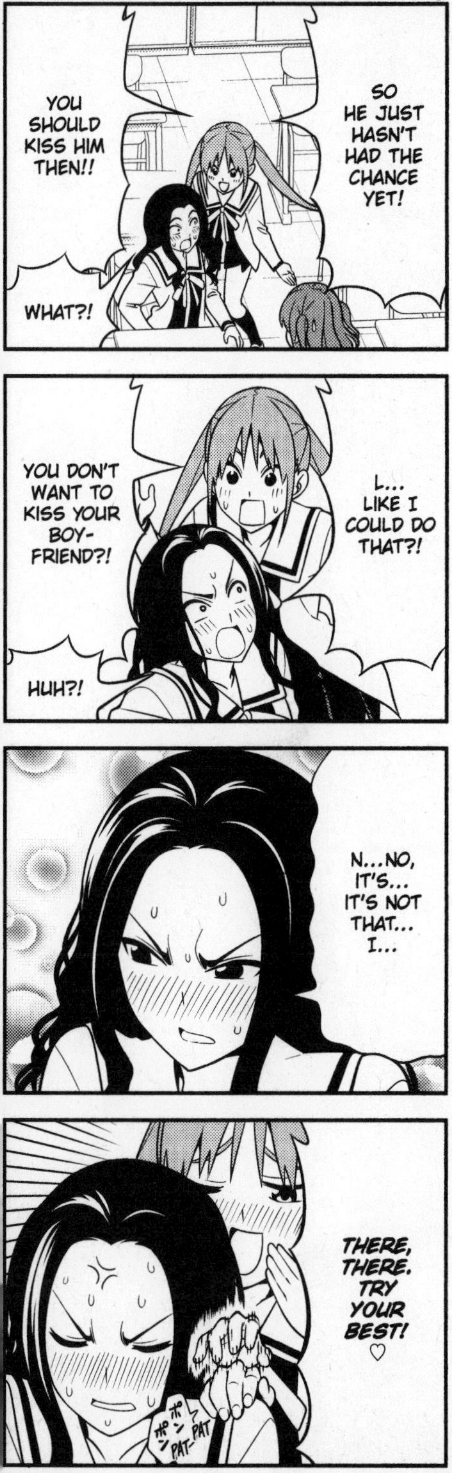
SO HE JUST HASN'T HAD THE CHANCE YET!
YOU SHOULD KISS HIM THEN!!
WHAT?!
L... LIKE I COULD DO THAT?!
YOU DON'T WANT TO KISS YOUR BOY-FRIEND?!
HUH?!
N...NO, IT'S... IT'S NOT THAT... I...
THERE, THERE. TRY YOUR BEST! ♡
ポン ポン
PAT PAT

Mind Made Up!

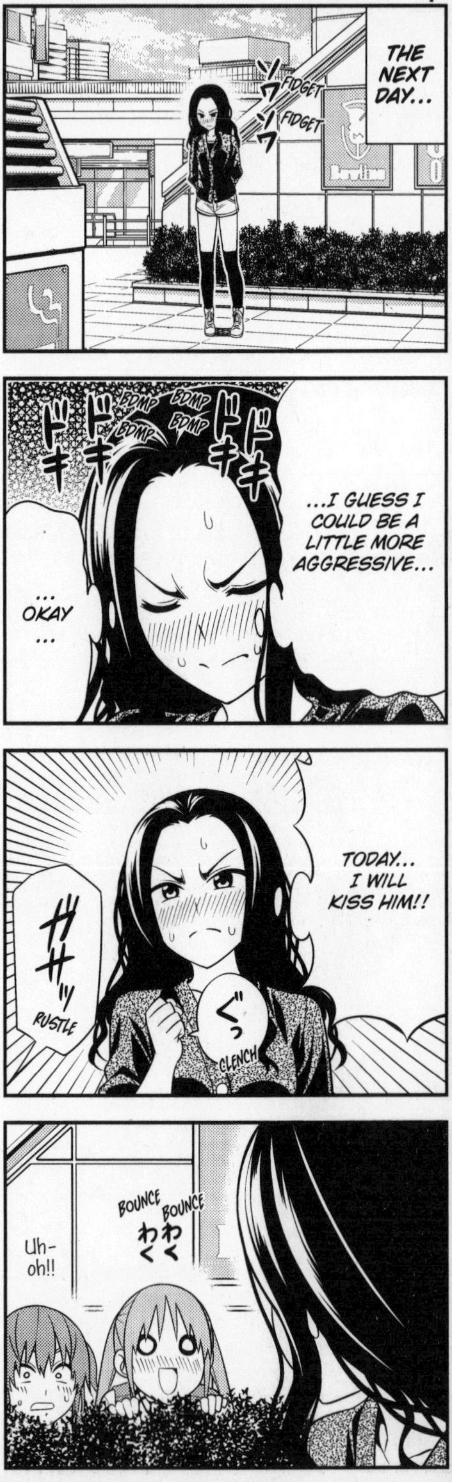

THE NEXT DAY...
ソワソワ
FIDGET
FIDGET
ドキドキ
ドキドキ
BDMP
BDMP
BDMP
BDMP
...I GUESS I COULD BE A LITTLE MORE AGGRESSIVE...
...OKAY...
TODAY... I WILL KISS HIM!!
ガサッ
RUSTLE
ぐっ
CLENCH
BOUNCE
BOUNCE
わくわく
Uh-oh!!


They Got Away!

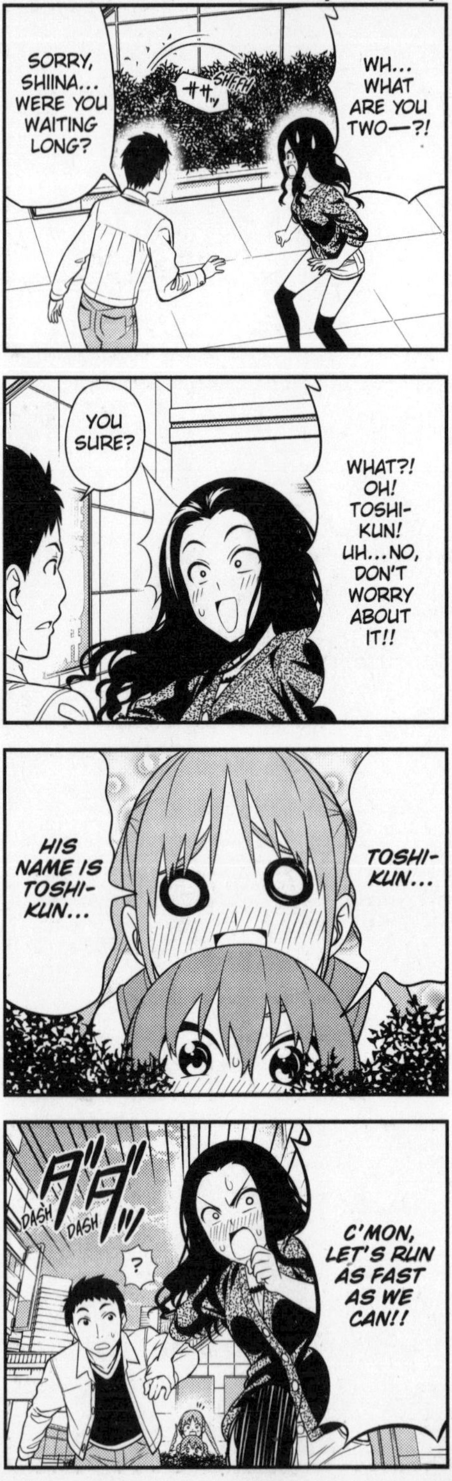

WH... WHAT ARE YOU TWO—?!
ササッ
SHFFH
SORRY, SHIINA... WERE YOU WAITING LONG?
WHAT?! OH! TOSHI-KUN! UH...NO, DON'T WORRY ABOUT IT!!
YOU SURE?
TOSHI-KUN...
HIS NAME IS TOSHI-KUN...
C'MON, LET'S RUN AS FAST AS WE CAN!!
ダダッ
DASH
DASH
?

## You Can't Escape!

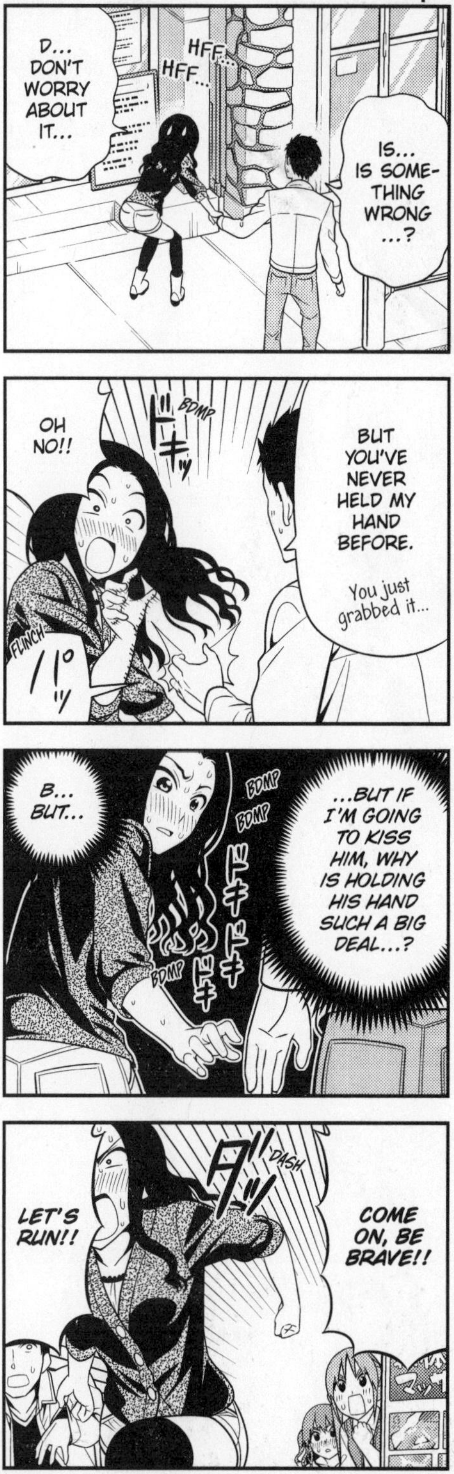
HFF... HFF...
IS... IS SOME-THING WRONG ...?
D... DON'T WORRY ABOUT IT...
BUT YOU'VE NEVER HELD MY HAND BEFORE.
You just grabbed it...
BDMP
OH NO!!
FLINCH
...BUT IF I'M GOING TO KISS HIM, WHY IS HOLDING HIS HAND SUCH A BIG DEAL...?
BDMP
BDMP
B... BUT...
BDMP
COME ON, BE BRAVE!!
DASH
LET'S RUN!!

## Relationship Advisor

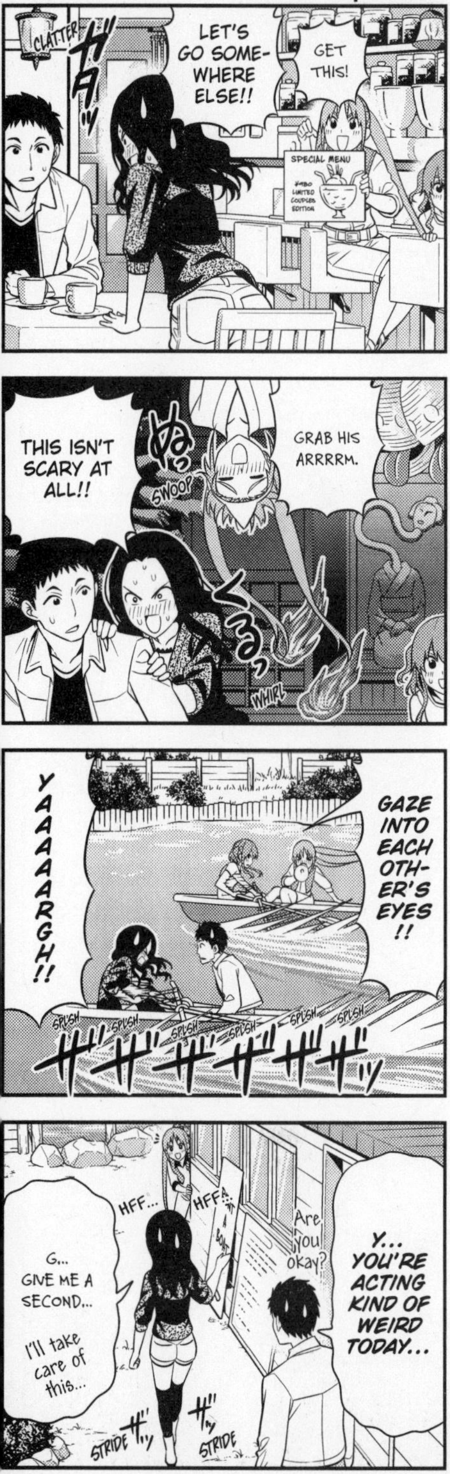
GET THIS!
LET'S GO SOME-WHERE ELSE!!
CLATTER
SPECIAL MENU
GRAB HIS ARRRRM.
SWOOP
THIS ISN'T SCARY AT ALL!!
WHIRL
GAZE INTO EACH OTH-ER'S EYES!!
YAAAAAARGH!!
SPLSH
SPLSH
SPLSH
SPLSH
SPLSH
SPLSH
Y... YOU'RE ACTING KIND OF WEIRD TODAY...
Are you okay?
HFF... HFF...
G... GIVE ME A SECOND...
I'll take care of this...
STRIDE
STRIDE

## Well, In All Honesty

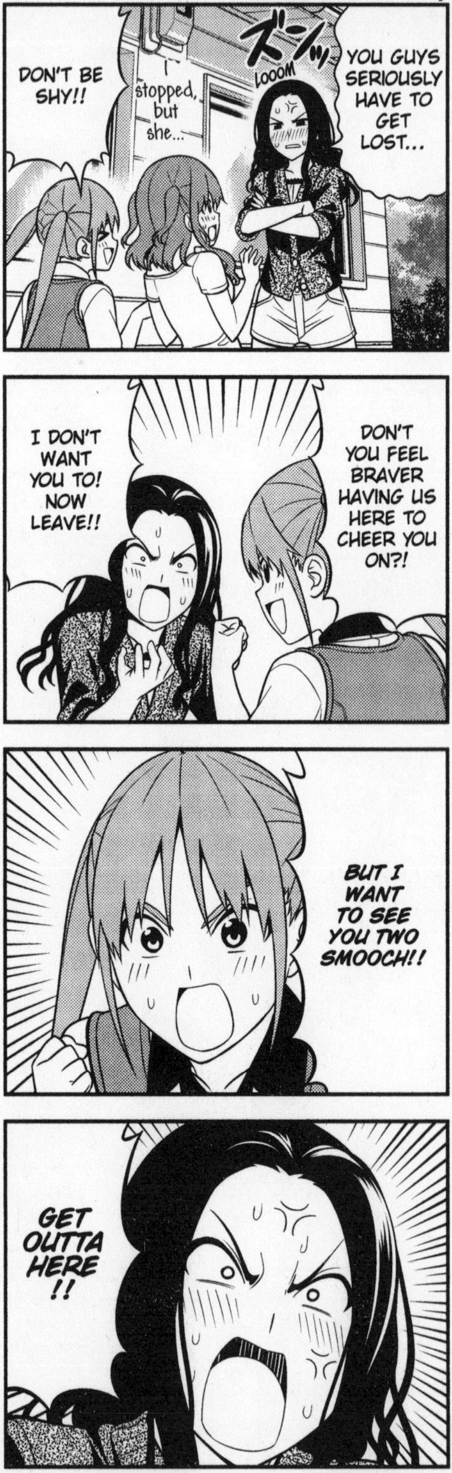
YOU GUYS SERIOUSLY HAVE TO GET LOST...
LOOOM
I stopped, but she...
DON'T BE SHY!!
DON'T YOU FEEL BRAVER HAVING US HERE TO CHEER YOU ON?!
I DON'T WANT YOU TO! NOW LEAVE!!
BUT I WANT TO SEE YOU TWO SMOOCH!!
GET OUTTA HERE!!

## Corrected Instantly

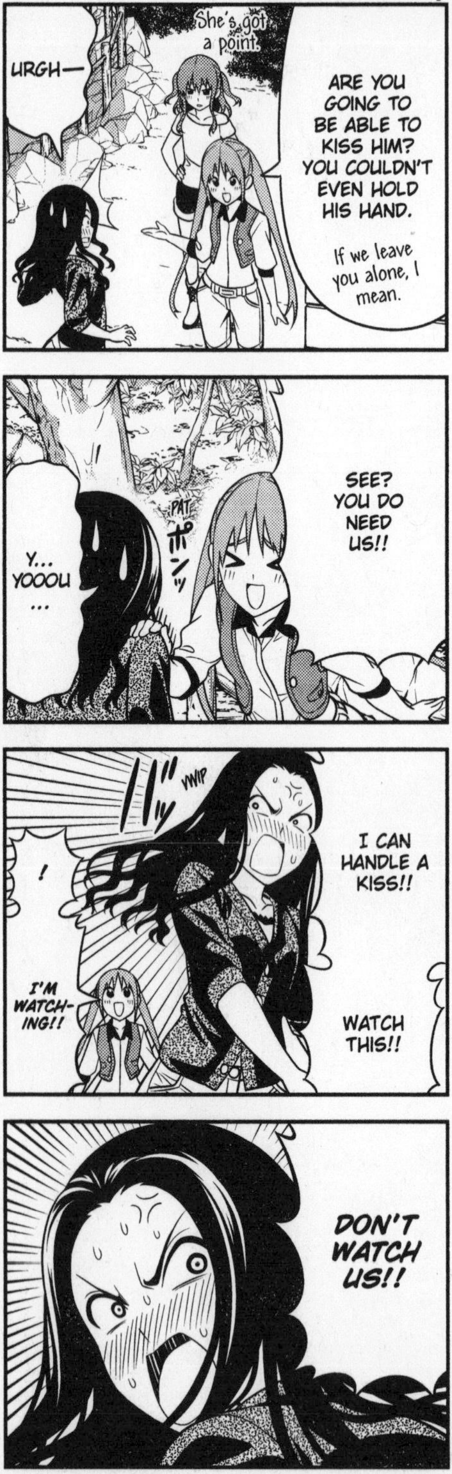
ARE YOU GOING TO BE ABLE TO KISS HIM? YOU COULDN'T EVEN HOLD HIS HAND.
If we leave you alone, I mean.
She's got a point.
URGH—
SEE? YOU DO NEED US!!
PAT
Y... YOOOU ...
I CAN HANDLE A KISS!!
WATCH THIS!!
VWIP
!
I'M WATCHING!!
DON'T WATCH US!!

Your Eyes Only

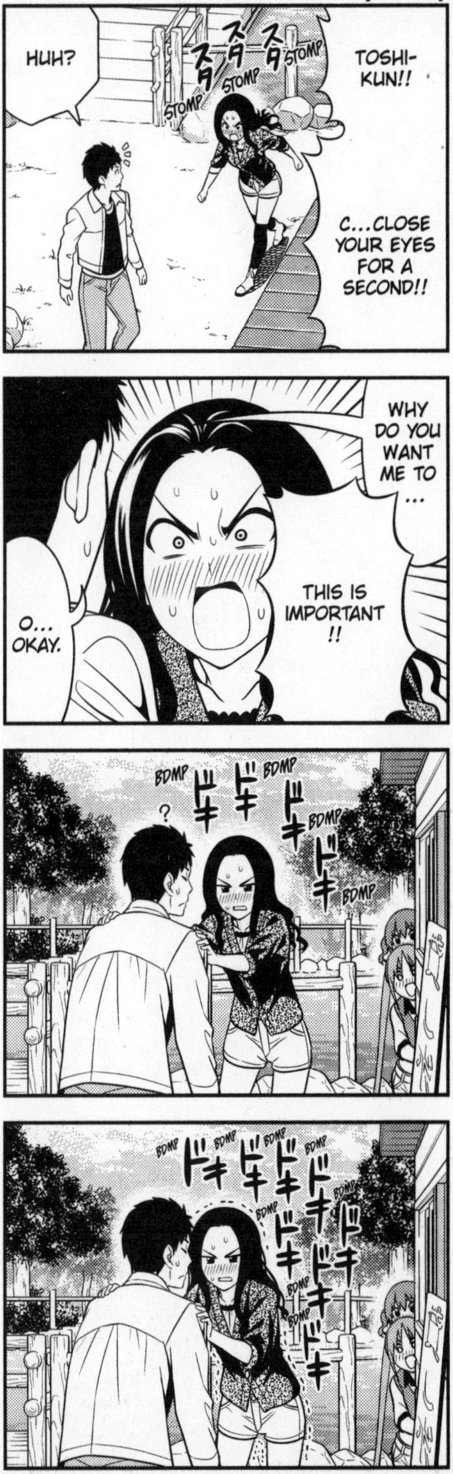
TOSHI-KUN!!
スタ STOMP
スタ STOMP
スタ STOMP
HUH?
C...CLOSE YOUR EYES FOR A SECOND!!
WHY DO YOU WANT ME TO ...
THIS IS IMPORTANT !!
O... OKAY.
BDMP ドキ
BDMP ドキ
BDMP ドキ
BDMP ドキ
?
BDMP ドキ
BDMP ドキ
BDMP ドキ
BDMP ドキ
BDMP ドキ
BDMP ドキ
BDMP ドキ
BDMP ドキ

Say Something

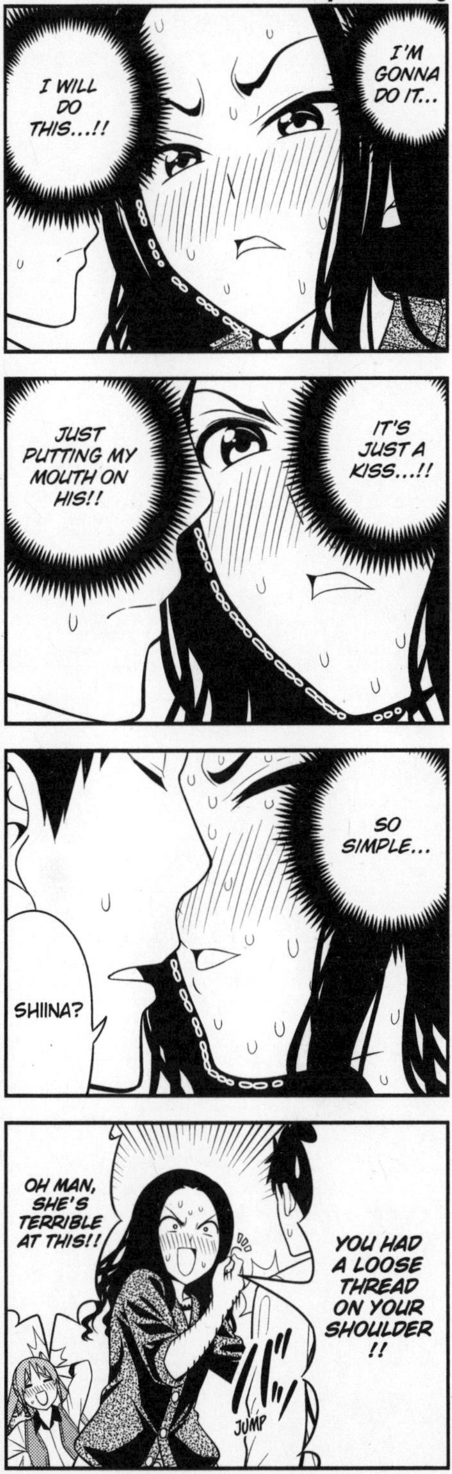
I'M GONNA DO IT...
I WILL DO THIS...!!
IT'S JUST A KISS...!!
JUST PUTTING MY MOUTH ON HIS!!
SO SIMPLE...
SHIINA?
YOU HAD A LOOSE THREAD ON YOUR SHOULDER !!
OH MAN, SHE'S TERRIBLE AT THIS!!
JUMP

Gal C Is Going to Be Mad

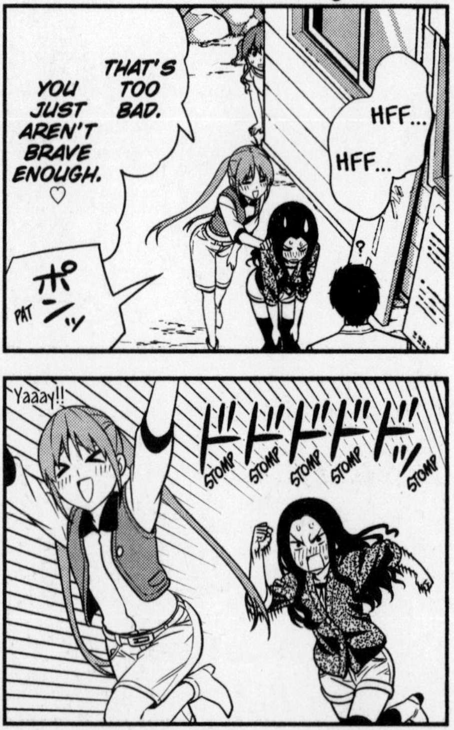
HFF...
HFF...
THAT'S TOO BAD.
YOU JUST AREN'T BRAVE ENOUGH. ♡
ポンッ PAT
ドドドドドッ
STOMP STOMP STOMP STOMP STOMP
Yaaay!!

(DANGEROUS ☆ Love Investigation)

# Aho-Girl

\\'ahô͵gərl\\ *Japanese, noun.*
A clueless girl.

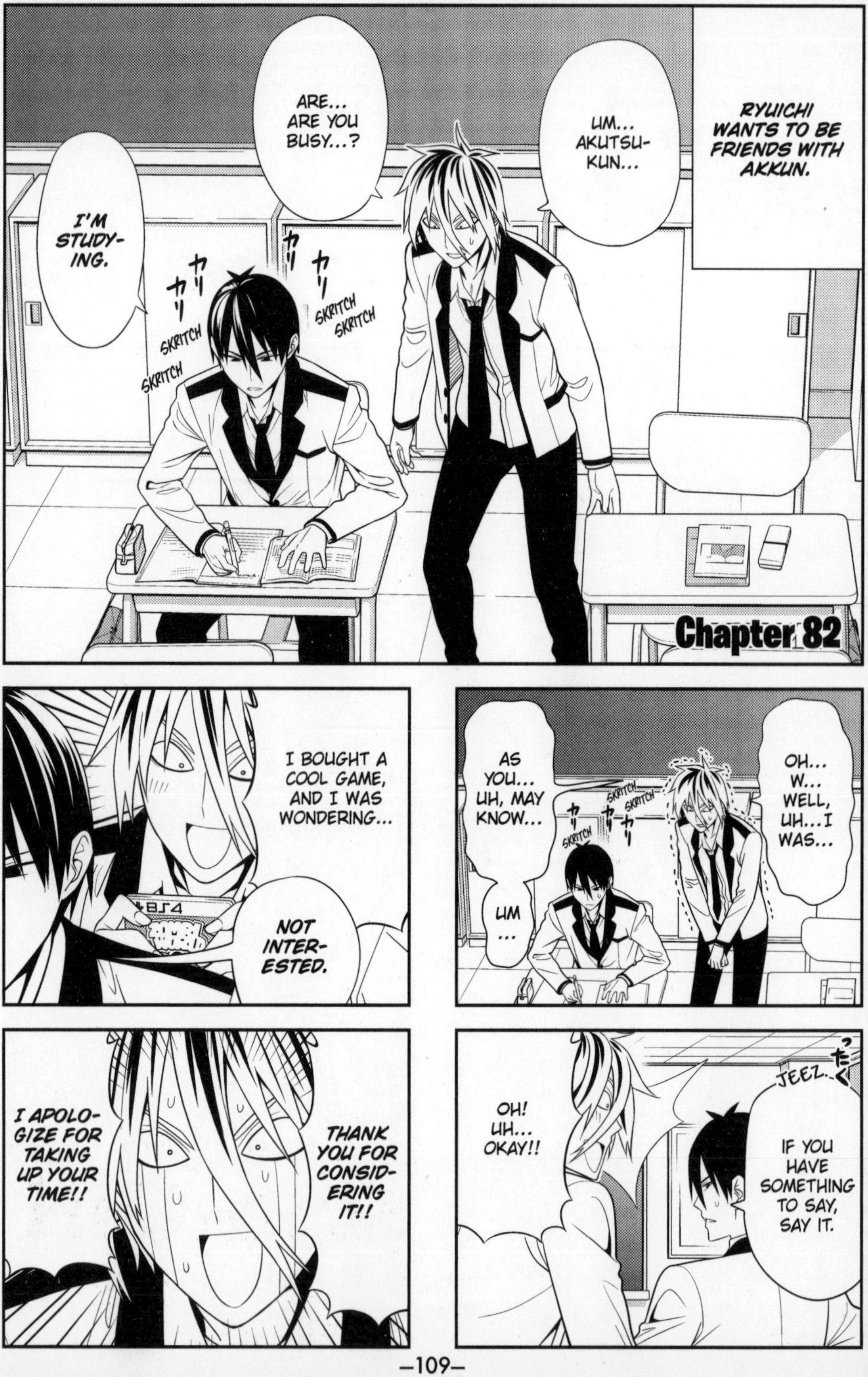
RYUICHI WANTS TO BE FRIENDS WITH AKKUN.
UM... AKUTSU-KUN...
ARE... ARE YOU BUSY...?
カリ カリ
SKRITCH SKRITCH
カリ カリ
SKRITCH SKRITCH
I'M STUDYING.
Chapter 82
OH... W... WELL, UH...I WAS...
カリ カリ
SKRITCH SKRITCH
カリ
SKRITCH
AS YOU... UH, MAY KNOW...
UM ...
I BOUGHT A COOL GAME, AND I WAS WONDERING...
NOT INTERESTED.
ったく
JEEZ.
IF YOU HAVE SOMETHING TO SAY, SAY IT.
OH! UH... OKAY!!
THANK YOU FOR CONSIDERING IT!!
I APOLOGIZE FOR TAKING UP YOUR TIME!!

## Caught in the Act

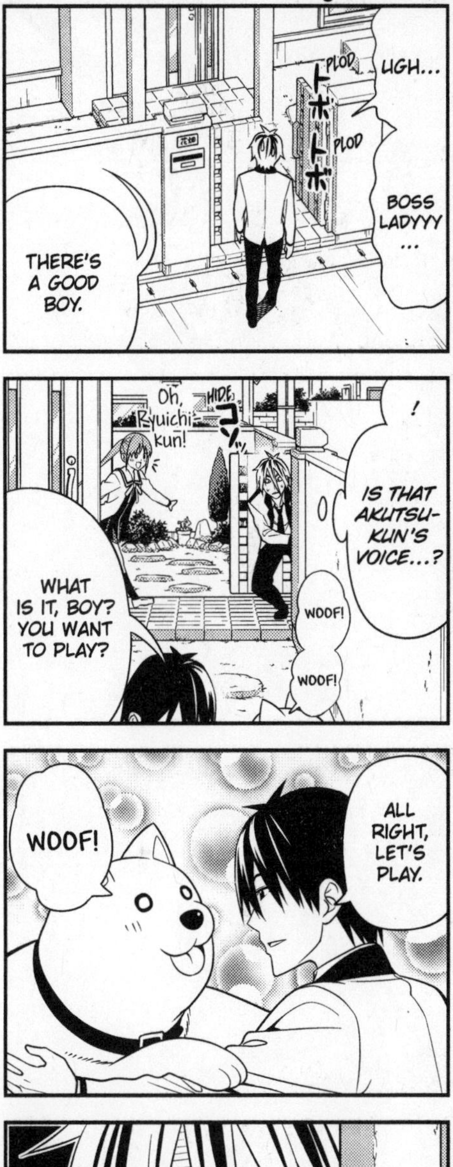
UGH...
トボトボ
PLOD
PLOD
BOSS LADYYY ...
THERE'S A GOOD BOY.
!
IS THAT AKUTSU-KUN'S VOICE...?
HIDE
コソッ
Oh, Ryuichi-kun!
WOOF!
WOOF!
WHAT IS IT, BOY? YOU WANT TO PLAY?
ALL RIGHT, LET'S PLAY.
WOOF!

## I Never Wanted to See This

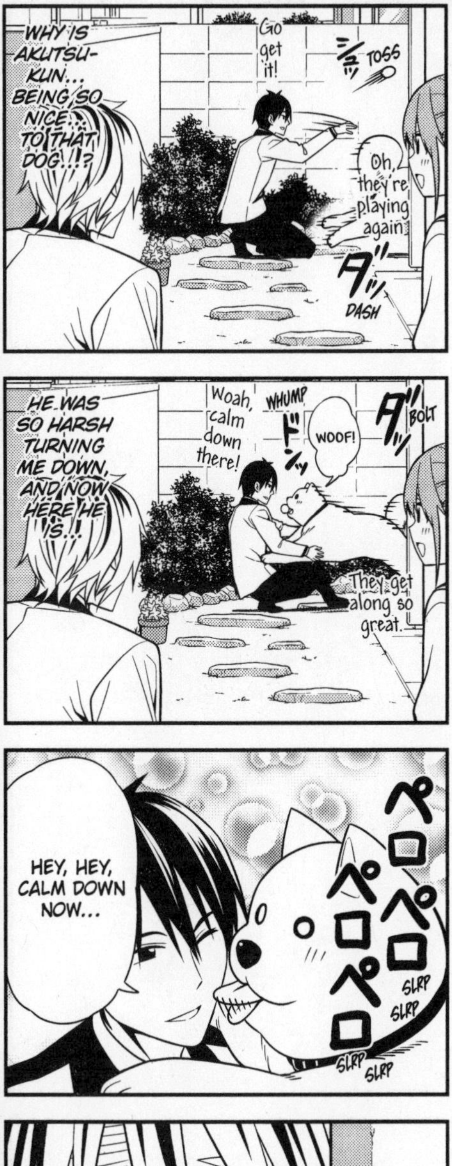
TOSS
Go get it!
WHY IS AKUTSU-KUN... BEING SO NICE... TO THAT DOG...!?
Oh, they're playing again.
ダッ
DASH
ダッ
BOLT
WOOF!
ドンッ
WHUMP
Woah, calm down there!
HE WAS SO HARSH TURNING ME DOWN, AND NOW HERE HE IS...
They get along so great.
ペロペロ
ペロペロ
SLRP
SLRP
SLRP
SLRP
HEY, HEY, CALM DOWN NOW...
I'VE NEVER SEEN HIM LOOK SO HAPPY.

Ready for an Immediate Answer

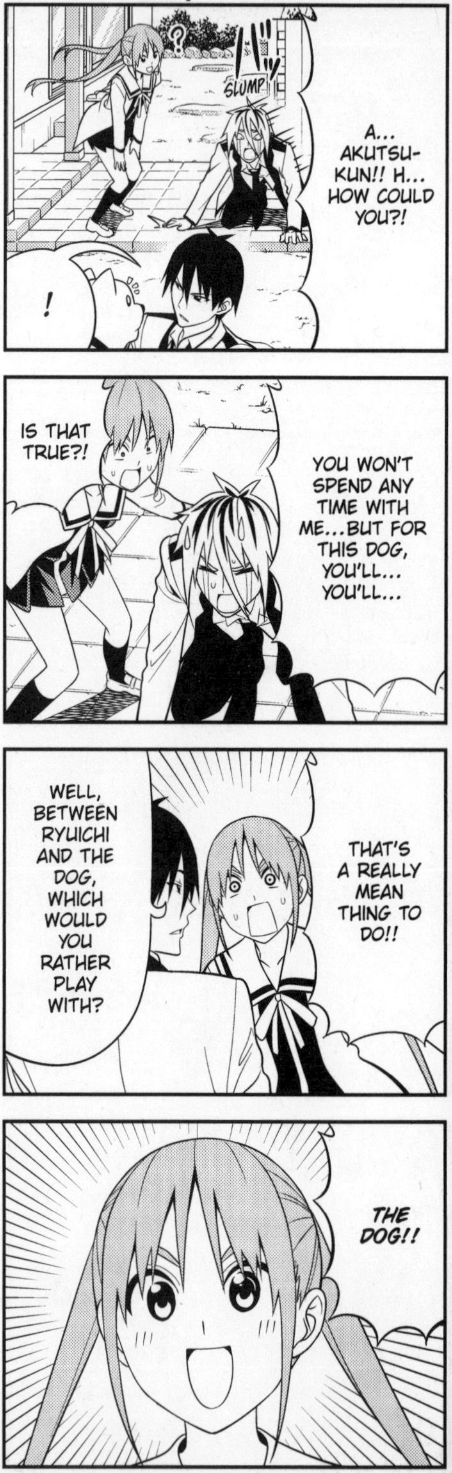
SLUMP
A... AKUTSU-KUN!! H... HOW COULD YOU?!
?
!
YOU WON'T SPEND ANY TIME WITH ME...BUT FOR THIS DOG, YOU'LL... YOU'LL...
IS THAT TRUE?!
THAT'S A REALLY MEAN THING TO DO!!
WELL, BETWEEN RYUICHI AND THE DOG, WHICH WOULD YOU RATHER PLAY WITH?
THE DOG!!

Shaken

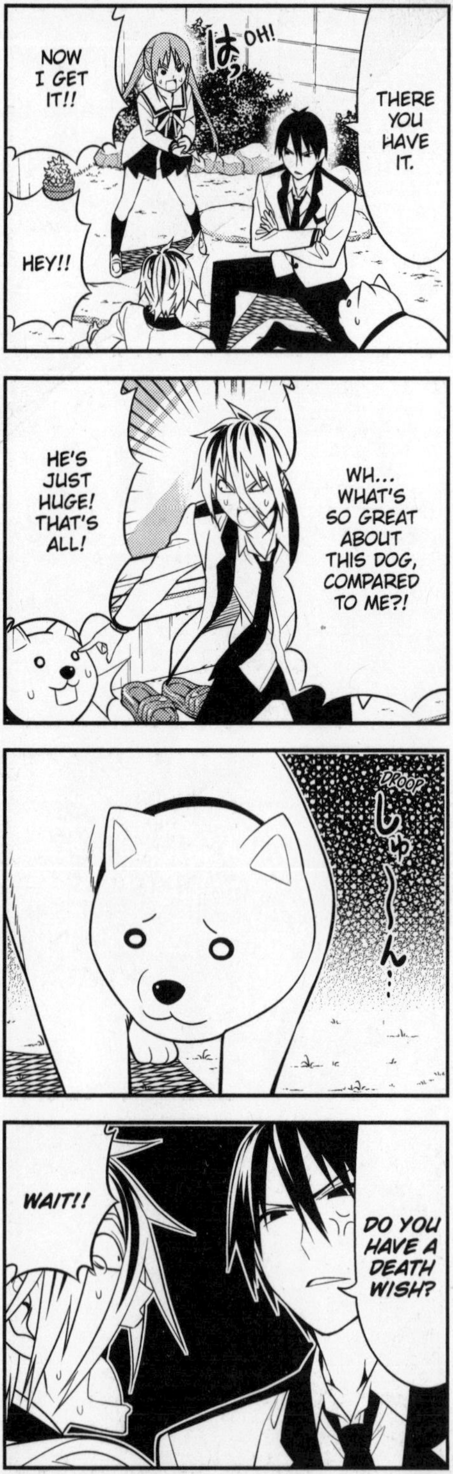
THERE YOU HAVE IT.
OH!
NOW I GET IT!!
HEY!!
WH... WHAT'S SO GREAT ABOUT THIS DOG, COMPARED TO ME?!
HE'S JUST HUGE! THAT'S ALL!
DROOP
DO YOU HAVE A DEATH WISH?
WAIT!!

**Going for the Diss**

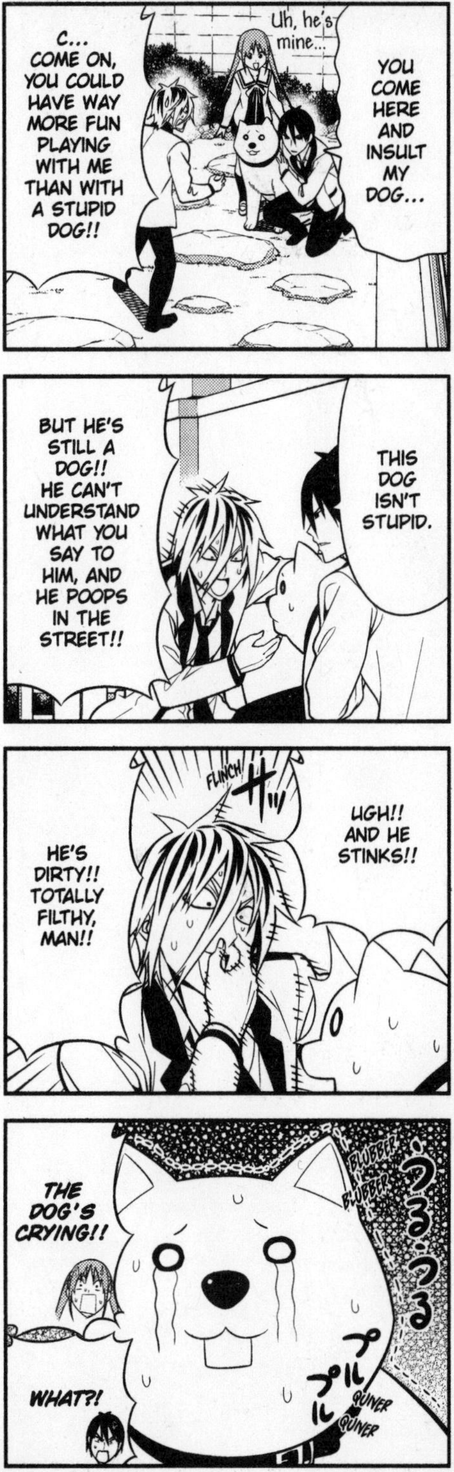
YOU COME HERE AND INSULT MY DOG...
Uh, he's mine...
C... COME ON, YOU COULD HAVE WAY MORE FUN PLAYING WITH ME THAN WITH A STUPID DOG!!
THIS DOG ISN'T STUPID.
BUT HE'S STILL A DOG!! HE CAN'T UNDERSTAND WHAT YOU SAY TO HIM, AND HE POOPS IN THE STREET!!
UGH!! AND HE STINKS!!
FLINCH!
HE'S DIRTY!! TOTALLY FILTHY, MAN!!
うるうる
BLUBBER BLUBBER
THE DOG'S CRYING!!
プルプル
QUIVER QUIVER
WHAT?!

**The Opposite of Special Treatment**

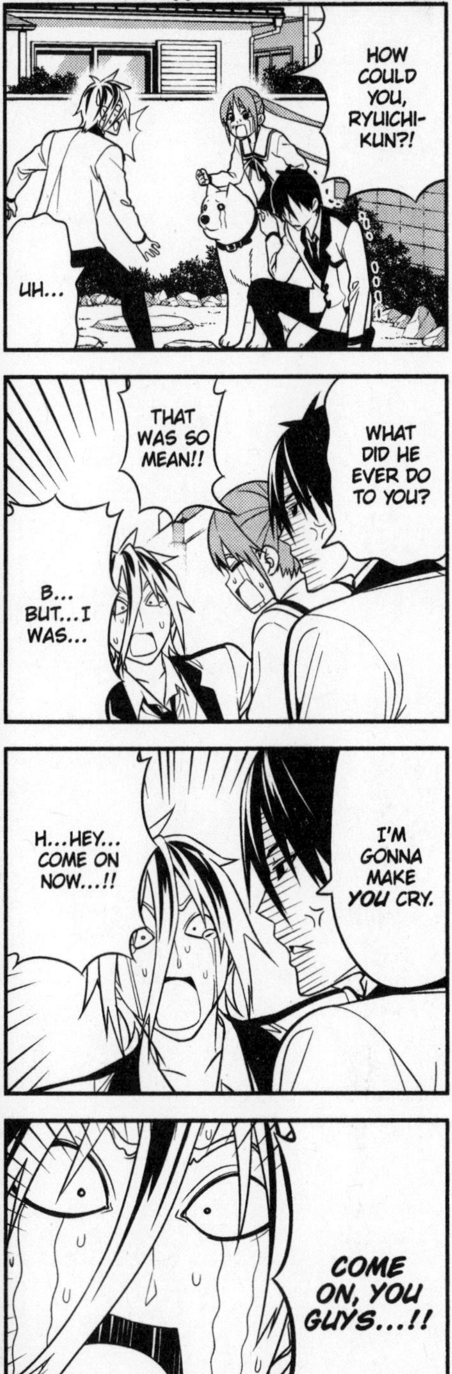
HOW COULD YOU, RYUICHI-KUN?!
UH...
WHAT DID HE EVER DO TO YOU?
THAT WAS SO MEAN!!
B... BUT...I WAS...
I'M GONNA MAKE *YOU* CRY.
H...HEY... COME ON NOW...!!
COME ON, YOU GUYS...!!

## Self-fulfilling Observation

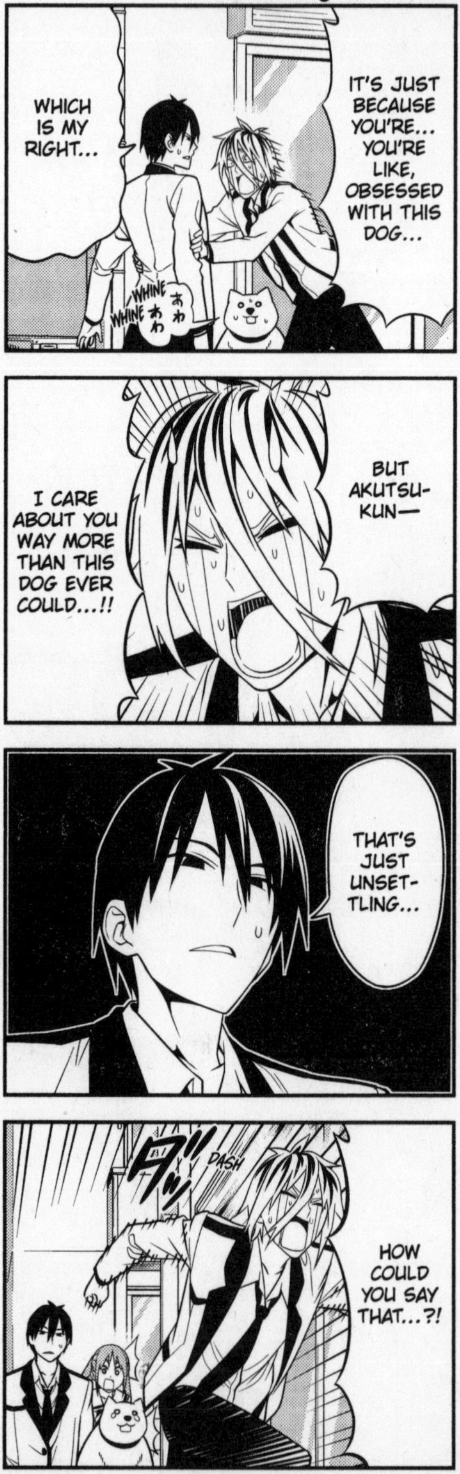
IT'S JUST BECAUSE YOU'RE... YOU'RE LIKE, OBSESSED WITH THIS DOG...
WHICH IS MY RIGHT...
WHINE WHINE あわあわ
BUT AKUTSU-KUN—
I CARE ABOUT YOU WAY MORE THAN THIS DOG EVER COULD...!!
THAT'S JUST UNSETTLING...
ダッ DASH
HOW COULD YOU SAY THAT...?!

## Dog and Ryuichi-kun

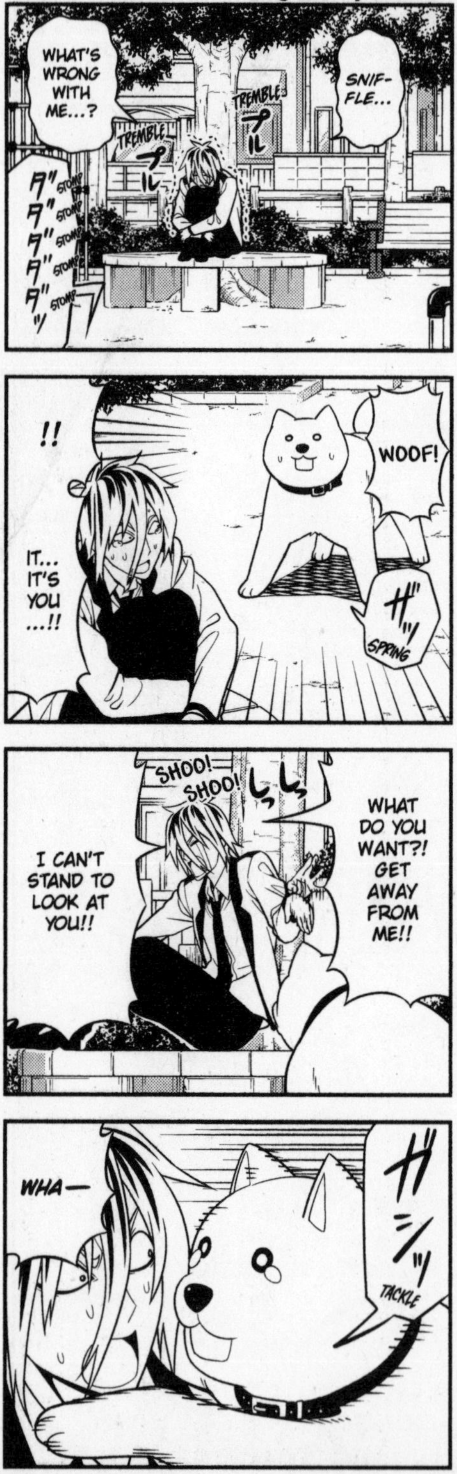
SNIF-FLE...
TREMBLE プル
TREMBLE プル
WHAT'S WRONG WITH ME...?
ダダダダダッ STOMP STOMP STOMP STOMP STOMP
WOOF!
ザッ SPRING
!!
IT... IT'S YOU...!!
WHAT DO YOU WANT?! GET AWAY FROM ME!!
SHOO! SHOO! しっしっ
I CAN'T STAND TO LOOK AT YOU!!
ガシッ TACKLE
WHA—

Dog's Feelings

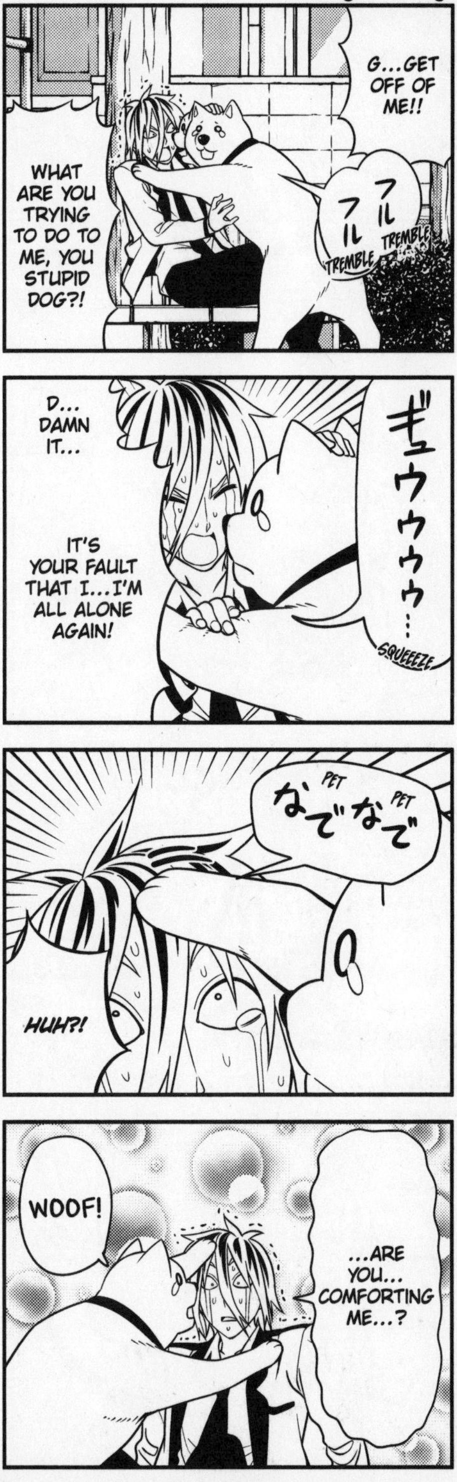
G...GET OFF OF ME!!
フル フル
TREMBLE TREMBLE
WHAT ARE YOU TRYING TO DO TO ME, YOU STUPID DOG?!
ギュウウウウ…
SQUEEEEZE
D... DAMN IT...
IT'S YOUR FAULT THAT I...I'M ALL ALONE AGAIN!
なでなで
PET PET
HUH?!
...ARE YOU... COMFORTING ME...?
WOOF!

Cocooned in Kindness

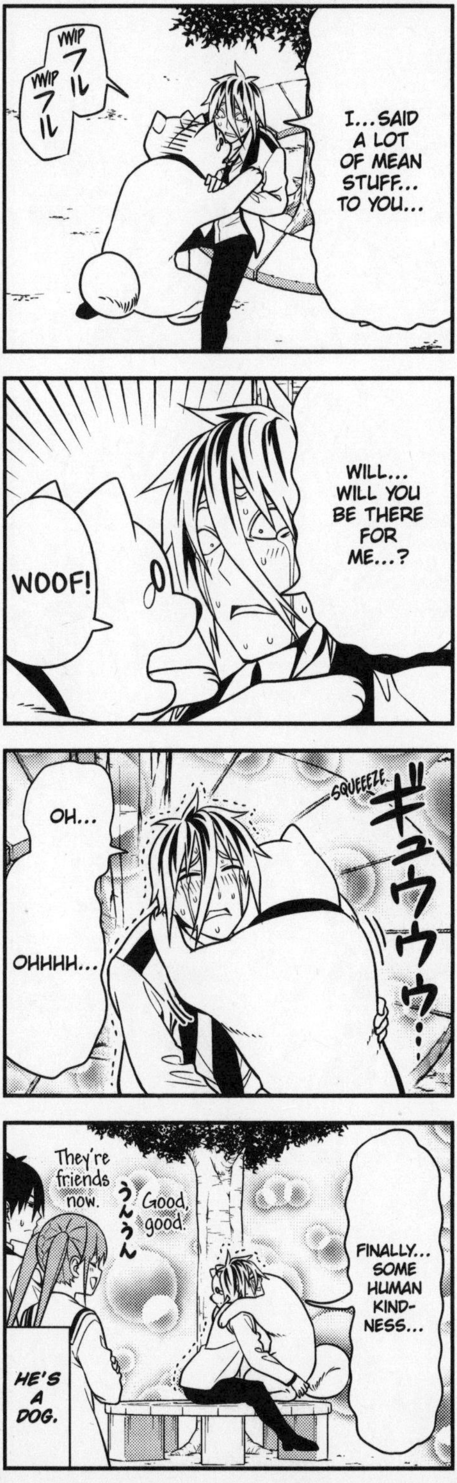
I...SAID A LOT OF MEAN STUFF... TO YOU...
フル フル
VWIP VWIP
WILL... WILL YOU BE THERE FOR ME...?
WOOF!
ギュウウウ…
SQUEEEZE
OH...
OHHHH...
FINALLY... SOME HUMAN KINDNESS...
Good, good.
うんうん
They're friends now.
HE'S A DOG.

Sayaka Notices

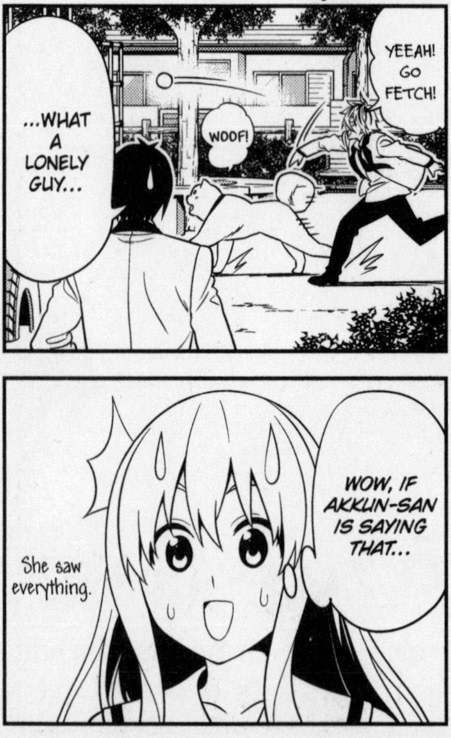
YEEAH! GO FETCH!
WOOF!
...WHAT A LONELY GUY...
WOW, IF AKKUN-SAN IS SAYING THAT...
She saw everything.

# Aho-Girl

\\'ahô͵gərl\ *Japanese, noun.*
A clueless girl.

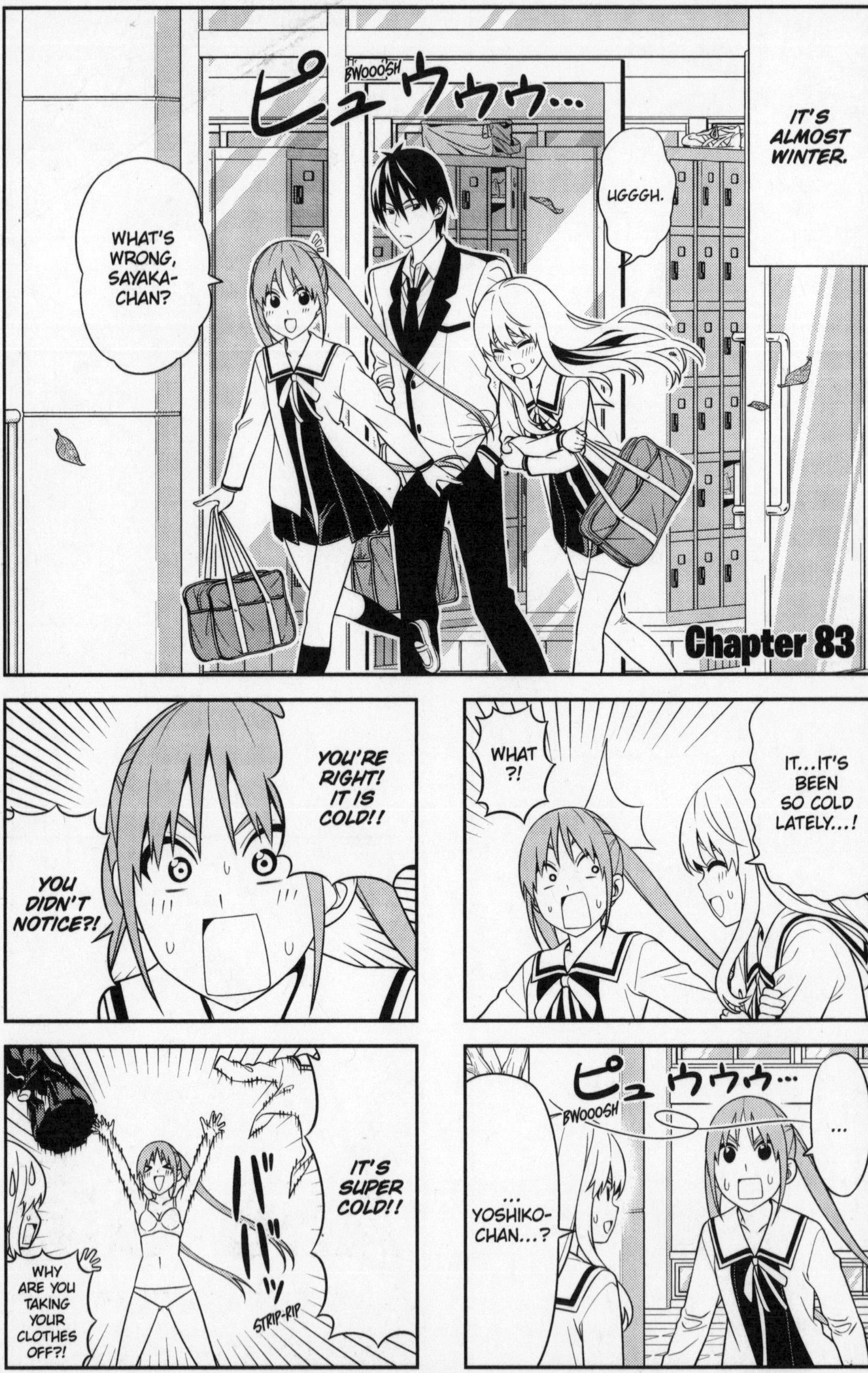
IT'S ALMOST WINTER.
ピュウウウ…
BWOOOSH
UGGGH.
WHAT'S WRONG, SAYAKA-CHAN?
Chapter 83
IT...IT'S BEEN SO COLD LATELY...!
WHAT ?!
YOU'RE RIGHT! IT IS COLD!!
YOU DIDN'T NOTICE?!
ピュウウウ…
BWOOOSH
...
...YOSHIKO-CHAN...?
IT'S SUPER COLD!!
ババッ
STRIP-RIP
WHY ARE YOU TAKING YOUR CLOTHES OFF?!

Typical Ice Bucket Challenge

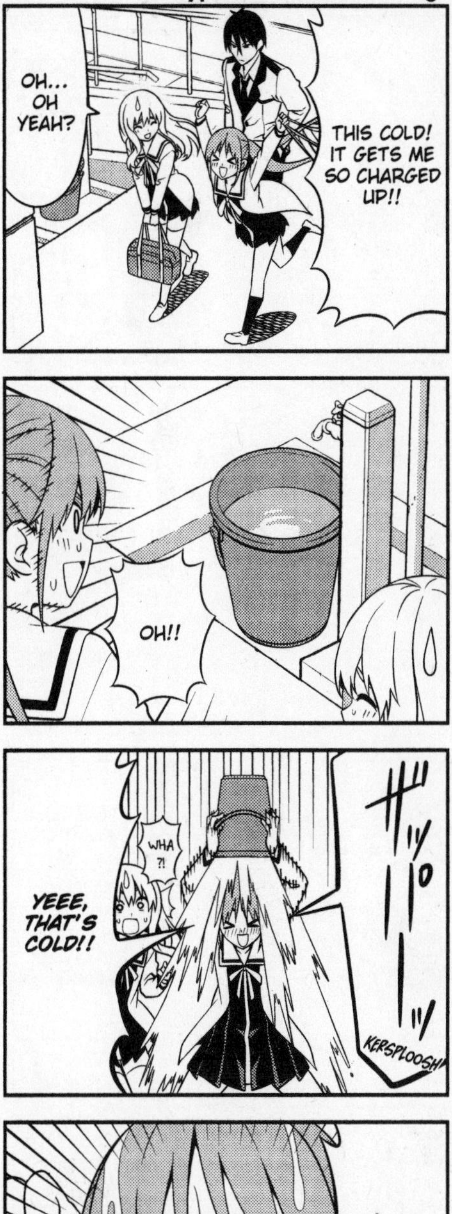
THIS COLD! IT GETS ME SO CHARGED UP!!
OH... OH YEAH?
OH!!
WHA ?!
YEEE, THAT'S COLD!!
KERSPLOOSH
GIVE ME AN-OTHER ONE!!

I Refuse to Engage in a Competition

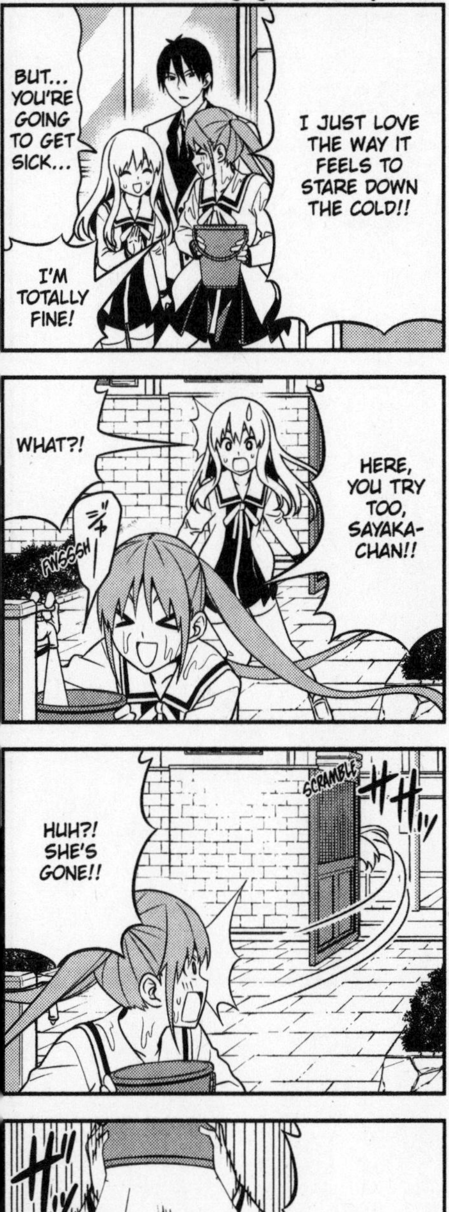
I JUST LOVE THE WAY IT FEELS TO STARE DOWN THE COLD!!
BUT... YOU'RE GOING TO GET SICK...
I'M TOTALLY FINE!
HERE, YOU TRY TOO, SAYAKA-CHAN!!
WHAT?!
FWSSSH
SCRAMBLE
HUH?! SHE'S GONE!!
THEN I GET TO DO IT AGAAAAIN!!
KERSPLOOOSH

## Well, That Figures

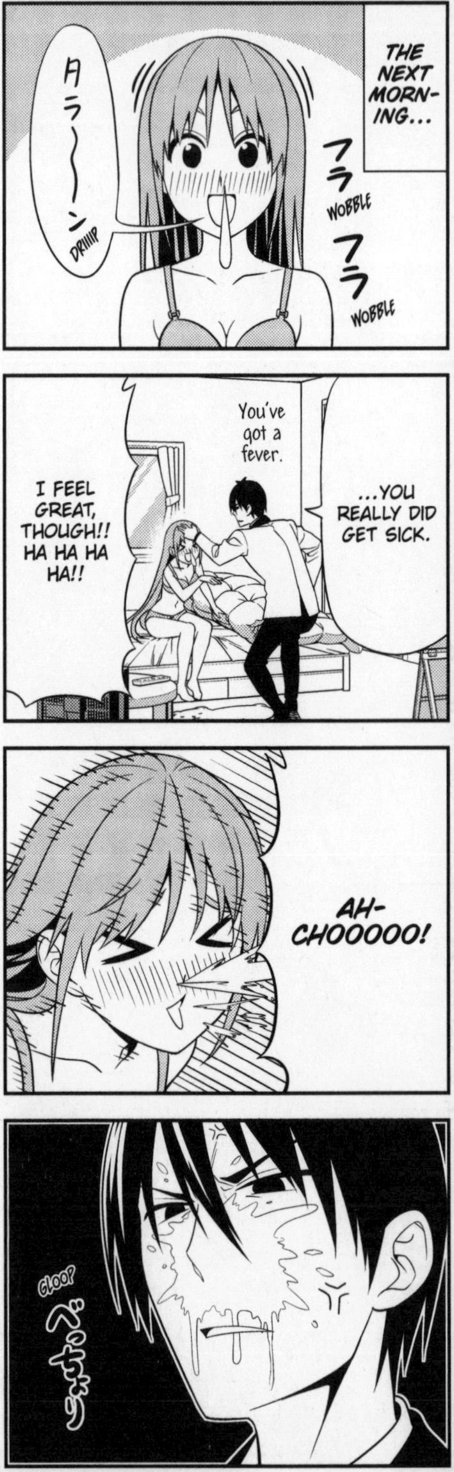
THE NEXT MORNING...
フラ
WOBBLE
フラ
WOBBLE
DRIIIP
...YOU REALLY DID GET SICK.
You've got a fever.
I FEEL GREAT, THOUGH!! HA HA HA HA!!
AH-CHOOOOO!
CLOOP
べっちょり

## She Believes the Superstition

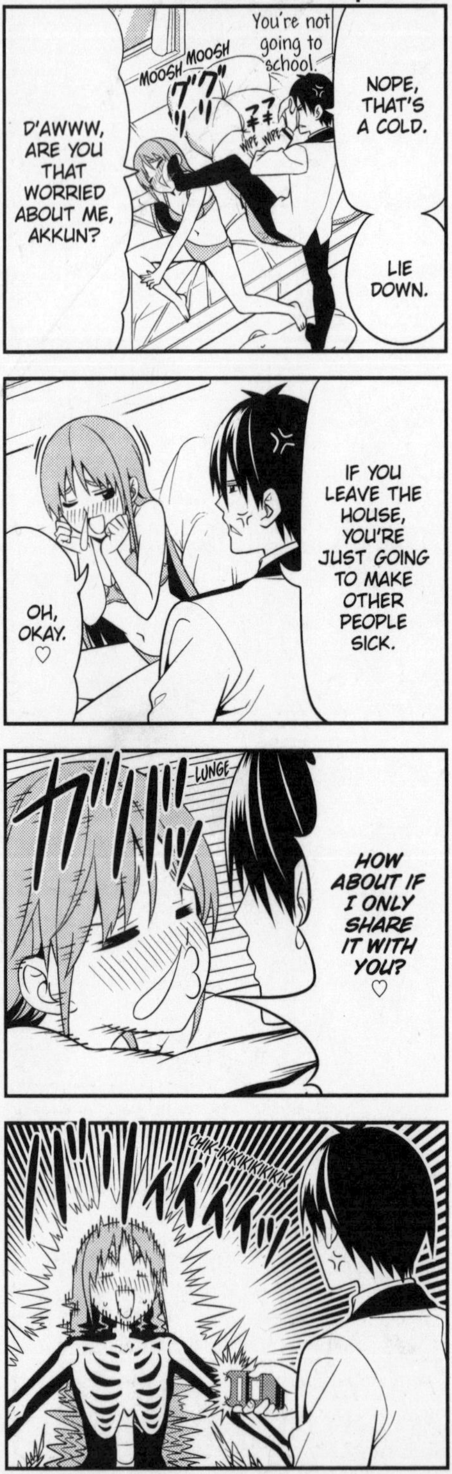
NOPE, THAT'S A COLD.
You're not going to school.
MOOSH MOOSH
WIPE WIPE
LIE DOWN.
D'AWWW, ARE YOU THAT WORRIED ABOUT ME, AKKUN?
IF YOU LEAVE THE HOUSE, YOU'RE JUST GOING TO MAKE OTHER PEOPLE SICK.
OH, OKAY. ♡
LUNGE
HOW ABOUT IF I ONLY SHARE IT WITH YOU? ♡
CHIK-IKIKIKIKIKIK

Warm Me in Your Embrace

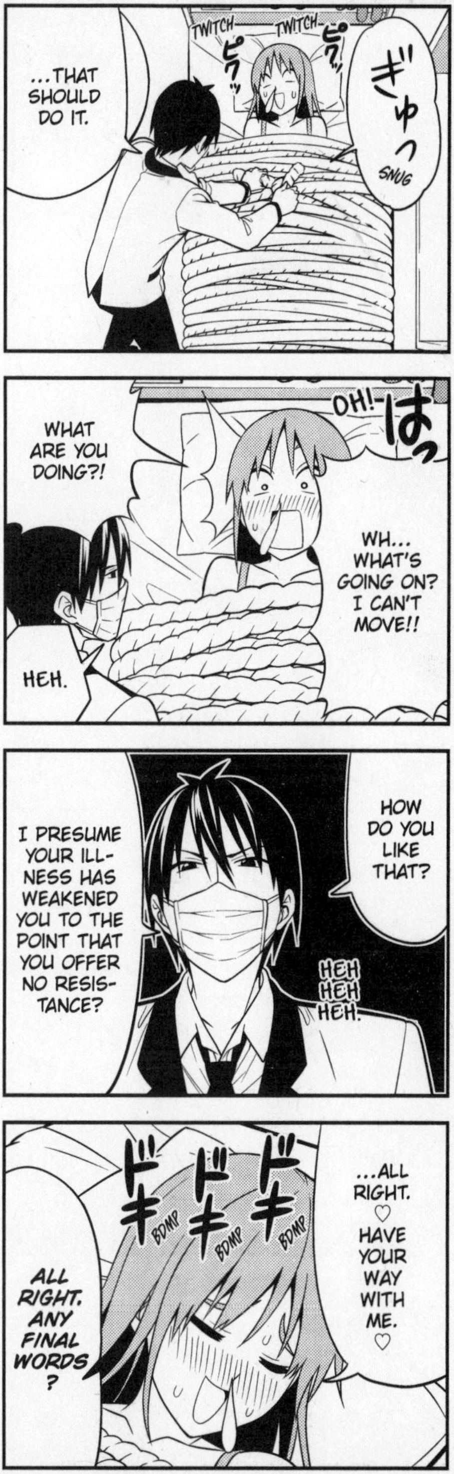
ぎゅっ
SNUG
TWITCH ピク
TWITCH ピクッ
...THAT SHOULD DO IT.
はっ
OH!
WH... WHAT'S GOING ON? I CAN'T MOVE!!
WHAT ARE YOU DOING?!
HEH.
HOW DO YOU LIKE THAT?
I PRESUME YOUR ILLNESS HAS WEAKENED YOU TO THE POINT THAT YOU OFFER NO RESISTANCE?
HEH HEH HEH.
...ALL RIGHT. ♡ HAVE YOUR WAY WITH ME. ♡
ドキ ドキ ドキ
BDMP BDMP BDMP
ALL RIGHT. ANY FINAL WORDS?

Mandatory Treatment

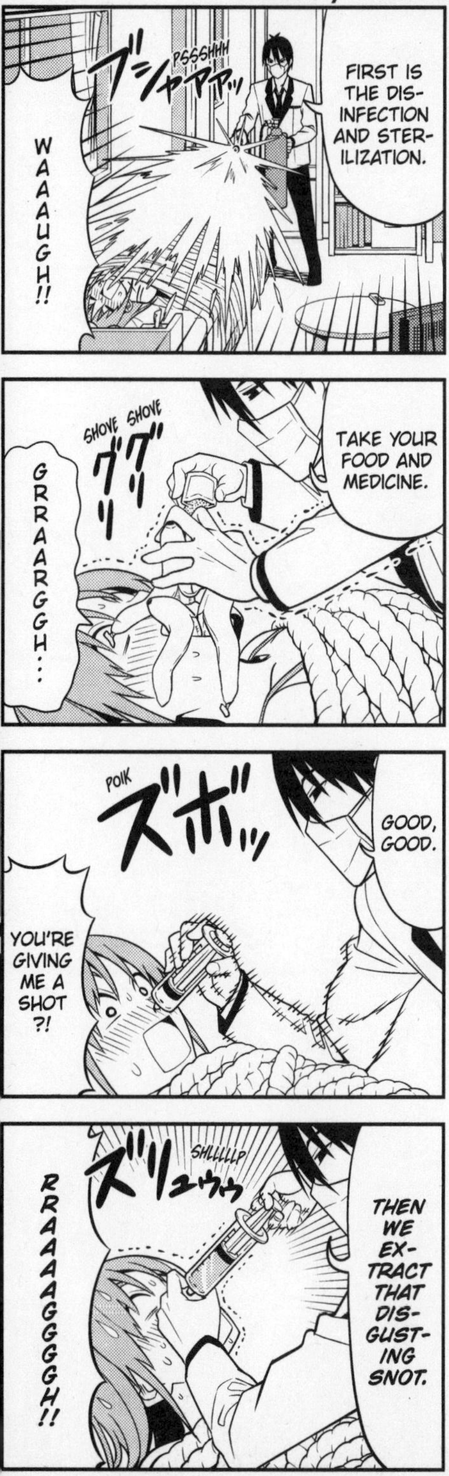
FIRST IS THE DISINFECTION AND STERILIZATION.
ブシャアアッ
PSSSHHH
WAAAAUGH!!
TAKE YOUR FOOD AND MEDICINE.
ググッ
SHOVE SHOVE
GRRAARGGH...
GOOD, GOOD.
ズボッ
POIK
YOU'RE GIVING ME A SHOT?!
THEN WE EXTRACT THAT DISGUSTING SNOT.
ズリュウウ
SHLLLLLP
RRAAAAAGGGGH!!

Only Effective in Weakened States

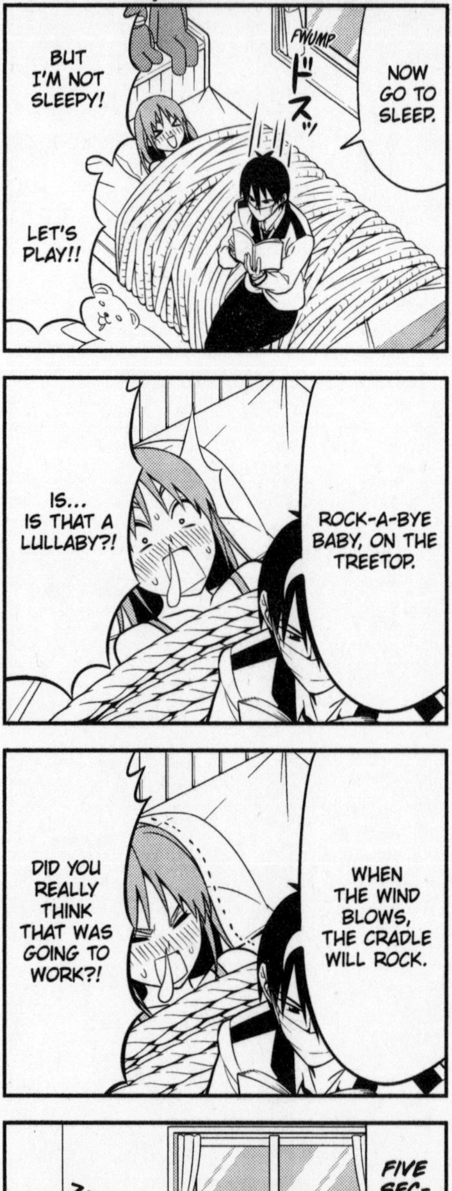
NOW GO TO SLEEP.
FWUMP
ドスッ
BUT I'M NOT SLEEPY!
LET'S PLAY!!
ROCK-A-BYE BABY, ON THE TREETOP.
IS... IS THAT A LULLABY?!
WHEN THE WIND BLOWS, THE CRADLE WILL ROCK.
DID YOU REALLY THINK THAT WAS GOING TO WORK?!
FIVE SECONDS LATER
ZZZZZ

REALLY Effective

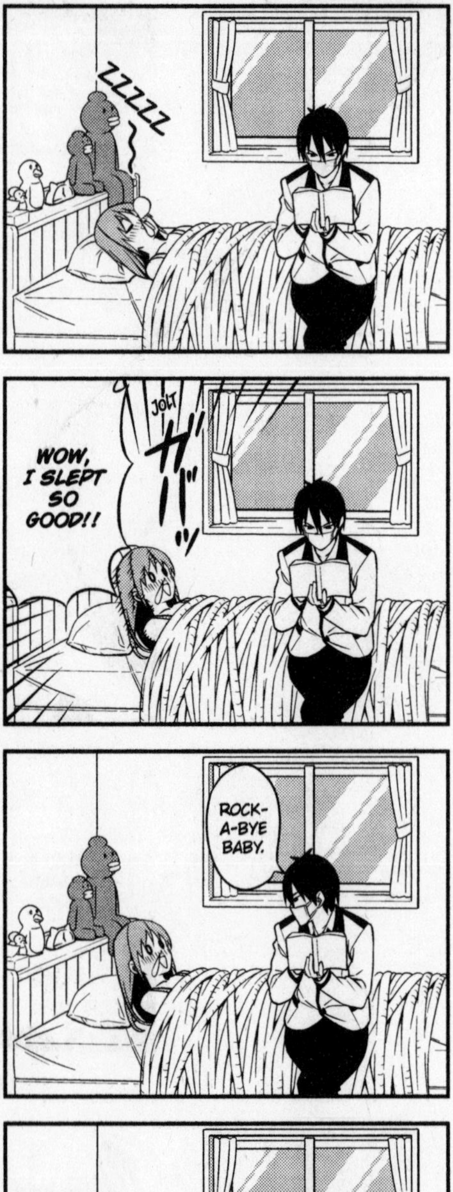
ZZZZZZ
JOLT
WOW, I SLEPT SO GOOD!!
ROCK-A-BYE BABY.
ZZZZZ

How Akkun Amuses Himself in His Spare Time

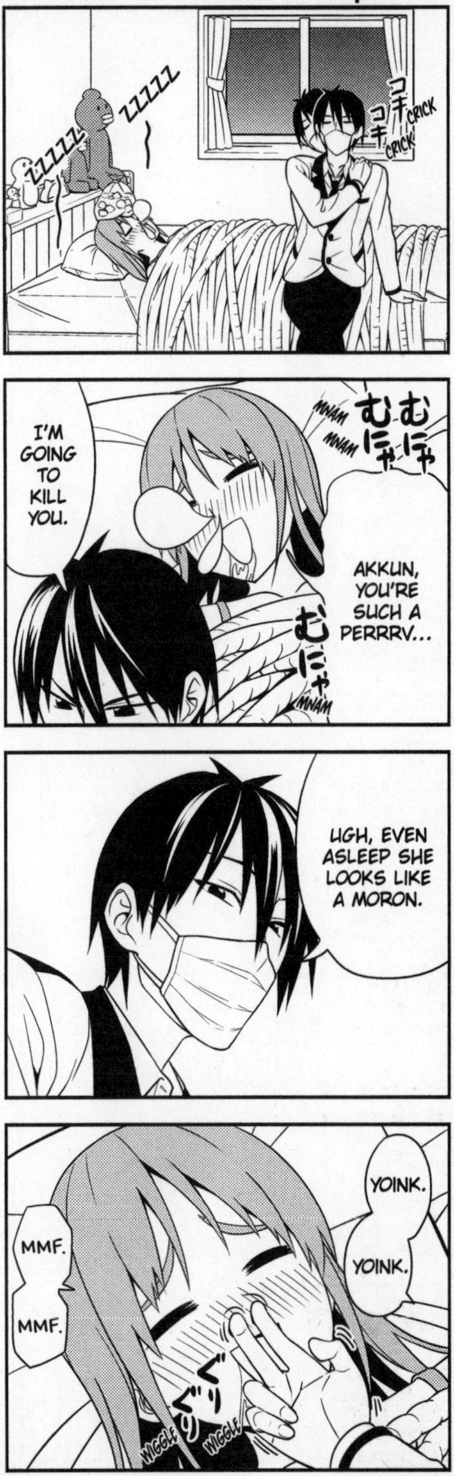
ZZZZZ~
ZZZZZ
コキ コキ
CRICK CRICK
むにゃ むにゃ
MNAM MNAM
AKKUN, YOU'RE SUCH A PERRRV...
むにゃ
MNAM
I'M GOING TO KILL YOU.
UGH, EVEN ASLEEP SHE LOOKS LIKE A MORON.
YOINK.
YOINK.
MMF.
MMF.
ぐりぐり
WIGGLE WIGGLE

Sorry to Hear That...

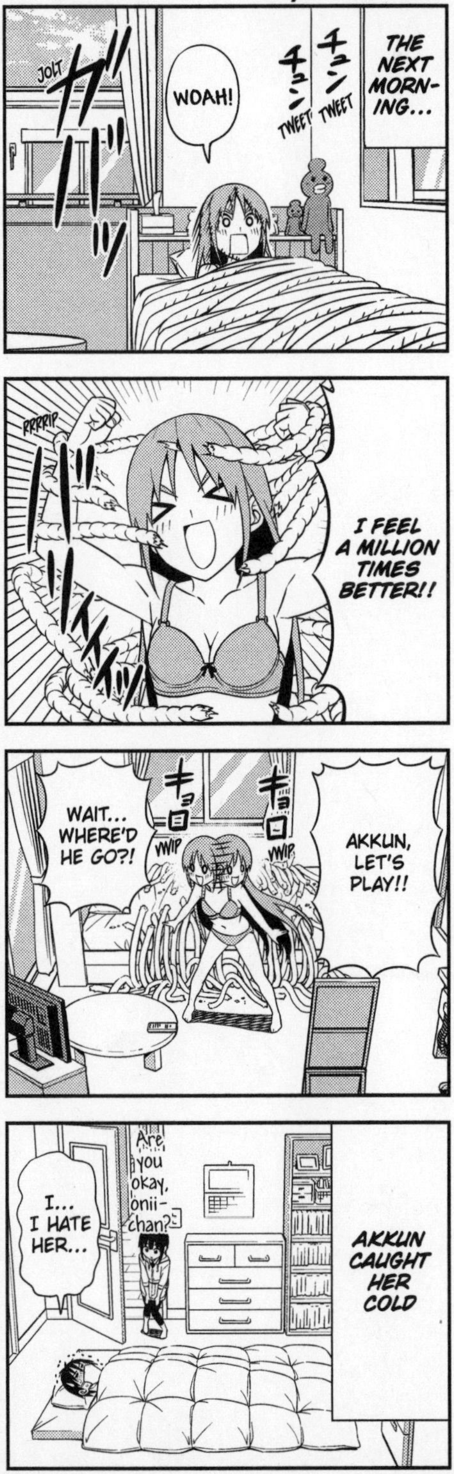
THE NEXT MORNING...
チュン チュン
TWEET TWEET
WOAH!
JOLT
I FEEL A MILLION TIMES BETTER!!
RRRRIP
AKKUN, LET'S PLAY!!
キョロ キョロ
VWIP VWIP
WAIT... WHERE'D HE GO?!
AKKUN CAUGHT HER COLD
Are you okay, onii-chan?
I... I HATE HER...

**My Only Wish**

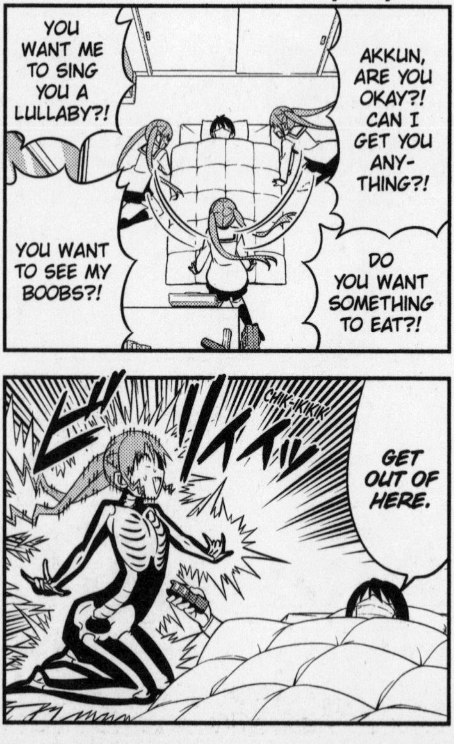
AKKUN, ARE YOU OKAY?! CAN I GET YOU ANYTHING?!
YOU WANT ME TO SING YOU A LULLABY?!
DO YOU WANT SOMETHING TO EAT?!
YOU WANT TO SEE MY BOOBS?!
CHIK-IKIKIK
GET OUT OF HERE.

(Before winter comes)

# Aho-Girl

\\'ahô͵gərl\\ *Japanese, noun.*
A clueless girl.

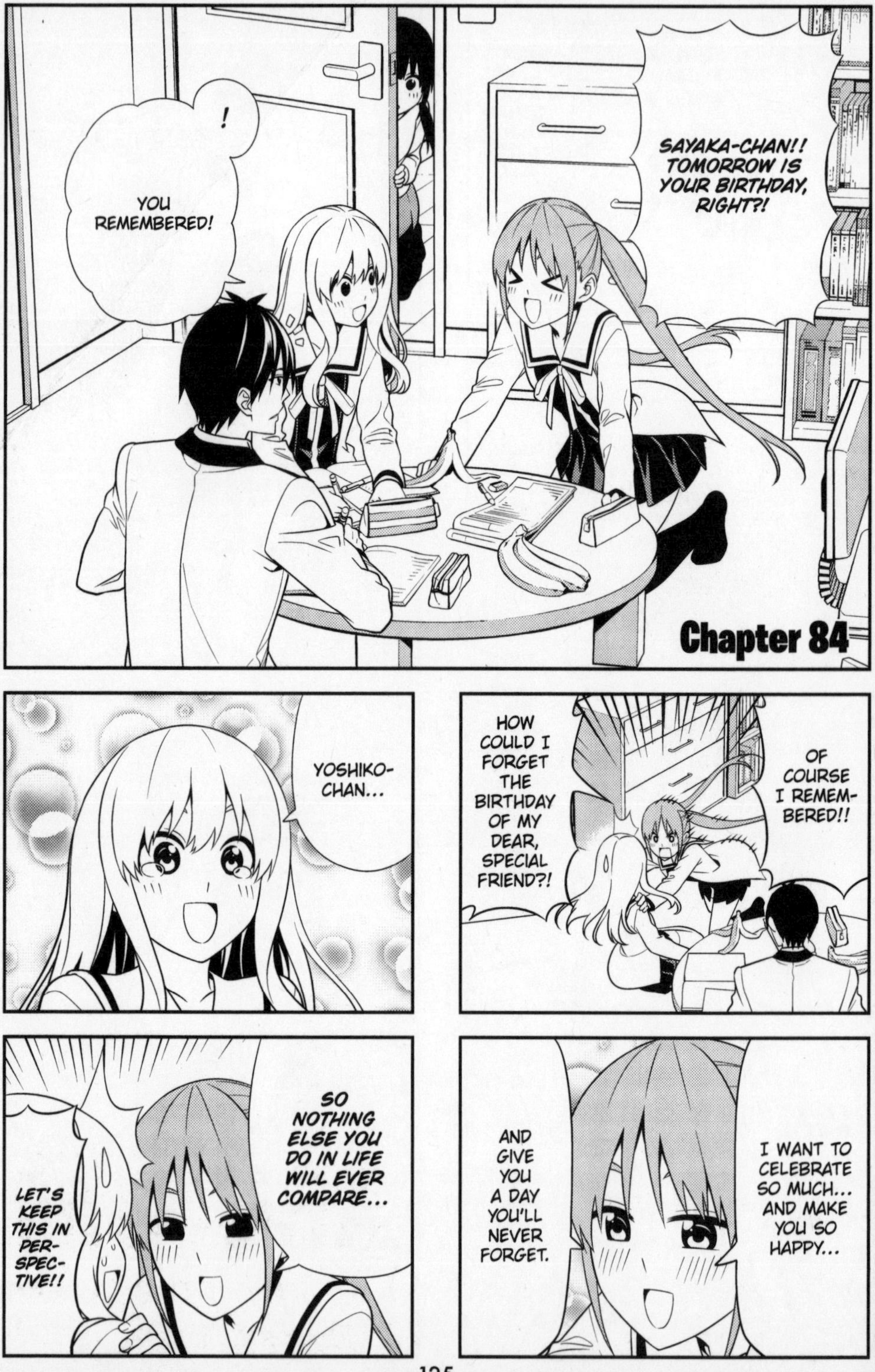
SAYAKA-CHAN!! TOMORROW IS YOUR BIRTHDAY, RIGHT?!
!
YOU REMEMBERED!
Chapter 84
OF COURSE I REMEMBERED!!
HOW COULD I FORGET THE BIRTHDAY OF MY DEAR, SPECIAL FRIEND?!
YOSHIKO-CHAN...
I WANT TO CELEBRATE SO MUCH... AND MAKE YOU SO HAPPY...
AND GIVE YOU A DAY YOU'LL NEVER FORGET.
SO NOTHING ELSE YOU DO IN LIFE WILL EVER COMPARE...
LET'S KEEP THIS IN PERSPECTIVE!!

## Earn the Approval

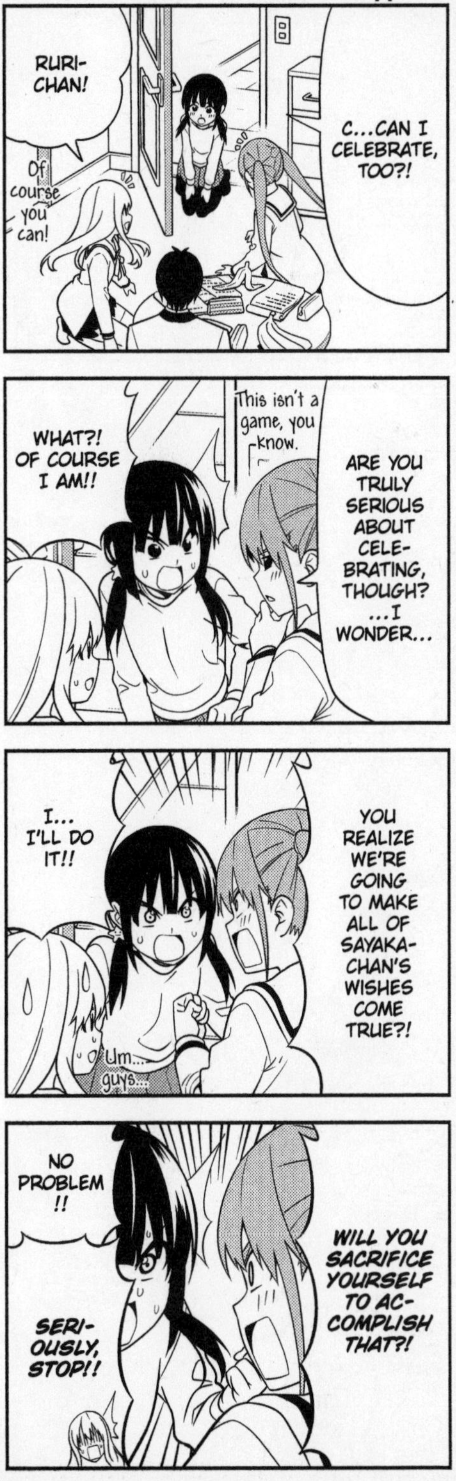

C...CAN I CELEBRATE, TOO?!
RURI-CHAN!
Of course you can!
ARE YOU TRULY SERIOUS ABOUT CELEBRATING, THOUGH? ...I WONDER...
This isn't a game, you know.
WHAT?! OF COURSE I AM!!
YOU REALIZE WE'RE GOING TO MAKE ALL OF SAYAKA-CHAN'S WISHES COME TRUE?!
I... I'LL DO IT!!
Um... guys...
WILL YOU SACRIFICE YOURSELF TO ACCOMPLISH THAT?!
NO PROBLEM!!
SERIOUSLY, STOP!!


## I Never Doubted You, Brother!

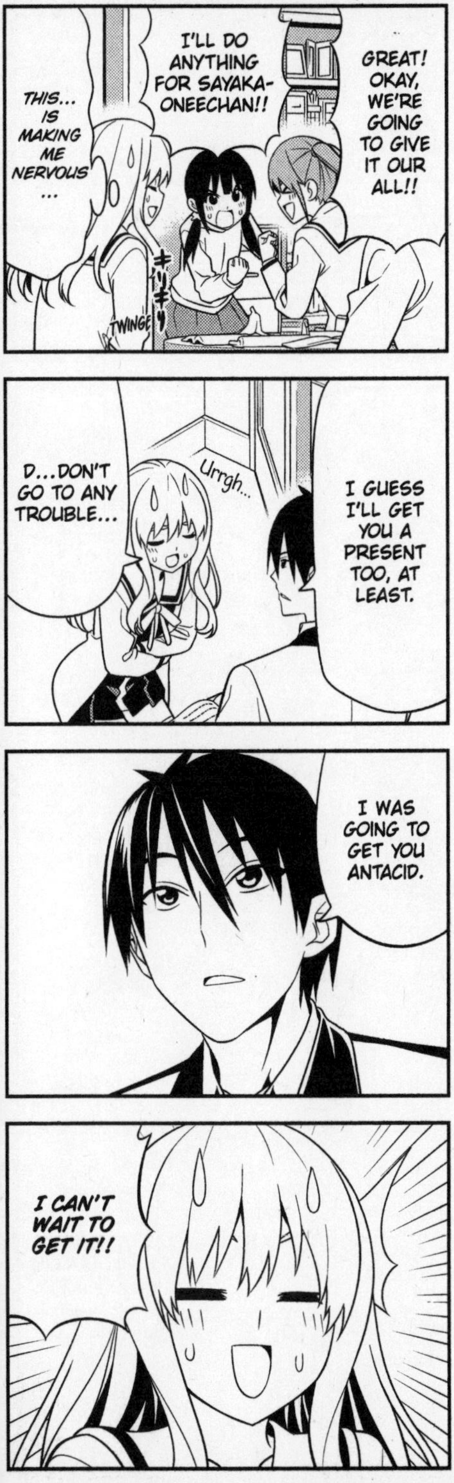

GREAT! OKAY, WE'RE GOING TO GIVE IT OUR ALL!!
I'LL DO ANYTHING FOR SAYAKA-ONEECHAN!!
THIS... IS MAKING ME NERVOUS...
キリキリ
TWINGE
I GUESS I'LL GET YOU A PRESENT TOO, AT LEAST.
Urrgh...
D...DON'T GO TO ANY TROUBLE...
I WAS GOING TO GET YOU ANTACID.
I CAN'T WAIT TO GET IT!!

On an Overwhelming Scale

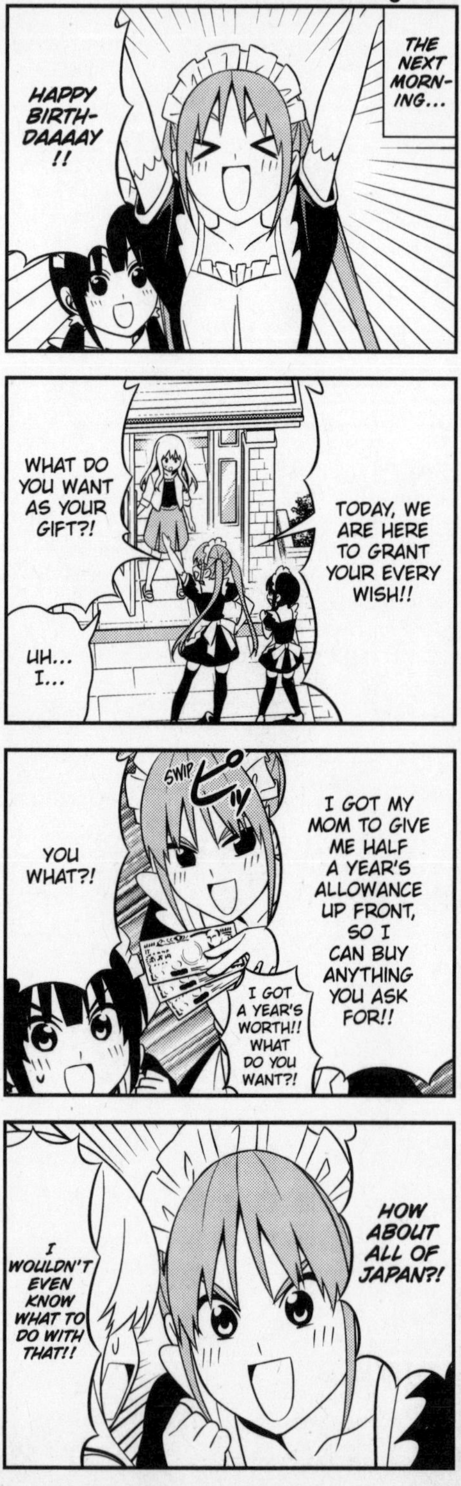
THE NEXT MORNING...
HAPPY BIRTHDAAAAY!!
TODAY, WE ARE HERE TO GRANT YOUR EVERY WISH!!
WHAT DO YOU WANT AS YOUR GIFT?!
UH... I...
SWIP
I GOT MY MOM TO GIVE ME HALF A YEAR'S ALLOWANCE UP FRONT, SO I CAN BUY ANYTHING YOU ASK FOR!!
YOU WHAT?!
I GOT A YEAR'S WORTH!! WHAT DO YOU WANT?!
HOW ABOUT ALL OF JAPAN?!
I WOULDN'T EVEN KNOW WHAT TO DO WITH THAT!!

One of Us Is Serious About This

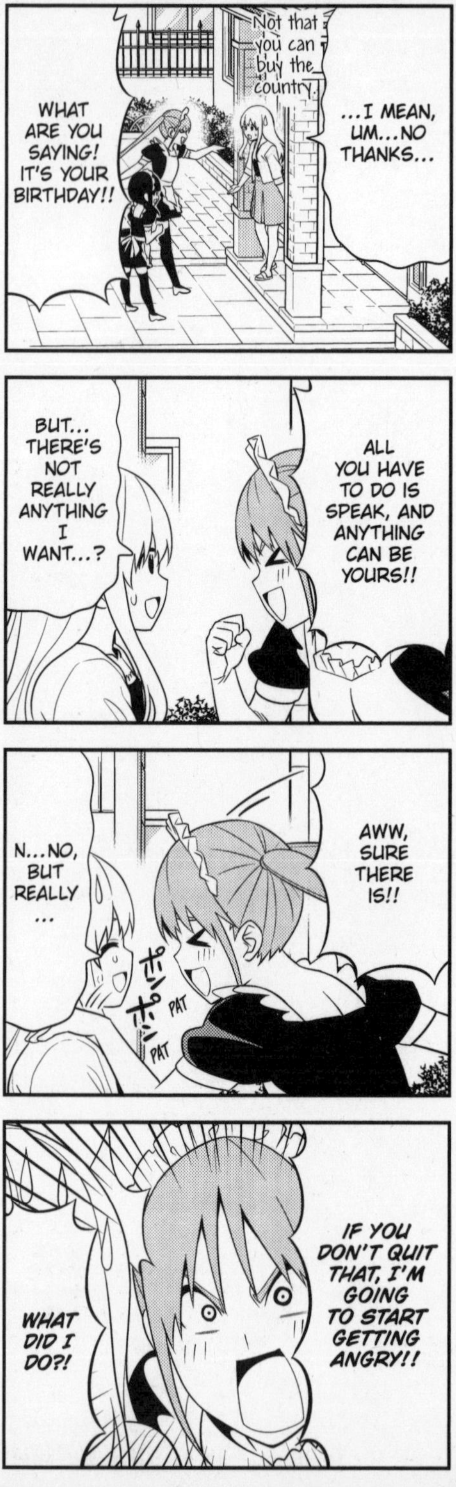
...I MEAN, UM...NO THANKS...
Not that you can buy the country.
WHAT ARE YOU SAYING! IT'S YOUR BIRTHDAY!!
ALL YOU HAVE TO DO IS SPEAK, AND ANYTHING CAN BE YOURS!!
BUT... THERE'S NOT REALLY ANYTHING I WANT...?
AWW, SURE THERE IS!!
PAT PAT
N...NO, BUT REALLY...
IF YOU DON'T QUIT THAT, I'M GOING TO START GETTING ANGRY!!
WHAT DID I DO?!

Little Late to Bring That Up

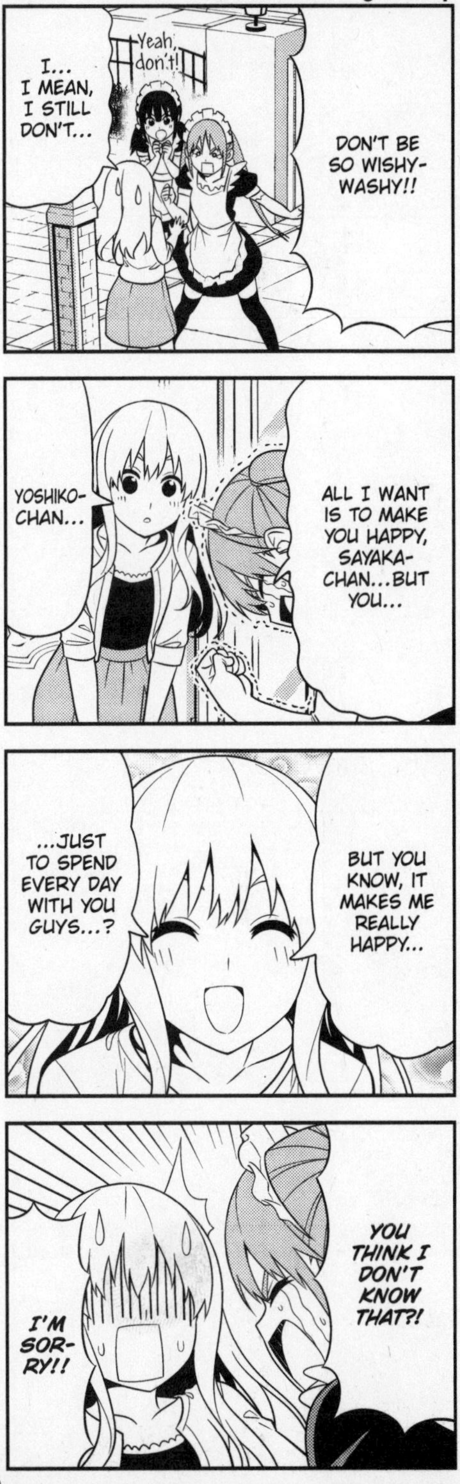
DON'T BE SO WISHY-WASHY!!
Yeah, don't!
I... I MEAN, I STILL DON'T...
ALL I WANT IS TO MAKE YOU HAPPY, SAYAKA-CHAN...BUT YOU...
YOSHIKO-CHAN...
BUT YOU KNOW, IT MAKES ME REALLY HAPPY...
...JUST TO SPEND EVERY DAY WITH YOU GUYS...?
YOU THINK I DON'T KNOW THAT?!
I'M SORRY!!

No Points

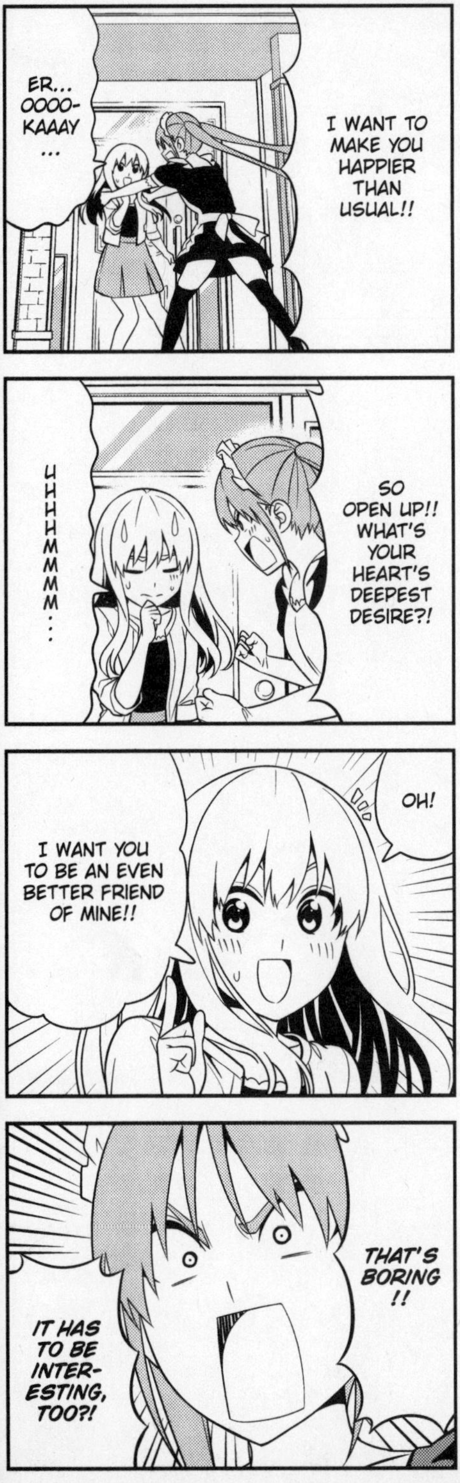
I WANT TO MAKE YOU HAPPIER THAN USUAL!!
ER... OOOO-KAAAY...
SO OPEN UP!! WHAT'S YOUR HEART'S DEEPEST DESIRE?!
UHHHHMMMM...
OH!
I WANT YOU TO BE AN EVEN BETTER FRIEND OF MINE!!
THAT'S BORING!!
IT HAS TO BE INTER-ESTING, TOO?!

Score!!

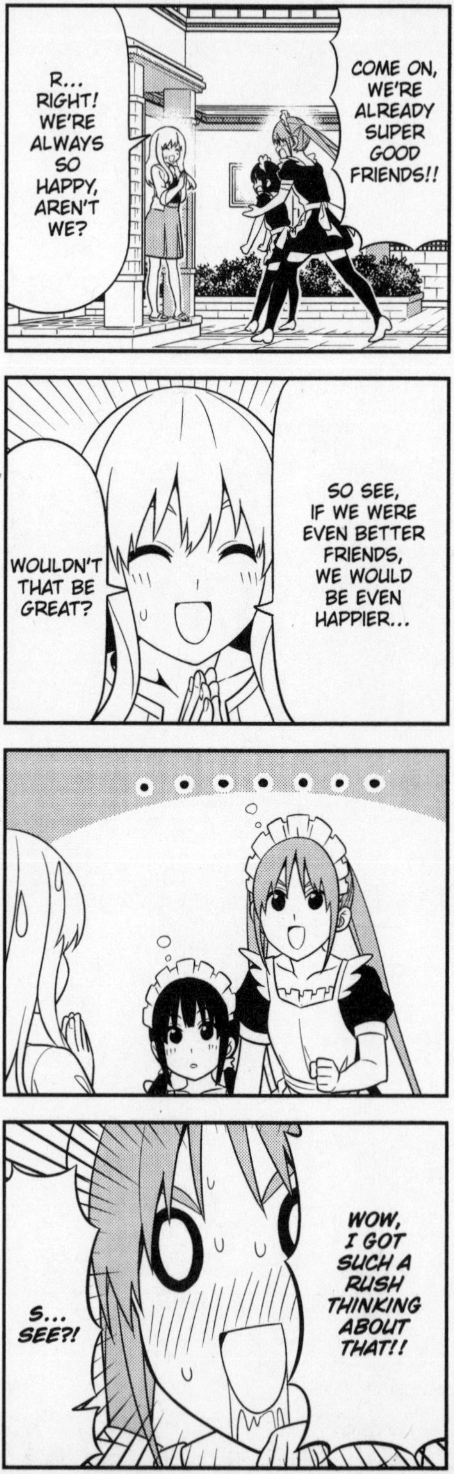
COME ON, WE'RE ALREADY SUPER GOOD FRIENDS!!
R... RIGHT! WE'RE ALWAYS SO HAPPY, AREN'T WE?
SO SEE, IF WE WERE EVEN BETTER FRIENDS, WE WOULD BE EVEN HAPPIER...
WOULDN'T THAT BE GREAT?
• • • • • • •
WOW, I GOT SUCH A RUSH THINKING ABOUT THAT!!
S... SEE?!

Mom Does This for Dad

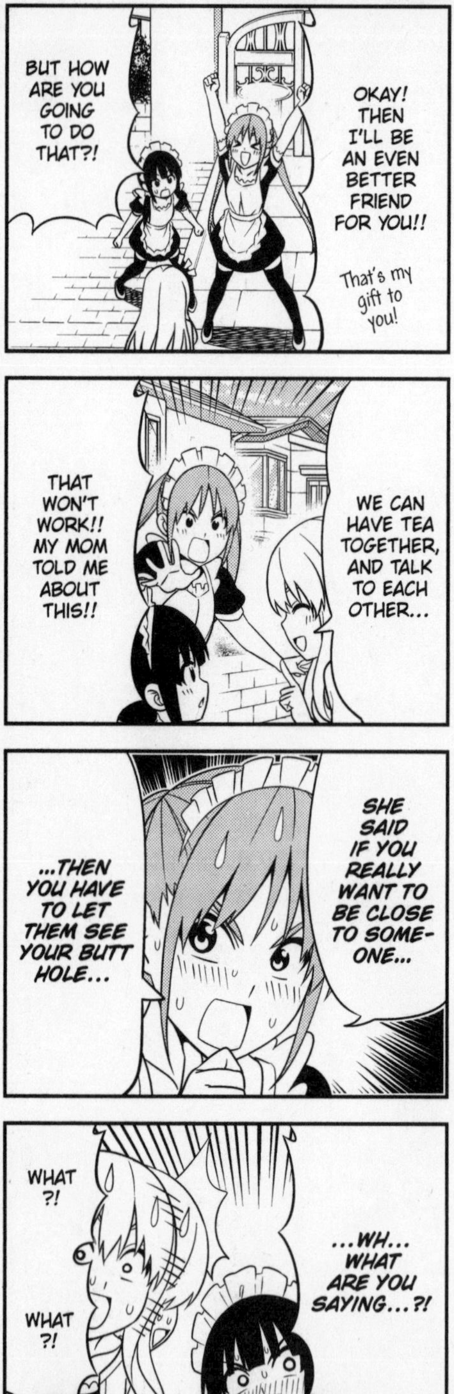
OKAY! THEN I'LL BE AN EVEN BETTER FRIEND FOR YOU!!
That's my gift to you!
BUT HOW ARE YOU GOING TO DO THAT?!
WE CAN HAVE TEA TOGETHER, AND TALK TO EACH OTHER...
THAT WON'T WORK!! MY MOM TOLD ME ABOUT THIS!!
SHE SAID IF YOU REALLY WANT TO BE CLOSE TO SOME-ONE...
...THEN YOU HAVE TO LET THEM SEE YOUR BUTT HOLE...
...WH... WHAT ARE YOU SAYING...?!
WHAT ?!
WHAT ?!

We're ALL Embarrassed, Okay?!

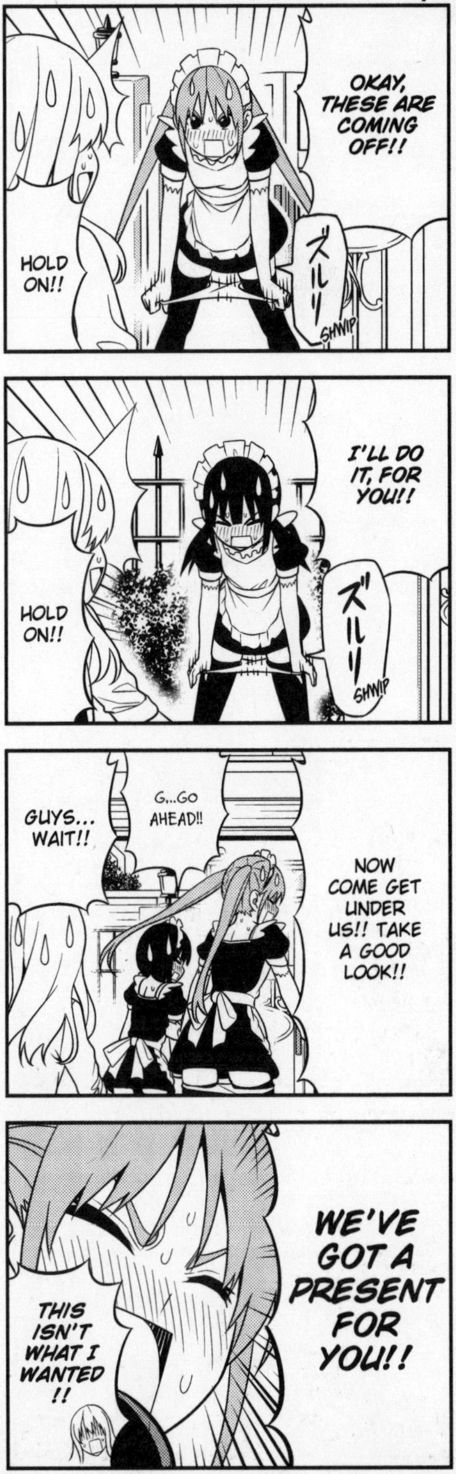
OKAY, THESE ARE COMING OFF!!
HOLD ON!!
ズルリ
SHWIP
I'LL DO IT, FOR YOU!!
HOLD ON!!
ズルリ
SHWIP
NOW COME GET UNDER US!! TAKE A GOOD LOOK!!
G...GO AHEAD!!
GUYS... WAIT!!
WE'VE GOT A PRESENT FOR YOU!!
THIS ISN'T WHAT I WANTED!!

Sayaka, Thinking on Her Feet

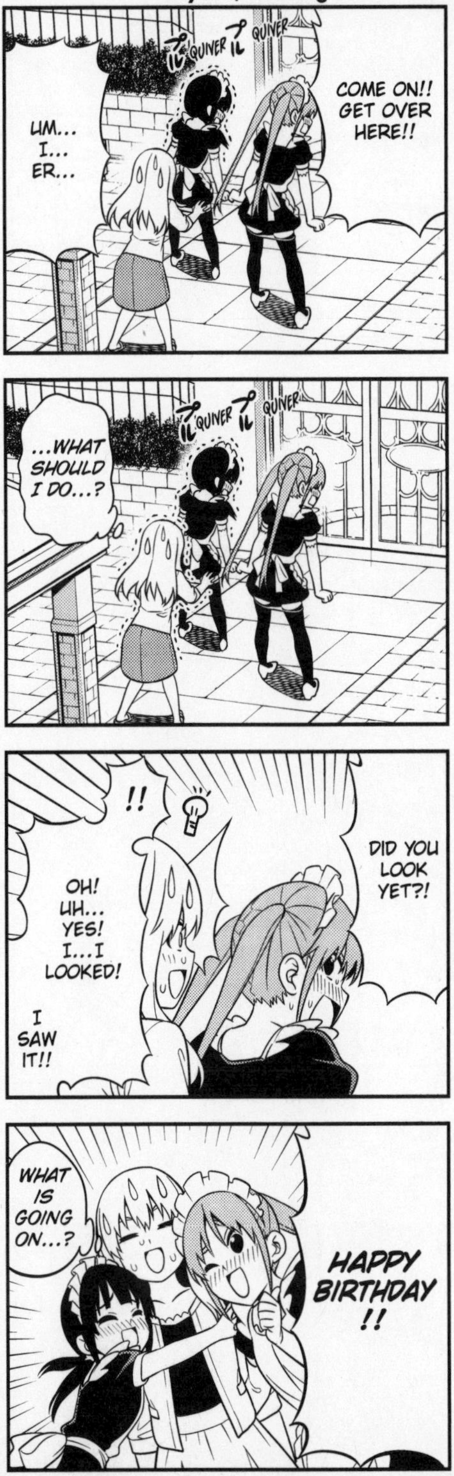
COME ON!! GET OVER HERE!!
プル QUIVER
プル QUIVER
UM... I... ER...
プル QUIVER
プル QUIVER
...WHAT SHOULD I DO...?
DID YOU LOOK YET?!
!!
OH! UH... YES! I...I LOOKED!
I SAW IT!!
HAPPY BIRTHDAY!!
WHAT IS GOING ON...?

**Good to Be Prepared**

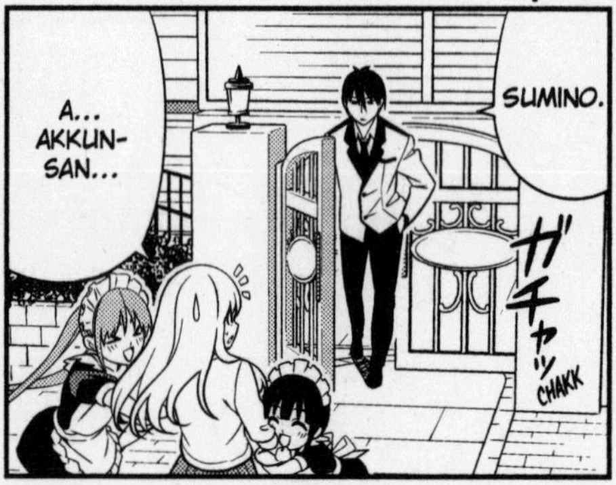
SUMINO.
ガチャッ
CHAKK
A... AKKUN-SAN...

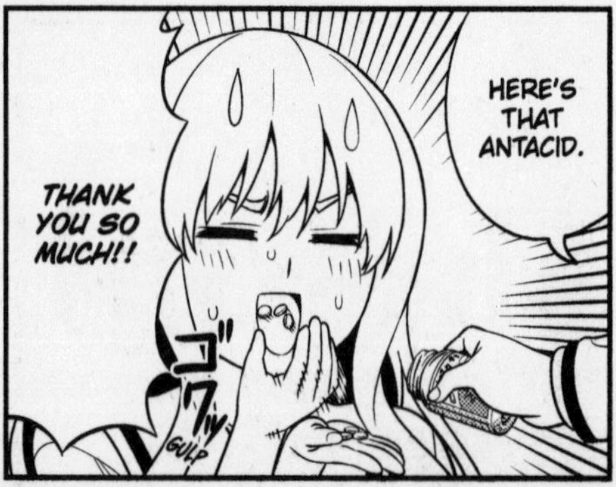
HERE'S THAT ANTACID.
THANK YOU SO MUCH!!
ゴクッ
GULP

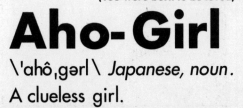

(You were born to be loved)

# Aho-Girl

\ˈahô͵gərl \ *Japanese, noun.*
A clueless girl.

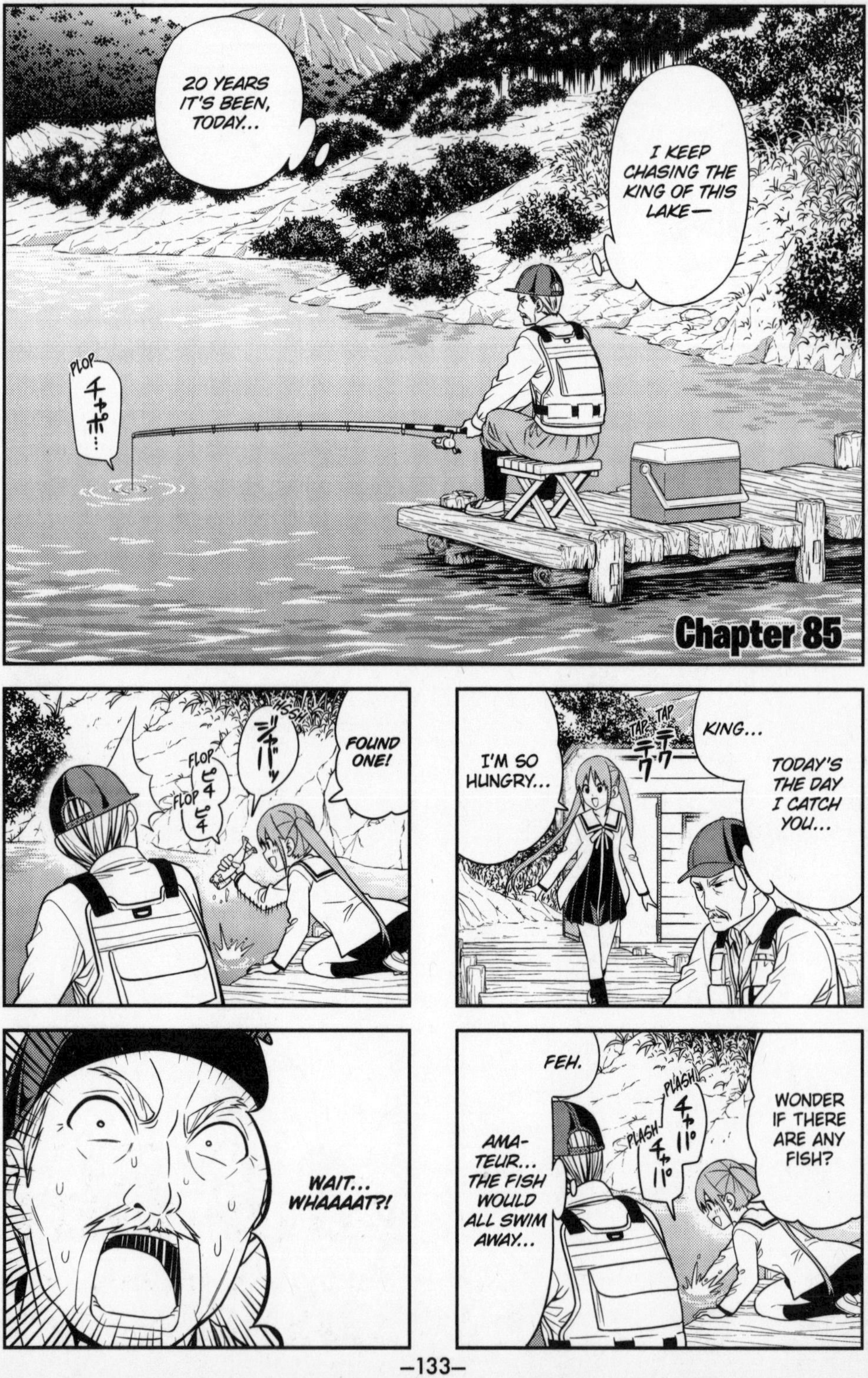
I KEEP CHASING THE KING OF THIS LAKE—
20 YEARS IT'S BEEN, TODAY...
PLOP チャポ…
Chapter 85
KING... TODAY'S THE DAY I CATCH YOU...
TAP TAP テクテク
I'M SO HUNGRY...
FOUND ONE!
HSSH ジャバッ
FLOP ピチ FLOP ピチ
WONDER IF THERE ARE ANY FISH?
PLASH チャパ PLASH チャパ
FEH.
AMATEUR... THE FISH WOULD ALL SWIM AWAY...
WAIT... WHAAAAT?!

## Could it Be

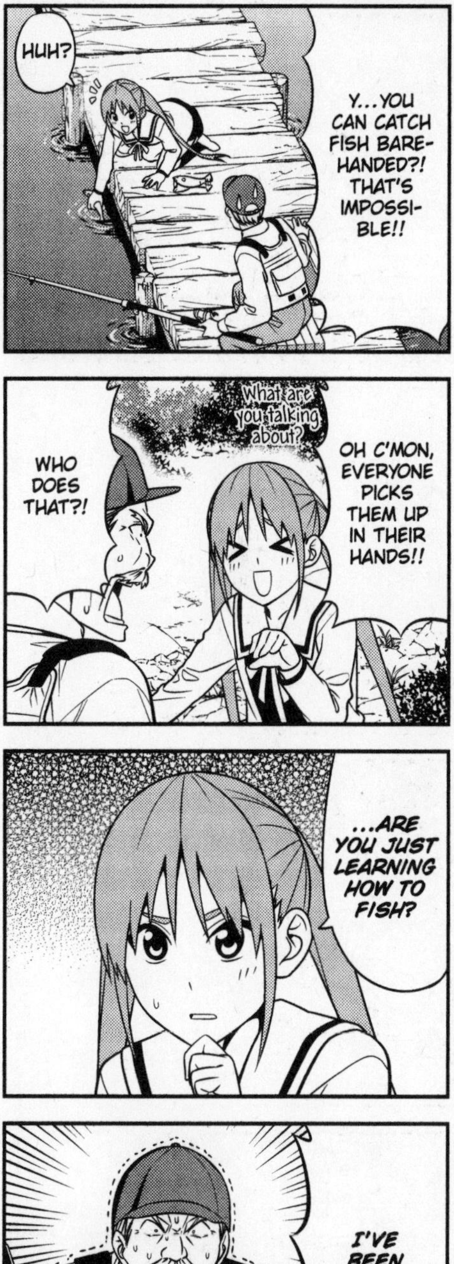
Y...YOU CAN CATCH FISH BARE-HANDED?! THAT'S IMPOSSIBLE!!
HUH?
OH C'MON, EVERYONE PICKS THEM UP IN THEIR HANDS!!
What are you talking about?
WHO DOES THAT?!
...ARE YOU JUST LEARNING HOW TO FISH?
I'VE BEEN DOING THIS FOR 20 YEARS!!

## That's Not the Point

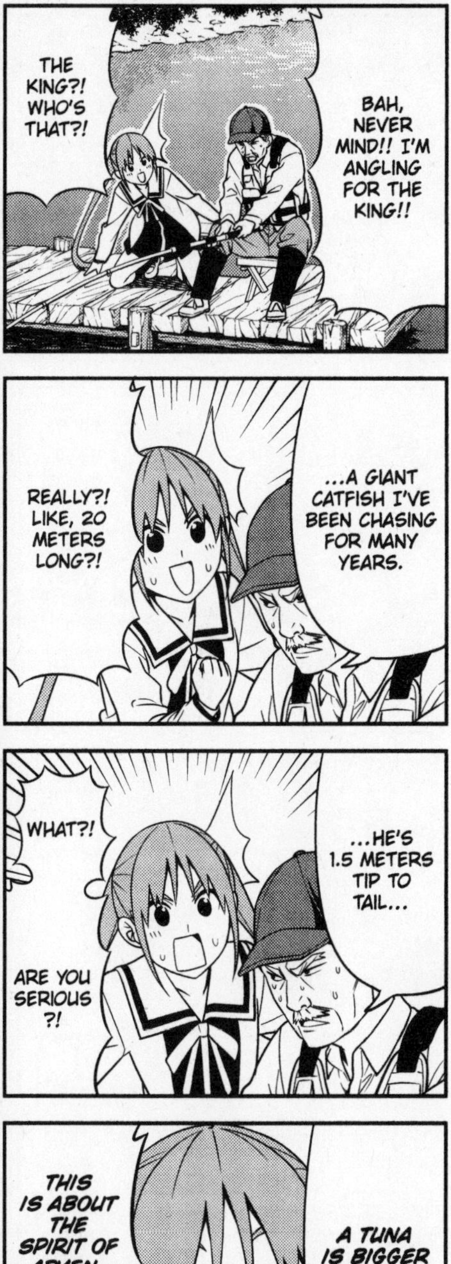
BAH, NEVER MIND!! I'M ANGLING FOR THE KING!!
THE KING?! WHO'S THAT?!
...A GIANT CATFISH I'VE BEEN CHASING FOR MANY YEARS.
REALLY?! LIKE, 20 METERS LONG?!
...HE'S 1.5 METERS TIP TO TAIL...
WHAT?!
ARE YOU SERIOUS?!
A TUNA IS BIGGER THAN THAT, THOUGH.
THIS IS ABOUT THE SPIRIT OF ADVENTURE, ALL RIGHT?!

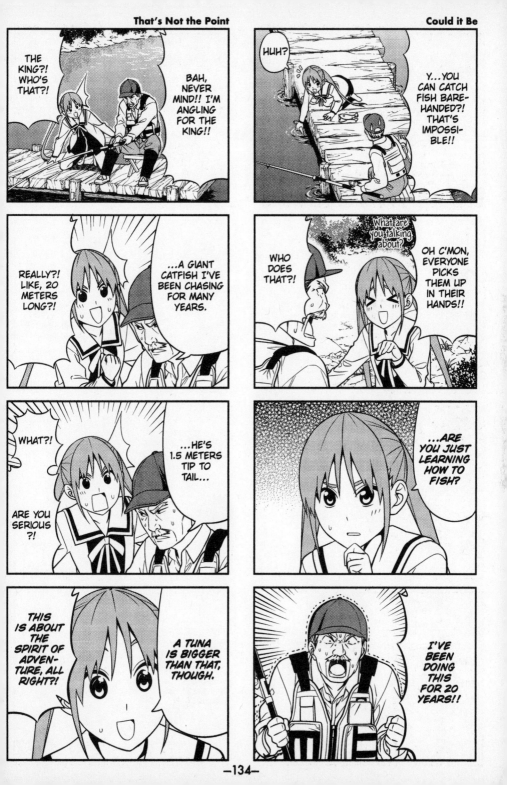

## Hello There, King-san

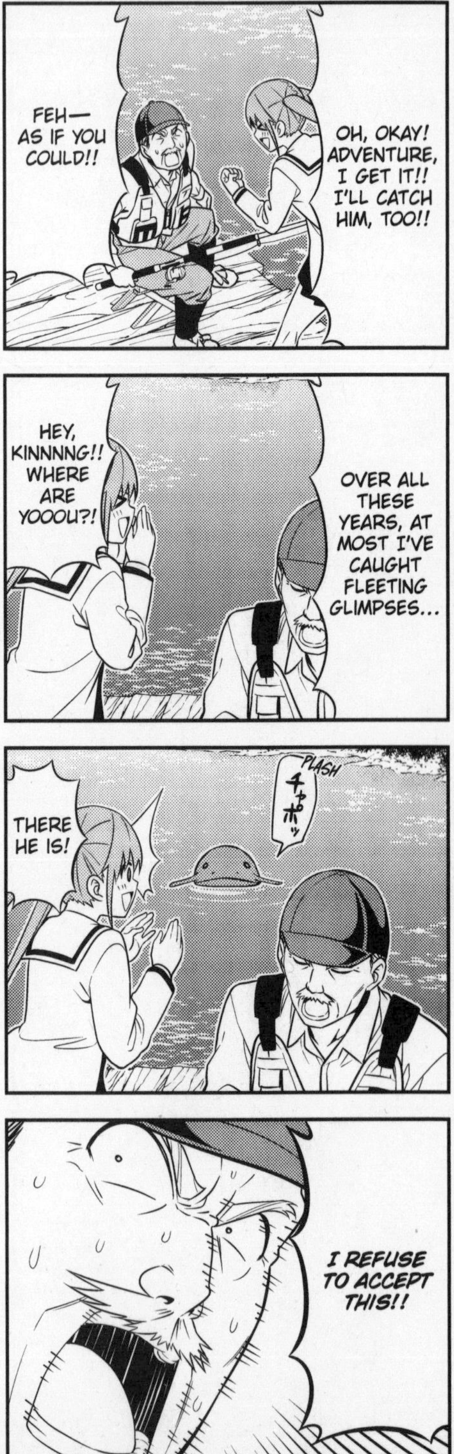

OH, OKAY! ADVENTURE, I GET IT!! I'LL CATCH HIM, TOO!!
FEH— AS IF YOU COULD!!
OVER ALL THESE YEARS, AT MOST I'VE CAUGHT FLEETING GLIMPSES...
HEY, KINNNNG!! WHERE ARE YOOOU?!
チャポッ
PLASH
THERE HE IS!
I REFUSE TO ACCEPT THIS!!


## This Is How You Use a Fishing Pole

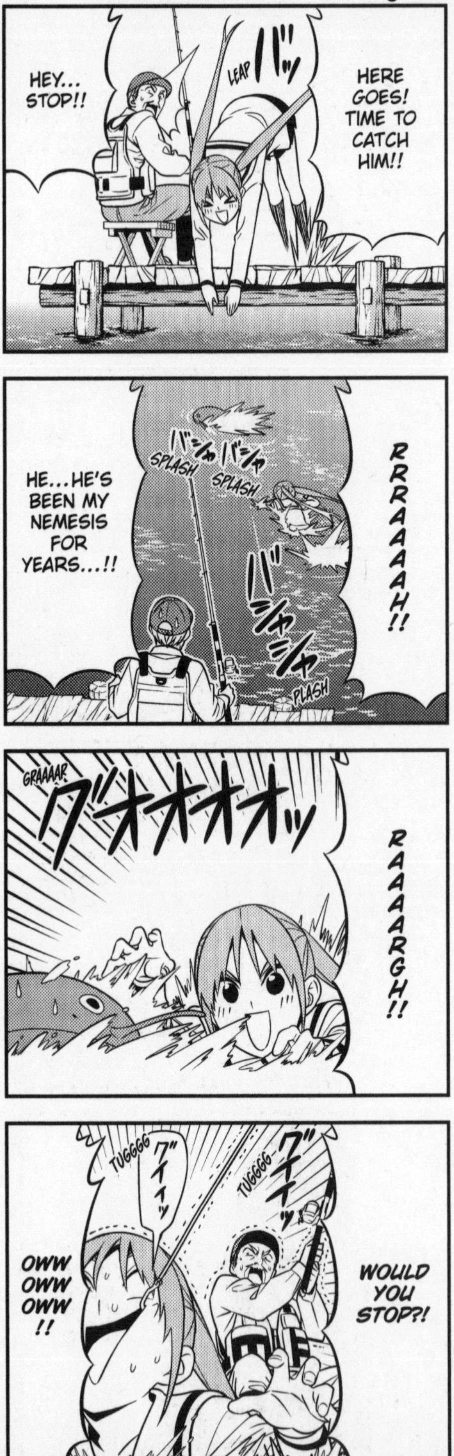

バッ
LEAP
HERE GOES! TIME TO CATCH HIM!!
HEY... STOP!!
RRRAAAAAH!!
バシャバシャ
SPLASH SPLASH
バシャシャ
PLASH
HE...HE'S BEEN MY NEMESIS FOR YEARS...!!
RAAAAARGH!!
グオオオオッ
GRAAAAR
WOULD YOU STOP?!
グイイッ
TUGGGG
グイイッ
TUGGGG
OWW OWW OWW !!

**That's Not It**

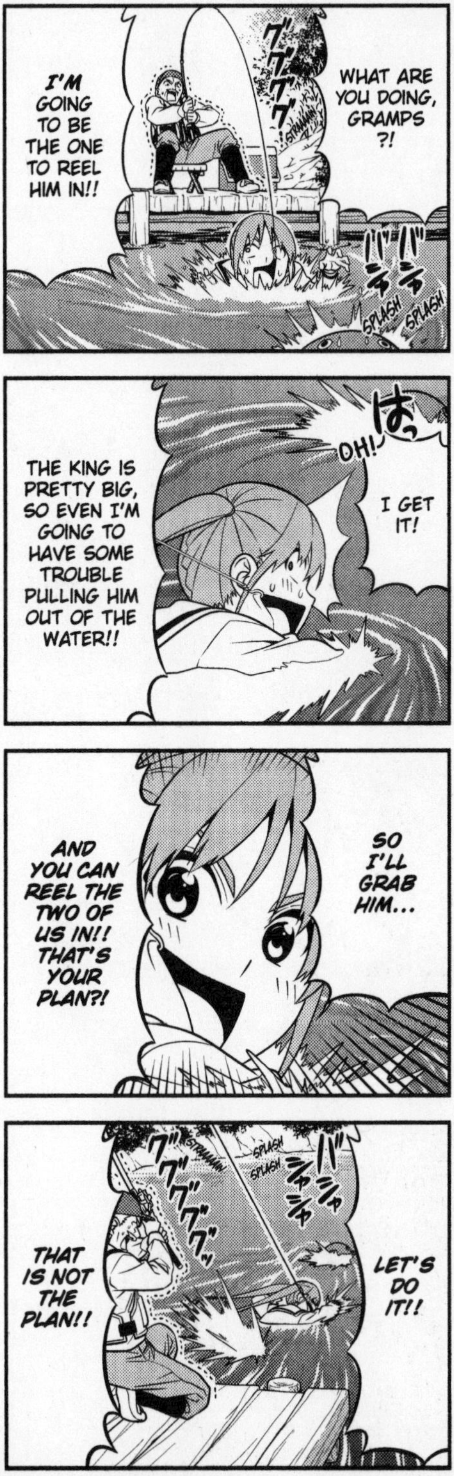
WHAT ARE YOU DOING, GRAMPS?!
STRAAAIN
I'M GOING TO BE THE ONE TO REEL HIM IN!!
SPLASH SPLASH
はっ
OH!
I GET IT!
THE KING IS PRETTY BIG, SO EVEN I'M GOING TO HAVE SOME TROUBLE PULLING HIM OUT OF THE WATER!!
SO I'LL GRAB HIM...
AND YOU CAN REEL THE TWO OF US IN!! THAT'S YOUR PLAN?!
SPLASH SPLASH
STRAAAIN
LET'S DO IT!!
THAT IS NOT THE PLAN!!

**Do You Understand the Words Coming Out of My Mouth?**

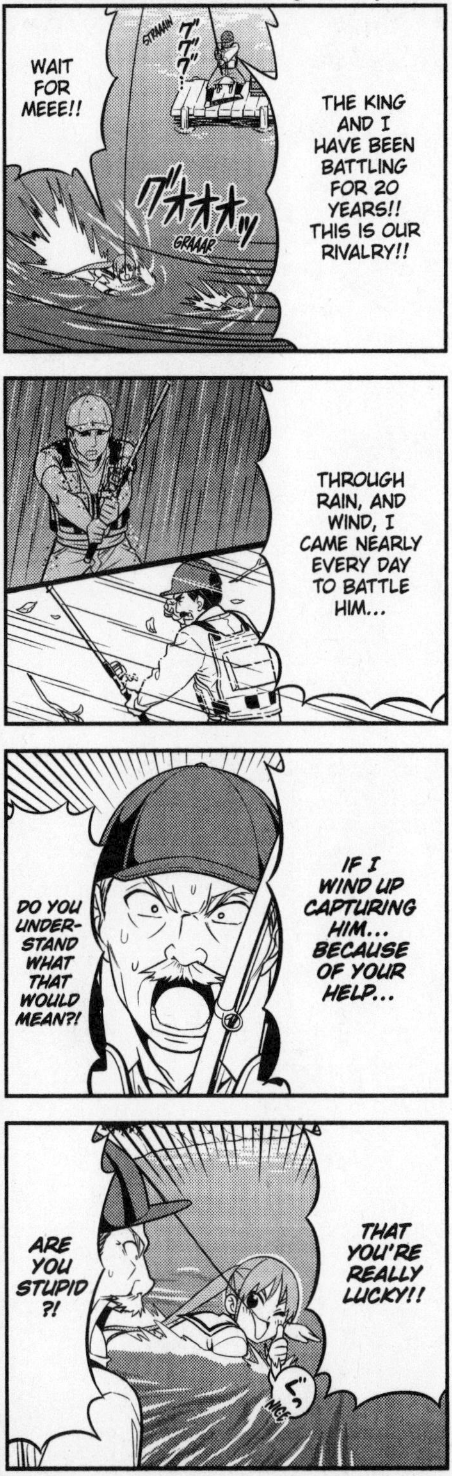
THE KING AND I HAVE BEEN BATTLING FOR 20 YEARS!! THIS IS OUR RIVALRY!!
STRAAAIN
WAIT FOR MEEE!!
GRAAAR
THROUGH RAIN, AND WIND, I CAME NEARLY EVERY DAY TO BATTLE HIM...
IF I WIND UP CAPTURING HIM... BECAUSE OF YOUR HELP...
DO YOU UNDER-STAND WHAT THAT WOULD MEAN?!
THAT YOU'RE REALLY LUCKY!!
NICE
ARE YOU STUPID?!

## Well, That Wasn't So Stupid

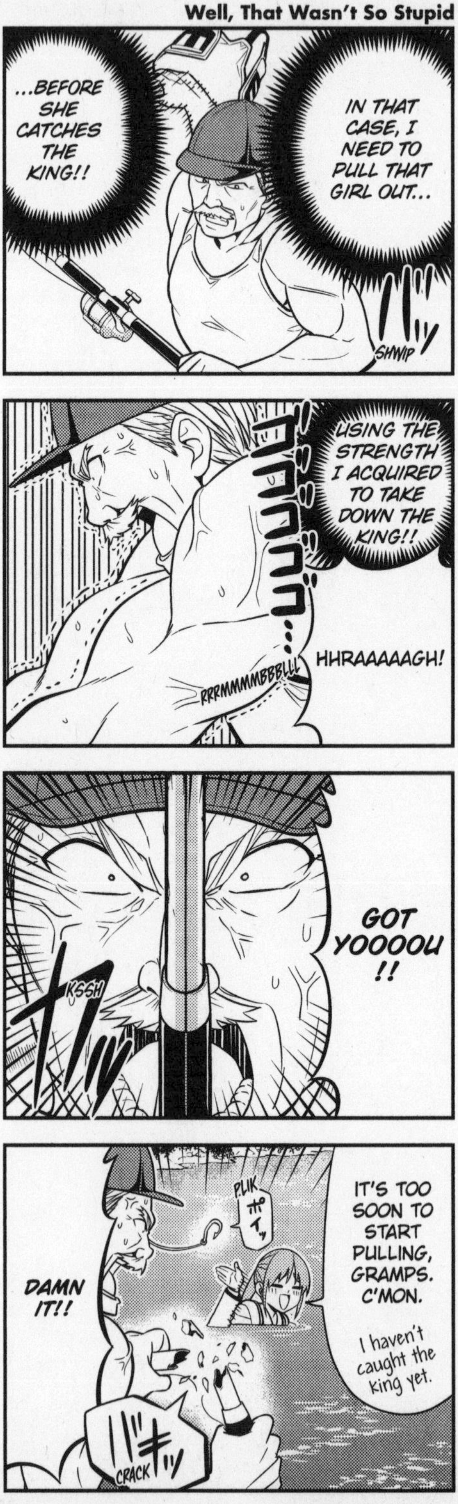
IN THAT CASE, I NEED TO PULL THAT GIRL OUT...
...BEFORE SHE CATCHES THE KING!!
バッ
SHWIP
USING THE STRENGTH I ACQUIRED TO TAKE DOWN THE KING!!
ゴゴゴゴゴ...
HHRAAAAAGH!
RRRMMMMBBBLLL
GOT YOOOOU !!
ガッ
KSSH
IT'S TOO SOON TO START PULLING, GRAMPS. C'MON.
I haven't caught the king yet.
PLIK
ポイッ
DAMN IT!!
バキッ
CRACK

## Fly, Old Man!! Fly!!

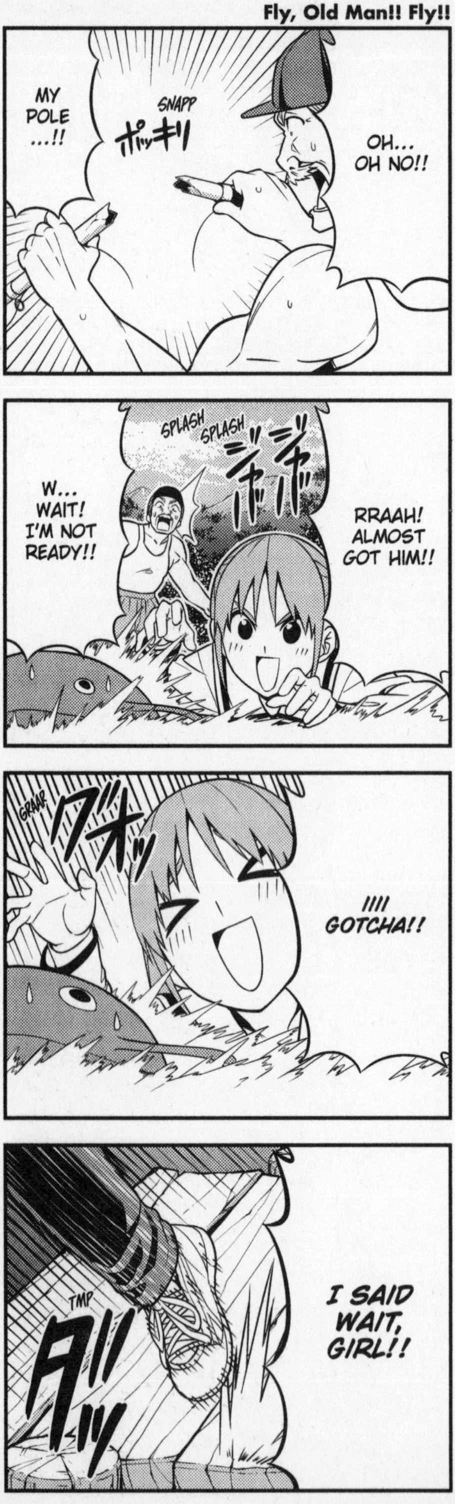
OH... OH NO!!
SNAPP
ポッキリ
MY POLE ...!!
RRAAH! ALMOST GOT HIM!!
SPLASH SPLASH
ジャバジャバ
W... WAIT! I'M NOT READY!!
GOTCHA!!
GRAAR
グオッ
I SAID WAIT, GIRL!!
TMP
ダッ

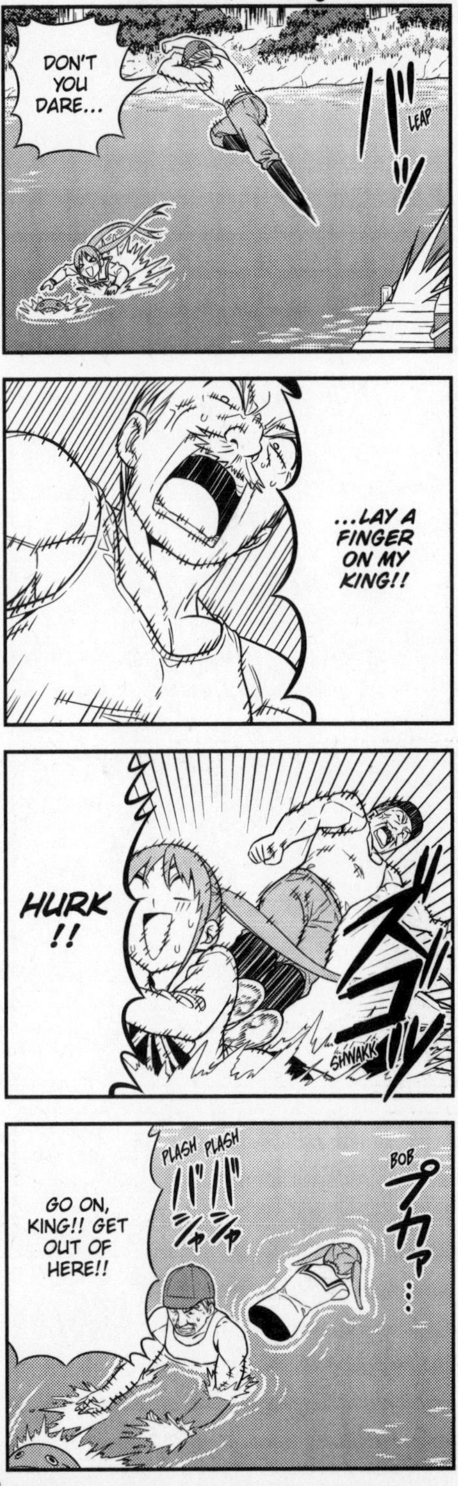
DON'T YOU DARE...
LEAP
...LAY A FINGER ON MY KING!!
SHWAKK
HURK!!
BOB
PLASH PLASH
GO ON, KING!! GET OUT OF HERE!!



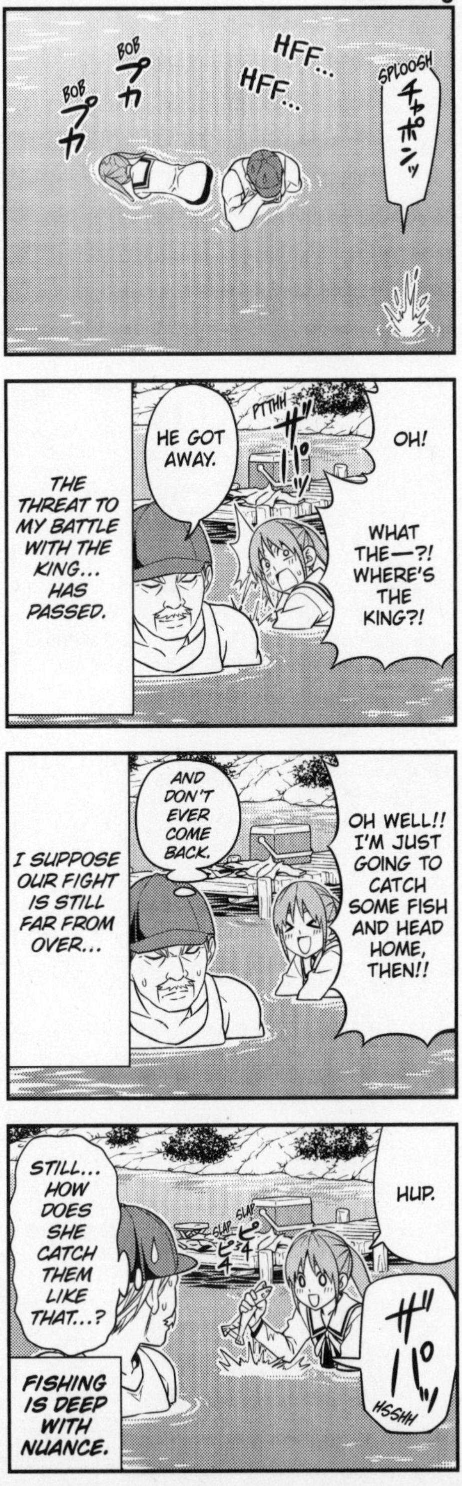
SPLOOSH
HFF...
HFF...
BOB
BOB
OH!
WHAT THE—?! WHERE'S THE KING?!
PTTHH
HE GOT AWAY.
THE THREAT TO MY BATTLE WITH THE KING... HAS PASSED.
OH WELL!! I'M JUST GOING TO CATCH SOME FISH AND HEAD HOME, THEN!!
AND DON'T EVER COME BACK.
I SUPPOSE OUR FIGHT IS STILL FAR FROM OVER...
HUP.
HSSHH
SLAP SLAP
STILL... HOW DOES SHE CATCH THEM LIKE THAT...?
FISHING IS DEEP WITH NUANCE.

Objective Attained

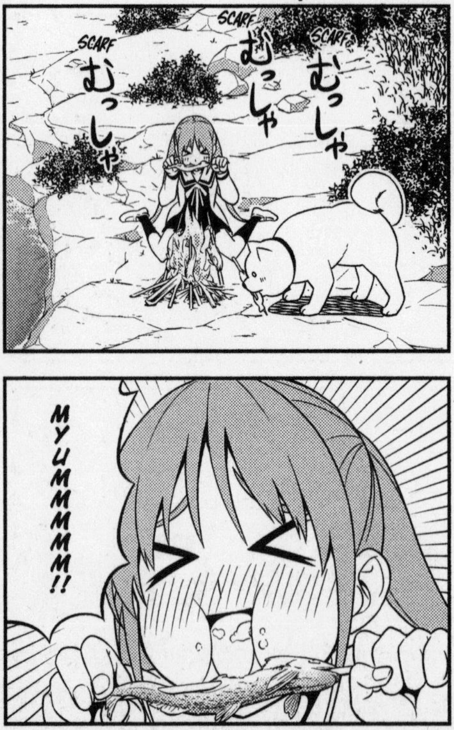
SCARF
むっしゃ
SCARF
むっしゃ
SCARF
むっしゃ
MYUMMMMM!!

(Yoshiko Hanabatake's J-style)

# Aho-Girl

\ˈahôˌgərl \ *Japanese, noun.*
A clueless girl.

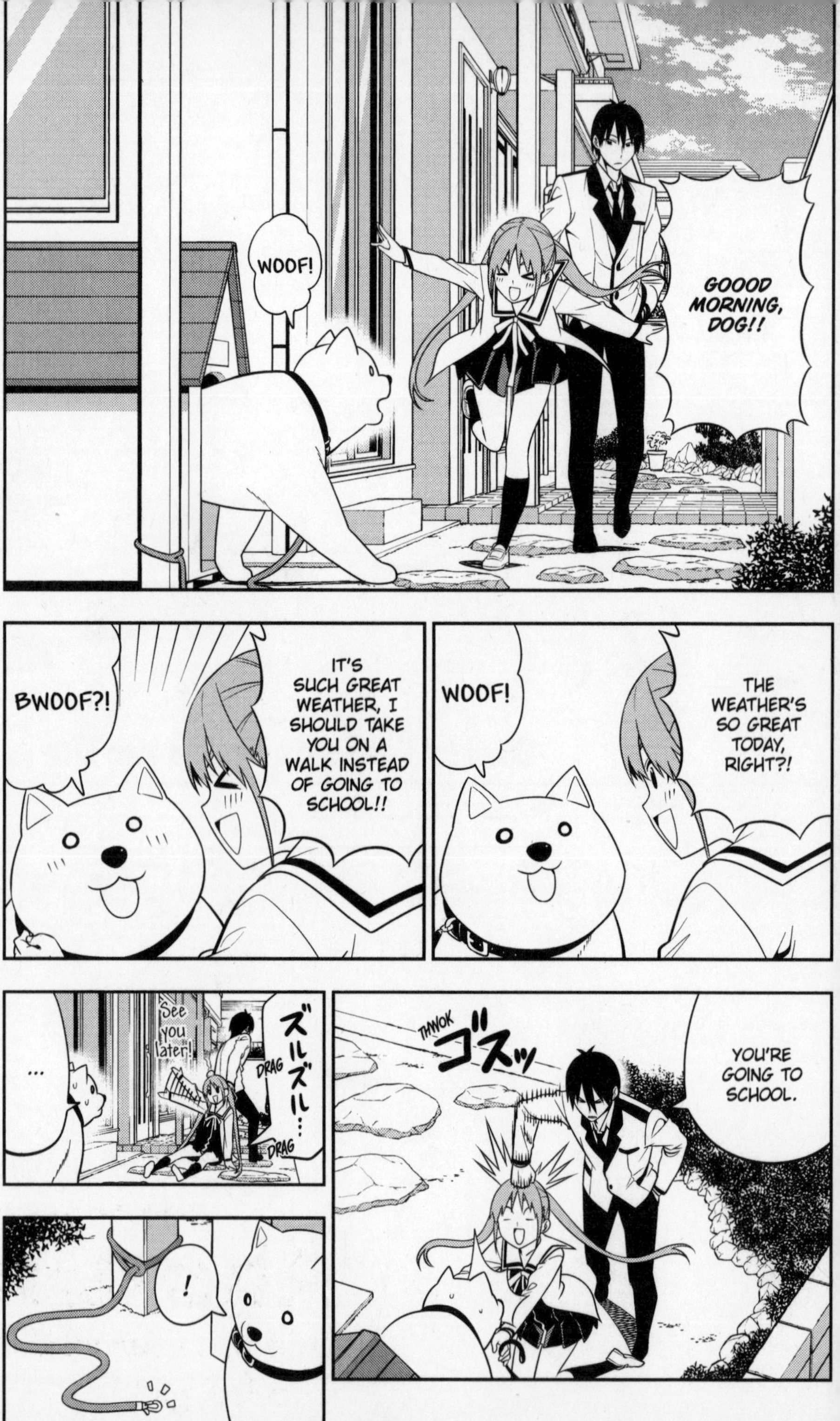
GOOOD MORNING, DOG!!
WOOF!
THE WEATHER'S SO GREAT TODAY, RIGHT?!
WOOF!
IT'S SUCH GREAT WEATHER, I SHOULD TAKE YOU ON A WALK INSTEAD OF GOING TO SCHOOL!!
BWOOF?!
YOU'RE GOING TO SCHOOL.
THWOK
ゴスッ
ズルズル…
DRAG
DRAG
See you later!
...
!

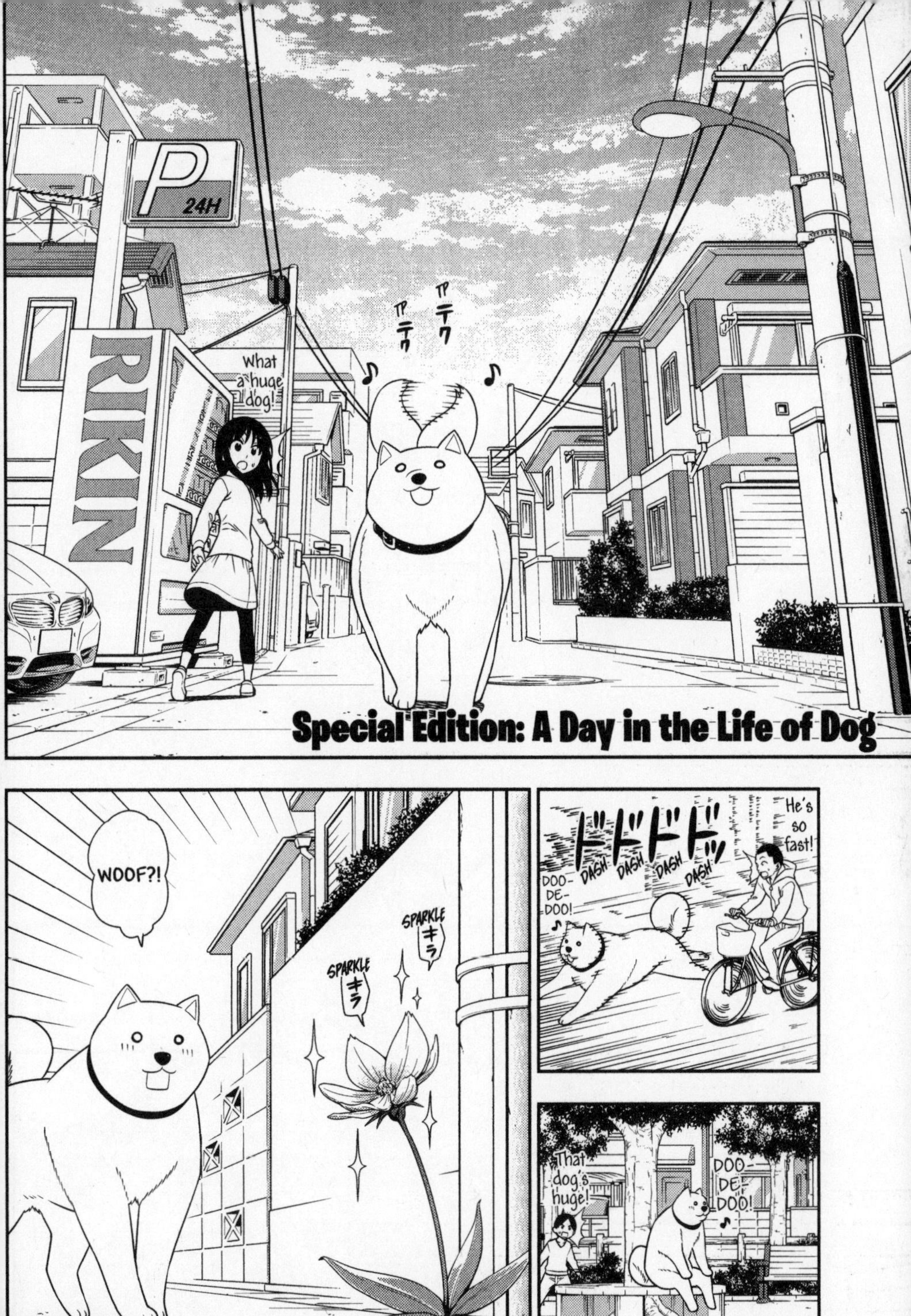
TP テク
TP テク
What a huge dog!
Special Edition: A Day in the Life of Dog
He's so fast!
ドドドドッ
DASH DASH DASH DASH
DOO-DE-DOO!
DOO-DE-DOO!
That dog's huge!
WOOF?!
SPARKLE キラ
SPARKLE キラ

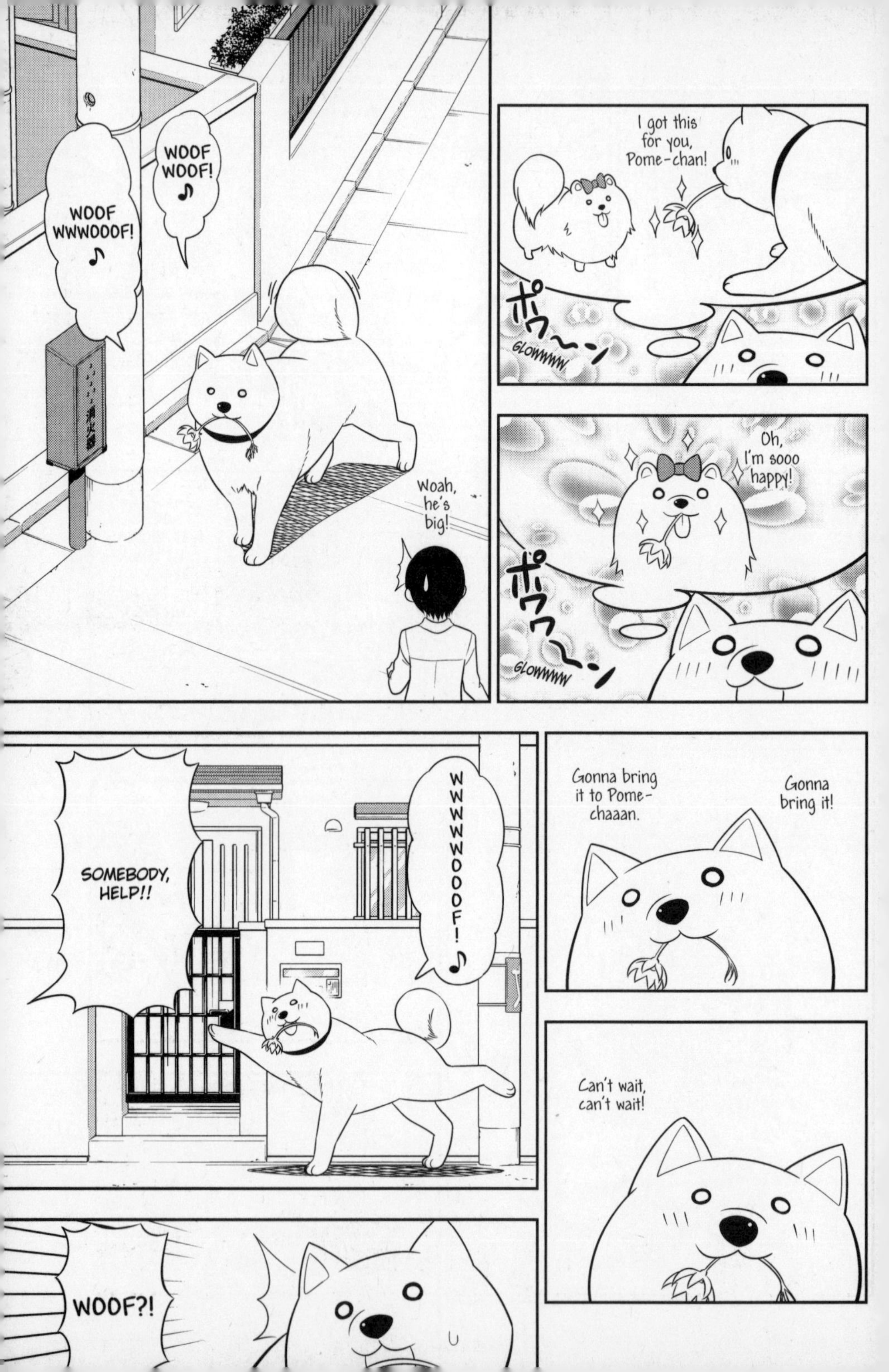
I got this for you, Pome-chan!
ポワ〜ン
GLOWWWW
Oh, I'm sooo happy!
ポワ〜ン
GLOWWWW
WOOF WOOF! ♪
WOOF WWWOOOF! ♪
Woah, he's big!
Gonna bring it!
Gonna bring it to Pome-chaaan.
Can't wait, can't wait!
WWWWWOOOOF! ♪
SOMEBODY, HELP!!
WOOF?!

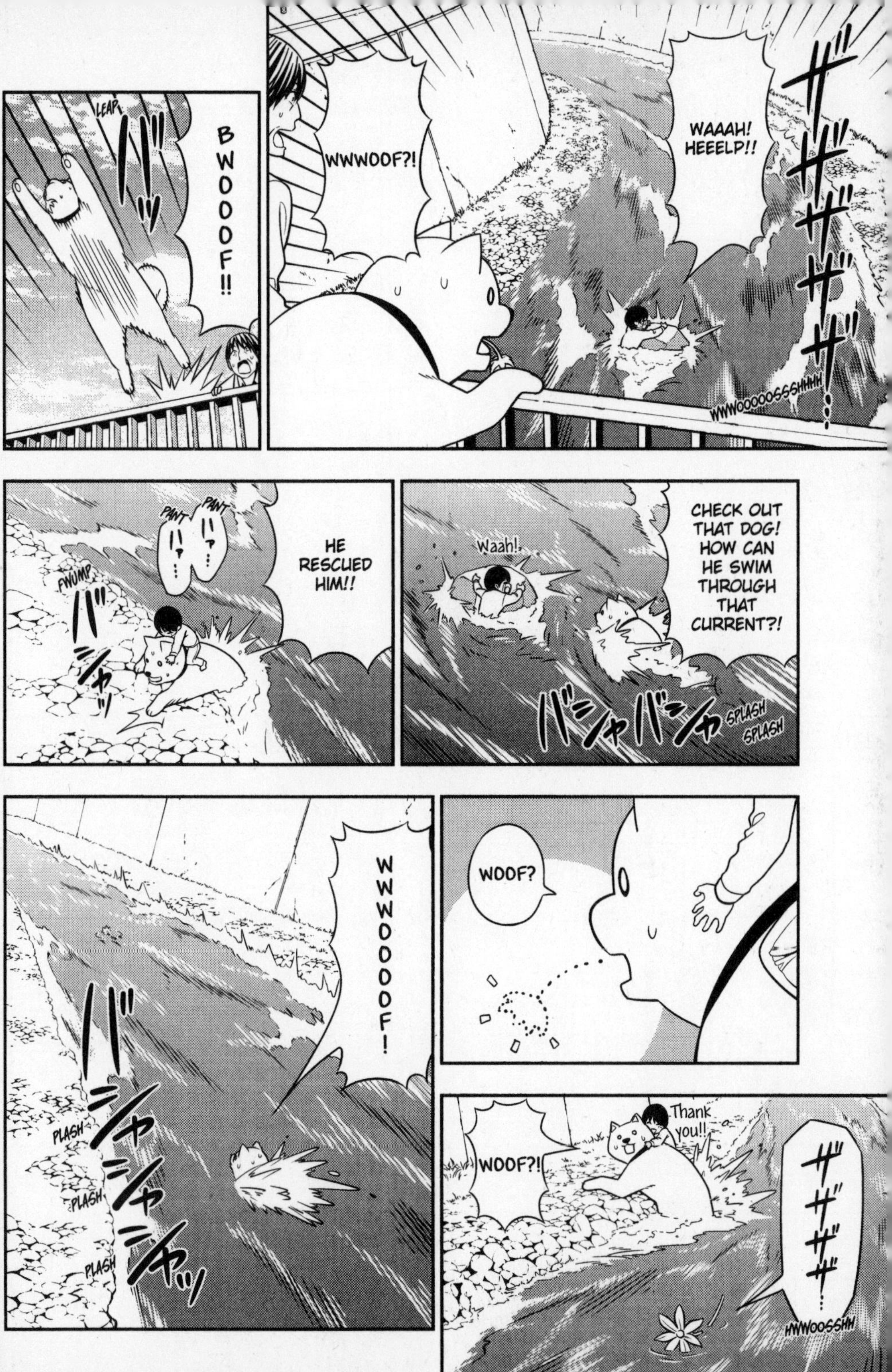
ザザザザザ…
WAAAH! HEEELP!!
WWWOOF?!
WWWOOOOOSSSHHHH
BWOOOOF!!
LEAP
バッ
CHECK OUT THAT DOG! HOW CAN HE SWIM THROUGH THAT CURRENT?!
Waah!
バシャバシャ
SPLASH SPLASH
HE RESCUED HIM!!
PANT PANT
ハァ… ハァ…
FWUMP
バシャッ
WOOF?
Thank you!!
WOOF?!
ザザザ…
HWWOOSSHH
WWWOOOOOF!
バシャシャシャッ
PLASH
PLASH
PLASH

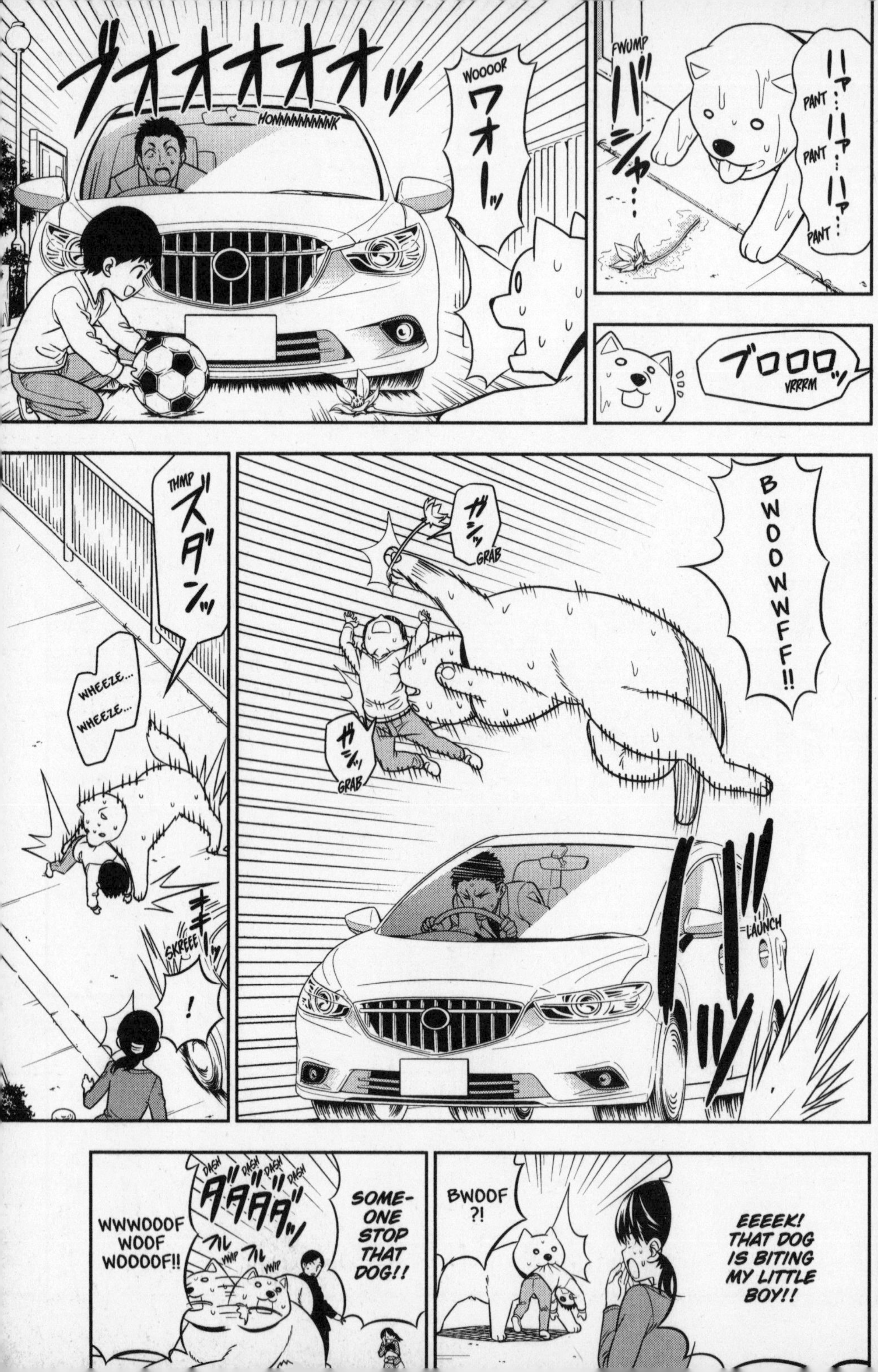

FWUMP
バシャ…
ハァ… ハァ… ハァ…
PANT PANT PANT
ブロロロッ
VRRRM
WOOOOR
ワオーッ
ブオオオオオオッ
HONNNNNNNNNK
BWOOWWFF!!
ガシッ
GRAB
ガシッ
GRAB
LAUNCH
THMP
ズダンッ
WHEEZE... WHEEZE...
キキッ
SKREEE
!
EEEEK! THAT DOG IS BITING MY LITTLE BOY!!
BWOOF ?!
SOME-ONE STOP THAT DOG!!
ダダダダッ
DASH DASH DASH DASH
WWWOOOF WOOF WOOOOF!!
フル WHIP フル WHIP

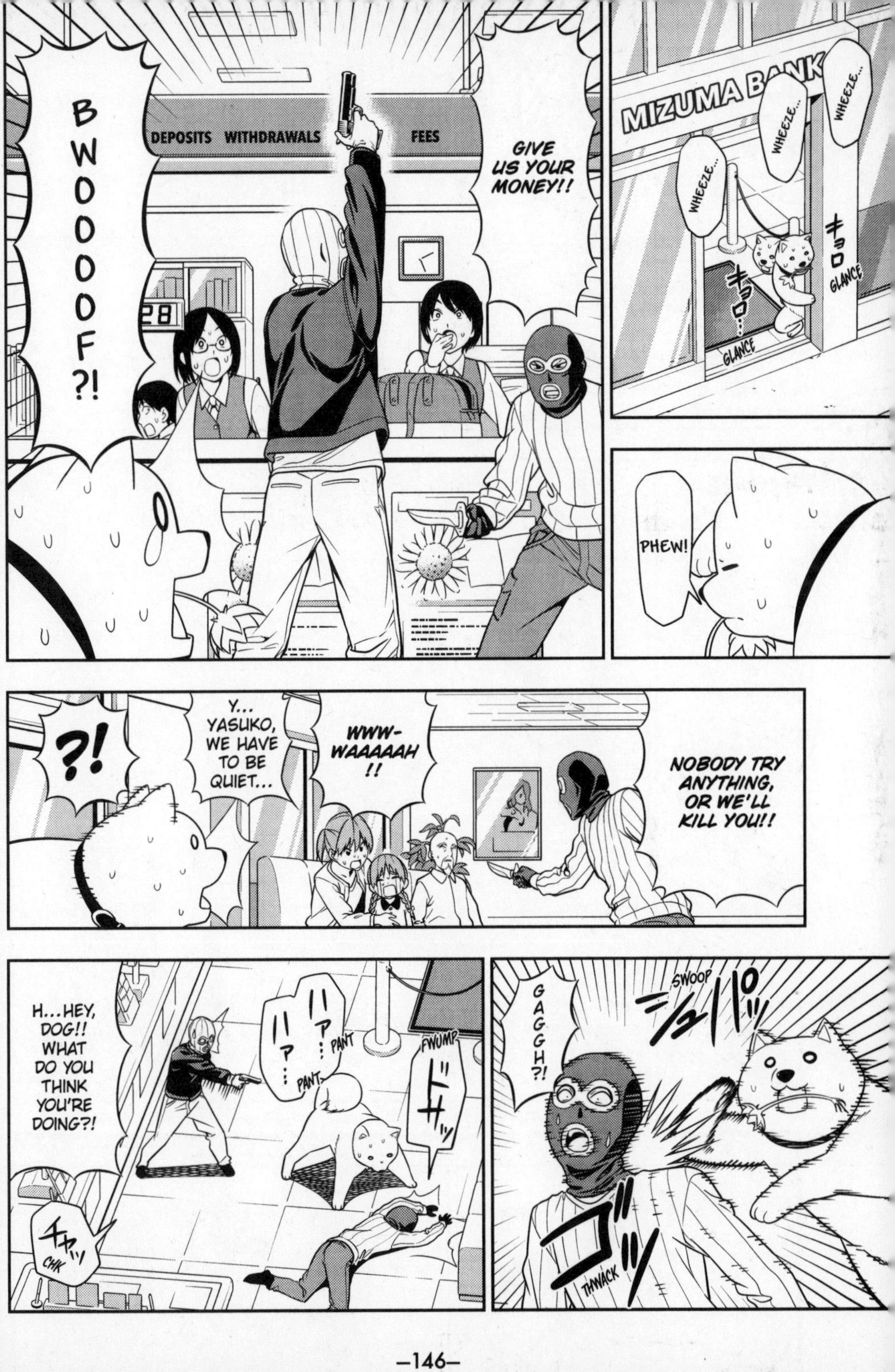
MIZUMA BANK
WHEEZE...
WHEEZE...
WHEEZE...
WHEEZE...
キョロ
GLANCE
キョロ...
GLANCE
PHEW!
GIVE US YOUR MONEY!!
DEPOSITS WITHDRAWALS FEES
BWOOOOOOF?!
NOBODY TRY ANYTHING, OR WE'LL KILL YOU!!
WWW-WAAAAAH!!
Y... YASUKO, WE HAVE TO BE QUIET...
?!
シュパッ
SWOOP
GAGGH?!
ゴッ
THWACK
ドザッ
FWUMP
ハァ... ハァ...
PANT PANT
H...HEY, DOG!! WHAT DO YOU THINK YOU'RE DOING?!
キャッ
CHK

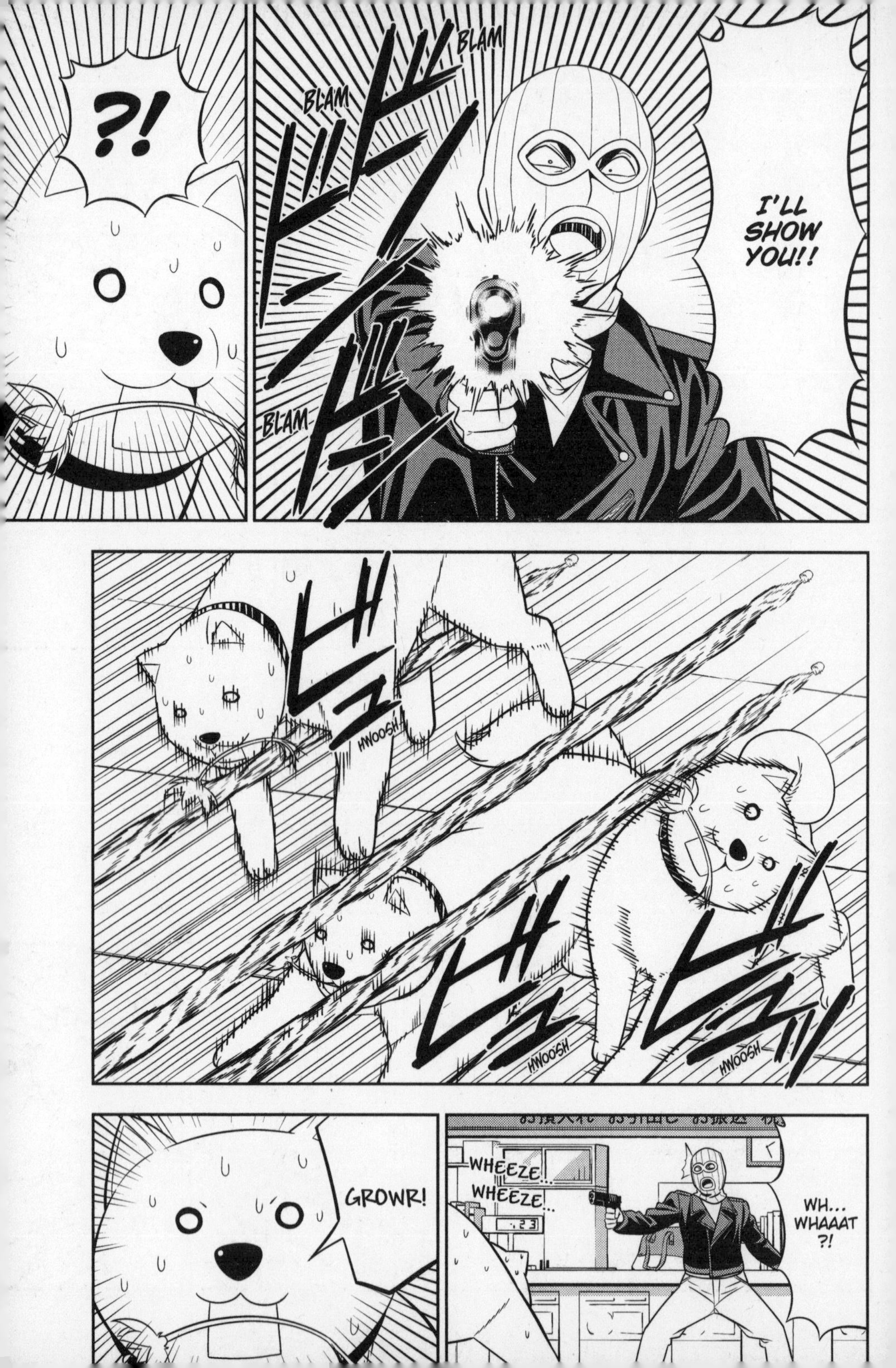
BLAM
BLAM
BLAM
I'LL SHOW YOU!!
?!
WHOOSH
WHOOSH
WHOOSH
WHEEZE...
WHEEZE...
WH... WHAAAT?!
GROWR!

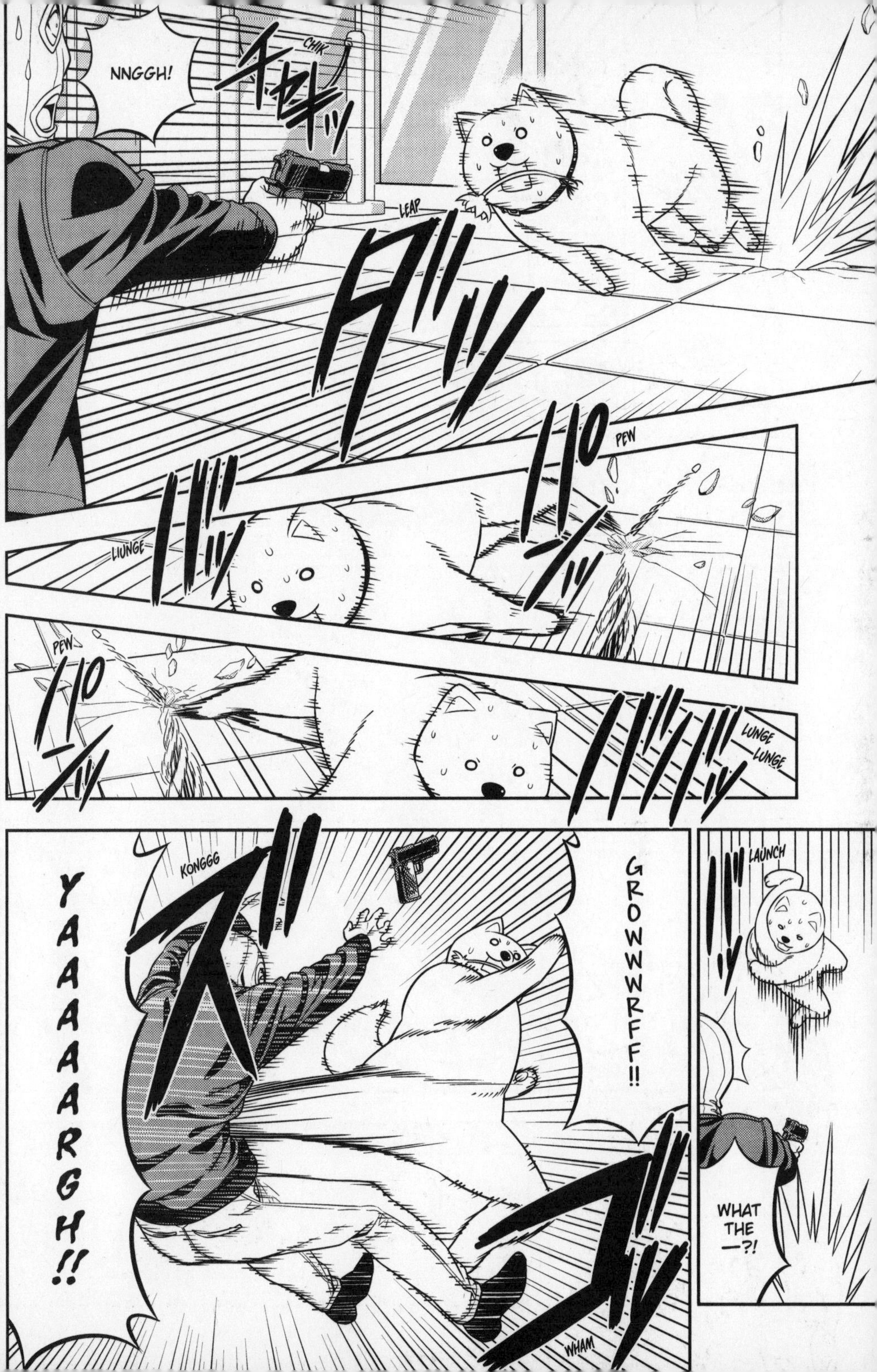
CHIK
NNGGH!
LEAP
PEW
LUNGE
LUNGE
LUNGE
PEW
LAUNCH
WHAT THE —?!
GROWWWRFF!!
KONGGG
YAAAAAARGH!!
WHAM

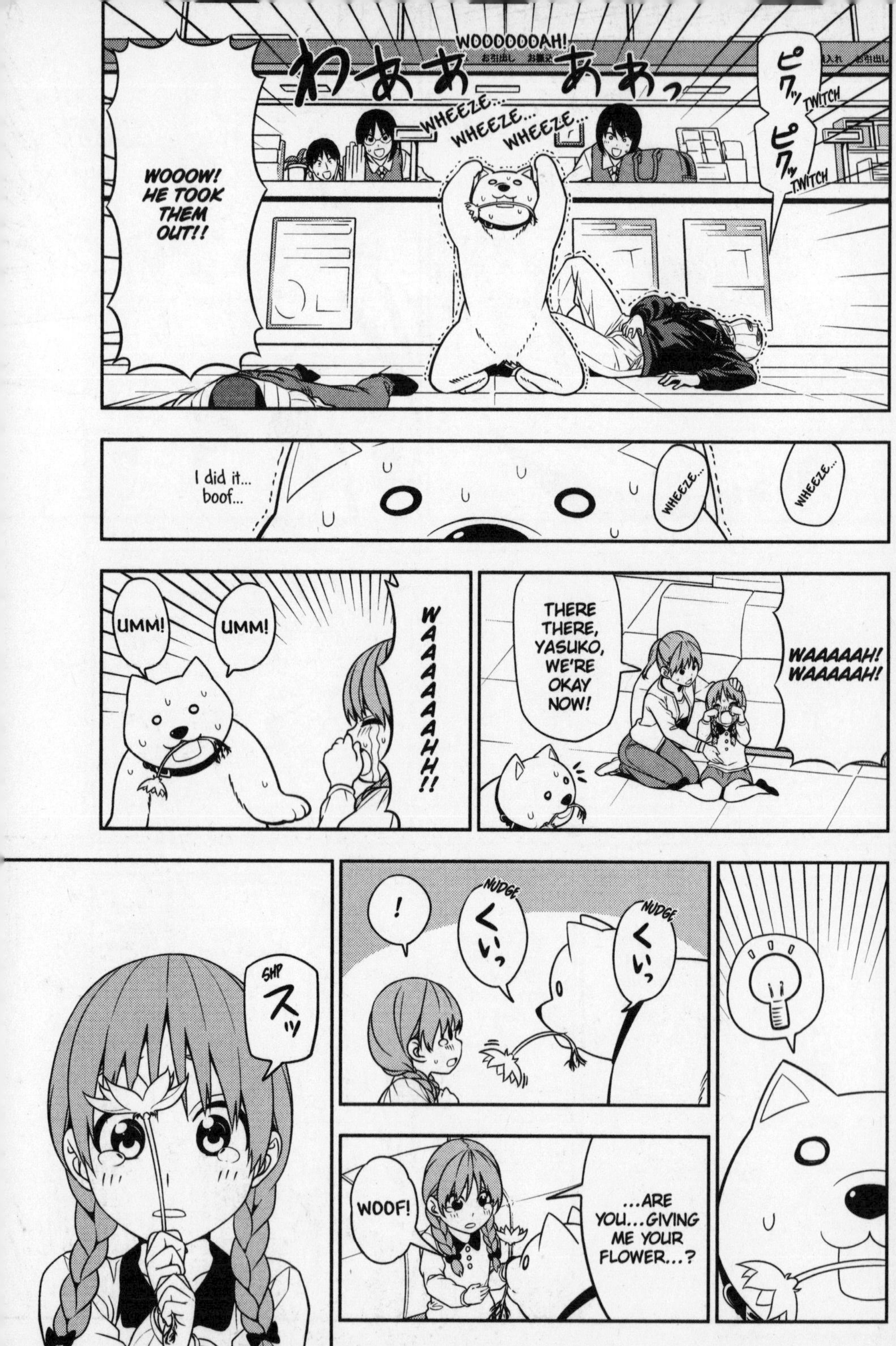
ピクッ
TWITCH
ピクッ
TWITCH
わあああ ああわっ
WOOOOOOAH!
WHEEZE...
WHEEZE...
WHEEZE...
WOOOW! HE TOOK THEM OUT!!
WHEEZE...
WHEEZE...
I did it... boof...
WAAAAAH! WAAAAAH!
THERE THERE, YASUKO, WE'RE OKAY NOW!
WAAAAAAAAHH!!
UMM!
UMM!
NUDGE
くいっ
NUDGE
くいっ
!
...ARE YOU...GIVING ME YOUR FLOWER...?
WOOF!
SHP
スッ

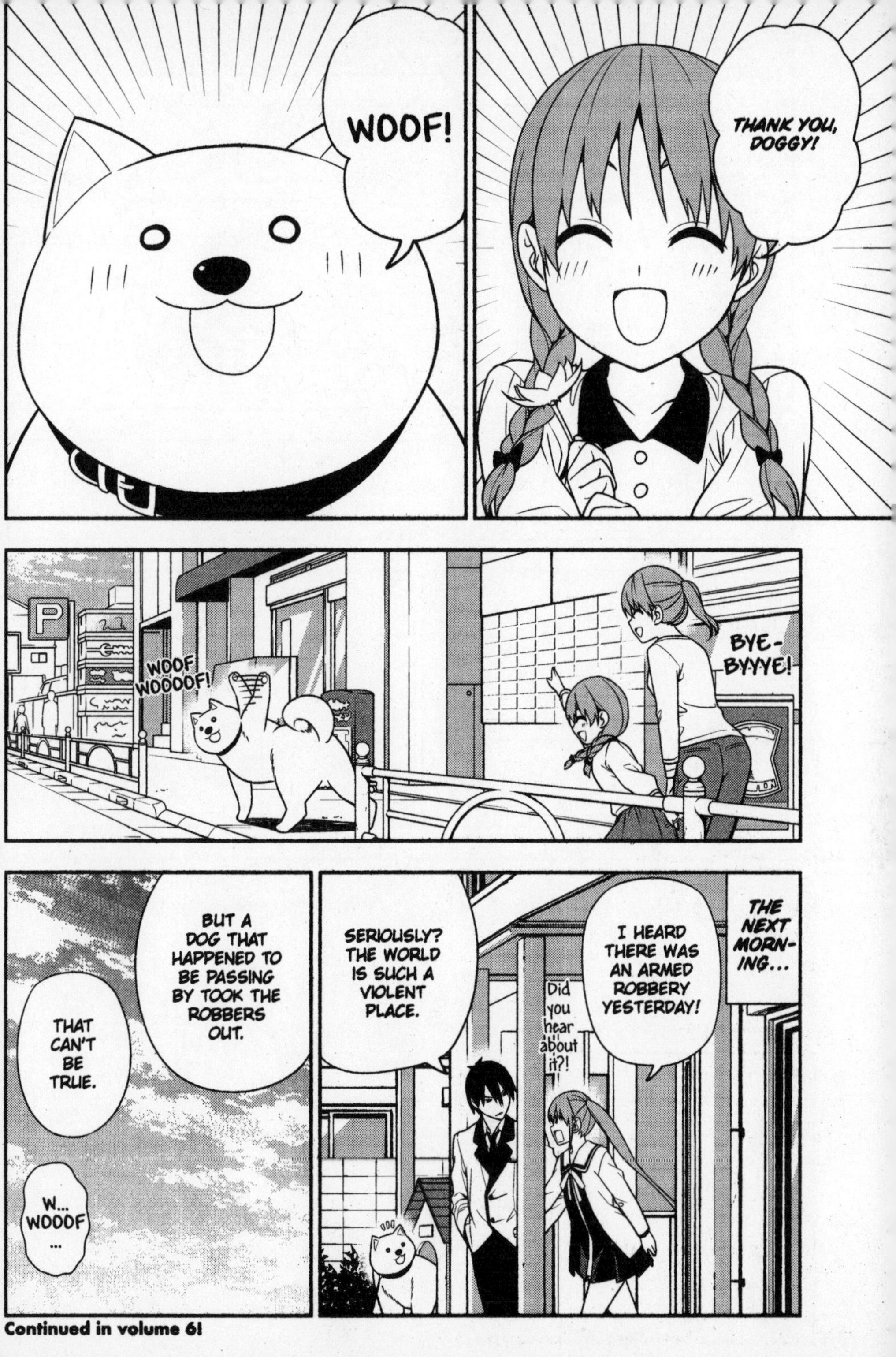
THANK YOU, DOGGY!
WOOF!
BYE-BYYYE!
WOOF WOOOOF!
THE NEXT MORNING...
I HEARD THERE WAS AN ARMED ROBBERY YESTERDAY!
Did you hear about it?!
SERIOUSLY? THE WORLD IS SUCH A VIOLENT PLACE.
BUT A DOG THAT HAPPENED TO BE PASSING BY TOOK THE ROBBERS OUT.
THAT CAN'T BE TRUE.
W... WOOOF ...

**Continued in volume 6!**

**Daily Training Makes You Strong**

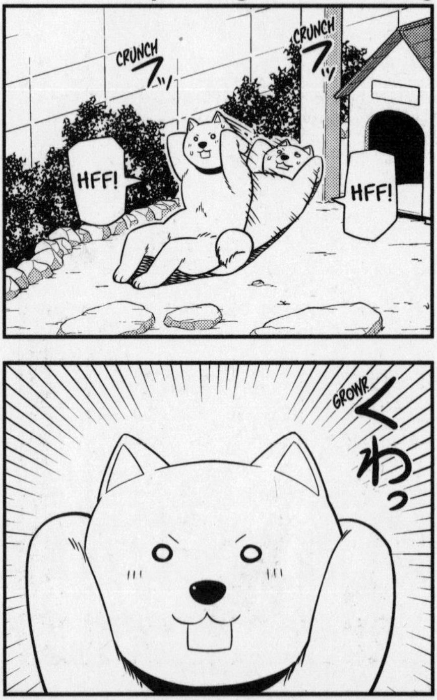
CRUNCH
ブッ
HFF!
CRUNCH
ブッ
HFF!
GROWR
くわっ

(Dog, Making a Break for)

# Aho-Girl

\ˈahôˌɡərl\ *Japanese, noun.*
A clueless girl.

# The Drama of How Hiroyuki Became a Manga-ka 4

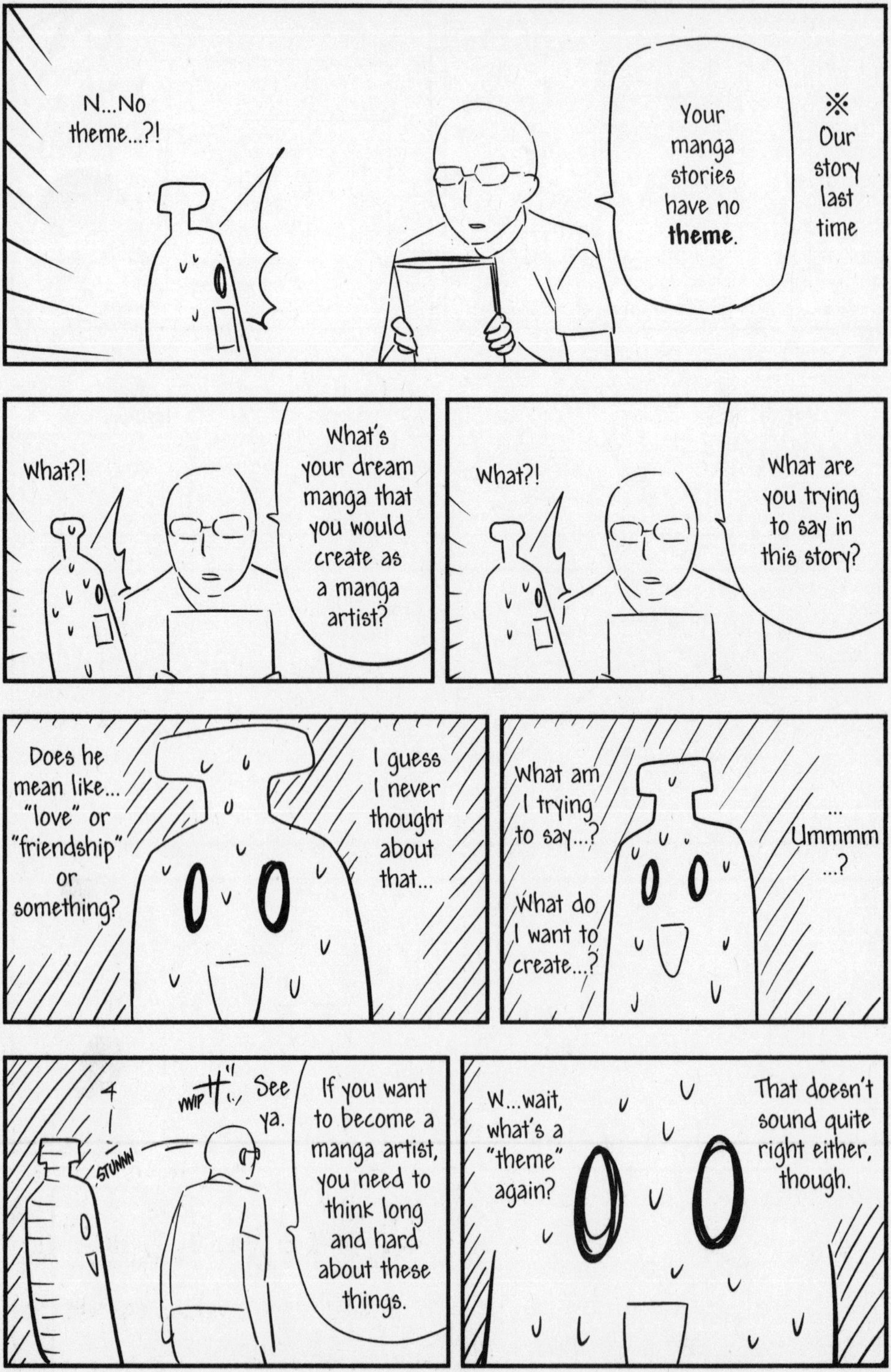

※ Our story last time
Your manga stories have no **theme**.
N...No theme...?!
What are you trying to say in this story?
What?!
What's your dream manga that you would create as a manga artist?
What?!
... Ummmm ...?
What am I trying to say...?
What do I want to create...?
I guess I never thought about that...
Does he mean like... "love" or "friendship" or something?
That doesn't sound quite right either, though.
W...wait, what's a "theme" again?
If you want to become a manga artist, you need to think long and hard about these things.
See ya.
VWIP
STUNNN

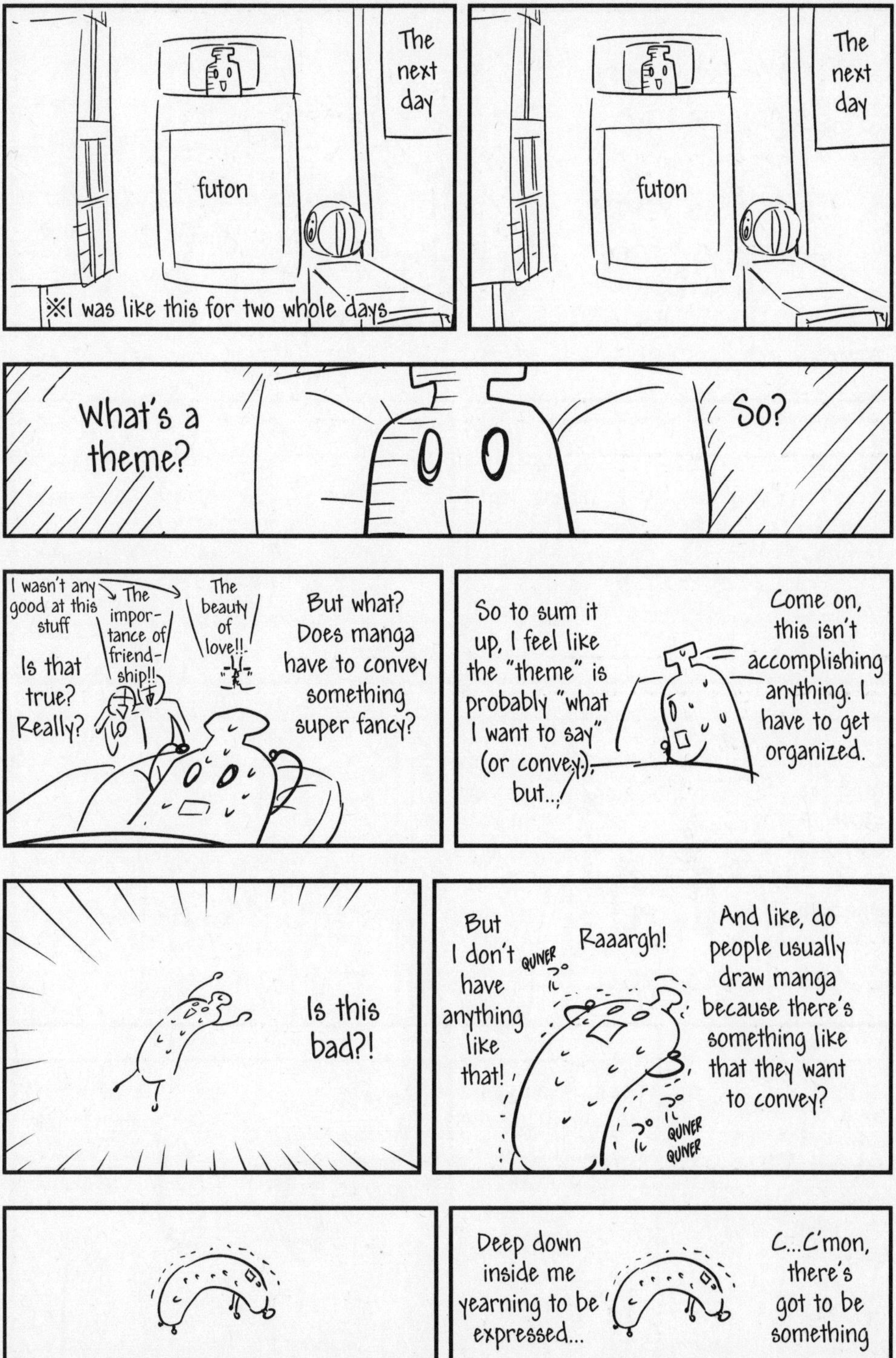
The next day
futon
The next day
futon
※I was like this for two whole days
So?
What's a theme?
Come on, this isn't accomplishing anything. I have to get organized.
So to sum it up, I feel like the "theme" is probably "what I want to say" (or convey), but...
But what? Does manga have to convey something super fancy?
The beauty of love!!
The importance of friendship!!
I wasn't any good at this stuff
Is that true? Really?
And like, do people usually draw manga because there's something like that they want to convey?
Raaargh!
QUIVER
But I don't have anything like that!
QUIVER QUIVER
Is this bad?!
C...C'mon, there's got to be something
Deep down inside me yearning to be expressed...

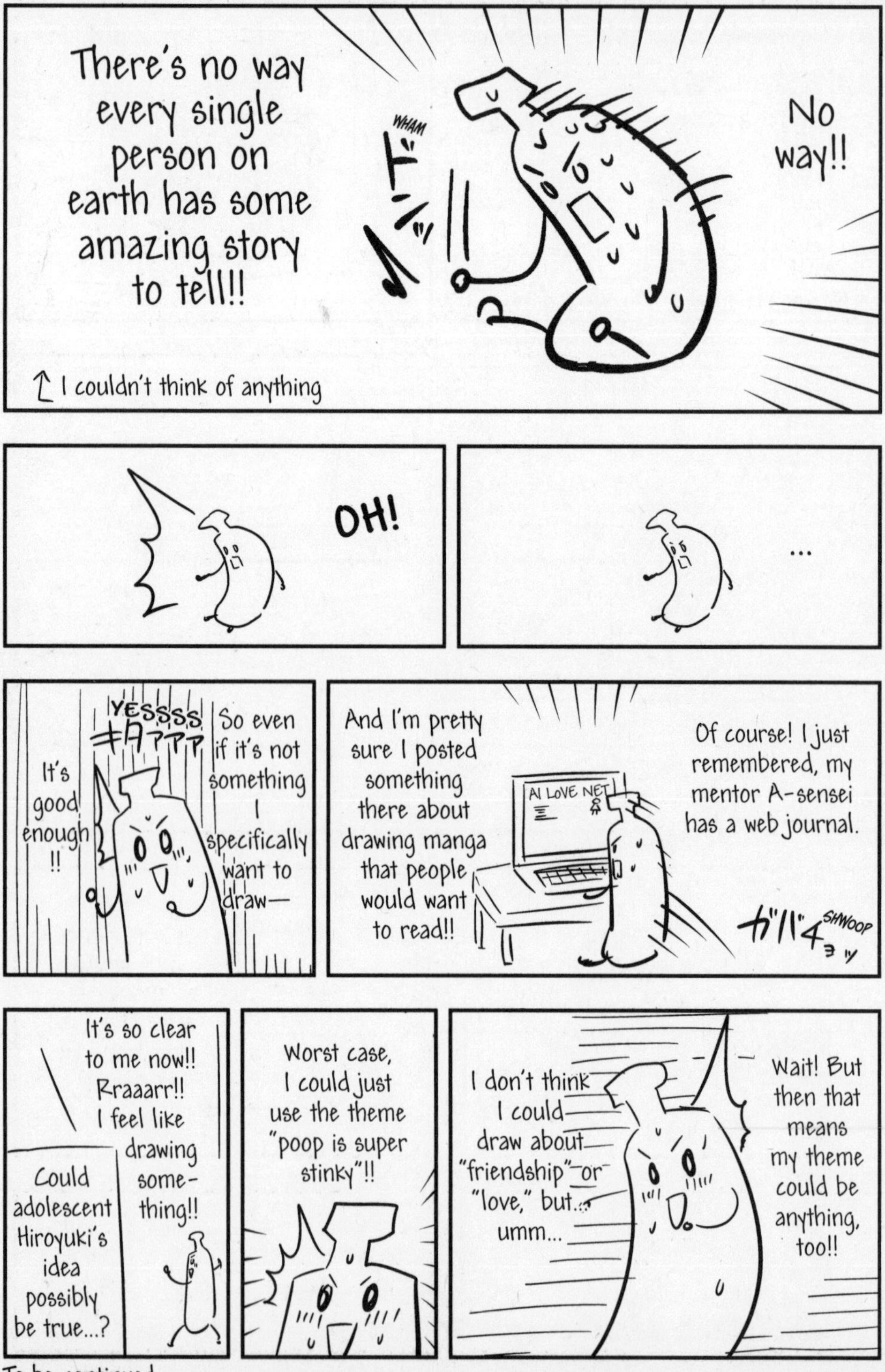
There's no way every single person on earth has some amazing story to tell!!
WHAM
No way!!
I couldn't think of anything
...
OH!
Of course! I just remembered, my mentor A-sensei has a web journal.
AI LOVE NET
And I'm pretty sure I posted something there about drawing manga that people would want to read!!
SHWOOP
So even if it's not something I specifically want to draw—
YESSSS
It's good enough!!
Wait! But then that means my theme could be anything, too!!
I don't think I could draw about "friendship" or "love," but... umm...
Worst case, I could just use the theme "poop is super stinky"!!
It's so clear to me now!! Rraaarr!! I feel like drawing something!!
Could adolescent Hiroyuki's idea possibly be true...?

To be continued

**I Guess They're the Same Shape?**

MAGAZINE SPECIAL UNCOLLECTED EXTRA! THE TOPIC IS "AMBITIONS/ DREAMS."

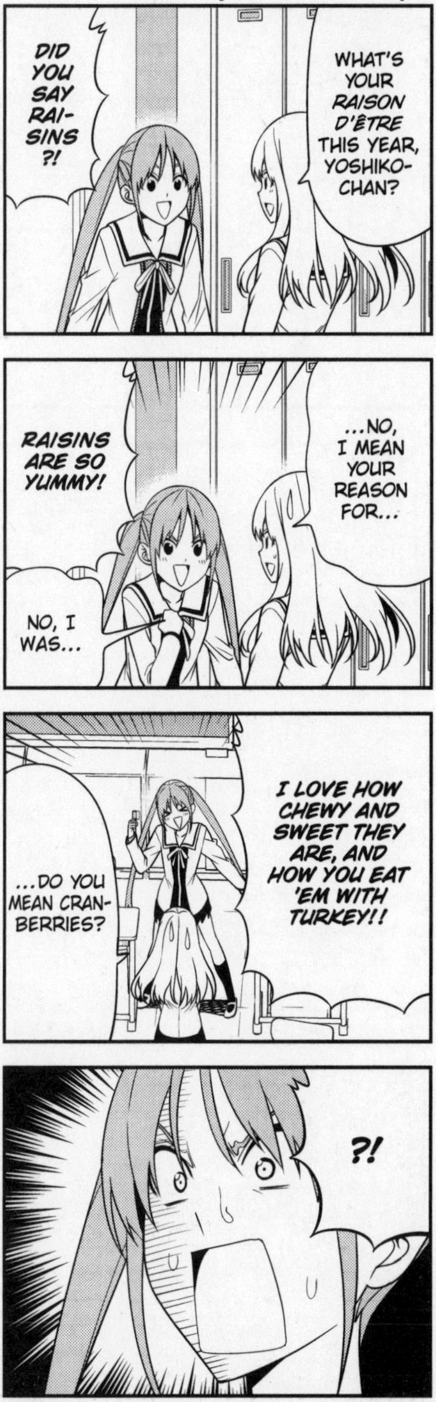
WHAT'S YOUR RAISON D'ÊTRE THIS YEAR, YOSHIKO-CHAN?
DID YOU SAY RAI-SINS?!
...NO, I MEAN YOUR REASON FOR...
RAISINS ARE SO YUMMY!
NO, I WAS...
I LOVE HOW CHEWY AND SWEET THEY ARE, AND HOW YOU EAT 'EM WITH TURKEY!!
...DO YOU MEAN CRAN-BERRIES?
?!

*MAGAZINE SPECIAL, PUBLISHED IN 2014 NO. 1*

## Anytime

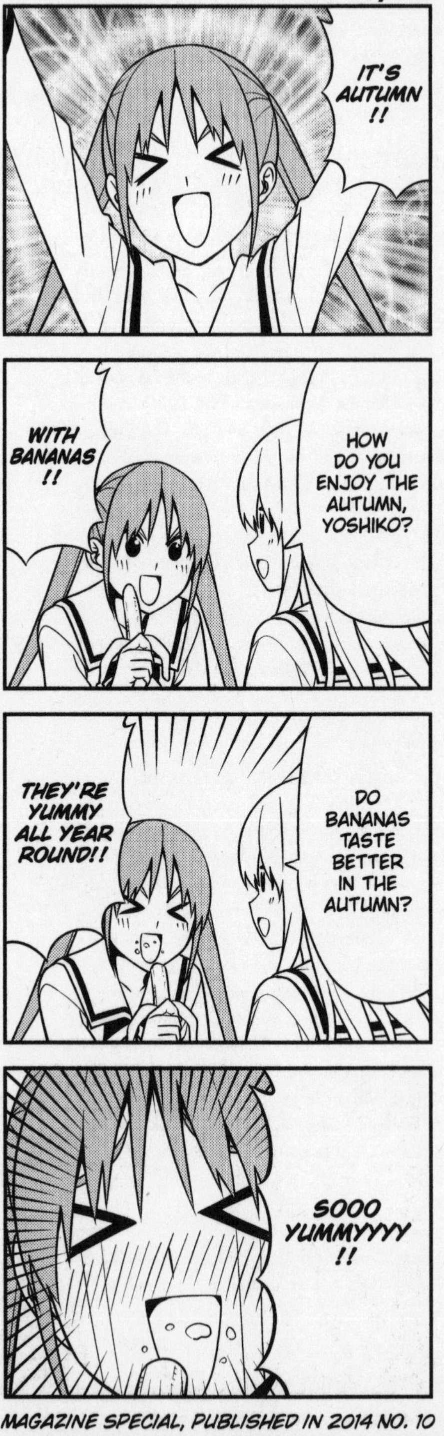
IT'S AUTUMN !!
HOW DO YOU ENJOY THE AUTUMN, YOSHIKO?
WITH BANANAS !!
DO BANANAS TASTE BETTER IN THE AUTUMN?
THEY'RE YUMMY ALL YEAR ROUND!!
SOOO YUMMYYYY !!

MAGAZINE SPECIAL, PUBLISHED IN 2014 NO. 10

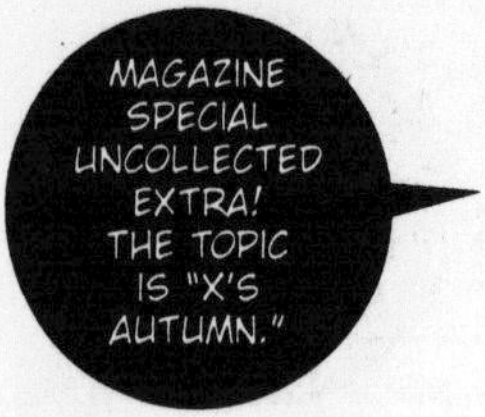
MAGAZINE SPECIAL UNCOLLECTED EXTRA! THE TOPIC IS "X'S AUTUMN."

**Page 2**
"Aggravated straight man"
This is an explanatory gloss of the Japanese term "tsukkomi." The tsukkomi and boke duo are a common trope in manzai-style stand-up comedy routines. The boke, like Yoshiko, draws over-the-top and just plain stupid conclusions to the tsukkomi's set-ups. The tsukkomi tries to remain calm and reasonable during the act, but is invariably pushed into extreme and sometimes violent reactions out of his frustration.

**Page 3**
"Head Monitor"
The head monitor's title in Japanese includes the word fuuki, which roughly translates to "moral order" or "discipline." She would not be merely checking for hall passes the way a hall monitor in a Western school might, and would be more broadly responsible for reporting anything in violation of the moral standards of the institution.

"G Cup"
Going by Japanese bra sizing conventions, the head monitor's "G cup" would be roughly equivalent to an American DDD.

**Page 6**
"You know the saying, you attract more with honey than with vinegar."
In the original, Sayaka references a Japanese saying "homejozu wa shitsukejozu," which literally translates to "good at praise means good at training."

**Page 7**
"What Kind of Blood Runs in Your Veins?!"
This is a reference to episode 46 of Fist of the North Star. When an overlord attempts to conquer a village, a young girl inspired by the main character's example resists the invaders, leading to her noble death. In response, the mercenary Rei screams at the overlord's soldiers "What kind of blood runs in your veins?!" before he attacks to avenge the girl's death.

**Page 12**
"Packed with nuts, sure to satisfy; when you're hungry, reach for"
This is a reference to a 1980s Snickers ad campaign in Japan.

**Page 21**
In Japan, people frequently leave their front doors unlocked. Solicitors, mail carriers, and other deliveries will open the front door and stand in the entry area (genkan) of the house, which is in many ways considered an extension of the outdoors. For example, this is where shoes are removed when entering the house. A visitor to the house will remain in the entry area and call out to alert the occupants of the house to their arrival.

**Page 23**
"¥20,000,000"
Equivalent to about $180,000 US.

"LEARN WITH PICTURES"
The original text refers to the Japanese art form of kamishibai (literally "paper theater"), in which a storyteller holds up a series of pictures illustrating scenes from the story as they occur. Street performance of this art goes back many centuries in Japan, and reached a peak of popularity during the depression of the 1930s and the post-war recovery of the 1940s and 50s. This practice was then supplanted by the growing availability of television, though it is still well-known and parodied.

**Page 28**
"It's incredibly important. They took care of my hospital stay, and"
This is a reference to an Aflac commercial for supplemental cancer insurance, where a real-life cancer survivor tells a person considering insurance about how Aflac's cancer insurance helped them during their illness.

**Page 36**
"In the trendy, popular "gal" mold"
The term "gal" (Japanese gyaru) refers to a broad segment of popular youth culture in Japan that began in the mid-1990s. The term encompasses many distinct subcultures with different stereotyped behaviors (such as extreme tanning, bleached-white hair, or casual dating in exchange for spending money) that are considered contrary to prevailing Japanese morality. In general, though, most people who are labeled by the term "gal" merely subscribe to a particular fashion aesthetic characterized by loose socks (the familiar slouchy socks that hang loose around the ankles), lightly bleached hair, extensive nail art or cell phone bangles, and—of particular relevance here—school uniform skirts that are rolled up at the waist to be scandalously short.

**Page 38**
"Barley tea"
The Japanese term is "mugicha." It has a toasty flavor, and in its chilled form is stereotypical of summer in Japan.

**Page 39**
In Japan, the gesture Yoshie is making here is a sign that refers to sexual intercourse.

on better.

## "...Was That a Mirage?!"
The Japanese refers to "zanzo," the word often used in battle manga when a character creates illusory copies of themselves, or moves so quickly that their opponent is deceived as to their true location.

## Page 69
## "I have Laid!!"
This is a localized version of the Japanese joke, which gives a very slightly altered name of a common household insecticide.

## Page 81
## "Yo-sei Watch"
This is a Japanese allusion to an anime series which is also broadcast in America, called *Yo-kai Watch*. The anime is in turn based on a video game (and full media empire) about a boy who goes exploring in the woods one day and finds a watch that lets him see and interact with Yo-kai (mischievous spirits). Here, the watch instead lets the wearer see Yo-sei (fairies).

## Page 83
## "ETO YOKATO"
This is a slightly altered name alluding to a famous chain of Japanese stores, Ito Yokado.

## Page 92
## "Watch! What time is it?"
This is a line from the theme song of the anime *Yo-kai Watch* (see note for page 81, above).

## Page 94
## "Oh hey, Akutsu-kun's address. That would be good to know."
How can the head monitor not know Akkun's address if she's right outside his house? Well...Japanese postal addresses are not precisely logical. Once you get beyond the city and prefecture, the rest of the address can seem somewhat arbitrary. Many streets (especially the smaller side streets that many people live on) do not have names, and building numbers do not go in order. When giving directions in Japan, people almost exclusively use landmarks to navigate, and this is presumably how the head monitor found Akkun's house. If being able to find his house is similar to seeing Akkun use a phone, then discovering his mailing address is like getting his cell phone number.

## Page 100
## "Good hunting"
This refers to the catchphrase "Good hunting, S.T.A.L.K.E.R." from the video game *S.T.A.L.K.E.R.*, a

## Page 40
## "Watch Carefully—What Do Your Senses Tell You?"
A reference to *Jojo's Bizarre Adventure*, and a fight between Jean-Pierre Polnareff and Mohammed Abdul.

## Page 47
## "That's my Papeco!!"
This is a slightly altered name for Papico, a sherbet-like frozen treat that comes in squeezable plastic bottles. Since each package contains two bottles stuck together, Papico is generally marketed as shareable. Young Akkun feels differently.

## Page 56
## "Kids Return"
This is the title of the "Beat" Takeshi Kitano movie that established his celebrity in Japan.

## Page 58
## "This is My Weak Arm"
This is a reference to the movie *Commando*, starring Arnold Schwarzenegger. While Schwarzenegger's character John Matrix is dangling the villain Sully over a cliff in one hand, he warns the man not to waste time and lie because "This is my weak arm."

## Page 62
## "Aniki"
This is a coarse but respectful form of address for a man who is slightly older, parallel to oniichan meaning "older brother." It is most commonly encountered in manga and anime being used by ruffians addressing their superiors in a gang, but is not exclusive to criminal lowlifes.

## Page 64
## "No way I can go see my clients like this, man. That'd be"
Originally from a commercial for clam extract capsules, this line became a running reference in pop culture. The series of commercials interviewed "people on the street" to try the capsules and experience their benefits. One such person was an extremely drunk office worker who uttered the above slurred line. One of the advertised benefits of the capsules is as a hangover cure, so everything turned out for the best.

## Page 67
## "Can't Fix Your Dimness"
This joke has been localized from the original Japanese of "todaimoto kurashi," which literally means "darkness at the base of the candle." Figuratively, the expression mirrors something being invisible "right under your nose." The effect is magnified because Yoshiko turns on the light precisely because she needs to see what's going

notices that last, unexpected quality and asks "...Do you mean konnyaku?" Konnyaku is a rubbery, gelatinous food made from a type of potato that is boiled into a paste and then shaped. Because of all these interwoven misunderstandings, the jokes have been massaged into a localized version.

series of first-person shooter survival horror games. The games take place in the fallout zone around Chernobyl in an alternate history where a second explosion occurred, unleashing various monsters, anomalies, and artifacts with unusual powers. Those who venture into the zone to recover such artifacts are known as "stalkers."

### Page 108
### "DANGEROUS ☆ Love Investigation"
This is a reference to a cell phone app dating simulation game, *ABUNAI ☆ Koi no Sosashitsu* or "DANGEROUS ☆ Love Investigation Bureau."

### Page 124
### "Before winter comes"
This is the title of a song by the Japanese band Kami Fusen ("paper balloons").

### Page 126
### "I Never Doubted You, Brother!"
This is a reference to *The Irregular in Magic High School* (Mahoka Koko no Rettosei), a Japanese light novel series that has also been adapted into an anime series and movie. In the series, the main characters are an extremely powerful brother and sister. The brother's extremely destructive magic is only kept in check by his profound affection for his sister, and she grows to adore him to a similar degree. This line is a catchphrase of sorts for her.

### Page 134
### "Like, twenty meters long?!"
Roughly 65 feet. 1.5 meters is approximately 5 feet.

### Page 136
### "Occhan"
An affectionate and/or familiar term for a much older man, parallel to "ojiisan" and analogous to "gramps."

### Page 140
### "Yoshiko Hanabatake's J-style"
This is a reference to a fishing show broadcast on Japanese TV called "Kenji Johjima's J-style Fishing TV," which filmed its last episode in 2013. The show was hosted by retired Major League Baseball catcher Kenji Johjima (aka "George McKenzie"), who played for the Seattle Mariners.

### Page 156
### "Raisins"
The word Sayaka uses is hofu, meaning "ambition, dream, goal," which is a somewhat advanced vocabulary word. Yoshiko mishears this as tofu, and begins expounding on all the things she loves about tofu. "It's so soft and spongy and tough to chew!!" But Sayaka

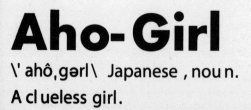

# Aho-Girl

\\' ahô,ɡərl\\ Japanese , noun.
A clueless girl.

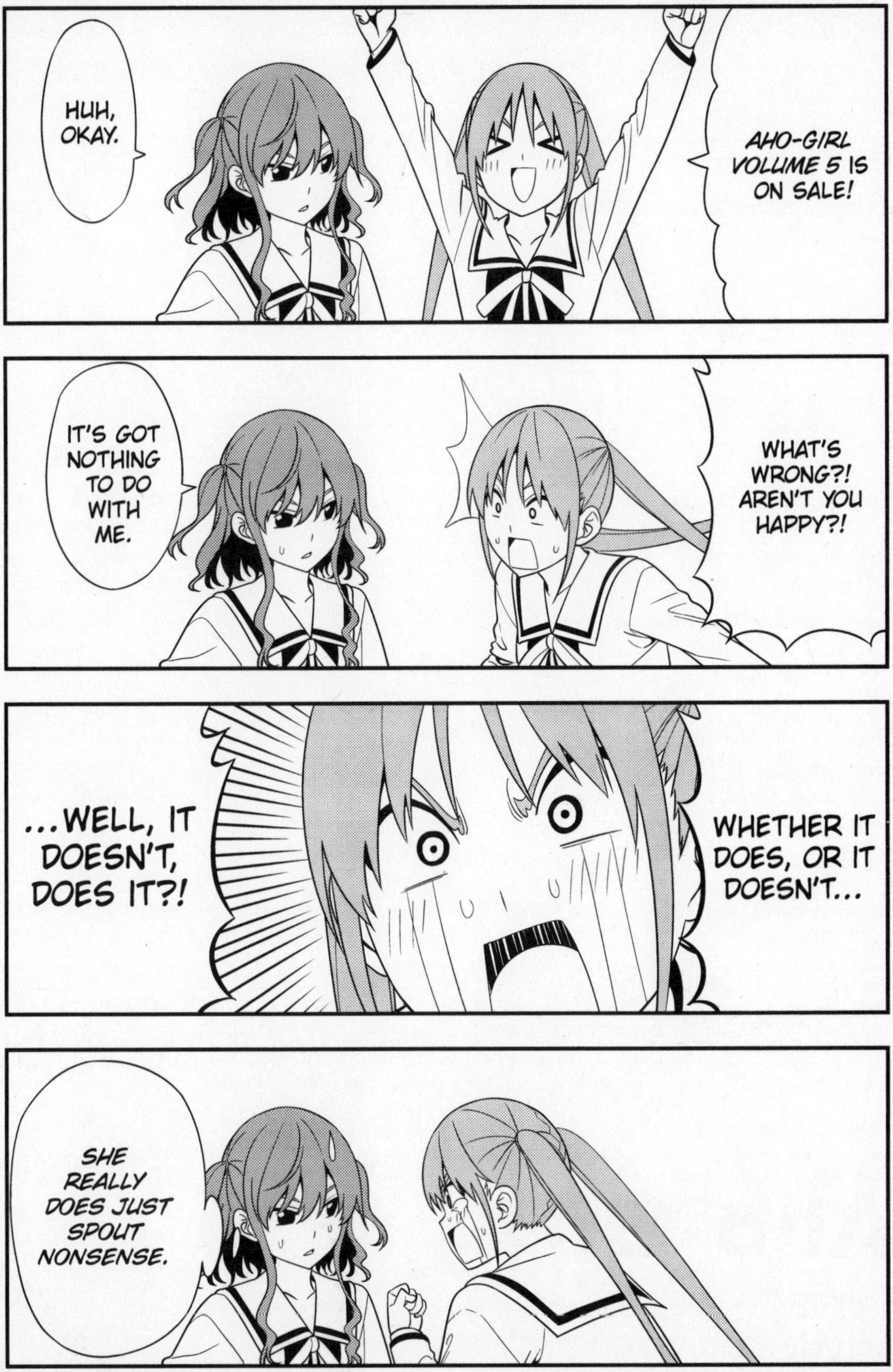
AHO-GIRL VOLUME 5 IS ON SALE!
HUH, OKAY.
WHAT'S WRONG?! AREN'T YOU HAPPY?!
IT'S GOT NOTHING TO DO WITH ME.
WHETHER IT DOES, OR IT DOESN'T...
...WELL, IT DOESN'T, DOES IT?!
SHE REALLY DOES JUST SPOUT NONSENSE.

A beautifully-drawn new action manga from Haruko Ichikawa, winner of the Osamu Tezuka Cultural Prize!

# LAND OF THE LUSTROUS

In a world inhabited by crystalline life-forms called The Lustrous, every gem must fight for their life against the threat of Lunarians who would turn them into decorations. Phosphophyllite, the most fragile and brittle of gems, longs to join the battle, so when Phos is instead assigned to complete a natural history of their world, it sounds like a dull and pointless task. But this new job brings Phos into contact with Cinnabar, a gem forced to live in isolation. Can Phos's seemingly mundane assignment lead both Phos and Cinnabar to the fulfillment they desire?

A new series from Yoshitoki Oima, creator of The New York Times bestselling manga and Eisner Award nominee *A Silent Voice*!

An intimate, emotional drama and an epic story spanning time and space...

# TO YOUR ETERNITY

An orb was cast unto the earth. After metamorphosing into a wolf, It joins a boy on his bleak journey to find his tribe. Ever learning, It transcends death, even when those around It cannot...

KC
KODANSHA
COMICS

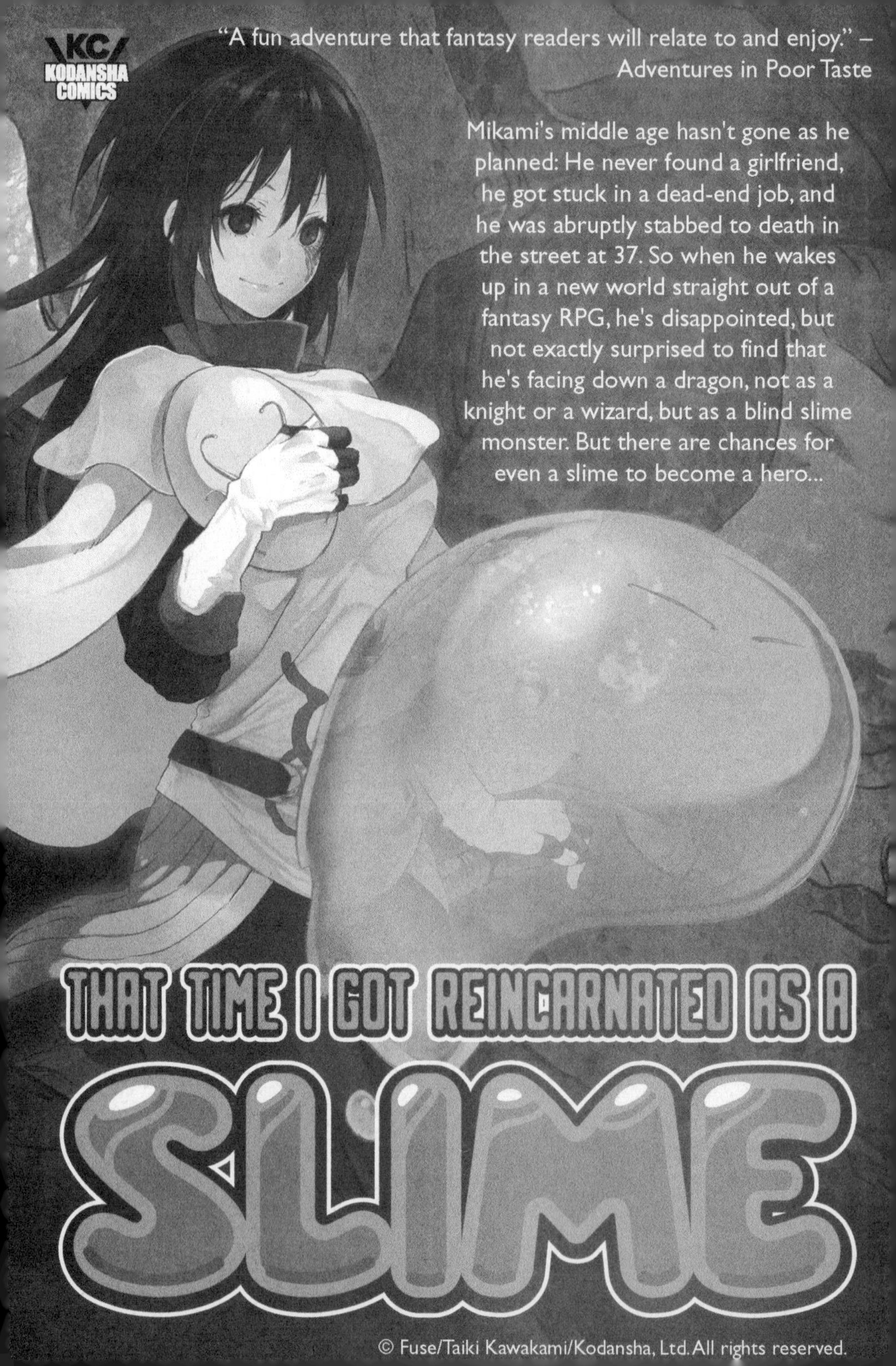
KC KODANSHA COMICS
"A fun adventure that fantasy readers will relate to and enjoy." – Adventures in Poor Taste
Mikami's middle age hasn't gone as he planned: He never found a girlfriend, he got stuck in a dead-end job, and he was abruptly stabbed to death in the street at 37. So when he wakes up in a new world straight out of a fantasy RPG, he's disappointed, but not exactly surprised to find that he's facing down a dragon, not as a knight or a wizard, but as a blind slime monster. But there are chances for even a slime to become a hero...
THAT TIME I GOT REINCARNATED AS A
SLIME
© Fuse/Taiki Kawakami/Kodansha, Ltd. All rights reserved.

# WELCOME TO THE BALLROOM

### By Tomo Takeuchi

Feckless high school student Tatara Fujita wants to be good at something—anything. Unfortunately, he's about as average as a slouchy teen can be. The local bullies know this, and make it a habit to hit him up for cash, but all that changes when the debonair Kaname Sengoku sends them packing. Sengoku's not the neighborhood watch, though. He's a professional ballroom dancer. And once Tatara Fujita gets pulled into the world of ballroom, his life will never be the same.

KC KODANSHA COMICS

**The award-winning manga about what happens inside you!**

"Far more entertaining than it ought to be... what kid doesn't want to think that every time they sneeze a torpedo shoots out their nose?"
—Anime News Network

Strep throat! Hay fever! Influenza! The world is a dangerous place for a red blood cell just trying to get her deliveries finished. Fortunately, she's not alone…she's got a whole human body's worth of cells ready to help out! The mysterious white blood cells, the buff and brash killer T cells, even the cute little platelets— everyone's got to come together if they want to keep you healthy!

# Cells at Work!

はたらく細胞

By Akane Shimizu

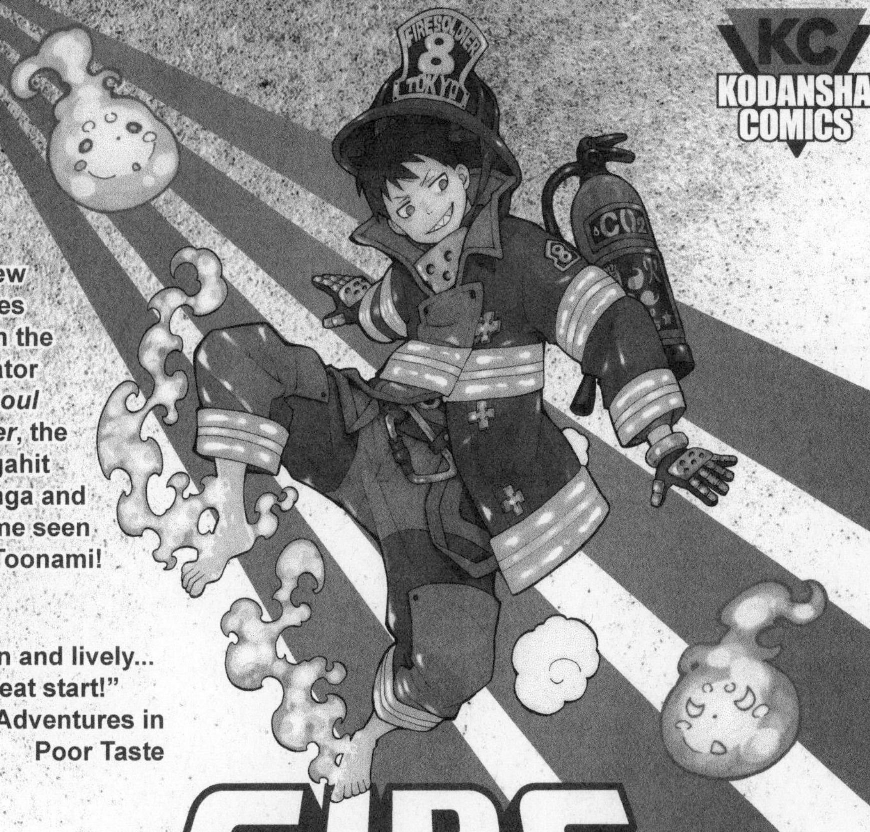

A new series from the creator of *Soul Eater*, the megahit manga and anime seen on Toonami!

"Fun and lively... a great start!"
-Adventures in Poor Taste

# FIRE FORCE

By Atsushi Ohkubo

The city of Tokyo is plagued by a deadly phenomenon: spontaneous human combustion! Luckily, a special team is there to quench the inferno: The Fire Force! The fire soldiers at Special Fire Cathedral 8 are about to get a unique addition. Enter Shinra, a boy who possesses the power to run at the speed of a rocket, leaving behind the famous "devil's footprints" (and destroying his shoes in the process). Can Shinra and his colleagues discover the source of this strange epidemic before the city burns to ashes?

# The Black Museum
# The Ghost and the Lady

### By Kazuhiro Fujita

Deep in Scotland Yard in London sits an evidence room dedicated to the greatest mysteries of British history. In this "Black Museum" sits a misshapen hunk of lead—two bullets fused together—the key to a wartime encounter between Florence Nightingale, the mother of modern nursing, and a supernatural Man in Grey. This story is unknown to most scholars of history, but a special guest of the museum will tell the tale of The Ghost and the Lady...

### Praise for Kazuhiro Fujita's *Ushio and Tora*

"A charming revival that combines a classic look with modern depth and pacing... **Essential viewing both for curmudgeons and new fans alike.**" — Anime News Network

"**GREAT!** The first episode of Ushio and Tora captures the essence of '90s anime." — IGN

Japan's most powerful spirit medium delves into the ghost world's greatest mysteries!

Story by Kyo Shirodaira, famed author of mystery fiction and creator of *Spiral*, *Blast of Tempest*, and *The Record of a Fallen Vampire*.

Both touched by spirits called yôkai, Kotoko and Kurô have gained unique superhuman powers. But to gain her powers Kotoko has given up an eye and a leg, and Kurô's personal life is in shambles. So when Kotoko suggests they team up to deal with renegades from the spirit world, Kurô doesn't have many other choices, but Kotoko might just have a few ulterior motives...

# IN/SPECTRE

### STORY BY KYO SHIRODAIRA
### ART BY CHASHIBA KATASE

# HAPPINESS

## ―ハピネス―

### By Shuzo Oshimi

### From the creator of *The Flowers of Evil*

Nothing interesting is happening in Makoto Ozaki's first year of high school. His life is a series of quiet humiliations: low-grade bullies, unreliable friends, and the constant frustration of his adolescent lust. But one night, a pale, thin girl knocks him to the ground in an alley and offers him a choice. Now everything is different. Daylight is searingly bright. Food tastes awful. And worse than anything is the terrible, consuming thirst...

### Praise for Shuzo Oshimi's *The Flowers of Evil*

"A shockingly readable story that vividly—one might even say queasily—evokes the fear and confusion of discovering one's own sexuality. Recommended." —The Manga Critic

"A page-turning tale of sordid middle school blackmail." —Otaku USA Magazine

"A stunning new horror manga." —Third Eye Comics

Based on the critically acclaimed classic horror manga

The first new *Parasyte* manga in over 20 years!

# NEO ParaSyte f

BY ASUMIKO NAKAMURA, EMA TOYAMA, MIKI RINNO, LALAKO KOJIMA, KAORI YUKI, BANKO KUZE, YUUKI OBATA, KASHIO, YUI KUROE, ASIA WATANABE, MIKIMAKI, HIKARU SURUGA, HAJIME SHINJO, RENJURO KINDAICHI, AND YURI NARUSHIMA

A collection of chilling new *Parasyte* stories from Japan's top shojo artists!

Parasites: shape-shifting aliens whose only purpose is to assimilate with and consume the human race... but do these monsters have a different side? A parasite becomes a prince to save his romance-obsessed female host from a dangerous stalker. Another hosts a cooking show, in which the real monsters are revealed. These and 13 more stories, from some of the greatest shojo manga artists alive today, together make up a chilling, funny, and entertaining tribute to one of manga's horror classics!

KC
KODANSHA
COMICS

*New action series from Hiroyuki Takei, creator of the classic shonen franchise Shaman King!*

In medieval Japan, a bell hanging on the collar is a sign that a ca has a master. Norachiyo's bell hangs from his katana sheath, but he i nonetheless a stray — a ronin. This one-eyed cat samurai travels across dishonest world, cutting through pretense and deception with his blade

# Nekogahara

## STRAY CAT SAMURAI

By
Hiroyuki Takei

*ceya*

A Kodansha Comics Trade Paperback Original.

*Aho-Girl* volume 5 copyright © 2015 Hiroyuki
English translation copyright © 2018 Hiroyuki

Published in the United States by Kodansha Comics, an imprint of Kodansha USA Publishing, LLC, New York.

Publication rights for this English edition arranged through Kodansha Ltd., Tokyo.

First published in Japan in 2015 by Kodansha Ltd., Tokyo, as *Aho Gaaru* volume 5.

ISBN 978-1-63236-533-0

Printed in the United States of America.

www.kodanshacomics.com

9 8 7 6 5 4 3 2 1

Translator: Karen McGillicuddy
Lettering: S. Lee
Editing: Paul Starr
Kodansha Comics edition cover design by Phil Balsman